Object-Oriented Frameworks Using C++ And CORBA

Gold Book

Vishwajit Aklecha

CORIOLIS

Publisher
Keith Weiskamp

Acquisitions Editor
Stephanie Wall

Marketing Specialist
Diane Enger

Project Editor
Melissa D. Olson

Technical Reviewer
Kimberly Kirk Ringer

Production Coordinator
Meg E. Turecek

Cover Design
Jesse Dunn

Layout Design
April Nielsen

CD-ROM Developer
Robert Clarfield

Object-Oriented Frameworks Using C++ And CORBA Gold Book

The Coriolis Group, LLC
14455 North Hayden Road, Suite 220
Scottsdale, Arizona 85260

480/483-0192
FAX 480/483-0193
http://www.coriolis.com

Library of Congress Cataloging-in-Publication Data
Aklecha, Vishwajit
    Object-oriented frameworks using C++ and CORBA gold book / by Vishwajit Aklecha.
        p.   cm.
    Includes index.
    ISBN 1-57610-403-6
    1. Object-oriented programming (Computer science)   2. C++ (Computer program language)   3. CORBA (Computer architecture)   I. Title.
QA76.64.A42   1999
005.1'17 — dc21   99-23782
                                                                          CIP

Printed in the United States of America
10 9 8 7 6 5 4 3 2 1

14455 North Hayden Road, Suite 220 • Scottsdale, Arizona 85260

Dear Reader:

Coriolis Technology Press was founded to create a very elite group of books: the ones you keep closest to your machine. Sure, everyone would like to have the Library of Congress at arm's reach, but in the real world, you have to choose the books you rely on every day *very* carefully.

To win a place for our books on that coveted shelf beside your PC, we guarantee several important qualities in every book we publish. These qualities are:

- *Technical accuracy*—It's no good if it doesn't work. Every Coriolis Technology Press book is reviewed by technical experts in the topic field, and is sent through several editing and proofreading passes in order to create the piece of work you now hold in your hands.

- *Innovative editorial design*—We've put years of research and refinement into the ways we present information in our books. Our books' editorial approach is uniquely designed to reflect the way people learn new technologies and search for solutions to technology problems.

- *Practical focus*—We put only pertinent information into our books and avoid any fluff. Every fact included between these two covers must serve the mission of the book as a whole.

- *Accessibility*—The information in a book is worthless unless you can find it quickly when you need it. We put a lot of effort into our indexes, and heavily cross-reference our chapters, to make it easy for you to move right to the information you need.

Here at The Coriolis Group we have been publishing and packaging books, technical journals, and training materials since 1989. We're programmers and authors ourselves, and we take an ongoing active role in defining what we publish and how we publish it. We have put a lot of thought into our books; please write to us at **ctp@coriolis.com** and let us know what you think. We hope that you're happy with the book in your hands, and that in the future, when you reach for software development and networking information, you'll turn to one of our books first.

Keith Weiskamp
President and Publisher

Jeff Duntemann
VP and Editorial Director

Look For These Other Books From The Coriolis Group:

Visual Basic 6 Object-Oriented Programming Gold Book

Visual C++ 6 Core Language Little Black Book

Visual C++ 6 Programming Blue Book

COM/DCOM Blue Book

I dedicate this book to my parents who gave me everything—
including love, inspiration, education, and freedom.
—Vishwajit Aklecha

About The Author

Vishwajit Aklecha has worked for many years in the area of object-oriented software development. His interests include distributed computing with CORBA, software reuse, and object-oriented frameworks.

He has a bachelor's degree in mathematics and a master's degree in computer science. He is employed with Hewlett-Packard's International Software Operation in Bangalore, India. He is currently involved in designing, building, testing, and evaluating object-oriented applications and frameworks.

Vishwajit can be reached at **vishwajit@technologist.com**.

Acknowledgments

First and foremost, the good people at The Coriolis Group deserve many thanks for making this book possible. In particular, Acquisitions Editor Stephanie Wall, Project Editor Melissa D. Olson, and Production Coordinator Meg Turecek deserve gratitude for their support in developing this book.

It was great fun to work with William F. McManus, a dedicated copyeditor who provided extremely valuable suggestions and hints to improve this book's quality. Excellent technical reviews by Kirky Ringer helped me to get this book in useful form.

Thanks are also due to my agent Martha D. Kaufman for her help and advice during the writing of this book.

I would also like to acknowledge my employer, Hewlett-Packard's International Software Operation, which provided me with a constructive environment to write this book. Ashok Waran deserves many thanks for all of his encouragement and technical help during this project. Also worthy of recognition are Anil, Vikarm, and my other colleagues at HP, who were nice enough to adjust their work to my schedule (due to my late night writing).

In addition, the technical and support people at Object Oriented Concepts, Inc., deserve recognition for implementing an excellent ORBacus product and for making this software freely available.

I would also like to thank the hundreds of people scattered throughout the world who did research in the field of programming languages, object orientation, design patterns, reuse, and frameworks. This book could not have been written without these people. I would especially like to acknowledge B. Stroustrup, S.B. Lippman, Paul Bassett, G. Booch, Ian Graham, Erich Gamma, Frank Buschmann, Ralph Johnson, Douglas Schmidt, Michael Mattsson, and Wolfgang Pree for their excellent contributions to the field of computing.

Last but not least, I owe an acknowledgment and apology to my family. Pramila, my wife, deserves an award. She was kind enough to tolerate and sanction my absence during the last 260 evenings and more than 35 weekends. Himalini, my 4-year-old daughter, merely knew that after I finished my book I would get holidays forever, and then, never disappear during in the evenings. Nishant, my son, is too young to complain; he just smiles (he has no choice anyway).

—Vishwajit Aklecha
    Bangalore, India
    Summer 1999

Contents At A Glance

Table Of Contents

Introduction

Today's business is driven by information; information is perhaps the most important asset of an organization. Information must be accurate and accessible across offices, buildings, and even international organizations. This means that an organization's computing infrastructure must consist of a set of computers connected via a *networking mechanism* that is capable of information transmission and reception. Consequently, a typical organization may have a large computing infrastructure consisting of a blend of operating systems and many networking protocols.

Distributed Components: CORBA Is The Answer

In theory, such a blend is necessary, so that an organization can deploy the best hardware/software combination available to meet its information management requirements. However, in practice, establishing the best combination isn't an easy task. For example, attempting to define and apply the right standards for interoperability and portability to deal with software components in a distributed and heterogeneous environment can be a complex and difficult task. Likewise, developing, integrating, deploying, maintaining, enhancing, and configuring the distributed components can cost an enormous amount of time and money.

Fortunately, these problems are addressed by the *Common Object Request Broker Architecture (CORBA)*. CORBA is a mechanism to create, deploy, and deal with object-oriented components in a distributed environment.

CORBA enables you to create specifications for a distributed component. You can encapsulate application data and the business logic within a component that then can be instantiated and interacted with from anywhere. In addition to providing you with the capability to write application components, CORBA provides numerous services and facilities to handle a component at runtime, such as locating a component, managing the lifecycle of a component, and so forth. CORBA services and facilities are critical to creating *component frameworks*.

Frameworks: Nirvana Of OOP And Reuse

Improving developer productivity is a major benefit that object-oriented programming (OOP) provides. You can take advantage of OOP to improve productivity and provide the development leverage to address the requirements of today's complex solutions. The success of OOP depends on its capabilities, such as *software reuse*, the process of creating software systems from predefined software components. Software reuse can reduce risks, development time, and costs, and should be practiced in virtually every software project.

The ultimate success of the OOP and software reuse paradigm, in my view, relates to the availability of object-oriented frameworks. A *framework* is a set of prefabricated software building blocks that you can use as a foundation on which to develop new applications. If you use a framework as a development foundation, you don't have to start from scratch each time you design and develop an application. Because frameworks consist of a set of classes that collaborate with each other in a well-defined manner, they provide the necessary foundation on which developers can design and deliver systems that are more reusable and maintainable.

C++, OOP, Frameworks, And CORBA: The Future Of Computing

C++ has already demonstrated that it is one of the most useful languages and that it can be used to build mission-critical systems that involve CORBA, OOP, reuse, and frameworks. With an increased demand and emphasis on object-oriented distributed systems, the combination of C++, CORBA, and object-oriented frameworks seems to be the future of computing. Considering all of the objective benefits that CORBA promises, I firmly believe that the techniques of object-oriented-based frameworks and CORBA are going to play a crucial role in the future of computing. Design patterns, the UML notation, and object-oriented methods will be handy tools for OOP and CORBA practitioners.

Framework-oriented development undoubtedly is the logical extension of OOP. CORBA, with its services and interfaces, already plays the role of a metaframework that can be used to derive full-fledged object-oriented applications and other metaframeworks and frameworks.

About This Book

This book brings together C++, OOP, CORBA, and frameworks to present approaches and techniques for developing object-oriented frameworks in C++ and CORBA. It explains C++ features that are useful for OOP and reusability and tells you how these features can be used to implement design patterns and object-oriented frameworks. This is not a theoretical book. It contains many practical C++ examples, a generic business component framework example, and useful descriptions for various CORBA concepts through C++ examples.

This is an intermediate- to advanced-level book, written for the following audience:

♦ Software architects

♦ Programmers

♦ Researchers and students

This book consists of 16 chapters that will help you to understand the following concepts:

♦ OOP and reusability in C++

♦ Generic programming in C++

♦ UML concepts

♦ Design patterns

♦ Frameworks and framework-development processes, with examples

♦ Application-development processes using frameworks

♦ Refactoring frameworks

♦ Integration of frameworks with legacy applications

♦ Distributed computing using CORBA

♦ Description of CORBA services, interface repository, and dynamic invocation interface

♦ Development of CORBA-based frameworks

I've provided a glossary of useful terms and a "Recommended Reading" list at the end of the book.

About The Examples In The Book

Examples in this book have been tested using ORBacus (version 3.1) and Visual C++ 5 on the Windows NT platform. ORBacus, from Object-Oriented Concepts, is a CORBA implementation that is compliant with the CORBA 2 specification. ORBacus is freely available for noncommercial use. Information on ORBacus, as well as a downloadable copy, is available on the Object-Oriented Concepts Web site, at **www.ooc.com/ob/**.

I have tried to make sure that of this book's all examples follow consistent coding styles. Names of all the example classes, global **typedef**s, and other global names start with the prefix **Co**. (Do not confuse **Co** with *component* or Microsoft's COM. **Co** is simply an abbreviation of *Coriolis*, the publisher of this book.)

Note that in the examples, some standard header inclusions (such as **iostream.h**, **stdio.h**, and so forth) are not shown, to save space. Similarly, I have not shown the **using namespace std;** statement in the example programs. In addition, I have not included defensive programming constructs, such as checking pointers for zero (**0**), memory allocation failures, and so forth.

Chapter 1

Object-Oriented Programming With C++

I f you want to model a car, your task is easier if you have the fundamental building blocks to model a car, such as wheels, a gearbox, a speedometer, and an accelerator. Your task is even easier if you have the proper interactions among those building blocks, such as applying the accelerator causes operations to take place on the wheels and speedometer. This cooperative and organized behavior is the result of a set of building blocks interacting under some predefined rules and conditions.

A *framework* dictates the architecture of a system. It defines the overall structure, its partitioning into objects, the key responsibilities of those objects, how the objects collaborate, and the thread of control. This chapter doesn't present a tutorial on frameworks—it simply conveys the concept, so that the term *framework* can be used freely throughout the chapter.

Building a good framework is not possible without an understanding of object-oriented (OO) concepts, as well as experience applying OO concepts in a real project by using a programming language. This chapter begins the book by presenting a few of the significant OO concepts, because understanding object-oriented programming is the prerequisite to framework programming.

Object orientation has become a buzzword with many meanings. It is a design methodology and a way of programming, referred to as *object-oriented programming (OOP)*. Similarly, the term *object* is quite generic and can be applied to almost any concept in the universe. Because terms such as *object* are misused and overused often, this chapter builds a conceptual and technical foundation from which you can read the rest of the book. Thus, this chapter starts by describing the basic concepts and vocabulary of object orientation. Next, it describes the C++ expressions that you need to understand to achieve and implement object orientation. The main C++ expressions to describe object orientation are *class, class derivation,* and *dynamic binding.* This chapter then explains C++'s manner of exception handling and memory management, because error and memory handling are important issues and strategies when you are designing frameworks. A section on runtime type information (RTTI) is presented toward the end of this chapter, because RTTI might influence your implementation of OO systems.

The concepts of object modeling (OM) and object-orientated analysis and design (OOAD) are not within the scope of this chapter. Reuse, which is a major benefit of OO, is another important idea that this chapter doesn't cover; it is covered in Chapter 3.

Expressions Of Object Orientation

Object-oriented technology has gained rapid acceptance among software developers and has become the preferred choice for designing and implementing software systems. This section introduces the vocabulary of object orientation. You must be aware that different authors sometimes use the terms associated with OO in subtly different ways. This section presents the terminology that is generally used and understood by a majority of programmers across the globe.

Objects In The Real World

The object model views the world as consisting of many objects that interact with each other to produce a collective behavior. In object modeling (OM), objects are considered concrete entities that exist in space and time. Objects are basic units of construction, whether for conceptualization, design, or programming. Objects from the real world can be represented in an object model with many of the attributes and behaviors deemed important in the natural world. This approach deals with systems from a perspective of simulating the real world, rather than looking at systems as a set of functions. Systems of high complexity become easier to understand with OM, because all parties talk about the objects based on real knowledge. An object model provides the following notions:

♦ *Objects everywhere*—OO views the word as being composed of objects with well-defined properties.

- *Objects form the design*—Objects are the basic units in OO design.

- *Objects have identity*—Identity is the property that distinguishes an object from all other objects. For example, you are not the same as the other readers of this book.

- *Object dynamics by message*—*Object dynamics* is the interaction among objects. Interactions are mediated by messages that objects exchange with each other. *Messages* are operations that act upon objects and that may modify the objects' states.

- *Objects have behavior*—The behavior of an object determines how an object acts or reacts in the context of other objects; in other words, *behavior* describes how the object interacts with the external world. Behavior is, in fact, a response to a message that is acting on an object.

Abstraction

Abstraction, which is key to OOP, characterizes an object and helps distinguish one object from other kinds of objects (for example, people are different from airplanes, but two people in different airplanes are still people). Abstraction represents the "outside view" of an object.

Two kinds of object abstraction are conceivable:

- *Real*—Objects closely resemble "real" objects (such as a *car* object, *monkey* object, and so forth).

- *Abstract*—Includes "abstract" objects that nobody has touched or seen yet (such as *shape* objects).

Abstraction helps you to design a solution for a problem. Abstraction is a process by which you can shape a vague problem into well-defined entities or narrow down a difficult problem into an abstract view, or *object model*, of the problem, as illustrated in Figure 1.1.

The *model* defines an abstract view to the problem. This implies that the model focuses only on problem-related characteristics and that you must try to capture the elements of the problem.

Encapsulation

The abstraction of an object captures the outside view of the object. *Encapsulation*, on the other hand, is the process of hiding all the internal details of an object. Why is encapsulation necessary?

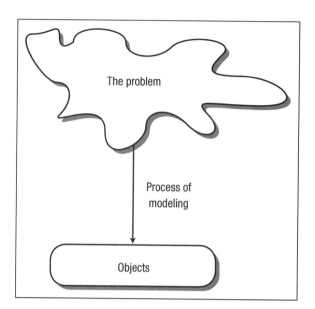

Figure 1.1
The process of modeling.

To answer this question, consider the following mathematical example in which an abstraction is defined for complex numbers. For this example, you need to know only that complex numbers consist of two parts: a real part and an imaginary part. Both parts are represented by real numbers. Complex numbers define several operations: addition, subtraction, multiplication, and division, to name a few. The user (or client) of a complex number doesn't need to know how the internal representation of a complex number is implemented. In the implementation, you can either define two float numbers, have dynamic pointers to two float numbers, or have an array of two float numbers. The user of the complex number is unaware of the data structure, because that structure is *encapsulated* within the complex object (along with the messages that the complex object supports).

Conceptual Structures To View The World

Object-oriented design may not be as straightforward as simply mimicking the outside world in the form of objects and their interactions. In reality, OO design may become quite complex and may not capture all the aspects of a problem space. To some people, many of the outside objects/interactions may seem to be irrelevant to the problem; to others, the outside objects/interactions may seem to be essential entities.

Some of the issues involved in OO design are how to identify the key abstractions in a specific OO design and how to determine the possible relationships among abstractions. For example, suppose that you want to design and implement a banking system. Various types of accounts and customer types can be used. Identification of the appropriate objects and their relationships is an initial activity of any OO design.

Generally, you will discover two types of relationships among objects: *inheritance* and *composition*, which are described in the next two sections.

Genetically Engineered Objects

Inheritance is a major strength of object orientation. Inheritance enables programmers to assemble relevant object abstractions into a hierarchy, to express hierarchical relationships, or *commonality*, among relevant abstractions. The abstraction at the top serves as the *super abstraction* for those abstractions below it in the hierarchy, which implies that a lower-level abstraction is a specialization of its super abstraction.

Inheritance is used as a method of *reusing* an implementation to create new abstractions. After a base abstraction is developed, it doesn't need to be reprogrammed or recompiled, but it can nevertheless be adapted to work in different situations. One result of reusability is the ease of distributing object frameworks, which generally depend on inheritance.

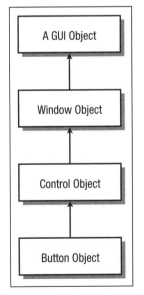

Figure 1.2
Hierarchy of abstractions.

As an example of inheritance, consider a button object of a graphical user interface (GUI) system. A button is a *button* at its own level of abstraction. At a higher level of abstraction, however, a button can be viewed as a *control* object. At still higher levels of abstraction, a control object is simply a kind of more-abstract *window* object. At the highest level of abstraction, a window is a *GUI* object. This example can (and should) be mapped to a hierarchy of abstractions as shown in Figure 1.2. Thus, inheritance is one of the conceptual ways with which you interact with the world.

Fusion Of Objects

Composition is the process of combining many related abstractions into a single abstraction. Whereas inheritance enables you to assemble relevant object abstractions into a hierarchy, to express hierarchical relationships, composition enables you to fabricate object abstractions, to form new abstractions. Consider the example car object. It is an object that, in turn, consists of many other objects, such as wheels, doors, a speedometer, and so forth. You actually operate on the car by operating on its composite objects. Composition is also used as a method of reusing an abstraction to create a new abstraction. Composition is a key concept in OO, because it maps very naturally to how things exist in the world.

Inheritance and composition are addressed again in Chapter 3, in the discussion of reuse.

Object Interface

Access to a particular object's application capabilities is mediated by the *interface* that it supports. An *object interface* is a set of messages that an object's client can use to access the object's capabilities. It represents a potential point of integration and interoperation between an object and its client. The object interface represents the underlying implementation.

Clients can be developed independently of an implementation. An object that implements a particular behavior represents its capabilities via its interface. For example, an **Account** object will support the interface that allows operations such as **withdrawMoney()** and **depositMoney()** to be performed. In other words, an object's application behavior is exposed to its client through the interface. An *abstract data type* (ADT) is an object that has the interface only and not the implementation.

Messaging

A running OO system is a collection of live objects in which objects are created, destroyed, and interact with one another. The dynamics of an OO system depend on the object interactions. This interaction is based on messages that are sent from one object to another, requesting the recipient to act, thus changing the recipient's states. A recipient's object interface determines which messages it can accept. Each object maintains its own state, and changes to its state do not proliferate to other objects in the system. Each object is responsible for initializing and destroying itself correctly. Consequently, the need to manage objects explicitly by using global functions no longer exists. This is a great advantage of using OOP rather than functional programming.

NOTE

Messages And Interfaces Are Not The Same

Some people use the words "message" and "interface" interchangeably. In this book, the term "interface" is used to mean "a collection of messages" that an object can support.

In Figure 1.3, the OO system consists of four objects that send messages to each other, as indicated by the direction lines. Note that the second object sends itself a message.

This view helps you to develop software, because it not only shows you what an individual object can do, but it also provides an overview of how the whole system runs and interacts. It gives you an abstraction of how to attack the problem by dividing it into smaller, manageable pieces. Typically, these pieces are the live objects in the system.

Polymorphism

Polymorphism is the most important of the key fundamental primitives of OOP. Polymorphism, which means *many forms*, provides a generic software interface so that an inheritance hierarchy of related objects can be manipulated consistently. Polymorphism enables different abstractions in the same hierarchy to use the same name for different messages. When a message is sent to an object, the OO system determines which message to use. Consider the collection of GUI objects that all are able to respond to the **repaint()** messages. The GUI collection might have a dialog box, a button, a pull-down menu, and so forth. If all GUI objects receive the same **repaint()** message, the polymorphism mechanism ensures that the correct **repaint()** messages are invoked on the recipient objects, based on the type of object encountered dynamically at runtime.

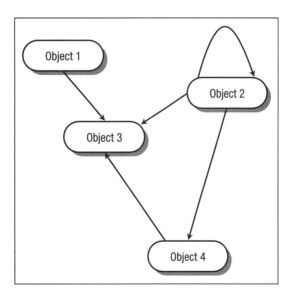

Figure 1.3
Objects sending messages to each other.

Together with inheritance, polymorphism brings the most power to OOP in terms of design-time and runtime flexibility. Whereas inheritance represents static generalization of an abstraction, polymorphism provides the runtime support for the object model.

Genericity

Genericity is a prime technique for defining objects of an OO system. Genericity represents the structural and behavioral similarity of objects. It is not the same as abstraction; however, it is key to avoiding the introduction of objects with duplicate behavior. Objects may operate on different types, but the way they operate may be similar. For example, in a banking system, maintaining a list of accounts and a list of employees may be a requirement. An abstraction, **AccountList**, for example, could be defined to encapsulate the list of accounts with the following object interface:

- ◆ Add an account

- ◆ Remove an account

- ◆ Iterate over the list

A similar interface is needed to define the list of employees, which is where genericity plays its role. Rather than duplicating the interface definition for various abstractions, a generic abstraction can be defined to represent all the list abstractions that might be needed in the system.

Genericity, when coupled with inheritance, can be a powerful tool for creating OO systems. Genericity signifies a generality across the types used, and inheritance signifies generality of representation and the object interface.

Generic programming is, roughly, a form of reusability, because after a generic abstraction is developed, it doesn't need to be reprogrammed, but can nevertheless be adapted to meet various designing or programming requirements.

C++ support of generic programming is discussed in Chapter 2.

Why Object Craftsmanship?

I have heard people ask a very basic question, "Why OO-based development?" I'm not surprised when these people claim that OO-based programs carry a great deal of overhead in terms of project execution and runtime performance. They say, "Abstractions, messaging, deep inheritance, and dynamic binding seem to be creating a kind of impedance or potential energy in the system, thus resulting in runtime costs." The reality is not so. Experience and experiments have shown that these factors don't cost any significant runtime performance. Often, a bad software architecture causes these problems. The bad architecture might be a result of the barriers to OOP, the mental blocks that build up from the habitual use of structural programming.

The following advantages of OOP show why object craftsmanship is so significant and useful:

♦ *Natural*—Object orientation is more than a design methodology or programming; OO is a natural way of thinking about problems and finding solutions to those problems. OO enables programmers to think about the real-world entities of any given problem. By beginning the design with concepts from the domain of real-world problems, the same concepts can be carried over to implementation, making the design and implementation cycle more seamless.

♦ *Simple*—The principle of "divide and conquer" has long been known as an efficient technique to overcome problems. Object orientation helps to decompose a complex application system into smaller, simpler pieces, enabling a problem to be divided and conquered.

♦ *Reusable*—Inheritance and composition enable programmers to *plug in* the existing objects to the new code that is being developed. A set of well-designed and quality-certified objects can provide an initial impulse to the application that you are developing. This is reusability.

♦ *Replaceable*—Existing objects can be readily replaced with new implementations, as long as the new object supports the same interfaces as the object that it replaces.

♦ *Extensible*—New capabilities can be added to existing objects. These capabilities can be represented by new object interfaces, without requiring changes to the existing interfaces. In addition, new objects with new capabilities can be added to an existing system in a modular and organized manner.

♦ *Strong cohesion*—*Cohesion* refers to how closely internals of an object are related. A well-designed object, by definition, is cohesive, because its data and behavior are always related. It provides internal integrity to the object.

♦ *Loose coupling—Coupling* refers to how closely objects of a system are related. Loose coupling is a complement to strong cohesion. OOP helps define objects with internal integrity (string cohesion) and visible and flexible relations with objects. The visible and flexible relationships among objects are represented by their object interfaces. The interfaces between objects define the objects' "contract" that enables loose coupling and independent development—as long as the contracts are respected.

C++ Expressions Of Object Orientation

C++ is an object-oriented programming language (OOPL). Because C++ is an OOPL, it possesses the following three benefits of object orientation:

♦ Implements "data abstraction" in a clean way.

♦ Tries to make parts of programs easily reusable and extensible.

♦ Tries to make existing code easily modifiable in a modular and organized manner.

All the expressions of object orientation are naturally captured in the C++ language. Object-oriented benefits, as previously mentioned, are characterized by the following three C++ features:

♦ *Class—*A way of defining a new data type, generally known as *user-defined data types* (UDT). This involves specifying the internal representation of that type, along with the operations that are used to manipulate the type. Classes are C++'s implementation of data abstraction.

♦ *Class derivation—*Involves the creation of a new type from an existing user-defined type in some hierarchical fashion. Class derivation is C++'s implementation of inheritance. Class derivation enables a class to be reusable and extensible.

♦ *Dynamic binding—*Provides a common interface for several different classes so that objects of those classes can be manipulated identically by the program. Dynamic binding is C++'s support to achieve polymorphism.

These three concepts are covered in more detail in the next few sections.

Classes

A class is an abstraction that summarizes the objects' common proper-ties (structure and behavior). Each object is always some instance of a class.

The C++ class mechanism enables users to define a new type of data according to the needs of the problem to be solved. A class type is also called an *abstract data type (ADT)*, or a UDT. A UDT in C++ is an aggregate of named data elements, possibly of different types, and a set of functions that is designed to manipulate that data. These types may add actions to an already existing type. A well-defined ADT doesn't differ from built-in types in the way that it is used—only in the way that it is created.

Data encapsulation refers to combining data and the functions that op-erate on that data into one composite type. In other words, the data and functions are packaged together in a superior and well-organized bundle (class). As a consequence, an object is no longer dependent upon any *external* (global) functions to alter its state or behavior, be-cause these functions are already part of the object itself. That is, it can receive messages (member function calls) and act upon those messages via its implementations of messages (member function definitions).

Classes normally are used to define notions that don't map logically into existing or derived data types. Typically, a class is used to intro-duce a new data type into the program; a well-designed class can be used as easily as a predefined data type.

A C++ class has three important associated constituents:

♦ *Data members*—A set of *data members* (also called *instance variables*) represents the state of the class. Generally, a class may include zero or more data members of *any* type.

Class Design Is Important

Designing classes is probably the most important activity in C++. In top-down procedural design, the core activity is the *function*. In data structures, the focus is on the *data*. On the other hand, the essence of OOP is the *class* and its mapping into real-world problems. Therefore, a C++ programmer should design a program as a set of associated abstractions, characterized by classes and objects, instead of as a cluster of isolated data structures and functions.

♦ *Member functions*—A set of *member functions* (also called *class methods*) is applied to alter the state of the class object. A class may include zero or more member functions, which are referred to collectively as the *class interface*. Member functions can be overloaded operator functions, conversion functions, constructors, or the destructor.

Data members and member functions of a class are referred to collectively as *class members* or *members of the class*.

♦ *Access specifiers*—Members of a class may be marked as **private**, **protected**, or **public**. These tags are referred to as *access specifiers*; they enforce the laws of information hiding.

Member Access Specifiers

Member access specifiers are used in C++ to enforce *information hiding*, a formal mechanism that is used to circumscribe user access to the internal representation of a class type. Information hiding is specified by labeled **public, private**, and **protected** compartments within the class body:

♦ A **public** member can be accessed by any function. The **public** functions of a class constitute the interface to objects of the class. Members of a **struct** or **union** are **public** by default.

♦ A **private** member can be accessed only by member functions and friends of the class in which it is declared. Class members are **private** by default.

♦ A **protected** member can be accessed by member functions and friends of the class in which it is declared, and by classes derived from the declared class.

Member Functions

A function (without the **friend** specifier) that is declared within the scope of a class is referred to as a *member function* of the class. Member functions provide the collection of operations that a user may carry out on the objects of a class type. This set of member functions is referred to as the *interface* of the class. The caliber of a class depends on how comprehensive and productive this set of member functions is.

Classification Of Member Functions

Class member functions generally can be classified in the following four ways:

Encapsulation, Information Hiding, And Abstraction

Information hiding, encapsulation, and abstraction are commonly used words in OO—no text on OO can be written without applying these words. Many authors use these words interchangeably to convey the OO concepts. Though these terms convey overlapping concepts, you need to understand the specific meaning of each term and how these terms are distinct from each other.

Encapsulation refers mostly to the packaging process that is characterized by a class in C++. Encapsulation is the process of bundling together, or packaging, the class member functions and class data members.

Encapsulation can be coupled with *information hiding* to restrict the visibility of objects from the user. What a user can access and what an object contains don't need to be the same set, and this is achieved by information hiding. In C++, information hiding is supported by the **public**, **protected**, and **private** keywords.

Encapsulation can be coupled with *abstraction* to define things, notions, or ideas. Abstraction encompasses more than what encapsulation does. You definitely need object-behavior and its characteristic to be abstract. Moreover, you need a common object-behavior that can be applied on a collection of classes. Abstraction gives you an opportunity to think more broadly in terms of extensibility and reusability. However, abstraction is a difficult word to grasp—it can't be understood without really understanding the motivation behind inheritance, polymorphism, composition, and reuse.

To recap—encapsulation is a packaging process; abstraction is a process that is used to organize the encapsulation hierarchically. You can't have abstraction with a single class—but you can have information hiding and encapsulation with a single class.

♦ *Manager function*—Manages class objects by controlling fundamental chores, such as initialization (constructors), cleanup (destructor), assignment, memory management, and type conversion. Manager functions usually are invoked implicitly by the compiler. If you don't provide the class-specific versions of these functions, the compiler will do so.

♦ *Implementor function*—Provides the actions associated with the class abstraction. Implementor functions make changes to the data members, which is how the state of an object can be modified. A **CoWindow** class, for example, may provide a **setActive()** function to activate a **CoWindow** object, thereby enabling the user to send messages to the object. These functions are also called *mutators*.

♦ *Accessor function*—A set of functions that provides read-access of the class abstraction to the user. Member functions that enable a user to read from otherwise **private** sections are referred to as *accessor functions*, which normally are declared to be **const**, because they aren't intended to modify the state of the object.

NOTE

Designing Of Inheritance Is Iterative

The reliable design of an inheritance hierarchy is a complex and laborious process. In the process of developing a trustworthy derivation hierarchy, the design of an abstract superclass will be altered and extended many times. Although the design process begins to exist with an *abstraction* and culminates with an *implementation*, the design may be required to undergo many feedback iterations.

♦ *Sidekick function*—Serves as a helper for the other class member functions. Generally, sidekick functions are declared as **private**. A **CoVector** class, for example, may define a **private** function, **checkRange()**, to carry out a safety action. Preferably, sidekick functions are declared as **const** functions, to guarantee that they don't make any kind of unintentional alterations to the data members.

Class Derivation

One of the basic characteristics of any OOP language is the capability to build other classes from existing classes, thereby reusing code. Inheritance enables existing types to be extended to an associated collection of subtypes. Inheritance is the process of creating new classes from existing classes. The new class is called a *derived class*, *subclass*, or *child class*. The existing class is called a *base class*, *superclass*, or *parent class*. The derived class inherits all the capabilities of the base class, but can add refinements of its own. The base class is unchanged by this process.

In C++, inheritance is implemented by the mechanism of *class derivation*. The implementations of reuse and polymorphism are the two primary uses of class derivation in C++. Polymorphism enables classes to respond to the same message differently. Reuse and polymorphism bring the most power to OOP in C++.

Polymorphic classes provide an identical interface, but can be implemented to serve different, specific requirements.

C++ provides three forms of derivation: **public**, **private**, and **protected**. These different forms are used to signify different relationships between objects.

Information Hiding Is Too Limiting

The concepts of encapsulation and data hiding dictate that nonmember functions shouldn't be able to access a class's non-**public** data. Any attempt by a nonmember function to access these data members directly (via an object) results in a compile time error.

In some instances, such rigid discrimination is too prohibitive. At the same time, changing the access levels of data members dishonors the whole notion of encapsulation and data hiding.

This dilemma can be solved by declaring a **friend** function (or a **friend** class) of the class in which the **private** data members are located. A **friend** of class **X** is a function or class that is not a member of **X**, but that is permitted to access the **private** and **protected** members of **X**. A function (or class) itself can't choose to become a **friend** of a class—only a class can grant friendships.

Public Derivation

In a **public** derivation, the derived class inherits **public** members as **public**, and **protected** members as **protected**. These members can be accessed by a new member function of the derived class. However, instances of the derived classes may access only the **public** members.

Protected Derivation

In a **protected** derivation, the derived class inherits **public** and **protected** members as **protected**. These members can be accessed by a new member function of the derived class. However, instances of the derived classes may access only the **public** members.

Private Derivation

In a **private** derivation, the derived class inherits **public** and **protected** members as **private**. These members can be accessed by a new member function of the derived class, but instances of the derived classes may not access the members. Also, **public** and **protected** members of the base class are *locked up* for subsequent derivations.

Standard Conversions Under Derivation

You must remember that when you instantiate a derived class object, the base class object is always constructed before the derived class object. The embodied base object in a derived object is referred to as a *sub-object*. A *complete object* is an object that is not a sub-object representing a base class.

A pointer (or reference) to a derived class may be converted to a pointer (or reference) to its accessible base class, provided that the conversion is unambiguous. The result of the conversion is a pointer (or reference) to the base class sub-object of the derived class object.

The following three predefined standard conversions are applied between a derived class and its accessible base classes:

♦ A derived class object is implicitly converted into an accessible, unambiguous base class sub-object.

♦ A derived class pointer (or reference) is implicitly converted into an accessible, unambiguous base class pointer (or reference).

♦ A pointer to a member of a base class is implicitly converted into a pointer to a member of a publicly derived class.

Information Hiding By A Destructor

If a class destructor is **protected** or **private**, the class can't be destroyed in a scope in which its destructor isn't visible, and thus can never be used within that scope. A **protected** destructor can be accessed only from derived classes and friends. This is a useful way to ensure that no instance of a base class is ever created; only derived classes and friends can generate its instances.

In addition to the preceding standard conversions, a pointer to any class object is implicitly converted into a pointer of type **void***. (A pointer to type **void*** always requires an explicit cast in order to assign it to a pointer of any other type.) As mentioned in the preceding list, a pointer to a member of a **public** base class can reliably be assigned to a pointer to a derived class member of the same type. A pointer to a derived class member, however, can't be assigned reliably to a pointer to its base class member. The reason is that the pointer to a class member, when invoked, is bound to an object of its class. The following is an example with simple class definitions:

```
class CoWindow
{
public:
    CoWindow();
    ~CoWindow();
    char* getTitle();
};

class CoButton:public CoWindow
{
public:
    CoButton();
    ~CoButton();
    char* getStatusAsString();
};
```

For example, **pfn1** is a **CoWindow** pointer to a class member function initialized to **CoWindow::getTitle()**:

```
typedef char*(CoWindow::*CO_WINDOW_FUNCTION)();

int main()
{
    CO_WINDOW_FUNCTION pfn1=&CoWindow::getTitle;
    CoWindow w;
    (w.*pfn1)(); //calls CoWindow::getTitle()
    return 0;
}
```

Because a **CoButton** object is guaranteed to contain a **CoWindow** sub-object, you can reliably assign the address of **CoWindow::getTitle()** to a **CoButton** pointer to a class member function, as the following demonstrates:

```
typedef char*(CoButton::*CO_BUTTON_FUNCTION)();

int main()
{
    CO_BUTTON_FUNCTION pfn2=&CoWindow::getTitle; //okay
    CoButton b;
    (b.*pfn2)(); //okay
    return 0;
}
```

Next, you can assign the address of the **CoButton** member function **getStatusAsString()** to **pfn1**. The assignment, because it is chancy, requires an explicit cast:

```
CO_WINDOW_FUNCTION pfn1=
    static_cast<CO_WINDOW_FUNCTION>(
        &CoButton::getStatusAsString);
```

pfn1 will always be invoked by binding it to a **CoWindow** class object. On the other hand, **CoButton::getStatusAsString()** may access members of **CoButton** that are not contained in a **CoWindow** class object. Whether the invocation of **pfn1** causes the collapse of the program depends on the actual type of the base class object. See the following example:

```
int main()
{
    CO_WINDOW_FUNCTION pfn1=
        static_cast<CO_WINDOW_FUNCTION>(
            &CoButton::getStatusAsString);

    CoWindow w;
    CoButton b;

    CoWindow* pw=&b; //pw addresses to CoButton
    (pw->*pfn1)(); //ok
    pw=&w; //pw addresses to an CoWindow
    (pw->*pfn1)(); //oops: disaster...!

    return 0;
}
```

The example uses the **static_cast** operator. The **static_cast** operator is explained in the section "Runtime Type Information (RTTI)" later in this chapter.

Casting From Base Object Into Derived Object

The conversion of a derived class object into an object of a base class is considered trustworthy. However, the conversion of a base class object into an object of a derived class is *not* reliable, because this conversion is an attempt to put a smaller object into a larger object. This conversion would leave a *void* inside the derived object containing *garbage*. This is why initialization, as well as assignment of a derived class to one of its base classes, requires that you explicitly apply the **dynamic_cast** operator. The **dynamic_cast** operator is explained in the section on "Runtime Type Information (RTTI)" later in this chapter.

Dynamic Binding

Dynamic binding (or *late binding*) refers to function resolution that takes place at runtime. In other words, dynamic binding indicates that all information needed to call a function is not known at compile time. On the other hand, *static binding* (or *early binding*) refers to a function call that has all the necessary information at compile time to execute the function. Examples of early binding are normal and C library function calls.

The main benefit of early binding is efficiency, because all information essential to call a function is available at compile time. The main drawback and inconvenience of early binding, however, is that you need to code a great deal of information in the code to take care of all possible function invocations that happen at runtime. In the following example of the typical GUI hierarchy classes, a **CoWindow** class serves as the base class of the entire GUI hierarchy. All the classes in the GUI hierarchy must have a **show()** function to display the GUI object on screen. Because the implementation of **show()** depends on the GUI object being operated on, you must provide an instance of **show()** in all the GUI classes. A skeleton implementation of a typical GUI hierarchy is shown in Listing 1.1.

Listing 1.1   An example of a typical GUI hierarchy.

```
class CoWindow
{
public:
    CoWindow();
    void show() const;
    //...
};

class CoDialogBox : public CoWindow
{
```

```
public:
    CoDialogBox();
    void show() const;
    //...
};

class CoButton : public CoWindow
{
public:
    CoButton();
    void show() const;
    //...
};

class CoRadioButton : public CoButton
{
public:
    CoRadioButton();
    void show() const;
    //...
};

class CoRadioGroup:public CoRadioButton
{
public:
    CoRadioGroup();
    void show() const;
    //...
};

void f(const CoWindow& w)
{
    w.show();
}

int main()
{
    CoDialogBox d;
    CoRadioButton b;
    CoRadioGroup g;

    f(d);
    f(b);
    f(g);

    return 0;
}
```

Unfortunately, **f()** defined in this style does not produce the expected results. For every call of **f()** in **main()**, **CoWindow::show()** is called, because the compiler sees only the type of **w** in the **f()** function. And, because type of **w** is **CoWindow**, all the function calls in **main()** result in **CoWindow::show()** being called. To invoke the correct **show()**, you should provide some sort of type-identification with each type that can be used at runtime, to manipulate the object being referred by **w**. Next, all the classes are reimplemented, as shown in Listing 1.2:

Listing 1.2   An example of implementing type identification for a GUI class hierarchy.

```
class CoWindow
{
public:
    enum TYPE_ID {DIALOG_BOX, RADIO_BUTTON, RADIO_GROUP};
    CoWindow();

    TYPE_ID typeId() const
    {
        return typeId_;
    }

    void show() const;
    //...

protected:
    TYPE_ID typeId_; //type identification code for the class
};

class CoDialogBox:public CoWindow
{
public:
    CoDialogBox()
    {
        typeId_=DIALOG_BOX;
        //...
    }
    void show() const;
    //...
};

class CoButton:public CoWindow
{
public:
    CoButton();
```

```
    void show() const;
    //...
};

class CoRadioButton:public CoButton
{
public:
    CoRadioButton()
    {
        typeId_=RADIO_BUTTON;
        //...
    }
    void show() const;
    //...
};

class CoRadioGroup:public CoRadioButton
{
public:
    CoRadioGroup()
    {
        typeId_=RADIO_GROUP;
        //...
    }
    void show() const;
    //...
};

void f(const CoWindow& w)
{
    typedef const CoDialogBox& RCD;
    typedef const CoRadioButton& RCB;
    typedef const CoRadioGroup& RCG;

    switch (w.typeId())
    {
        case CoWindow::DIALOG_BOX:
            RCD(w).show();break;
        case CoWindow::RADIO_BUTTON:
            RCB (w).show();break;
        case CoWindow::RADIO_GROUP:
            RCB(w).show();break;
    }//switch
```

Now, it works! However, dispatching a message to whatever instance happens to be pointed to by a reference (or pointer) is one of the very basic objectives of OOP. The moment that you become concerned about the type of a reference (or pointer), you are far from object-oriented programming. Also, you must realize that this method of coding is impractical. Functions written in this style depend on the implementation details of the derivation hierarchy. Functions such as **f()** must *know about* all the kinds of **CoWindow**s that exist. Therefore, the code for any such function grows each time that a new **CoWindow** is added to the system—it thus leads to maintenance problems. Moreover, you will not be able to extend or customize the hierarchy unless you have access to the source code. This definitely violates the principles of information hiding.

Therefore, you need a C++ technique to delay until runtime the selection of which member function gets executed. This binding technique must enable you to encapsulate the implementation details of the derivation hierarchy from the programmer. User code must no longer be subjected to change with each change to the hierarchy. Fortunately, C++ provides such a technique, called *late* (or *dynamic*) *binding*, that enables you to create objects that can respond to events that occur at runtime, without having to make a compile time resolution as to which function gets called.

By using dynamic binding, you can add a new **CoWindow** derived class to the derivation without having to modify existing code. The general **f()** function remains unchanged, regardless of how the hierarchy is modified, and does not need to know about future **CoWindow** derivation.

You can implement dynamic binding by using a **virtual** function. Dynamic binding is also referred to as *polymorphism*. A polymorphic class declares or inherits at least one **virtual** function. Polymorphic classes provide an identical interface, but can be implemented to serve different specific requirements.

Virtual Function

A **virtual** function is a special member function invoked through a **public** base class reference or pointer. A **virtual** function is declared by prefacing a member function declaration with the C++ **virtual** keyword.

Because a **virtual** function is bound dynamically at runtime, it allows derived classes to provide different versions of a base class function. The interpretation of a **virtual** function call depends on the type of the object it is called for. On the other hand, with non-**virtual** function

TIP

Making Virtual Functions Inline

Recall that C++ provides the *inline function* mechanism in which the explicit function calls can be avoided to reduce runtime overheads. An **inline** function is a function whose code gets expanded at the point of its call during compilation.

If some possibility exists of early binding of a **virtual** function, then making it an **inline** function has an advantage. However, if the **virtual** function will always be invoked as a consequence of dynamic binding, then making it **inline** is purposeless, because the compiler doesn't know which version of the function will ultimately be called, and therefore can't expand the code at compile time.

calls, the interpretation depends only on the type of the pointer or reference denoting the object for which it is called. You declare a **virtual** function in a base class and then redefine it in any derived class. A redefined **virtual** function is said to *override* the base class function; for example:

```
class CoWindow
{
public:
    virtual void show(); //virtual function
    //...
};
```

Two important points should be noted about the **show()** member function:

♦ It is declared as a member function of **CoWindow**, because it provides a functionality that the entire **CoWindow** hierarchy must provide.

♦ It is declared as a **virtual** function, because **CoWindow::show()** can't implement the **show()** functionality of the entire hierarchy. The actual implementation details depend on the derived class type; and the details aren't known yet.

The selection of the call of a **virtual** function happens at runtime, based on the type of the object for which it is called, whereas a non-**virtual** function is bound with the type of the pointer or reference at compile time.

Abstract Classes

Very often, a base class **virtual** function isn't intended to be invoked—it simply serves as a placeholder for the still-unknown derived class types. For example, a **CoWindow** class designer may decide to mark **show()** as a placeholder, and may not want to provide any implementation, because a **CoWindow** class is just an abstraction. Such functions

Polymorphism Or Overloading

Some authors say, "C++ provides three different types of polymorphism—**virtual** functions, function name overloading, and operator overloading." This book, however, doesn't use the word polymorphism to denote function name overloading and operator overloading. Polymorphism should be referred to only as a result of dynamic binding. Therefore, using so many different words to mean polymorphism doesn't make sense.

are referred to as *pure **virtual*** functions. A **virtual** function can be denoted *pure* by initializing its declaration to zero, possibly followed by the keywords **const** and **throw**. For example, in

```
class CoWindow
{
public:
    virtual void show()=0;
    //...
};
```

show() is a pure **virtual** function. A class with a pure **virtual** function is referred to as an *abstract* class. An abstract class can't be instantiated as a complete object, which makes sense, because an abstract class is just a notion or concept—it has yet to become concrete in the form of a derived class. Similarly, you can't use an abstract class as an argument type or as a function return type. It can be used only as a base class for subsequent derivations, which means that sub-objects of an abstract class can be created. Because pointers and references are not instances, you can declare pointers or references to an abstract class; for example:

```
CoWindow* pw1; //ok: pointer
CoWindow* pw2= new (nothrow) CoWindow; //error
CoWindow w; //error
CoWindow aw[8]; //error
void e(CoWindow w); //error
void f(const CoWindow& w); //ok
void g(CoWindow* w); //ok
CoWindow& h(); //ok: reference return type
```

If a definition of a **virtual** function is provided in a base class, it serves as a default instance for subsequent class derivation. If the derived class doesn't provide its own implementation of the **virtual** function, and its pointer (or reference) receives a call for this function, then the message will be *passed up* to its base class automatically. For example, if class **CoRadioButton** does not define its own instance of **show()**, then the following call, as shown in Listing 1.3, will invoke **CoButton::show()**:

Listing 1.3   Not overriding a base-class virtual function.
```
class CoWindow
{
public:
```

NOTE

Hiding The Virtual Mechanism

If a base class **virtual** function and a derived class function with the same name have different function signatures, a compiler considers them different, and the **virtual** function mechanism is ignored. A compiler may give a warning about that situation, but if you happen to ignore that warning, your program may give very awkward results. In a small program, it might be easy to catch such a mistake, but in a large project, such a mistake can be quite painful to debug. Remember, the derived class function with a different signature will *hide* the **virtual** function. It isn't the same as overriding a **virtual** function.

```
    CoWindow();
    virtual void show()=0;
};

class CoButton:public CoWindow
{
public:
    CoButton();
    void show(); //overrides
    //...
};

class CoRadioButton:public CoButton
{
public:
    CoRadioButton();
    //does not override CoButton::show()
    //...
};

void f(CoWindow* w)
{
    w->show();
}

int main()
{
    CoRadioButton* pb=new (nothrow) CoRadioButton;
    f(pb); //invokes CoButton::show()

    return 0;
}
```

Non-**Public Virtual** Functions

The access level of a **virtual** function is determined by the base class type, which means that a **public** implementation of a **private virtual** function isn't callable via a base class pointer or a reference. As an example, the following code makes **show()** protected in **CoWindow**:

```
class CoWindow
{
public:
    CoWindow();
```

```
protected:
    virtual void show()=0;
};

class CoButton:public CoWindow
{
public:
    CoButton();
    void show();
};

void f(CoWindow* w)
{
    w->show(); //error: protected function
}
```

On the other hand, if a **virtual** function has been declared **public** in the base class, it is always callable via a pointer or reference of the base class type—no matter what the access level of the same function is in the derived classes. For example:

```
class CoWindow
{
public:
    CoWindow();
    virtual void show()=0;
};

class CoButton:public CoWindow
{
public:
    CoButton();

protected:
    void show();
};
```

Even though **CoButton::show()** is **protected**, the following call is legal:

```
CoButton* pb= new (nothrow) CoButton;
f(pb); //ok: invokes CoButton::show()
```

On the other hand, the following call is illegal because

CoButton::show() is a protected function that can't be accessed directly:

```
pb->show(); //error: can't access protected CoButton::show()
```

Virtual Destructors

Take a look at the following code segment:

```
void f(CoWindow* w)
{
    w->show();
    delete w;
}
```

The explicit deletion of the **w** pointer causes the **CoWindow** destructor to be applied to the object to which **w** points. However, the object may not be pointing to a **CoWindow** object, but instead to some subsequently derived class type, such as **CoButton**. To invoke the destructor for the actual class type, an explicit typecasting might help, as follows:

```
void f(CoWindow* w)
{
    typedef CoDialogBox* PCD;
    typedef CoRadioButton* PCB;
    typedef CoRadioGroup* PCG;

    switch (w->typeId())
    {
        case CoWindow::DIALOG_BOX:
            PCD(w)->~CoDialogBox();break;
        case CoWindow::RADIO_BUTTON:
            PCB(w)->~CoRadioButton();break;
        case CoWindow::RADIO_GROUP:
            PCG(w)->~CoRadioGroup();break;
    }//switch

} //end of f()
```

Explicit typecasting such as **PCD(w)**, however, can undo all the advantages of dynamic binding. The notion of *virtual destructor* extends dynamic binding to destructors. Although destructors have different names, they can be declared as **virtual**; for example:

```
class CoWindow
```

```
{
public:
    CoWindow();
    virtual ~CoWindow();
    //...
};

void f(CoWindow* w)
{
    w->show();
    delete w; //ok
}

int main()
{
    CoRadioGroup* prg= new (nothrow) CoRadioGroup;
    f(prg);
    return 0;
}
```

The statement

```
delete w;
```

in the f() function will correctly invoke the destructor for the **CoRadioGroup** class.

The destructors can also exhibit dynamic binding in case of explicit invocation depending on how the destructor is invoked. For example,

```
CoRadioGroup* prg= new (nothrow) CoRadioGroup;
prg->~CoWindow();
```

uses the **virtual** destructor. On the other hand, the call

```
prg->~CoWindow::CoWindow();
```

calls **CoWindow**'s destructor.

After a base class declares its destructor to be **virtual**, every destructor in the entire derivation hierarchy becomes **virtual**. Furthermore, a destructor, even though it can be **virtual**, can never be made into a pure **virtual** function.

TIP

Always Declare A Destructor Virtual

Specifying the destructors in a derivation hierarchy as **virtual** guarantees that the appropriate destructor is invoked whenever **delete** is applied to a base class pointer. Hence, as a general standard of the hierarchy design, the destructor of an abstract class should always be specified as **virtual**.

Exception Handling

An important issue for the design of frameworks is the strategy of exception handling. The exception handling mechanism may be considered a runtime ally of the compile-time-type checking mechanism. Exception handling makes the design process of frameworks more significant and produces code that has a much better prospect of executing as predicted. Because exception handling has a great influence on the design and implementation of a framework, you need to read this section carefully, which presents concepts of error handling in C++. Also, this section examines whether the C++ error handling mechanism supports the idioms of OOP.

Exception handling in C++ provides a wonderful method by which the caller of a function can be informed that some error condition has occurred in the called function. C++'s exception handling mechanism is designed to address any kind of programming problem, whether it is memory allocation failure or improper typecasting at runtime. Exception handling provides a way of transferring control and information from the error-point to an *exception handler*. When a function that finds a problem it can't cope with *throws* an exception, hoping that its caller (direct or indirect) can handle the problem, a function that wants to handle that kind of problem can indicate its willingness to *catch* that exception.

C++ Support To Exception Handling

C++ provides three keywords to support exception handling in a program:

♦ **try**—The section of code in which an exception can take place must be prefixed by the keyword **try**. Following the **try** keyword is a block of code enveloped by curly brackets. This code block announces that the program is ready to test for the existence of exceptions.

Exception Handling Is A Good Style

C++ provides uniform syntax and style to support exception handling; in C, exception handling can be accomplished only informally and incompletely. In this way, according to Dr. Bjarne Stroustrup, C++ exception handling supports *good programming style* in C++ in the same manner that other C++ features do. Also, the C++ exception handling standard supports the notion of object-oriented design, by allowing the use of polymorphic objects to define exceptions. It is possible to design a good hierarchical exception model for a given system.

- **throw**—An exception is indicated by the keyword **throw**. Throwing an exception transfers control to a handler. An object is passed and the type of that object determines which handlers can catch it.

- **catch**—The section of code in which an exception is handled must be prefixed by the keyword **catch**. Following the **catch** keyword is a block of code enclosed by curly brackets. The construct

```
catch (/*...*/)
{/*...*/}
```

is referred to as an *exception handler*. It can be used only after a block prefixed with the keyword **try** or immediately after another exception handler.

How *try-throw-catch* Mechanisms Work

Throwing an exception transfers control to the nearest handler of an appropriate type. An object is passed and the static type of that object determines which handler can catch it. Listing 1.4 presents an example to show how to throw and catch an exception:

Listing 1.4   Throwing and catching exceptions.

```
typedef void (*CO_PFN)();

void fn()
{
    cout<<"in fn()"<<endl;
    //some handling stuff
}
void f(int i)
{
    try
    {
        if (i==0) throw "Help!";
        if (i==13) throw 13;
        if (i==169) throw fn;
    } //try block
    catch(const char* pChar)
    {
        cout<<"Please "<<pChar<<endl;
        //some handling stuff
    }
    catch(int v)
    {
        cout<<"oops..."<<v<<endl;
```

```
        //some handling stuff
    }
    catch (CO_PFN pfn)
    {
        pfn();
    }
    //some processing stuff
    return;
}

int main()
{
    f(0);
    f(13);
    f(169);

    return 0;
}
```

The call

```
f(0);
```

executes the statement

```
throw "Help!";
```

The statement transfers the control to the handler (**catch**-block) of type **const char***. Hence, you will see the following output:

```
Please Help!
```

Similarly, the calls

```
f(13);
f(169);
```

output

```
oops...13
in fn()
```

The exception handling mechanism provides an elegant way to interrupt the program flow (when an exception occurs). The following is the sequence of steps taken:

1. The program searches for a matching handler.

2. If a handler is found, the stack is unwound to that point and program control is transferred to the handler.

3. If no handler is found, the program calls the **terminate()** function. If no exceptions are thrown, the program executes in the normal fashion.

Object-Oriented Exceptions

Although C++ allows an exception to be of any type, throwing exceptions of a class type is useful. An exception of type **E** can be caught by a handler of type **T** if **T** is an accessible base class of **E** at the throwpoint. This enables you to define exceptions in a hierarchical manner and, by applying polymorphism, to represent the exception model of a system uniformly and elegantly; for example:

```cpp
class CoWindowException
{
public:
    CoWindowException();
    virtual int repaint();
};

class CoDialogException:public CoWindowException
{
public:
    CoDialogException();
    virtual int repaint();
};

showWindow()
{
    //something goes wrong here!
    throw CoDialogException();
    //...
}

void f()
{
    try
    {
        showWindow();
    }
    catch(CoWindowException& WinExc)
```

```
    {
        WinExc.repaint();
    }
}
```

The call of **showWindow()** in **f()** may generate an exception that
throws **CoDialogException**. The **catch** block of **f()** will call the **virtual** function **repaint()** of **CoDialogException**—not that of
CoWindowException.

Rethrowing An Exception

Having caught an exception, it is not unusual for a handler to conclude that it really can do nothing about the error. In that case, the
exception typically is tossed again (known as *rethrowing*), with the op-
timism that some other handler can do a superior job. A rethrow is
shown by an empty **throw** expression, which can occur only within a
catch handler. For example:

```
void f()
{
    try
    {
        showWindow(); //throws CoDialogException
    }
    catch(CoWindowException& WinExc)
    {
        WinExc.repaint();
        throw; //rethrows
    }
}

void g()
{
    try
    {
        f();
    }
    catch(CoDialogException&)
    {/*...*/}
    catch(CoWindowException&)
    {/*...*/}
}
```

In the preceding code, the rethrow is handled by the **CoDialogException** handler of **g()**. Even though the exception **CoDialogException** is rethrown by the **CoWindowException** handler of **f()**, it is dealt with by the **CoDialogException** handler of **g()**.

An inferior form of **catch** is available—an ellipsis **(...)** in **catch** provides a kind of *catch-all*. For example, the following **f()** function catches all the exceptions and rethrows:

```
void f()
{
    try
    {
        showWindow();
    }
    catch(...) //catch any exception
    {
        //...
        throw;
    }
}
```

Note that a rethrow throws the object without copying it.

Carrying Additional Information In An Exception Object

The exception object is treated exactly the way any other object is treated. An exception object can carry information from the throw-point to the catch-point. This is information that the program user wants to know when the program encounters some abnormality at runtime. For example, a program user might need to know the index of a vector that provoked a range error as shown in Listing 1.5.

Listing 1.5   Exception object can carry information.
```
class CoVector
{
public:
    CoVector(int);
    class Range;
    int& operator[](int i);

protected:
    int* pInt_;
```

```
        int theSize_;
};

class CoVector::Range
{
public:
    CoVector::Range(int);
    int index_;
};

CoVector::Range::Range(int i):index_(i)
{/*...*/}

int& CoVector::operator[](int i)
{
    if(0<=i && i<theSize_) return pInt_[i];
    throw Range(i);
}

void f(const CoVector& v)
{
    try
    {
        int temp=v[169];
    }
    catch(const CoVector::Range& r)
    {
        cout<<"bad index="<<r.index_<<endl;
    }
}
```

The statement in parentheses after **catch** is, in fact, a declaration and is similar to a formal argument declaration for a function.

Order Of Handlers

The handlers are attempted in sequence. Because a derived exception can be caught by more than one handler, some care must be used while enumerating **catch** handlers for a **try** block. Moreover, no priority is given to an exact match over a match that requires the application of a standard conversion. For example, the following order of **catch** handlers is not considered skillful:

```
class CoWindow
{/*...*/};
```

```
class CoButton:public CoWindow
{/*...*/};

void f(int v)
{
    typedef void (*PCF)(const char*);

    try
    {
        if (v) throw &v;
    } //try
    catch(void*) {/*...*/}
    catch(PCF) {/*...*/}
    catch(const CoWindow&) {/*...*/}
    catch(const CoButton&) {/*...*/}
    catch(...) {/*...*/}

    return;
}
```

In the previous example, the **void*** handler will never allow the next handler, **PCF**, to be caught. Similarly, the **CoButton&** handler will never invoke, because the **CoWindow&** handler will always be caught. A compiler may issue a warning when a handler for a type **D** that is derived from type **B** is specified after a handler for **B**. However, if the **(...)** handler is not the concluding handler, a compile time error is generated.

Construction And Destruction During Exceptions

When program flow is interrupted by an exception, all automatic objects are destroyed that have been constructed since the beginning of the **try**-block was entered. The effect of calling destructors for automatic objects is referred to as *stack unwinding*. This is explained in Listing 1.6.

Listing 1.6 Invocations of constructors and destructors when an exception is thrown.

```
class CoClass
{
public:
    int v_;
    CoClass(int v=0):v_(v)
```

```cpp
        {
            cout<<"CoClass(int): "<<v_<<endl;
        }
        ~CoClass()
        {
            cout<<"~CoClass(): "<<v_<<endl;
        }
};

class CoError
{
public:
    int v_;
    CoError(int v=0):v_(v)
    {
        cout<<"CoError(int): "<<v_<<endl;
    }
    CoError(const CoError& ve):v_(ve.v_)
    {
        cout<<"CoError(const CoError&): "
            <<ve.v_<<endl;
    }
    ~CoError()
    {
        cout<<"~CoError(): "<<v_<<endl;
    }
};

int f(int v)
{
    if (v==13)
    {
        CoClass vc(0); //auto object
        throw CoError(v);
    }
    return v;
}

int main()
{
    try
    {
        CoClass vc(169); //auto object
        f(13);
    }
    catch(const CoError& e)
```

NOTE

**Exceptions
In A Constructor**

If the exception is thrown during construction of some objects, destructors are not invoked for those objects that are semiconstructed. For example, if an array of objects is under construction when an exception is thrown, destructors are invoked only for those array elements that are fully constructed.

```
    {
        cout<<"Caught : "<<e.v_<<endl;
    }
    return 0;
}
```

This example produces the following output:

```
CoClass(int): 169
CoClass(int): 0
CoError(int): 13
CoError(const CoError&): 13
~CoError(): 13
~CoClass(): 0
~CoClass(): 169
Caught: 13
~CoError(): 13
```

A Function's Exception Specifications

The argument list of a function is referred to as the *signature* of the function, because the argument list is often used to differentiate one instance of a function from another. A function consists of four parts: a return type, the function name, the signature, and the function body. The first three parts are collectively referred to as *function prototype*. The function prototype provides the compiler with the type information necessary for it to perform compile time type checking. Typically, the user of a function is aware only of the function's prototype. But, if the user is supposed to write exception handlers to receive all the exceptions that the function may throw, the user obviously must also know the types of the thrown expressions.

To solve this problem, a function's prototype (or definition, if it replaces the prototype) may include *exception specifications* that list exceptions that it might directly or indirectly throw. These specifications appear as a suffix to the function declaration; for example:

```
void f() throw(v1,v2,v3);
void g();
void h() throw();
void e() throw(WClass*);
```

The declaration of **f()** specifies that the function may throw exceptions of types **v1**, **v2**, and **v3**, as well as exceptions derived from these types (and no other types); if the function does throw another type of exception, a compiler-generated runtime error occurs. Function **g()** is declared without an exception specification, which means that it may throw any exception. Function **h()** will not throw any exception. Function **e()** can throw exceptions of type **WClass***, or a pointer to a class publicly derived from **WClass**.

The function's suffix is not considered to be part of the function's pointer type. However, a pointer to a function assigned to a pointer to a function only allows exceptions that are allowed by the pointer being assigned to. For example:

```
void (*pf1)();    //no exception specification
void (*pf2)() throw(int);

void f()
{
    pf1 = pf2;  //ok: pf1 is less restrictive
    pf2 = pf1;  //error: pf2 is more restrictive
}
```

Unexpected And Uncaught Exceptions
The definition

```
void f() throw(v1,v2,v3)
{
    SomeAction();
}
```

is equivalent to writing the following:

```
void f()
{
    try
    {
        SomeAction();
    }
    catch(v1)
    {
        throw; //rethrows
    }
    catch(v2)
    {
        throw; //rethrows
    }
    catch(v3)
```

```
    {
        throw; //rethrows
    }
    catch(...)
    {
        unexpected(); //declared in <exception>
    }
}
```

The **unexpected()** function is called when a function throws an exception that is not listed in its exception specification. The function **unexpected()**, by default, calls any user-defined function that is registered by **set_unexpected()**. If no function is registered with **set_unexpected()**, the **unexpected()** function then calls **terminate()**. The prototypes of these three functions are as follows:

```
void unexpected();
typedef void (*unexpected_handler)();
unexpected_handler set_unexpected(unexpected_handler) throw
();
void terminate();
```

The return value of **set_unexpected()** is the previous function given to **set_unexpected()**.

The function **terminate()** can be called by **unexpected()** or by the program when a handler for an exception can't be found. The default action by **terminate()** is to call **abort()**. Such a default mechanism causes immediate program termination. You can modify the way that your program terminates when an exception occurs that isn't enumerated in the exception specification. If you don't want the program to conclude with a call to **abort()**, you can define a function to be called instead. Such a function (called a *terminate function*) will be called by **terminate()** if it is registered with **set_terminate()**. The declaration of **set_terminate()** is as follows:

```
typedef void (*terminate_handler)();
terminate_handler set_terminate(terminate_handler) throw();
```

The return value is the previous function given to **set_terminate()**.

The **<exception>** header file contains the declarations and prototypes for exception-handling functions and classes, their data members, and member functions.

Virtual Functions With Exception Specifications

A **virtual** function may have an exception specification. The exception specification for the overriding member function cannot be less restrictive than the exception specification of the overridden **virtual** function; for example:

```
class CoWindow
{
public:
    virtual void show() throw (int);
    virtual void getFocus() throw(int, char);
};

class CoDialogBox : public CoWindow
{
public:
    //error: less restrictive
    void show() throw (int, char);

    //ok: more restrictive
    void getFocus() throw (int);
};
```

The compiler gives an error for the overridden **CoDialogBox::show()** function, because at runtime, this function can throw either an **int** or a **char**, whereas the original specification for this function allows only **int** to be thrown. On the other hand, **CoDialogBox::setFocus()** is a valid overriding function, because its exception specification is more restrictive than the original specification.

Exception Specifications, Or Not?

Some programmers argue that exception specifications shouldn't be used in production code. The problem, according to this argument, is that the runtime effects of an exception specification are almost never what is desired (usually immediate termination), and in complex systems, it is almost impossible to maintain exception specifications so that they are always up to date. In my opinion, this argument doesn't have merit, because if new exceptions are being introduced without proper handling, the chances of a crash or undesired behavior still exist. In fact, exception specifications provide a basis for standards of quality assurance in the areas of system design and implementation. Any exception-related mistakes must be caught by this standard. It, therefore, guarantees a more robust system if done properly.

NOTE

realloc() Or calloc() In C++?

The **new** and **delete** operators are enhanced versions of the standard C library functions **malloc()** and **free()**. However, **new** and **delete** do not support the functionality of **realloc()** and **calloc()**.

Memory Management

To achieve a high degree of reliability and to address space-optimization related issues, a framework must perform memory management in a highly proficient way. This section conveys the fundamentals of C++ memory management, as well as a few issues and techniques related to memory handling in a program.

You may allocate memory in a C++ program at execution time from a domain referred to as the program's *free store*, or *heap*. Such memory is addressed by a pointer that contains the starting address of the object. Note that this memory is still *engaged* even when the function in which it is allocated exits. This mechanism of runtime allocation is supported by two C++-specific operators: **new** and **delete**. These operators take advantage of C++ features (such as constructors, destructors, operator overloading, and so forth) and make dynamic memory handling easy.

The new Operator

Like the **malloc()** function in C, the **new** operator in C++ is used to allocate contiguous, unnamed memory dynamically. Unlike **malloc()**, however, the **new** operator no longer needs to use the **sizeof()** operator to specify the exact number of bytes required. The fact that different types occupy different amounts of memory is manipulated by the compiler. If successful, the **new** operator returns a pointer of the correct type instead of the **void*** which **malloc()** returns. The pointer returned by the statement

```
new T;
```

is of the correct type (in other words, a pointer to **T**) without the need for explicit casting as needed when you use **malloc()**. For example,

```
int* pInt=new int;
```

allocates one object of type **int**, and

```
T* pT=new T(13);
```

allocates a **T** class object and calls the **T** constructor that accepts an **int**. The parentheses following the class name, if present, supply arguments to the class constructor. If the parentheses are not present, as in

```
T* pT1=new T;
```

NOTE

Garbage Collection In C++

C++ does not have a standard *garbage collector* to look out for unreferenced objects and make them accessible to **new** for reuse. Consequently, if you forget to apply the **delete** operator to something that was earlier allocated with **new**, leaving a *stray* (or more precisely, *orphan*) memory block, the amount of memory consumed will have an adverse effect on the system. This situation is referred to as a *memory leak*.

the class must define either a constructor that does not require arguments or no constructors at all.

Array Allocation

An array can be allocated from the free store by following the type specifier with a bracket-enclosed dimension. The dimension can be any expression; for example:

```
char* TwofoldArray=new char[2*Extent];
```

Arrays of class objects can also be allocated, for example:

```
T* pT=new T[SomeExtent];
```

When **new** Fails

The program's free store isn't unlimited; during the process of program execution, it may become exhausted. If not enough memory exists to allocate a requested type, **new** throws a **bad_alloc** exception that is declared in the **<new>** header file. Therefore, you must not ignore the fact that **new** can throw **bad_alloc**. For example:

```
bool reserve(unsigned long Amount)
{
    double* ptr;
    try
    {
        ptr=new double[Amount];
    }
    catch(const bad_alloc&)
    {
        cerr<<"Free store is not adequate"<<endl;
        return false;
    }
    //...
}
```

The delete Operator

The storage duration of the object that is allocated through use of the **new** operator is from the point of its creation until it is explicitly released by the programmer.

The **delete** operator offers dynamic memory deallocation, releasing a memory block allocated by a call to **new**. The **delete** operator is similar but superior to the standard library function **free()**. It is applied to a

Using new And delete Correctly

It is legal to use **malloc()**, **delete**, **new** and **free()** in the same program, but they must be used in the proper combination. The **delete** operator must be applied only to memory that has been allocated by the **new** operator. Applying the **delete** operator to memory that is not allocated on the free store (using **new**) is likely to bring about an undefined and problematic display of the program during execution. For example, it is not legal to call **delete** on a pointer allocated using **malloc()**. Similarly, it is not legal to call **free()** with a pointer allocated using **new**.

The effect of accessing a deleted object is undefined. The effect of deleting an array with plain **delete** syntax is undefined, as is deleting an individual object with the **delete[]** syntax.

Application of the **delete** operator to a pointer set to zero is *always* safe.

pointer addressing the dynamic object. A request for nonarray deallocation uses the global function **operator delete()**. The following is an example:

```
void store()
{
    int* pInt=new int;
    //...
    delete pInt;
    return;
}
```

Array Deallocation

Arrays are deleted by the **delete[]** operator. The array dimension doesn't need to be specified within the brackets. For example:

```
T* pT=new T[extent];
//...
delete[] pT;
typedef
int (*CO_ACTION)();
CO_ACTION* actions=new CO_ACTION[13];
//...
delete[] actions;
```

In the case of an array, **delete** destroys the elements in order of decreasing address (that is, in reverse order of construction).

Deleting void*

An object can't be deleted by using a pointer of type **void***, because the type of the object allocated is unknown. In such a case, either delete the object by using the allocated type or call the **delete** operator directly. For example:

```
class CoClass
{
public:
    CoClass()
    {
        cout<<"In the constructor"<<endl;
    }
    ~CoClass()
    {
        cout<<"In the destructor"<<endl;
    }
```

```
};

int main()
{
    void* pv=new (nothrow) CoClass;
    //delete  pv; //error
    //operator delete(pv); //just deletes.
                            //does not call destructor
    delete (CoClass*)pv; //deletes. calls destructor
    return 0;
}
```

set_new_handler()

The C++ library provides the **set_new_handler()** mechanism to take action when an attempt to allocate memory by using **new** fails. The declaration of **set_new_handler()**, found in the header file **<new>**, looks as follows:

```
typedef void (*new_handler)();
new_handler set_new_handler(new_handler new_p) throw();
```

set_new_handler() installs the function to be called when the global **operator new()** or **operator new[]()** can't allocate the requested memory. If **new** can't allocate the requested memory, it calls the **new_p** handler that was set by a previous call to **set_new_handler()**. If no handler installed by **set_new_handler()** exists, **new** throws **bad_alloc**. **set_new_handler()** returns the old handler, if one has been registered.

The **new_p** function should specify the actions to be taken when **new** can't satisfy a request for memory allocation. The **new_p** function generally performs one of the following:

♦ Makes more memory available for allocation and then returns

♦ Throws an exception of type **bad_alloc** or a class derived from **bad_alloc**

♦ Calls either **abort()** or **exit()**

In summary, the purpose of **set_new_handler()** is to provide access to a function that is to be called only under the exceptional condition that the free store is exhausted. For example:

```
#include <new> //essential

void FauxPas()
{
```

```
        cout<<"Free store is empty"<<endl;
        //...
}
int main()
{
        set_new_handler(FauxPas);
        //...
        return 0;
}
```

No-Throw And Placement Forms Of new

The C++ standard header file **<new>** provides the following useful forms of **new**:

```
//form# 1
void* operator new(size_t size, const nothrow_t&) throw();
//form# 2
void* operator new[](size_t size, const nothrow_t&) throw();
//form# 3
void* operator new  (size_t size, void* ptr) throw();
//form# 4
void* operator new[](size_t size, void* ptr) throw();
```

Forms 1 and 2 are called *no-throw forms* of **new**. They do not throw the exception **bad_alloc** when memory allocation fails. Instead, they return zero. The following example demonstrates the use of form 2:

```
#include <new>

f()
{
    for (;;)
    {
        int* pi=new (nothrow) int[10000];
        if (!pi)
        {
            cout<<"new failed!"<<endl;
            break;
        }
    }
}
```

The header **<new>** declares **nothrow** as a constant of type **nothrow_t**:

```
struct nothrow_t{};
const nothrow_t nothrow;
```

Forms 3 and 4 of **new** can be useful for constructing an object at a known address (**ptr**). They are referred to as *placement forms* of **new**. In the following example, an object is placed at a specific address by using the placement argument. This facility lets you preallocate memory that later will contain objects:

```
#include <new>

class CoString
{
public:
    CoString(const char*);
    //...

protected:
    int theLength_;
    char* theCoString_;
};

char* Spot=new char[sizeof(CoString)];

int main()
{
    CoString* ps=new (Spot) CoString("simplify life");
    //...
    ps->~CoString(); //explicit destructor call
    return 0;
}
```

The deinitialization is done by destroying the object explicitly, because the global **delete** operator cannot be used with the pointer allocated using the placement **new**.

Overloading new And delete For A Class

The allocation and deallocation operators for a class can be overloaded. This overloading enables you to put all instances of a particular class on a class-specific heap. You can then take control of allocation, either for efficiency or to accomplish other memory management functions, such as garbage collection.

The following is an example of overloaded **new** and **delete** operators for a class (the global **new** and **delete** operators are used to make the code simple):

```
class CoClass
{
public:
    CoClass(int v=0)
    {
        val_=v;
    }
    ~CoClass()
    {
        cout<<"~CoClass():"<<val_<<endl;
    }
    void* operator new(size_t TypeSize)
    {
        cout<<"CoClass()::new():"<<val_<<endl;
        return ::operator new(TypeSize);
    }
    void operator delete(void* pType)
    {
        cout<<"CoClass()::delete():"<<val_<<endl;
        ::operator delete(pType);
    }

private:
    static int val_;
};

int CoClass::val_=13; //static variable's
                      //definition
int main()
{
    CoClass* pv1=new CoClass(169);
    delete pv1;
    return 0;
}
```

This example produces the following output:

```
CoClass()::new():13
~CoClass():169
CoClass()::delete():169
```

Class-specific **new** and **delete** operator functions are always **static**, even if they aren't explicitly declared to be **static**. Hence, they may only access other **static** members of the class—and thus, they can't be **virtual** functions. In the example, the **new** and **delete** operator functions use the **static** member **val_**. The functions simply use global versions of **new** and **delete** operators to implement class-specific versions. However, an array of the **CoClass** class instances will use global definitions of **new[]** and **delete[]** because they aren't overloaded for the class.

Memory Leaks

The problem of undeleted memory in a function can become quite intense in an application that runs for a long time, because whenever the user uses the function, a small chunk of memory may vanish. Inevitably, the amount of memory consumed has an adverse effect on the system. This situation, referred to as a *memory leak*, can be caused by the following:

♦ Forgetting to apply **delete** on something that has been allocated on the free store.

♦ Failing to observe that code may sidestep a **delete** statement under certain circumstances.

♦ Assigning the result of the **new** operator to a pointer that was already pointing to an allocated object.

The following tips show ways of avoiding these problems:

♦ C++ lets programmers delete a null (0) pointer. Nothing happens, but you are relieved from the inconvenience of checking whether the pointer refers to something valid. Instead of writing this:

```
if (pObject) delete pObject;
```

you may write only this:

```
delete pObject;
```

♦ When you use pointers in a class, initialize them to null (0) in the constructor and delete them in the destructor.

♦ You must provide a copy constructor and an assignment operator if your class contains pointer members.

♦ You must delete a pointer that is previously pointing to an allocated object, before assigning the result of a **new** statement to it; for example:

```
void setUp()
{
    int* pArray=new int[13];
    //...
    delete[] pArray; //required
    pArray=new int[Size];
    //...
}
```

◆ If you need to delete a pointer other than in a destructor, set it to null (0) afterward. For example:

```
void shutDown()
{
    //...
    delete[] pArray;
    pArray=0; //required
    return;
}
```

◆ You must supply your version of **delete** whenever you redefine the **new** operator.

Runtime Type Information (RTTI)

A C++ class is a compile time entity that defines the form of all objects (instances) of the class. An RTTI facility of the C++ standard provides some support for introspection. The RTTI mechanism enables you to determine the actual type of a data object at runtime, even when the code has access only to a pointer or reference to that object. The RTTI mechanism also enables you to check whether two objects are of the same type. This mechanism provides a **typeid** operator that enables you to determine the RTTI of an object. A **<typeinfo>** header file also is available that contains the declarations and prototypes for the RTTI classes: **type_info** and **bad_typeid**.

The typeid Operator

The **typeid** operator is a C++-specific operator that can be used to get runtime identification of types and expressions. Its usage is similar to that of the **sizeof()** operator. A call to **typeid** returns a reference to a constant object of class **type_info (const type_info&)**. The returned object represents the type of the **typeid** operand:

♦ If the **typeid** operand is a *dereferenced pointer* or a reference to a polymorphic type, the result refers to a **type_info** object that represents the dynamic type of the actual object pointed or referred to.

♦ If the operand is nonpolymorphic, the result refers to a **type_info** object that represents the static type.

♦ You can use the **typeid** operator with fundamental data types (**int**, **char**, and so forth) and constructed types (class, arrays, pointers, and so forth). When **typeid**'s operand is obtained by applying the unary * operator to a pointer and the pointer is a null pointer value, it throws a **bad_typeid** exception.

♦ When **typeid()** is applied to a result of **typeid()**, the result refers to a **type_info** object representing the type of the **type_info()** itself.

The type_info Class

The **type_info** class provides information about a type, as follows:

```
class type_info
{
public:
    virtual ~type_info();
    bool operator==(const type_info&) const;
    bool operator!=(const type_info&) const;
    bool before(const type_info&) const;
    const char * name() const;

private:
    type_info(const type_info&);
    type_info& operator=(const type_info&);
    // implementation details
    const char *theName;
    //...
};
```

Only a **private** constructor is provided, which means that you can't create **type_info** objects. **type_info** references are generated by the **typeid** operator. The **type_info** class provides you with the ability to make comparisons of objects. It provides three types of comparison operations:

♦ The member operator functions **operator==()** and **operator!=()** are used to determine where two objects are of the same type.

♦ The member function **name()** is used to determine the type name of an object. The output of **name()** is implementation-dependent.

♦ The member function **before()** is used to compare the lexical order (not to be confused with declaration order or hierarchical order) of types.

Example Of The **name()** Function

Here is an example that uses the **name()** function on polymorphic types:

```
#include <iostream.h>
#include <typeinfo>

class CoControl //polymorphic class type
{
    virtual void paint(){}
    //...
};

class CoButton : public CoControl
{
    //...
};

int main()
{
    CoButton b;
    CoControl* pb;
    pb=&b;

    cout<<"Name of *pb is:" <<typeid(*pb).name()<<endl;
    cout<<"Name of CoControl is:"
        <<typeid(CoControl).name()<<endl;

    return 0;
}
```

This example produces the following output:

```
Name of *pb is:class CoButton
Name of CoControl is:class CoControl
```

Because the **pb** pointer is actually pointing to an object of type **CoButton**, the call **typeid(*pb).name()** gives **clsss CoButton** and not **class CoControl**.

Example Of The Member Operator Functions
Here is an example that uses the member operator functions on polymorphic types:

```
#include <iostream.h>
#include <typeinfo>

class CoControl //polymorphic class type
{
    virtual void paint(){}
    //...
};

class CoButton : public CoControl
{
    //...
};

int main()
{
    CoButton b;
    CoControl* pb;
    pb=&b;

    if (typeid(*pb)==typeid(CoButton))
        cout<<"Name is " <<typeid(*pb).name()<<endl;

    if (typeid(*pb)!=typeid(CoControl))
        cout<<typeid(*pb).name()<<
        " is not same as "<<
        typeid(CoControl).name()<<endl;

    return 0;
}
```

This example produces the following output:

```
Name is class CoButton
class CoButton is not same as class CoControl
```

Note the use of the operator **==** to compare the types of ***pb** and **CoButton**. The following is another way of comparison that can be used:

```
if (!strcmp(typeid(*pb).name(),"class CoButton"))
    //...
```

However, such an approach may not work on all compilers, because the output of **typeid().name()** depends on the compiler's implementation.

Example Of The *before() Function*

Here is an example that uses the **before()** function on polymorphic classes:

```
#include <typeinfo>

class CoWindow //polymorphic class type
{
public:
    virtual void paint()
    {}
    //...
};

class CoDialogBox:public CoWindow
{
public:
    virtual void paint()
    {}
    //...
};

void f(const CoWindow& w1,const CoWindow& w2)
{
    cout<<typeid(w1).name()<<" before "<<
    typeid(w2).name()<<" : "<<
    typeid(w1).before(typeid(w2))<<endl;

    return;
}

int main()
{
    CoWindow* pw= new (nothrow) CoWindow;
    CoWindow* pd= new (nothrow) CoDialogBox;
    f(*pw,*pd); //performed at runtime
```

```
                              return 0;
                          }
```

This example produces the following:

```
class CoWindow before class CoDialogBox : 0
```

Dereferenced Pointer As A *typeid* Operand

When **typeid()** is applied to a dereferenced pointer whose type is a polymorphic class type, the result refers to a **type_info** object representing the dynamic type of the object to which the pointer refers. The following example demonstrates this concept:

```cpp
#include <typeinfo>
#include <iostream.h>

class CoBase
{
public:
    virtual void f() //to make CoBase polymorphic
    {
        //...
    }
};

class CoDerived:public CoBase
{
public:
};

CoBase* f()
{
    cout<<"in f()"<<endl;
    return (new (nothrow) CoDerived);
}

int main()
{
    cout<<typeid(f()).name()<<endl; //static-type: does
                                    //not run f()
    cout<<"------------------------"<<endl;
    cout<<typeid(*f()).name()<<endl; //dynamic-type:
                                     //runs f()
    return 0;
}
```

This example produces the following output:

```
class CoBase *
-------------------------
in f()
class CoDerived
```

The first call

```
cout<<typeid(f()).name()<<endl;
```

produces the static type of **f()**'s return type because it is a pointer. However, the call

```
cout<<typeid(*f()).name()<<endl;
```

produces the dynamic type of **f()**'s return type because the returned pointer has been deferenced.

typeid Vs. Virtual Functions

Although the **typeid** operator is a useful feature, there is a danger of overusing it to supersede **virtual** functions; for example:

```
#include <typeinfo>

class CoWindow
{
public:
    virtual int setup(); //at least one virtual
                          //function is essential
    void paint(); //non-virtual
    //...
};

class CoDialogBox:public CoWindow
{
public:
    void paint();
    //...
};

f(CoWindow& w)
{
```

```
    typedef CoDialogBox* PDIALOG;

    if (typeid(w)==typeid(CoWindow))
        w.paint();
    else
    if (typeid(w)==typeid(CoDialogBox))
        PDIALOG(&w)->paint();
}

int main()
{
    CoWindow* pw= new (nothrow) CoWindow;
    CoWindow* pd= new (nothrow) CoDialogBox;
    f(*pw); //invokes CoWindow::paint()
    f(*pd); //invokes CoDialogBox::paint()
    return 0;
}
```

The previous code is a good example of bad programming. In the function **f()**, explicit type checking such as **typeid(w) ==typeid(CoWindow)** and explicit typecasting such as **PDIALOG(&w)** can undo all the advantages of dynamic binding. The better way to write this program is to declare the **paint()** function **virtual**. However, if you know that a **CoDialogBox** object has unique function (say, a **disableControls()** function) that is not shared by all derived **CoWindow** objects, instead of burdening all classes derived from **CoWindow** with empty definitions of the **disableControls() virtual** function, the following could be done:

```
#include <typeinfo>

class CoWindow
{
public:
    virtual void paint();
};

class CoDialogBox:public CoWindow
{
public:
    void disableControls(); //unique to CoDialogBox
};
```

```
void f(CoWindow& w)
{
    typedef CoDialogBox* PDIALOG;

    if (typeid(w)==typeid(CoDialogBox))
        PDIALOG(&w)->disableControls();
    return;
}
```

In the previous example, the **f()** function makes a runtime decision to call the **disableControls()** function. Since the **disableControls()** function is not declared in the **CoWindow** class, the address of argument **w** is typecast to **CoDialogBox*** before the **disableControls()** function is invoked.

Safe And Smart Typecast Operators

Sometimes you need to convert a value from one type to another in a program where the compiler will not perform it implicitly. Type conversions specified by you are referred to as *cast* The following two notations

```
Type(ExprList); //function style cast
(Type)ExprList;  //C style cast
```

are used for casts. They represent an explicit request by you to convert **ExprList** into **Type**. These notations are referred to as *old-style casts*. C++ provides four *new-style*, *safe*, and *smart* typecast operators to perform typecasting from one type to another type:

- **dynamic_cast**, for safe navigation of an inheritance hierarchy

- **reinterpret_cast**, to perform type conversions on unrelated types

- **static_cast**, to convert one type to another type

- **const_cast**, to cast away the "**const**-ness" or "**volatile**-ness" of a type

These typecast operators are specific to the C++ language. Each one returns an object converted according to the rules of the operator. They use the syntax

```
cast_operator <T>(expr);
```

where the **cast_operator** is one of the following:

NOTE

dynamic_cast At Compile Time

The conversion from a derived class pointer or reference to a base class pointer or reference is resolved at compile time and results in a pointer or reference to the sub-object of the base class.

- ♦ **dynamic_cast.**

- ♦ **static_cast.**

- ♦ **reinterpret_cast.**

- ♦ **const_cast.**

The **T** argument is the type being cast to, and the **expr** argument is the expression or object being cast from.

The new typecast operators are intended to remove some of the ambiguity and danger inherent in old-style casts, by providing the following:

- ♦ *Improved syntax*—Casts have clearly readable syntax, which makes casts easier to understand and locate. The old-style casts are difficult to locate in a program.

- ♦ *Improved semantics*—The intended meaning of a cast is no longer ambiguous. The old-style casts do not convey the semantic purpose to perform a cast.

- ♦ *Type-safe conversions*—At runtime, you can check whether a particular cast is successful. The old-style casts do not perform a cast at runtime.

dynamic_cast

The **dynamic_cast** operator takes the following form:

```
dynamic_cast<T> (expr);
```

It can be used only for pointer or reference types to navigate a class hierarchy. The **dynamic_cast** operator can be used to perform the following casts:

- ♦ Casting a base class pointer (reference) to a derived class pointer (known as *downcast*)

- ♦ Casting a derived class pointer (reference) to another derived (sibling) class pointer (known as *cross-hierarchy cast*)

These conversions are resolved at runtime.

The **dynamic_cast** operator is actually part of C++'s RTTI. You can use the **dynamic_cast** operator only when the base class is polymorphic (the base class must contain at least one **virtual** function). The **dynamic_cast** operator can be used to determine at runtime whether a base class reference (or pointer) refers to an object of a derived class.

If a pointer cast using **dynamic_cast** fails, the returned pointer has the value zero. If a cast to a reference type fails, the **bad_cast** exception is thrown.

Listing 1.7 presents an example to demonstrate downcast and cross-hierarchy cast using the **dynamic_cast** operator:

Listing 1.7   Using the dynamic_cast operator.

```
#include <typeinfo>
#include <iostream.h>

class CoControl //polymorphic class type
{
public:
    virtual void paint() {}
    //...
};

class CoGif
{
    //...
};

class CoGifButton:public CoControl, public CoGif
{
    //...
};

int h()
{
    try
    {
        CoControl* pc= new (nothrow) CoGifButton;
        //attempt downcasting
        CoGifButton* pb=dynamic_cast<CoGifButton*>(pc);
        if (pb)
        {
            cout<<
            "The resulting pointer's type:"<<
            typeid(pb).name()<<endl;
        }
        else throw bad_cast();
        //attempt cross-hierarchy casting
        CoGif* pp=dynamic_cast<CoGif*>(pc);
```

```
        if (pp)
        {
            cout<<
            "The resulting pointer's type:"<<
            typeid(pp).name()<<endl;
        }
        else throw bad_cast();
    }//end of try block
    catch (const bad_cast&)
    {
        cout<<"dynamic_cast() failed"<<endl;
        return 1;
    }
    catch (...)
    {
        cout<<
        "Exception handling error."<<endl;
        return 1;
    }
    return 0;
}

int main()
{
    h();
    return 0;
}
```

This example produces the following output:

```
The resulting pointer's type:class CoGifButton *
The resulting pointer's type:class CoGif *
```

In the previous example, the conversion

```
CoGifButton* pb=dynamic_cast<CoGifButton*>(pc);
```

doesn't fail because **pc** pointer points to an object of type **CoGifButton**. The result of the conversion is the **pb** pointer that points to a complete object of type **CoGifButton**.

Similarly, the conversion

```
CoGif* pp=dynamic_cast<CoGif*>(pc);
```

is valid because **CoGif** is a base class of **CoGifButton** and **pc** is pointing to an object of type **CoGifButton**. The result is a pointer **pp** that points to a sub-object of type **CoGif**.

static_cast

Unlike **dynamic_cast**, the **static_cast** operator makes no runtime check and isn't restricted to base and derived classes in the same polymorphic class hierarchy. **static_cast** is the most general operator and is intended as a replacement for most C-style casts. The static_cast operator takes the form

```
static_cast<T> (expr);
```

to convert the expression **expr** to type **T**. Such conversions rely on static (compile time) type information.

The **static_cast** operator can be used in a non-polymorphic class hierarchy. A pointer to a class **X** can be explicitly converted to a pointer to some class **Y** by using **static_cast**, if **X** is a base class for **Y**. A static conversion can be made only under the condition that **X** is not a **virtual** base class. Here is an example:

```
class CoWindow
{
    //...
};

class CoView
{
    //...
};

class CoViewWindow:public CoWindow, public virtual CoView
{
    //...
```

---

typeid Vs. dynamic_cast

Although the **dynamic_cast** operator, like **typeid**, can tell you that an object is of a specified class or of a class derived from the specified class, the **dynamic_cast** operator, unlike **typeid**, has the following limitations associated with it:

♦ To use the **dynamic_cast** operator, the specified class needs at least one **virtual** member function.

♦ The **dynamic_cast** operator does not work with intrinsic types.

NOTE

The static_cast Operator Does Not Make A Runtime Check

It is easy to make mistakes when the **static_cast** operator is used. Since **static_cast** doesn't perform a runtime check, it can produce results that can't be checked whether they are correct. For example, when you use a **static_cast** on a base class pointer that doesn't point to a derived object, you are likely to get extremely unfavorable results. The **static_cast** operator requires you to make sure that the usage is safe.

```
};

int h()
{
    CoWindow* pb1= new (nothrow) CoViewWindow;
    CoViewWindow* pd=static_cast<CoViewWindow*>(pb1);
    if (pd)
    {
        cout << "The resulting pointer's type:["<<
            typeid(pd).name()<<"]"<<endl;
    }
    return 0;
}

int main()
{
    h();
    return 0;
}
```

This example produces the following:

```
The resulting pointer's type:[class CoViewWindow *]
```

In the previous example **CoWindow** is not a **virtual** base class of **CoViewWindow**, and **pb1** pointer points to an object of type **CoViewWindow**. Hence, the cast works correctly. On the other hand, because **CoView** is a **virtual** base class of **CoViewWindow**, you can't use the **static_cast** operator on a **CoView** pointer.

reinterpret_cast

The **reinterpret_cast** operator replaces most inconsistent uses of the old-style cast. The **reinterpret_cast** operator takes the form

```
reinterpret_cast<T> (expr);
```

and is used to perform conversions between two unrelated types. For example, if you need to cast between a nonpointer, such as an **int** and a pointer, you can use the **reinterpret_cast** operator. The result of the conversion is usually implementation-dependent and, therefore, not likely to be portable. You should use this type of cast only when absolutely necessary. Note that the cast is resolved at compile time.

Here is an example to demonstrate that to use the converted value, you are required to convert it back to the original type:

```
void foo(void* pv)
{
    //cast back from pointer type to integral type
    int v=reinterpret_cast<int>(pv); //works well
    //...
}

int main()
{
    typedef void (*PFV)();

    //cast from an integral type to pointer type
    foo(reinterpret_cast<void*>(13));
    //cast from a pointer to function of one type
    //to pointer to function of another type
    PFV pfunc=reinterpret_cast<PFV>(foo);
    pfunc(); //may not work
    //...
    return 0;
}
```

const_cast

The three cast operators just discussed don't cast away **const**-ness of an operand. To cast away **const**-ness of an operand, the **const_cast** operator is used, which adds or removes the **const** or **volatile** modifier from a type.

In the expression,

```
const_cast<T>(expr);
```

T and **expr** must be of the same type, except for the **const** and **volatile** modifiers. No other conversions are performed explicitly using **const_cast**. The result of the expression **const_cast<T>(expr)** is of type **T**. Note that the cast is resolved at compile time. Here is an example:

```
class CoClass
{
public:
    CoClass(int v): count_(v){}
    ~CoClass()
    {
```

reinterpret_cast Vs. static_cast

Because the **reinterpret_cast** operator allows the programmer to cast between objects that are not related, using it is risky. You should know the semantic purpose of applying **reinterpret_cast**, just as you should when you use old-style casts. To use the converted value, you are required to convert it back to the original type; otherwise, it may not behave as expected.

You must *always* use **static_cast**, as long as the compiler does not disagree; otherwise, it may be that **reinterpret_cast** must be used to change the underlying bit-interpretation of the operand.

Use **reinterpret_cast** and **static_cast** as a last resort, because these operations present the same dangers as old-style casts. However, they are still necessary to completely replace old-style casts.

```
            cout<<"count_="<<count_<<endl;
    }
    void changeCount() const;

private:
    int count_;
};

void CoClass::changeCount() const
{
    //count_++; //error
    const_cast<CoClass*>(this)->count_++; //ok
}

int main()
{
    CoClass v(13);
    v.changeCount();
    v.changeCount();
    v.changeCount();
    return 0;
}
```

Within the **const** member function **changeCount()**, the statement

```
count_++; //error
```

is commented, because in a **const** member function you can't modify a data member of the class. To be able to modify **count_**, you must cast away **const**-ness of the **this** pointer:

```
const_cast<CoClass*>(this)->count_++; //ok
```

New-Style Cast Vs. Old-Style Cast

New-style casts are fast becoming *standard*, and succeeding the old-style C++ typecast style. C++ still supports the old-style casts, but their application is discouraged and they will gradually vanish, as new programs supersede old ones. The old-style cast is known to be unreliable, error-prone, and painful to locate when reading the programs.

The **const** object **this** is cast to a non-**const** object of the **CoClass*** type, thereby allowing you to modify the data member **count_**. Thus, this example produces the following:

```
count_=16
```

Chapter Recap

Designing good OO systems (such as class libraries and frameworks) isn't possible without a deep understanding of OO concepts and experience applying OO concepts in a real-life project by using a programming language. Abstraction and polymorphism play significant roles in creating reusable and extensible OO systems. Object orientation is a truly powerful and elegant way of developing software systems. Languages such as C++ enable you to develop systems by using the OO paradigm, thus enabling you to design your software while maintaining a real-world view of the system.

This chapter presented a few significant OO and C++ notions and features, including the following:

♦ The object model provides a very natural language for modeling the world, one that can closely mimic in software most of the concepts and ideas that exist in nature.

♦ The principle of abstraction is the basic pillar in object-oriented design. When you encounter a design problem, the first thing that you typically do is analyze the problem, to isolate necessary details from unnecessary ones.

♦ Object-oriented building blocks are flexible, permitting subclassing to satisfy users' specialized needs.

♦ C++ is an object-oriented programming language (OOPL). Because C++ is an OOPL, it possesses the benefits of OO and is a powerful tool to write OO programs powered by exception handling, flexible memory management, and RTTI, which themselves support the idioms of OO.

- The implementation of reuse and polymorphism are two primary uses of class derivation in C++. Polymorphism enables classes to respond to the same message differently. Reuse and polymorphism bring the most power to OOP in C++.

- Exception handling is an important strategy for the design of frameworks. The exception handling mechanism is considered a runtime ally of the compile-time-type checking mechanism. Exception handling makes the design process more significant and produces code that has a much better prospect of executing as predicted.

- To achieve a high degree of reliability and address space optimization, a framework must perform memory management in a highly proficient way. C++ memory-management techniques are good enough to meet this requirement.

- The C++ RTTI mechanism enables you to determine the actual type of a data object at runtime, even when the code has access only to a pointer or reference to that object.

- The **dynamic_cast** operator is part of C++'s RTTI. The **dynamic_cast** operator provides a way to determine at runtime whether a base class reference (or pointer) refers to an object of a specified derived class or to an object of a class derived from the specified class.

Chapter 2
Generic Programming With C++

Key Topics:

- *Generic-programming concepts*

- *C++ templates*

- *Smart pointers*

- *Standard Template Library (STL)*

Genericity is facilitated by good class libraries. These libraries provide the generic code to use in your code to construct new classes and functions at compile time. Abstraction and polymorphism do not play any significant role in creating generic class libraries. However, genericity, when coupled with inheritance, can be a powerful tool to create object-oriented (OO) frameworks. Roughly, Generic programming is a form of reusability, because generic components and algorithms can be adapted to meet various programming requirements. Generic class libraries are very significant and useful for development in C++. They generally contain ready-to-use generic algorithms and components in a program. C++ templates are used to construct the generic libraries. C++'s Standard Template Library (STL) is a well-designed and efficient generic library. This chapter presents a tutorial on templates and related notions and conveys STL concepts through examples.

Expressions Of Generic Programming

As mentioned in Chapter 1, *genericity* is a prime technique to define objects of an OO system. It represents the structural and behavioral similarity of objects. Genericity is not the same as abstraction; genericity is, however, key to avoiding the introduction of objects with duplicate behavior. Objects may operate on different types, but the way that they operate may be similar. Two kinds of genericity are possible—*generic types* and *generic functions*.

Generic Types

Generic types enable you to define a pattern for similar types. For example, in a banking system, a requirement may be to maintain a list of accounts and a list of employees. An abstraction—**CoAccountList**, for example—could be defined to encapsulate the list of accounts, with the following object-interface:

♦ Add an account

♦ Remove an account

♦ Iterate over the list

The banking system needs a similar interface to define the list of employees—which is where generic type plays its role. Rather than duplicating the interface definition for various abstractions, a *generic abstraction* can be defined to represent all the list abstractions that might be needed in the system.

Generic Functions

Generic functions provide you with the capability to write a single function that can be used to generate similar functions. For example, a banking system may need to sort a list of account numbers and a list of customer names. A function **sort()**, for example, could be defined to sort a list of various types. The **sort()** function is referred to as a generic function.

The concepts of generic types and generic functions are well supported by C++. The following section presents them in detail.

C++ Expressions Of Genericity

C++ supports generic programming by using templates and STL. *Templates* (also called *generic*, or *parameterized*, *types*) are used to construct a family of related classes or functions. C++ supports two kinds of generic types: class templates and function templates.

Class Templates

A *class template* (also called a *generic class* or *class generator*) enables you to define a pattern for class definitions. STL container classes are a good example of class templates.

A Simple Stack Class Template

A *stack* is a data structure in which items are entered at one end (the *top*) and removed at the same end. Whether you have a stack of integers or any other type, the basic operations performed on the type are the same. The operations upon a stack consist of the following:

◆ Add an element to the top of the stack:

```
void push(element);
```

◆ Remove an element from the top of the stack:

```
element pop();
```

◆ Determine the size of the stack:

```
size_t size();
```

Listing 2.1 presents a simple implementation of a stack class template in which the **element** type is treated as a generic **T** type.

Listing 2.1   An example of creating a class template.

```
template <class T>
class CoStack
{
public:
    CoStack(size_t s)
    {
        v_=pT_=new (nothrow) T[theSize_=s];
    }
    ~CoStack()
    {
        delete[] v_;
    }
    void push(T a)
    {
        *pT_++=a;
    }
    T pop()
    {
        return *--pT_;
    }
    size_t size() const
    {
        return (pT_-v_);
    }
```

```
//...

protected:
    T* v_;
    T* pT_;
    size_t theSize_;
};
```

In Listing 2.1, the **template <class T>** prefix specifies that a template is being *declared*, in which type **T** represents some generic type. **T** is referred to as *type parameter*. The scope of **T** extends to the end of the declaration that **template <class T>** prefixes. The argument list enclosed in angle brackets (**<** and **>**) is referred to as the *formal parameter list* of the template. It cannot have a repeated generic type. For example:

```
template <class T,class T> //error
class CoBadStack
{/*...*/};

template <class T,class U> //ok
class CoDoubleStack
{/*...*/};
```

In a template's formal parameter list, **<class T>**, the keyword **class** indicates that the type **T** is a generic or parameterized type. The use of the **class** keyword has nothing to do with the keyword that is used to create a user-defined type. Within a class template, **T** is used exactly like other type names. The class template becomes a real class with real types when its objects are created. This process is referred to as *template instantiation*. For example, the syntax

```
CoStack<char> sc(13); //CoStack of characters
```

instantiates a **CoStack<char>** class and defines an **sc** object, which is a stack of characters having 13 elements. During template instantiation, all references to the argument **T** are replaced with **char**.

The member functions don't need to be defined within the scope of the enclosing class; the **push()** function can equally well be defined as follows:

```
template <class T>
void CoStack<T>::push(T a)
{
```

```
        *pT_++=a;
}
```

The following example instantiates a stack of pointers to integers. The instantiated class will have an argument that is a pointer to an **int**:

```
CoStack<int*> si(13);
int i=169;
si.push(&i);
cout<<*(si.pop())<<endl; //displays 169
```

During template instantiation in the preceding example, all references to the argument **T** are replaced with **int***. Hence, the call **si.pop()** returns **int***. It is, therefore, required to use the dereference operator (*****) on **si.pop()** to access the **int** value.

A **CoStack** of user-defined types can also be defined. The following example instantiates stacks using a class **CoClass**:

```
class CoClass
{/*...*/};

int main()
{
    CoStack<CoClass> sc(13); //stack of CoClass
    CoStack<CoClass*> spc(13); //stack of pointers to CoClass
    //...
    return 0;
}
```

In the preceding example, **sc** and **spc** are stacks of type **CoClass** and **CoClass***, respectively.

CoStack is used just like any other type in C++. The following example uses a reference and pointer to a **CoStack** of integers:

```
void f(CoStack<int>& si, size_t size)
{
    for(size_t i=0; i<size; ++i)
    {
        si.push(i);
        cout<<si.pop()<<endl;
    }
}
```

```
int main()
{
    const size_t size=13;
    CoStack<int>* psi=new (nothrow) CoStack<int>(size);
    f(*psi,size);
    delete psi;
    return 0;
}
```

Default Parameter For A Template Type

You may provide a default value for a type parameter; for example:

```
template <class T=int>
class CoVector
{
public:
    CoVector();
    //...
};

int main()
{
    CoVector<> v1; //creates a CoVector<int>
    CoVector<char> v2; //creates a CoVector<char>
    //...
    return 0;
}
```

This way of providing a default parameter for a template type is used in C++'s Standard Template Library (STL). For example, STL container **map**'s declaration looks like this:

```
template <class Key, class T, class Compare = less<Key>,
          class Allocator = allocator<T> > class map;
```

The **map** class is a class template that takes four type parameters: **Key**, **T**, **Compare**, and **Allocator**. **Compare** determines the sorting order of the elements in a **map**. If no **Compare** is provided when a **map** object is instantiated, **Compare**'s default type **less<Key>** will be used to sort the **map**'s elements. The map class is described in the section on STL, later in the chapter.

Specializing A Class Template

Sometimes, a class template may not provide the required, or proper, semantics for all parameter types that might be used to instantiate the class template. In such cases, it is generally preferred to hand code the required class, rather than generating it using the class template. As an example, consider the following class:

```
template <class T>
class CoLess //primary class template
{
public:
    CoLess(const T& t1,const T& t2): t1_(t1), t2_(t2){}
    bool operator()()
    {
        return (t1_<t2_);
    }
    void show()
    {
        cout<<t1_<<":    <<t2_<<endl;
    }
    //...

private:
    T t1_;
    T t2_;
};
```

The following instantiation of **CoLess**

```
CoLess<char*> c("one", "two");
```

may cause the following statement of **operator()()**

```
return (t1_<t2_);
```

to fail at runtime, because **char*** does not have the expected semantics for the < operator.

This problem can be resolved by providing a specialized instance of **CoLess** for **char***. This process is referred to as an *explicit specialization* of a class template. The following example demonstrates how to define an explicit specialization of the **CoLess** class for the **char*** type parameter:

```
#include <string>

template <>
class CoLess<char*>
```

TIP

Blocking A Class

You may choose to block
the **CoLess<char*>**
class by providing a
private constructor, and
let the user use the
CoLess<string>
instance.

```
{
public:
    CoLess(const char* t1,const char* t2): t1_(t1), t2_(t2){}
    bool operator()()
    {
        return (t1_<t2_);
    }
    void show()
    {
        cout<<t1_<<":"<<t2_<<endl;
    }
    //...
private:
    string t1_;
    string t2_;
};
```

The **CoLess<char*>** class has been defined explicitly by using the syntax **template <>**. Therefore, **CoLess<char*>** will be used directly instead of being instantiated from the class template. Other types, however, use the class template. Here, the C++ standard **string** is used to implement the entire specialized class for **char***.

Explicit specialization of a member function of a class template is also possible by using a similar syntax, such as the following:

```
template <>
bool CoLess<char*>::operator()()
{
    return (strcmp(t1_,t2_)<0);
}
```

If you specialize a member function of a class for a type parameter, you do not have to specialize the entire class for the same type parameter. An instance of that class will use the specialized member function. Other member functions, however, will be generated by the compiler.

Function Templates

A *function template* enables you to define a pattern for function definitions. Function templates provide you with the capability to write a single function for constructing a family of similar functions.

NOTE

Function Objects

A template class that overloads the function call operator is referred to as a *generic function object*. This concept is used in the Standard Template Library. Function objects are described in more detail in the section on STL, later in this chapter.

A Simple Global Function Template

A function template characterizes a family of functions in the same way that a class template characterizes a family of classes. The following example, which provides a general **isMin()** function, illustrates the notion of global function templates:

```
template <class T>
bool isMin(T t1, T t2)
{
    return (t1<t2);
}

int main()
{
    int i1=10;
    int i2=20;

    cout<<isMin(i1,i2)<<endl;

    float f1=10.1;
    float f2=20.2;

    cout<<isMin(f1,f2)<<endl;

    return 0;
}
```

In the preceding example, a global **isMin()** function template is defined. This function is invoked by the **main()** function, which actually instantiates **isMin()** with types **int** and **float**. When the compiler sees the call **isMin(i1,i2)**, it generates a function **isMin(int, int)** and calls it.

A Simple Member Function Template

In addition to global template functions, member function templates can be defined within a class. They are referred to as *member templates*. The following example, which provides a partial declaration of the standard **auto_ptr** class, illustrates how to declare member function templates:

```
template<class T>
class auto_ptr
{
```

NOTE

**Modifiers For A
Template Function**

A global function
template name may be
preceded by any of the
normal modifiers, such
as **inline**, **extern**, **static**,
and so forth.

A member function
template name may be
preceded by **inline**. It,
however, can't be
declared **virtual**.

```
public:
    explicit auto_ptr(T* p =0) throw();
    auto_ptr(const auto_ptr&) throw();

    //member function template
    template<class U>
    auto_ptr(const auto_ptr<U>&) throw();

    ~auto_ptr(); //destructor

    auto_ptr& operator=(const auto_ptr&) throw();

    //member function template
    template<class U>
    auto_ptr& operator=(const auto_ptr<U>&) throw();

    //...
};
```

The member function template

```
template<class U> auto_ptr&
operator=(const auto_ptr<U>&) throw();
```

makes it possible to assign an **auto_ptr<U>** object to an **auto_ptr<T>**
object. The calls

```
auto_ptr<int> ai;
auto_ptr<float> af;
ai=af;
```

will instruct the compiler to generate the following function definitions:

```
auto_ptr<int>::auto_ptr(int *)
auto_ptr<float>::auto_ptr(float *)
auto_ptr<int>::~auto_ptr()
auto_ptr<float>::~auto_ptr()
auto_ptr<int>::operator =<(const auto_ptr<float> &)
```

Specializing A Function Template

Given a global function template definition of

```
template <class T>
bool isMin(T t1, T t2)
{
```

```
        return (t1<t2);
}
```

the following call of **isMin()**

```
const char* c1="one";
const char* c2="two";
cout<<isMin(c1, c2)<<endl;
```

causes the following statement of **isMin()** to fail:

```
return (t1<t2);
```

because **const char*** does not have the expected semantics for the < operator.

This problem can be resolved by providing a specialized instance of **isMin()** for **char***:

```
template <>
bool isMin(const char* pc1, const char* pc2)
{
        return (strcmp(pc1, pc2)<1);
}
```

The **isMin(const char*, const char*)** function has been defined explicitly by using the syntax **template <>**. Therefore, it will be used directly instead of being instantiated from the generic **isMin(T, T)** function. Other types, however, will use generic functions:

```
const char* c1="one";
const char* c2="two";
cout<<isMin(c1, c2)<<endl; //ok: calls specialized instance
cout<<isMin(1,2)<<endl; //ok: calls generated instance
```

Template Function Overloading Resolution

When the compiler instantiates a function template, implicit type conversions are not applied to the arguments. Instead, new variants of template functions are introduced whenever permissible. For example:

```
template <class T>
T Sqr(T);

class CoComplex
{
```

```
public:
    CoComplex(int);
    CoComplex(double);
    CoComplex(const CoComplex&);
};

void f(int i,double d,CoComplex c)
{
    CoComplex c1=Sqr(i); //Sqr(int)
    CoComplex c2=Sqr(d); //Sqr(double)
    CoComplex c3=Sqr(c); //Sqr(CoComplex)
}
```

This code instantiates a **Sqr()** function from the function template for each of the three argument types. You must not demand something particular—for example, a call of **Sqr(double)**, given an **int** argument. To get that specifically, you must use an explicit type conversion in the argument:

```
CoComplex c4=Sqr(double(i)); //Sqr(double)
```

A template function may be overloaded either by nontemplate functions of its same name or by other template functions of the same name, provided that each signature is unique in either the number or types of its arguments. The process of overloading resolution for nontemplate functions and other template functions of the same name goes through three phases:

1. Examine all nontemplate instances of the function to find an exact match; if found, call it.

2. Examine all template instances of the function to find a template function that can generate a function with an exact match; if found, call it.

3. Examine all nontemplate instances of the function by trying *ordinary* overloading resolution for the functions; if a function is found, call it. If no match is found, the call is an error.

In each case, if more than one selection applies, the call is ambiguous.

The following is an example that demonstrates how a function template can be overloaded by a nontemplate function:

```
#include <iostream.h>
```

```
template <class T>
void f(T* pT)
{
    cout<<"f(T*):"<<pT<<endl;
}

void f(int i) //overloads function template f(T*)
{
    cout<<"f(int):"<<i<<endl;
}

int main()
{
    int i=13;
    f(i);
    f(&i);
    f("V");
    f(13.169);
    return 0;
}
```

The preceding example produces the following output (on a particular machine):

```
f(int):13
f(T*):0x0012FF7C
f(T*):V
f(int):13
```

In the preceding example, the call **f(i)** resolves the nontemplate function **f(int)** as per Phase 1. The calls **f(&i)** and **f("V")** resolve the function template **f(T*)** as per Phase 2. Again, the call **f(13.169)** resolves the nontemplate function **f(int)** as per Phase 3.

Template Arguments To Functions And Classes

Each template argument of a function template must appear at least once in the signature of the function. This ensures that functions can be selected and generated based on their arguments. Of course, no constraint exists on how many times each generic and nongeneric type can appear in the signature, as the example in Listing 2.2 demonstrates.

Listing 2.2   An example of template arguments.

```
class CoComplex
{
    //...
};

template <class T>
class CoVector
{
    //...
};

template <class T>
class CoIndex
{
    //...
};

template <class T> void f1(T); //ok
template <class T> void f2(T*); //ok
template <class T> T f3(int); //error
template <class T,class V> void f4(T); //error
template <class T> void f5(const T&,CoComplex); //ok
template <class T> void f6(CoVector<CoIndex<T> >); //ok

int main()
{
    int i=13;
    f1(i);
    f2(&i);
    f3(i);
    f4(i);
    f5(i, CoComplex());
    f6(CoVector<CoIndex<int> >());
    return 0;
}
```

Listing 2.2 contains two errors:

♦ The error in **f3()** occurs because the type parameter **T** is not used in the function signature.

♦ The error in **f4()** occurs because only the type parameter **T** is used in the function signature and **V** is not used.

The use of a type parameter in the signature of the function template must justify its appearance in the *formal parameter list* (bracketed by **<** and **>**). However, no such compulsion exists on arguments to class templates, which must be specified whenever that class is instantiated.

Commingling Parameterized And Fixed Types

A template argument doesn't have to be a generic type name. In addition to generic type arguments, compile time constant expressions can be used. These arguments are referred to as *expression parameters* or *nontype template parameters*; for example:

```
class CoComplex
{/*...*/};

template <class T,size_t theSize>
class CoVectorAsArray
{
public:
    CoVectorAsArray();

protected:
    T v_[theSize];
    //...
};

void f()
{
    const size_t v1=13;
    size_t v2=169;
    CoVectorAsArray<char,13*v1> vect1; //ok
    CoVectorAsArray<CoComplex,v2> vect2; //error
    //...
}
```

Making **theSize** an argument of the template **CoVectorAsArray** itself rather than of its constructor implies that the size of a **CoVectorAsArray** is known at compile time, such that a **CoVectorAsArray** instance (such as **vect1**) can be allocated without use of the **new** operator. The declaration of **vect2** invoked a compile time error because **v2** is not a constant expression; the expression parameter must be capable of being evaluated at compile time. Similarly, the following instantiation is illegal, because the **new** operator is invoked at runtime:

```
CoVectorAsArray<CoComplex,*new size_t(13)> Vect3; //error
```

Here is another example to demonstrate that the expression parameter must be capable of being evaluated at compile time:

```
template<class T, const char* p>
class CoClassX
{
public:
    CoClassX();
    // ...
};


char p[]="abc";

int main()
{
    //string literal as template-argument
    CoClassX<int,"abc"> x1; //error:

    CoClassX<int,p> x2; // ok
    return 0;
}
```

Types Generated From A Common Template

Although two types generated from a common template are similar, they are not identical unless their template arguments are the same; for example:

```
class CoComplex
{
public:
    operator size_t(); //returns truncated modulus
    //...

protected:
    double rd_;
    double id_;
};

template <class T, size_t theSize>
class CoVector
{/*...*/};
```

```
void f()
{
    CoVector<int,13> v1;
    CoVector<int,169> v2;
    CoVector<CoComplex,13> v3;
    CoVector<char,13> v4;
    CoVector<int,13> v5;
    v1=v2; //error
    v1=v3; //error
    v1=v4; //error
    v1=v5; //ok
}
```

Here, only **v1** and **v5** are of the same type, because their template arguments are identical.

Although an implicit conversion exists from **CoComplex** to **size_t**, that relationship does not express an implicit conversion from **CoVector<CoComplex,13>** to **CoVector<int,13>**. Similarly, no implicit conversion exists from **CoVector<char,13>** to **CoVector<int,13>**. Furthermore, even **CoVector<int,13>** and **CoVector<int,169>** are treated as different types and don't have any relationship.

Template Classes Under Derivation

The alliance of derivation and templates can be an effective mechanism. A template signifies a generality across the types used as template arguments, and a base class signifies a generality of the representation and calling interface.

A template class can serve as the following:

♦ A base class for a nontemplate class

♦ A derived class with a nontemplate base class

♦ As both a base class and a derived class

For example:

```
template <class T>
class CoVector //template class
{/*...*/};

class CoAnotherVector //nontemplate class
{/*...*/};
```

```
class CoMatrix0:public CoVector<int> //template base class
{/*...*/};

//template derived class
template <class T>
class CoMatrix1:public CoAnotherVector
{/*...*/};

template <class T>
class CoMatrix2:public CoVector<T> //both
{/*...*/};

int main()
{
    CoMatrix0 pm0;
    CoMatrix1<int> pm1;
    CoMatrix2<float> pm2;
    //...
    return 0;
}
```

A template argument can also serve as a base class:

```
template <class T>
class CoMatrix3:public T
{/*...*/};

int main()
{
    CoMatrix0 pm0;
    CoMatrix3<CoMatrix0> pm30; //ok
    CoMatrix3<int> pm31; //error
    //...
    return 0;
}
```

In the preceding example, the instantiation **CoMatrix3<int>** causes an error because **int** can never be a base class.

Two types generated from a common template do not express any inheritance relationship, as shown in the following example:

```
template <class T>
class CoVector
{/*...*/};
```

```
template <class T>
class CoMatrix:public CoVector<T>
{/*...*/};

template <class T>
class CoClass
{/*...*/};

void f()
{
    CoVector<int> vec;
    CoMatrix<int> mat;
    vec=mat; //ok
    CoClass<CoVector<int> > v1;
    CoClass<CoMatrix<int> > v2;
    v1=v2; //error: no conversion
}
```

Although an implicit conversion exists from **CoMatrix** to **CoVector**, that relationship does not express an implicit conversion from **CoClass<CoMatrix<int> >** to **CoClass<CoVector<int> >**.

Type Names In A Class Template

A name used in a template is assumed *not* to name a type, unless the C++ **typename** keyword is used in template declarations to specify that a "qualified" name is a type, not a class member. This construct can be used to access a nested class in the template parameter class as a type in a declaration within the template; for example:

```
template<class T>
class CoClass1
{
public:
    //error: T is a type, but T::CoClass2 is not
    T::CoClass2* p_;

    //ok: the keyword typename flags
    //the qualified name T::CoClass2 as a type
    typename T::CoClass2* q_;
};

class CoClass
{
public:
```

```
        class CoClass2
        {/*...*/};
        //...
    };
    int main ()
    {
        CoClass1<CoClass> c;
        //...
        return 0;
    }
```

Generic Smart Pointers

Smart pointers objectify the pointers, yet they have a pointerlike interface by having overloaded -> and * operators defined. Smart pointers are mostly developed as wrapper classes for pointers. Because a danger of memory leaks always exists when you allocate pointers dynamically in your programs, a mechanism is needed that automates the deallocation of pointers—which is the role of smart pointers. Smart pointers provide proper destructor operations and other semantically meaningful operations. By templatizing a smart pointer, you can make smart pointers more useful. Standard C++ provides an implementation of a smart pointer called **auto_ptr**. A partial class interface of the **auto_ptr** class looks like this:

```
template<class T> class auto_ptr
{
public:
    explicit auto_ptr(T* p =0) throw(); //constructor
    auto_ptr(const auto_ptr&) throw(); //constructor
    ~auto_ptr(); //destructor

    auto_ptr& operator=(const auto_ptr&) throw();
    T& operator*() const throw();
    T* operator->() const throw();
    T* get() const throw();
};
```

Listing 2.3 presents an example of using **auto_ptr**.

Listing 2.3   An example of using auto_ptr.
```
#include <memory>

struct CoInt
{
```

NOTE

Auto Pointer's Ownership

The implementations of **auto_ptr**'s constructors and assignment operator provide the semantics of object ownership. Once an **auto_ptr** object is instantiated, it owns the object to which it holds a pointer. Copying an **auto_ptr** object copies the pointer and transfers the object ownership to the target object. If more than one **auto_ptr** owns the same object simultaneously, the program may even crash.

```
      int i_;
};

void g()
{
    auto_ptr<CoInt> a(new (nothrow) CoInt);
    auto_ptr<CoInt> b;

    a->i_=13;

    cout<<"a->i_="<<a->i_<<endl;

    if (b.get()==0)
    {
        cout<<"b is null"<<endl;
    }

    b=a;

    cout<<"b->i_="<<b->i_<<endl;

    if (a.get()==0)
    {
        cout<<"a is null"<<endl;
    }
}
```

This program produces the following output:

```
a->i_=13
b is null
b->i_=13
```

The member functions **get()** and **operator ->()** both return the pointer to the encapsulated data.

When the program in Listing 2.3 dies, the allocated pointer on heap (**new CoInt**) is deallocated by the destructor of **auto_ptr**.

Why Templates?

The next section presents the Standard Template Library (STL). However, before actually presenting STL, you need to understand the advantages of using templates over other techniques of implementing genericity. These advantages really reflect the reason behind selecting template features to implement generic containers and algorithms in STL.

Function Templates Vs. Function Overloading And Macros

The fundamental convenience of function overloading is that it relieves the users of a library from having to master several different names of the matching functions (either global or class scope) that essentially perform the same action. Unfortunately, overloaded functions, while a magnificent improvement over what is available in C, are not the last solution to the problem of implementing generic functions.

For example, a function—such as **CoMax()**—has to be overloaded continually to serve the various types of arguments that can possibly be used to invoke it:

```
int CoMax(int v1,int v2)
{
    return (v1>v2)?v1:v2;
}


double CoMax(double v1,double v2)
{
    return (v1>v2)?v1:v2;
}
//...
```

Even though function overloading has been used, this example has a problem with redundant coding. One way around this problem is to use a macro:

```
#define CoMax(v1,v2) ((v1>v2)?v1:v2)
```

However, using the **CoMax()** macro may ignore the C++ type-checking mechanism, and it is possible to perform a comparison between an **int** and an **int***, which are incompatible types. Another problem with the macro technique is that substitution is performed where you don't want it to be performed. For example, the call

```
int i=0;
int j=0;

int k=CoMax(++i,j);
```

produces undesirable results. The reason is that the **CoMax()** macro substitutes the code as follows:

```
int k=((++i>j)?++i:j);
```

Obviously, you do not want such substitutions to happen. In addition, macros are handled by the preprocessor, which makes debugging more painful.

A *function template* solves these problems by enabling you to define a pattern for a family of related functions whose tasks are similar. At the same time, full type checking is performed at compile time.

Class Templates Vs. Class Wrapper Types

Using the **void** pointer is a popular technique to implement genericity in C. The same technique can be extended to C++ to implement generic classes:

```
class CoList
{
public:
    void insert(void*);
    void* peek();
    //...
};
```

However, a problem exists with the **CoList** class definition: Because no type checking occurs on what is inserted, you have no technique to determine what results you will get. You can solve this problem by writing a *wrapper class*:

```
class CoClass1;
class CoClass2;
class CoClass3;

class CoList1:public CoList
{
public:
    void insert(CoClass1* pv)
    {
        CoList::insert(pv);
    }
    CoClass1* peek()
    {
        return (CoClass1*)CoList::peek();
```

```
        }
        //...
};
```

This syntax is type-safe—**CoList1::insert()** takes arguments only of type **CoClass1*** or **CoClass1**'s derived class pointer, and **CoList1::peek()** can be assigned only to a **CoClass1*** or **CoClass1**'s derived class pointer. This means that you have created a real **CoList1**. Now, to create a similar type-safe list for a **CoClass2**, a **CoClass3**, and so on, you require repeated individual class definitions. You can solve this problem by writing a class template, as demonstrated in Listing 2.4.

Listing 2.4   An example of using a template to create a type-safe list.

```
template <class T>
class CoGenericList:public CoList
{
public:
    void insert(T* pt)
    {
        CoList::insert(pt);
    }
    T* peek()
    {
        return (T*)CoList::peek();
    }
    //...
};

int main()
{
    // create a list of CoClass1 class
    CoGenericList<CoClass1> List1;

    // create a list of CoClass2 class
    CoGenericList<CoClass2> List2;

    // create a list of CoClass3 class
    CoGenericList<CoClass3> List3;
    //...
    return 0;
}
```

As Listing 2.4 shows, you can instantiate whatever type-safe lists you need. Also, the type conversions (**T*** to **void*** and vice-versa) don't impose any runtime overhead, because each type conversion is performed at compile time. Generally, when you need to create a set of nearly similar objects, you must consider using templates. The next section also discusses avoidance of runtime overhead by using templates.

Making *Virtual* Calls Unnecessary By Using Templates

You can include *actual* member objects and avoid using base-class pointers by using class templates, thereby making pointers nonessential in a class. This can reduce the number of **virtual** function calls required, because the compiler knows the actual types of the objects. This is advantageous if the **virtual** functions are sufficiently small to be inlined. Recall that you can't inline **virtual** functions when they are invoked dynamically, because the compiler can't determine the actual types of the objects. For example:

```
class CoClass
{/*...*/};

template <class T>
class CoGeneric
{
public:
    //...

private:
    T TObject_;
};

class CoActualObject:public CoGeneric<CoClass>
{/*...*/};
```

All the functions in class **CoGeneric<CoClass>** can call functions defined in **CoClass** through **TObject_;**, thereby making pointers to **CoClass** unnecessary. If you can inline any of the functions in **CoClass**, you will get better speed performance, because class templates permit them to be inlined.

Standard Template Library (STL)

Generic class libraries are another significant development in C++. These libraries generally contain ready-to-use generic algorithms and components in a program. C++'s Standard Template Library is a well-designed and efficient generic library. This section uses examples to explain a few conceptual building blocks of STL. This section doesn't go into great detail about the STL building blocks, but it should give you a foundation from which to consider STL programming techniques in the domain of generic programming.

Introduction To STL

STL is a relatively new C++ library that provides a set of easily composable C++ container classes and generic algorithms in the form of template functions. STL is designed for use with a style of programming called *generic programming*. The essential idea of generic programming is to create components that can be reused easily in various combinations, without losing any performance. The advantages of STL are presented later in the chapter.

STL Components

STL is a component library that provides self-sufficient objects. STL consists of six main components. The following three components, in particular, are the core components of the library:

♦ *Container*—Object that keeps and manages a set of memory locations of arbitrary types.

♦ *Generic algorithm*—Computational procedure that is able to work on different containers. The generic algorithms include a broad range of fundamental algorithms for the most common kinds of data manipulations, such as searching, sorting, merging, copying, and transforming.

♦ *Iterator*—Abstraction to provide a mechanism for traversing and examining the elements in a container.

The remaining three components of STL are also essential parts of the library. They provide portability and extensibility for the three core components mentioned earlier:

♦ *Function object*—A class that can be used like a function to generate and test data and to apply operations to the data.

♦ *Adaptor*—Provides an existing component with a different interface (for example, makes a **stack** out of a **list**).

♦ *Allocator*—Encapsulates the information about the memory model for a container.

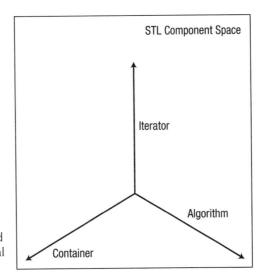

STL Component Space

Iterator

Algorithm

Container

Figure 2.1
Containers, algorithms, and
iterators form an orthogonal
component space in STL.

How STL Components Work Together

The core concept behind STL is shown in Figure 2.1.

Imagine STL software components as a three-dimensional space. One dimension represents the algorithms, the second dimension represents the iterators, and the third dimension represents the containers. Algorithms have been decoupled from the containers and can only interact with a container via traversal by an iterator. This concept is referred to as *orthogonal decomposition* of STL components. In spite of the minimal coupling between components, they interoperate with each other very well, as explained here:

♦ *Containers, algorithms, and iterators*—Most STL algorithms work on a variety of containers, and even on ordinary C++ arrays. A key factor in the library design is the consistent use of iterators as links between algorithms and containers.

♦ *Containers and allocators*—*Containers* store objects of compile time types and are parameterized by allocators. *Allocators* are objects that encapsulate information about the memory model used and provide memory handling routines to access memory uniformly. Containers internally use allocators to access memory. This means that the usage of a container object remains uniform under different memory models.

♦ *Algorithms, iterators, and function objects*—An STL *algorithm* is a computation procedure. Thus, two algorithms should differ in the computations that they perform, not in the access method used to read input data and write output data. An algorithm can be developed without worrying about an access method only when data is accessed in a uniform manner. This is where STL iterators play their role. They provide a uniform data access mechanism for STL algorithms. Different iterators provide different access modes. Function objects, on the other hand, are used in combination with algorithms to extend the algorithms' utility.

♦ *Adaptors and other components*—*Adaptors* are interface mappings; they implement new objects with different or enhanced functionality on the basis of existing components.

Advantages Of STL

Code-reuse is a major motivation behind creating STL. STL is a significant feature of C++ because it contains ready-to-use generic components that embody all the major requirements that a component must possess in order to be called reusable. Chapter 3 provides a recap on STL in the realm of reuse.

Because of its generic nature and excellent design, STL offers many advantages:

♦ *Efficiency*—Generic programming makes it possible to avoid using base-class pointers by using class templates, thereby making pointers nonessential in a class. This can reduce the number of **virtual** function calls required and moves the runtime effort to compile time.

♦ *Flexibility*—Templates enable STL components to work with built-in types and user-defined types in a seamless way. That guarantees the interoperability between all built-in and user-built components.

♦ *Simplicity of development*—The clean, orthogonal, and transparent design of the library is expected to simplify software development by decreasing development times, simplifying debugging and maintenance, and increasing understanding.

♦ *Portability of code*—STL solves the common memory-related portability problems by encapsulating the information about the memory model in allocators.

♦ *Set standards*—STL provides a basis for quality-assurance standards in the areas of system design and implementation.

The STL components are illustrated with examples in the following sections.

Introduction To Containers

Containers are data structures that manage a collection of elements and that are responsible for managing the memory of contained elements. One of these containers is a class called **vector**, which behaves like an array, but can expand itself, as necessary.

Elements are stored in containers as whole objects; no pointers are used to access the elements in a container. Containers use certain basic properties of the objects (ability to copy, and so forth), but otherwise don't depend on the type of object that they contain. Therefore, the containers are type-safe and efficient. STL containers may contain pointers to objects. This feature can take advantage of polymorphism and can be used to build various design patterns. This is illustrated in the section "Examples Of Typical Applications Of STL" later in this chapter.

Note that built-in containers (C arrays) can also be used as an STL container.

STL has two types of containers—*sequence containers* and *associative containers*.

Sequence Containers

Sequence containers store elements in sequential order by grouping a finite set of elements of the same type in a linear arrangement. STL provides three basic kinds of sequence containers:

- ◆ *Vector*—Allows fast insertion at the end, and provides random access.

- ◆ *List*—Allows fast insertion anywhere, but provides sequential access only.

- ◆ *Deque* (abbreviation for *double ended queue*)—Allows insertion at either end, and provides random access.

Here is an example of a **vector** of integers:

```
#include <vector>

int main()
{
    vector<int, allocator<int> > v;
    for (int i=0; i < 13; ++i)
        v.push_back (i);
    return 0;
}
```

This example uses the **push_back()** function of the **vector** container. The **push_back()** function inserts elements.

Associative Containers

Associative containers store elements, based on a key value. They are implemented as class templates and their internal data-structures are red-black trees. Associative containers allow fast retrieval of data based on keys. The elements are sorted, so fast binary searches are possible for data retrieval. STL provides the following four basic kinds of associative containers:

♦ *Map*—Supports unique keys and provides fast retrieval of values of another type based on the keys. It provides one-to-one mapping from one type (the key type) to another type (the value type).

♦ *Multimap*—Supports multiple copies of keys and provides fast retrieval of values of another type based on the keys.

♦ *Set*—Supports unique keys and provides fast retrieval of the keys.

♦ *Multiset*—Supports multiple copies of keys and provides fast retrieval of the keys.

If the key value must be unique in the container, then **set** and **map** can be used. If multiple elements are going to be stored using the same key, **multiset** and **multimap** must be used. A partial class declaration for the **map** class is presented in Listing 2.5 to give you an idea about the comprehensiveness of STL classes.

Listing 2.5   The class declaration for the map class.

```
template <class Key, class T, class Compare = less<Key>,
         class Allocator = allocator<T> >
class map
{
public:
    //types:
    typedef Key key_type;
    typedef T mapped_type;
    typedef pair<const Key, T>value_type;
    typedef  <red_black tree implementation> iterator;
    typedef <red_black tree implementation>const_iterator;

    //construct/copy/destroy:
    explicit map(const Compare& comp = Compare(),
    const Allocator& = Allocator());
    ~map();
```

```
    map<Key,T,Compare,Allocator>&
    operator=(const map<Key,T,Compare,Allocator>& x);

    //iterators:
    iterator begin();
    const_iterator begin() const;
    iterator end();
    const_iterator end() const;

    //capacity:
    bool empty() const;
    size_type size() const;
    size_type max_size() const;

    //access_ element access:
    reference operator[](const key_type& x);

    //modifiers:
    pair<iterator, bool> insert(const value_type& x);
    size_type erase(const key_type& x);
    void clear();

    //map operations:
    iterator find(const key_type& x);
    const_iterator find(const key_type& x) const;
    size_type count(const key_type& x) const;
};
```

This chapter does not present detailed descriptions of STL classes; it provides simple examples to convey the concepts.

The following is an example of a **map** of a **string** and an **int**:

```
#include <string>
#include <map>

int main()
{
    map<string,int,less<string>, allocator<int> > m;
    m["first"]=1;
    m["second"]=2;
    return 0;
}
```

The preceding example uses the subscript operator of **map** to store elements.

As the previous two examples show, STL containers are templatized, so that you can have a **vector** of integers or a **set** of **CoWindow**s.

Table 2.1 presents a summary of STL containers.

Introduction To Iterators

Containers, by themselves, do not provide access to their elements. Instead, *iterators* are used to traverse the elements within a container. Iterators are very similar to smart pointers and have increment (**++**), dereferencing (*****), and comparison (**==** and **!=**) operations. Because iterators are a generalization of pointers, every template function that takes iterators as arguments is assumed to work with regular pointers, too.

The following example declares two iterators, **i1** and **i2**:

```
#include <vector>

int main()
{
    vector<int, allocator<int> > v;

    vector<int, allocator<int> >::iterator i1 = v.begin();
    vector<int, allocator<int> >::iterator i2 = v.end();

    return 0;
}
```

These declarations generally are written using **typedef**s:

```
typedef vector<int, allocator<int> > VEC_INT;
typedef VEC_INT::iterator VEC_INT_ITER;

VEC_INT v;

VEC_INT_ITER i1 = v.begin();
VEC_INT_ITER i2 = v.end();
```

Table 2.1 **Summary of STL containers.**

Sequence Containers	Associative Containers
Vector	**Set**
Deque	**Multiset**
List	**Map** and **Multimap**

To iterate through a **vector** of integers, you should write (using the previous **typedef**s):

```cpp
#include <vector>

int main()
{
    typedef vector<int, allocator<int> > VEC_INT;
    typedef VEC_INT::iterator VEC_INT_ITER;

    VEC_INT v;

    for (int i=0; i < 13; ++i)
    v.push_back (i);

    VEC_INT_ITER last=v.end();
    for (VEC_INT_ITER iter  = v.begin(); iter != last;
        ++iter)
    {
        cout << *iter << endl;
    }

    return 0;
}
```

Note that each time through the loop, you dereference the iterator (***iter**) to obtain the value that the iterator is pointing at. The increment operator (**++**) is used to advance the iterator through the **vector**.

STL also provides **const** iterators so that iterators may be used with **const** containers, as in the following example:

```cpp
#include <list>

typedef list<int, allocator<int> > LIST_INT;
typedef LIST_INT::const_iterator LIST_INT_CONST_ITER;

void showList (const LIST_INT& l)
{
    LIST_INT_CONST_ITER last=l.end();

    for (LIST_INT_CONST_ITER iter = l.begin(); iter != last;
        ++iter)
    {
        cout << *iter << endl;
    }
}
```

Categories Of Iterators

Iterators are the foundation of STL design and are one of the core components of STL. Iterators give STL its flexibility. STL provides five categories of iterators (according to the operations defined on them): *input, output, forward, bidirectional,* and *random access.* Instead of developing algorithms for a specific container, they are parameterized by a specific iterator category. This strategy enables programmers to use the same algorithm with a variety of different containers.

STL provides a hierarchy of iterator categories, as shown in Figure 2.2. This hierarchy means that the iterators at the top of the hierarchy are the most general, and the iterators at the bottom are the most restricted and support fewer operations. An iterator satisfies all the requirements of the iterator below it:

♦ Forward iterators provide all the functions of the input and output iterators. You can use a forward iterator whenever input and output iterators are specified.

♦ Bidirectional iterators provide all the functions of the forward iterators. You can use a bidirectional iterator whenever a forward iterator is specified.

♦ Random access iterators provide all the functions of bidirectional iterators. You can use a random access iterator whenever a bidirectional iterator is specified.

Table 2.2 shows the iterators that can be used with STL containers.

This section does not present detailed descriptions of the iterators. However, the following are simple definitions for STL iterators:

Figure 2.2
Iterators in STL form a hierarchy.

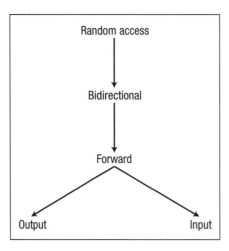

Table 2.2   Iterators that can be used with STL containers.

Container	Iterator Category
Vector	Random-access iterators
List	Bidirectional iterators
Deque	Random-access iterators
Map	Bidirectional iterators
Multimap	Bidirectional iterators
Set	Bidirectional iterators
Multiset	Bidirectional iterators

◆ *Input iterator*—Input iterators can be moved forward and can be used to read the elements of the container. Moving the iterator from one element of the container to another element takes a length of time proportional to the distance between the two.

◆ *Output iterator*—Output iterators can be moved forward and can be used to write the elements of the container.

◆ *Forward iterators*—Forward iterators can be moved forward and can be used to read or write the elements of the container.

◆ *Bidirectional iterators*—Bidirectional iterators can be moved forward or backward and can be used to read or write the elements of the sequence. All STL containers provide at least bidirectional iterators.

◆ *Random-access iterators*—Random-access iterators can be moved from any place to any other place in constant time and can be used to read or write the elements of the supported container. STL containers' C array, **vector**, and **deque** provide the random access iterators.

Introduction To Algorithms

STL algorithms are C++ function templates that are used to perform operations on containers. STL algorithms are decoupled from the particular containers that they operate on and, instead, are parameterized by iterator types. For example, STL's **count()** algorithm, which counts the number of elements in a container with a particular value, looks like this:

STL Iterators Vs. Non-STL Iterators

STL's iterator model differs from most iterator models. STL iterators are very transparent with regard to the type of containers that they traverse. The iterator traversing doesn't know what kind of container it is operating. Another difference is that STL provides past-the-end iterators (**end()**) to indicate the end of a container whereas other iterator models use the **NULL** value to examine a container's end.

```
template<class InputIterator, class T>
iterator_traits<InputIterator>::difference_type
count(InputIterator first, InputIterator last,
      const T& value);
```

As you can see in the preceding declaration, the **count()** algorithm doesn't take any container type as an argument. Instead, **count()** is parameterized by **InputIterator** type. Thus, all containers within the **InputIterator** category can utilize the **count()** algorithm. For example, to count the number of elements equal to 13 in a **vector v**, you can write:

```
#include <vector>
#include <algorithm>

int main()
{
    typedef vector<int, allocator<int> > VEC_INT;

    VEC_INT v;

    cout<<count(v.begin(), v.end(), 13)<<endl;

    return 0;
}
```

STL provides many fundamental algorithms, including the following:

♦ *Nonmutating sequence operations*—Algorithms such as **for_each()**, **count()**, and **search()** that don't modify the iterator or its associated container

♦ *Mutating sequence operations*—Algorithms such as **copy()**, **reverse()**, or **swap()** that are used to modify a container

♦ *Searching and sorting*—Sorting, searching, and merging algorithms, such as **sort()**, **binary_search()**, and **merge()**

♦ *Set operations*—Set operations, such as **set_union()**, **set_difference()**, and **set_intersection()**, to work on sorted containers

♦ *Heap operations*—Including **push_heap()**, **make_heap()**, and **sort_heap()**

♦ *Min/Max operations*—Including **min()**, **max()**, and **min_element()**

♦ *Permutation operations*—Operations to generation permutations such as **next_permutation()** and **prev_permutation()**

Using A Container, An Iterator, And An Algorithm

Listing 2.6 is a complete program that demonstrates how a container, an iterator, and an algorithm work together in a program.

Listing 2.6   An example of using a container, an iterator, and an algorithm.

```
#include <iostream>
#include <algorithm>
#include <vector>

main ()
{
    typedef vector<int, allocator<int> > VEC_INT;
    typedef VEC_INT::iterator VEC_INT_ITER;

    VEC_INT v;

    int input;
    while (cin >> input)    // while not end of file
    v.push_back (input);  // append to vector

    sort(v.begin(), v.end());

    VEC_INT_ITER last= v.end();

    for (VEC_INT_ITER iter  = v.begin(); iter != last;
        ++iter)
    {
        cout << *iter << endl;
    }

    return 0;
}
```

The **sort()** algorithm takes two random iterators and sorts the elements between them. Listing 2.6 demonstrates the decoupling between the three core components of STL.

Introduction To Function Objects

Function objects generalize C++ functions. A *function object* is an instance of a class that overloads the function call operator (()). A function object can be used like a function. A template-based function object is referred to as a *generic function object*. Consider the following example, which uses the **operator()()** function call:

```
class CoLess
{
public:
    CoLess (int v) : val_ (v) {}
    int operator () (int v)
    {
        return v < val_;
    }

private:
    int val_;
};
```

The **operator()** on a function object is applied, as follows:

```
int main()
{
    CoLess lessThan_10(10);
    cout << "7 is less than 10: " << lessThan_10(7)<<endl;
    return 0;
}
```

The program produces the following output:

```
7 is less than 10: 1
```

Function objects are more useful than normal function pointers, for the following reasons:

- They are type-safe, because the resolution of function objects happens at compile time.

- They are more efficient than using a normal function pointer or a **virtual** function.

- They can be inlined to achieve runtime efficiency.

When you use STL, you often have to pass function objects as arguments to algorithms and as template arguments when instantiating containers. For example, in the declaration

```
map<string,int,less<string>, allocator<int> > m;
```

less is a function object.

Function objects are STL's way of representing executable data. Suppose that you want to remove from a **list** all the **int**s that are a multiple of 3. You can use STL's **remove_if()** function and supply your own predicate, called **CoThreeMult**, as a function object. The actual logic goes in the body of **operator()**, which returns a **bool**:

```
struct CoThreeMult
{
    bool operator() (int& v)
    {
        return (v % 3 == 0);
    }
};
```

A new **list, m**, is created as the predicate is applied to each element of the **list** by **remove_copy_if()**:

```
#include <list>
#include <algorithm>

int main()
{
    typedef list<int, allocator<int> > LIST_INT;

    LIST_INT l;
    LIST_INT m;

    remove_copy_if (l.begin(), l.end(),  back_inserter(m),
                    CoThreeMult());

    return 0;
}
```

In STL, function objects are used for three main purposes: generating data, testing data (predicates), and applying operations.

Introduction To Adaptors

Adaptors are used to create a new interface by mapping the interface of an existing class to a new requirement. Adaptors generally apply the object composition technique to reuse an existing implementation. (Chapter 3 describes object composition and offers examples.) Other than providing an interface map, adaptors may provide new functionality, by adding new member functions, or adaptors may hide the original member functions.

STL adaptors are template classes that are used to create new interfaces for containers or iterators. Container adaptors are discussed next.
A special function pointer adaptor **ptr_fun** is also presented.

Container Adaptors

Container adaptors are used to create a new container by mapping the
interface of an existing container to that of the new container. STL
provides three container adaptors—**stack, queue,** and **deque**—which
are described and shown in the following:

♦ *Stack*—A **stack** can be instantiated with either a **vector, list,** or
  deque. Its declaration looks like this:

```
template <class T, class Container = deque<T> >
class stack
{
public:
    typedef typename Container::value_type value_type;
    typedef typename Container::size_type size_type;
    typedef typename Container container_type;

protected:
    Container c;

public:

    explicit stack(const Container& = Container());
    bool empty() const { return c.empty(); }
    size_type size() const { return c.size(); }
    value_type& top() { return c.back(); }
    const value_type& top() const { return c.back(); }
    void push(const value_type& x) { c.push_back(x); }
    void pop() { c.pop_back(); }
    //…
};
```

The default container for **stack** is **deque**. For the comparison of two
stacks, **operator==()** and **operator<()** are provided. (They are not
shown in the preceding declaration.)

Here is an example that demonstrates how to instantiate different
types of **stack**s:

```
#include <vector>
#include <list>
```

```
#include <deque>
#include <stack>

int main()
{
    typedef allocator<int> ALLOC_INT;
    typedef vector<int, ALLOC_INT> VEC_INT;
    typedef list<int, ALLOC_INT> LIST_INT;
    typedef deque<int, ALLOC_INT> DEQUE_INT;

    stack<int, VEC_INT, ALLOC_INT> s1;
    stack<int, LIST_INT, ALLOC_INT>   s2;
    stack<int, DEQUE_INT, ALLOC_INT>   s3;

    s1.push(10); s1.push(5);
    cout << s1.top() << endl;
    s1.pop();
    cout << s1.size() << endl;
    s1.empty()? cout << "empty" : cout << "not
empty"<<endl;

    return 0;
}
```

This example produces the following output:

```
5
1
not empty
```

♦ **Queue**—A **queue** can be instantiated with a **list** or a **deque**. Its declaration looks like this:

```
template <class T, class Container = deque<T> >
class queue
{
public:
    typedef typename Container::value_type value_type;
    typedef typename Container::size_type size_type;
    typedef typename Container container_type;

protected:
    Container c;

public:
    explicit queue(const Container& = Container());
```

```
        bool empty() const { return c.empty(); }
        size_type size() const { return c.size(); }
        value_type& front() { return c.front(); }
        const value_type& front() const { return c.front(); }
        value_type& back() { return c.back(); }
        const value_type& back() const { return c.back(); }
        void push(const value_type& x) { c.push_back(x); }
        void pop() { c.pop_front(); }
        //...
};
```

The default container for **queue** is **deque**. As with the **stack**, two **queue**s can be compared by using **operator==()** and **operator<()**. (These operators are not shown in the preceding declaration.)

Here is an example that demonstrates how to instantiate different types of **queue**s:

```
#include <list>
#include <deque>
#include <queue>

int main()
{
    typedef allocator<int> ALLOC_INT;
    typedef list<int, ALLOC_INT> LIST_INT;
    typedef deque<int, ALLOC_INT> DEQUE_INT;

    queue<int, LIST_INT, ALLOC_INT>   q1;
    queue<int, DEQUE_INT, ALLOC_INT>  q2;

    return 0;
}
```

◆ **Priority_queue**—A **priority_queue** can be instantiated with a **vector** or a **deque**. The elements of a **priority_queue** are sorted by using a comparison function object, such as **less**, as shown in the following:

```
template <class T, class Container = vector<T>,
class Compare = less<Container::value_type> >
class priority_queue
{
public:
    typedef typename Container::value_type value_type;
```

```
    typedef typename Container::size_type size_type;
    typedef typename Container container_type;

protected:
    Container c;
    Compare comp;

public:
    explicit priority_queue(const Compare& x = Compare(),
    const Container& = Container());

    bool empty() const { return c.empty(); }
    size_type size() const { return c.size(); }
    const value_type& top() const { return c.front(); }
    void push(const value_type& x);
    void pop();
    //...
};
```

The default container for **priority_queue** is **vector**. Note that no comparison operators for **priority_queue**s are provided.

Here is an example that demonstrates how to instantiate different types of **priority_queue**s:

```
#include <queue>
#include <functional>

int main()
{
    typedef allocator<int> ALLOC_INT;
    typedef vector<int, ALLOC_INT> VEC_INT;
    typedef deque<int, ALLOC_INT> DEQUE_INT;

    priority_queue<int, VEC_INT, less<int>, ALLOC_INT>
    p1;

    priority_queue<int, DEQUE_INT, greater<int>,
        ALLOC_INT>   p2;

    VEC_INT v(5, 1);

    priority_queue<int, DEQUE_INT, less<int>,
        ALLOC_INT > p3 (v.begin(), v.end());

    return 0;
}
```

The preceding example declares the following three **priority_queue**s:

♦ The **q1** object is a **priority_queue** using **less** as a comparison object.

♦ The **q2** object is a **priority_queue** using **greater** as a comparison object.

♦ The **q3** object is a **priority_queue** out of a **vector** and uses **less** as a comparison object.

Adaptors For Pointers To Functions

C++ provides *function pointer adaptors* to allow pointers to functions (unary and binary) to work with function adaptors STL provides. In other words, if a usual C++ function is going to be used, it has to be wrapped in a function pointer adaptor.

The **ptr_fun** function takes a unary or binary function and returns the corresponding function object. The function-call operator of these function objects simply calls the function with the arguments provided.

Listing 2.7 demonstrates how the binary **strcmp()** function can be transformed into a comparison object and then can be used to sort elements of a **vector**.

Listing 2.7   An example of using a function pointer adaptor.

```
#include <vector>
#include <algorithm>
#include <functional>
#include <string.h>

int main()
{
    typedef vector<const char*, allocator<char*> > VEC_STRING;

    const char* c1 = "one";
    const char* c2 = "two";
    const char* c3 = "three";

    VEC_STRING v;

    v.push_back (c1);
    v.push_back (c2);
    v.push_back (c3);

    sort (v.begin(), v.end(), ptr_fun (strcmp) );

    return 0;
}
```

In Listing 2.7, the **strcmp()** function is wrapped in the **ptr_fun** function pointer adaptor.

Introduction To Allocators

Portability is one of C++'s strengths. The inability to encapsulate memory-model information is a common problem in portability. If you are a C++ programmer and develop applications for DOS and 16-bit Microsoft Windows environments, you must be familiar with the multitude of memory models such as near, far, and huge pointers.

STL provides a special class, called an *allocator*, to encapsulate memory-model-related information, which includes:

♦ The knowledge of pointer types

♦ The type of their difference (difference type is typically **ptrdiff_t**)

♦ The type of the size of objects in a memory model (size type is typically **size_t**)

♦ Routines to handle raw memory; such routines are typically **allocate()**, **deallocate()**, **construct()**, and **destroy()**

All STL containers are parameterized in terms of allocators. Containers, therefore, are separated from the dependencies of the underlying memory model of the machine architecture.

Changing the memory model for a container is as simple as changing allocator types in a container declaration. The **allocator<>** allocator is used as a default allocator object. The compiler vendors are expected to provide allocators for the memory models supported by their respective products.

Examples Of Typical Applications Of STL

STL supports a wide variety of computational tasks and is a very useful collection of C++ classes and routines, designed to solve general structural and algorithmic needs. In my experience, once you start using STL, you can't live without STL. In the world of complex software solutions, STL really provides a foundation upon which you can build many vital structures and design patterns of your application. Containers such as **vector**, **set**, **list**, and **map** generally are very useful to store runtime information. Some of your software components may interact with these containers later to access the runtime information. Two vital and useful applications of these containers are the following:

♦ To develop composite objects

♦ To develop name-value pairs

The following two sections explain composite objects and name-value pairs.

Vector: In Developing Composite Objects

A composite object consists of many different objects. A Web page, for example, may consist of text and pictures. A picture, in turn, may be a composition of a GIF, BMP, JPG, and another picture, as illustrated in Figure 2.3. Repainting the Web page may require repainting the text and all the pictures. Repainting a picture invokes some kind of recursion; in other words, repainting the elements that make up the *big* picture.

A picture object can easily map to a composite object, because a picture object consists of many similar objects. At runtime, a composite object appears as a tree of objects, as shown in Figure 2.3. The behavior of a composite object depends on the execution of polymorphic messages that pass through the tree. Listing 2.8 demonstrates the skeletal implementation of the picture example.

Listing 2.8 An example of implementing a composite object by using vector.

```
#include <vector>

class CoPicture
{
public:
    virtual void paint()=0;
};

class CoCompositePicture : public CoPicture
{
public:
    typedef vector<CoPicture*, allocator<CoPicture*> >
PICTURE_VECTOR;
    typedef PICTURE_VECTOR::iterator PICTURE_ITERATOR;

public:
    void addImage(CoPicture* anImage);
    virtual void paint();
```

```
private:
    PICTURE_VECTOR pictures_;
};

void CoCompositePicture::addImage(CoPicture* anImage)
{
    pictures_.push_back(anImage);
}

void CoCompositePicture::paint()
{
    PICTURE_ITERATOR last=pictures_.end();

    for (PICTURE_ITERATOR iter=pictures_.begin(); iter!=last;
        ++iter)
    {
        (*first)->paint();
    }
}
```

The preceding listing shows that polymorphism plays an important role in defining a composite object. When you iterate a composite object, you send the messages across the tree by using a **virtual** function. You can also implement composite objects by using a **list**, **deque**, or **set**, depending on your requirements.

Map: In Developing Name-Value Pairs

Many frameworks and applications use *name-value pairs*. Name-value pairs are a collection of objects that have their own runtime identity. The notion is very similar to that of composite types, the only difference being the identity that is missing from the composite types.

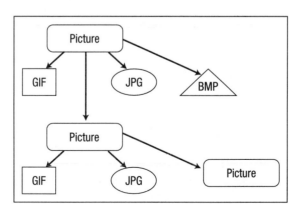

Figure 2.3

A picture consists of many pictures.

Map is an obvious choice for implementing name-value mechanisms.
Listing 2.9 is an extension of the previous example.

**Listing 2.9   An example of implementing name-value pairs by
                 using map.**

```
#include <string>
#include <map>

class CoPicture
{
public:
    virtual void paint()=0;
    void setName(const string& name);
    const string& getName() const;

private:
    string name_;
};

void CoPicture::setName(const string& name)
{
    name_=name;
}

const string& CoPicture::getName() const
{
    return name_;
}

class CoCompositePicture : public CoPicture
{
public:
    typedef
        map<string, CoPicture*, less<string>,
            allocator<CoPicture*> PICTURE_MAP;

    typedef PICTURE_MAP::iterator PICTURE_ITERATOR;

public:
    void addImage(CoPicture* anImage);
    virtual void paint();

private:
    PICTURE_MAP pictures_;
};
```

```
void CoCompositePicture::addImage(CoPicture* anImage)
{
    pictures_[anImage->getName()]=anImage;
}

void CoCompositePicture::paint()
{
    PICTURE_ITERATOR last=pictures_.end();

    for (PICTURE_ITERATOR iter=pictures_.begin(); iter!=last;
        ++iter)
    {
        ((*iter).second)->paint();
    }
}
```

In Listing 2.9, a **map** is used to store the runtime identity of an object. You can't use runtime type information (RTTI) to implement this concept, because RTTI does not provide the object identity. It just supports the type information. In Listing 2.9, the functions **setName()** and **getName()** are introduced to implement runtime object-identity.

Chapter Recap

Suppose that you want to use a list of integers in your program. Doing so is much more convenient if you have a generic list that can be instantiated to generate a list of integers. Generic types encapsulate the generic behavior for similar types. STL provides a rich generic library with such generic types and algorithms. STL components can be applied in your program to solve many general problems. This chapter presented a few significant C++ template features that are used to implement genericity in C++ programs. Also, a few important ideas about generic programming using STL were also conveyed.

The following summarize the highlights of this chapter:

♦ A C++ template is a powerful tool to write generic types and algorithms.

♦ An important design goal of STL is to provide a set of easy-to-use, efficient, and portable container classes. The user of STL should be independent from a specific memory model.

♦ STL provides containers, such as **vectors**, that are reusable building blocks for your programs.

Chapter 3

Concepts Of Reusability In C++

Almost every programmer practices *reuse* by recycling old information in some ad hoc fashion. You save time by modifying existing software or a software component to make it fit your current need, which is referred to as an *opportunistic reuse*. Opportunistic reuse has many disadvantages—issues such as testing, configuration management, maintenance, and documentation have to be addressed. By contrast, *systematic reuse* focuses on using frozen assets, or unmodified software components, which means that you don't alter the source files of the component being reused. If behavior modifications are necessary, you make them all through parameter passing, generic instantiations, inheritance, or composition. This chapter (and book) focuses on systematic reuse.

Chapters 1 and 2 cover the concepts of object-oriented programming and generic programming in C++. These two features of C++ enable *reuse* in C++. Another reuse technique, *composition*, is also supported in C++ by using member objects in a class. This chapter describes the attributes of C++ that promote the development of reusable classes. Before actually presenting C++ support for reuse, the chapter presents reuse concepts in general terms. To understand this chapter better, you need to have already read the previous two chapters. In a few places, this chapter quotes and *reuses* a few things from the previous two chapters.

This chapter presents concepts of reuse at the class level. *Class reuse* is the lowest level of reuse. *Design patterns* and *frameworks*, on the other hand, embody higher levels of reuse. Chapters 5 and 6 address higher levels of reuse. For this chapter, the focus is on class-level reuse, because class-level reuse is the key to understanding pattern- and framework-level reuse.

119

Expressions Of OO-Based Reuse

Object-oriented (OO) technology has gained rapid acceptance among software developers and has become the preferred choice for designing and implementing software systems. The primary reason for OOP's success is that it enables *software reuse*, the process of creating software systems from predefined software components. Software reuse has two phases:

♦ Development of reusable components by *reuse producers*

♦ Reuse of these components by *reuse consumers*

By using OOP, you can define reusable abstract data types that package data with the functions that manipulate that data. Apart from defining reusable abstract data types, the bigger benefits of OO-based reuse are derived from design patterns and frameworks; they provide better form and higher levels of reuse. Again, this chapter focuses on reusable classes.

Reuse Is Not The Same As Copy, Modify, Or Use

Does using the C **printf()** function in a program constitute reuse of **printf()**? Is a teacup a reusable component because you use it many times before it is broken? Both of these examples actually convey the question, "What is *use?*" The activity of *using* should not be confused with the activity of *reusing*. In software engineering, use and reuse have clearly distinct activities. Use is a *runtime* activity. Reuse is a *building-time* activity. When you run a program, the program uses many components at runtime. However, when you develop the program, you reuse many software components.

Reuse Is An Advanced Form Of Object-Oriented Programming

A reusable component should have the following features:

♦ *Usability*—A reusable component should be usable. Usability is a runtime property of a reusable component. Unless a component provides acceptable functionality and efficiency, it cannot be used, and hence cannot be reused.

♦ *Generality*—A reusable component must have a broad scope of applicability. If a component can be reused only once, it is not a reusable component. A reusable component should evolve to have the maximum scope of applicability that is appropriate to a given information domain. For example, components that function in the computing platforms domain tend to be more general, hence more reusable, than those focused on a single business domain, such as inventory control. Higher levels of reuse, such as design patterns and frameworks, usually possess the attribute of generality. (Chapter 6 presents this topic in the realm of frameworks.) Because information domain boundaries change, it is important to understand that reusable components evolve, too. This process needs to be managed to ensure that a component's generality never diminishes. This includes protecting existing reuses of a component from the effects of evolutionary changes. Some evolutionary changes reflect the *adaptability* of the component. You evolve a reusable component by either updating a reusable component with better implementations or composing new interfaces on it.

♦ *Adaptability*—A reusable component is not used as-is, because of its generality property. It has to be modified through proper programming techniques. Often, other reusable components will automate the adaptation of a component to suit a given context, making the adaptability problem trivial. Adaptability means *ease of use*, and clearly is an important yardstick in making a reusable component. A framework without a good degree of adaptability can't be used (and thus can't be reused). Chapter 14 discusses this topic in more detail.

Based on the preceding information, the **printf()** function clearly isn't an example of a reusable component, because it is not general enough to be adapted to meet many different programming requirements.

An object-oriented language provides four features: an object interface, inheritance, polymorphism, and composition. These four features encourage software reuse in several ways. These topics are discussed in Chapters 1 and 2, so the following sections provide only a short recap of these features in the context of reuse.

Object Interface

The specification of an object is given by its *object interface*, the set of messages that can be sent to it. In other words, access to an object's capabilities is mediated by the object interface that the object supports. Objects with an identical object interface are interchangeable at runtime. An object interface represents a potential point of integration and interoperation between an object and its user. An object interface conveys an object's runtime behavior or functionality.

Object interface, in fact, expresses an object's usability. A collection of well-designed object interfaces is the key to express the functionality of an OO system.

While *sending a message* is the most common terminology in OO, C++ programmers refer to this as *calling a **virtual** function*.

Inheritance

As mentioned in Chapter 1, inheritance is a major strength of object-orientation. Inheritance enables programmers to assemble relevant object abstractions into a hierarchy to express relationships between abstractions; that is, to express commonality between relevant abstractions. The abstraction at the top serves as a *super abstraction* for those below; an abstraction below is a specialization of its super abstractions. This implies that inheritance is a method of *reusing* an implementation to create new abstractions. After a base abstraction is developed, it doesn't need to be reprogrammed or recompiled, but it can nevertheless be adapted to work in different situations.

In addition to reuse, object inheritance helps form the families of standard object interfaces that are so important for reuse. All the specialized objects inherit operations from the super abstraction. So, specialized objects share the object interface of the super abstraction.

Polymorphism

Operations are performed on objects by sending them a generic message. Message sending causes polymorphism. Polymorphism enables the correct operation in the receiver object to be invoked. Polymorphic calls mean that objects require less information about each other, and thus require only the right object interface. A polymorphic call is easier to reuse than a non-polymorphic call, because a polymorphic call works with a wider range of objects.

Composition

Chapter 1 defines *composition* as a process of combining many related abstractions into a single abstraction. Object composition is one of the most common techniques of reusing functionality in OO systems. It is, in fact, used as an alternative to inheritance. While inheritance enables you to assemble relevant object abstractions into a hierarchy to express relationships, composition enables you to fabricate relevant object abstractions to form new abstractions. Therefore, composition is used as a method of reusing an abstraction to create new abstractions. By using composition, complex objects can be created by interconnecting the compatible objects. For example, you can compose Engine, Doors, and so forth to make a Car.

Why OO-Based Reuse?

Would you volunteer to be the inaugural traveler on an airplane whose components have just come out of the R&D shop? Or, would you prefer to fly knowing that the aircraft is designed and constructed with components that have successfully been used for years?

Practicing engineers, whether they specialize in civil, mechanical, electrical, or aerospace engineering, believe in reusability as a fundamental principle of engineering. Even in software engineering, reuse can cut risks, development time, and costs. Reuse should be practiced in virtually every software project. A few major reasons for practicing OO-based reuse include the following:

♦ *Increase software productivity*—Reuse of prefabricated components, such as vectors and windows, enhances productivity and usually improves reliability and lowers risks.

♦ *Produce software that is more standardized and portable*—Reusing standard components, such as Standard Template Library (STL) components, makes the system more standardized, thus reducing porting efforts.

♦ *Reduce development costs and time*—Reuse reduces and hides complexity. Standardization helps people to understand the code better, thereby lowering training costs. Therefore, reuse enables companies to move personnel more easily from project to project, and software development can be accomplished with fewer people. Reuse also shortens software-development time, because a good deal of the code has already been written and is simply reused.

♦ *Produce higher-quality software*—Reusing a pretested and quality-certified component leads to an overall higher-quality system.

♦ *Provide easier maintenance*—One of the reasons that software developers have rapidly accepted object-oriented technology as their preference for designing and implementing software systems is that software reuse is becoming more important. Developing new systems is expensive, and maintaining them is even more expensive. Class inheritance permits a new version of a program to be built without affecting the old version. For example, rather than change a program by adding runtime flag parameters, you can almost always make a derived class for each differential and have the derived classes override the methods. This is referred to as *programming-by-difference*. Programming-by-difference reduces the number of functions, and thus reduces the overall size of the program that the software maintenance engineer has to understand. Programming-by-difference is explained later in the chapter.

♦ *Provide better interoperability*—Interoperability between software modules or components is determined by their interfaces. Reusing standard interfaces provides better interoperability among components.

C++ Expressions Of Reuse

Languages such as C++ reduce not only development time but also the cost of maintenance, thus simplifying the creation of new systems and new versions of old systems. C++ provides a powerful springboard for developing reusable objects. Many of the techniques for reusing software that is written in conventional languages are paralleled by C++. For example, program skeletons are represented by abstract classes. Copying and editing a program is analogous to deriving a class and overriding some of its member functions. Table 3.1 sets forth the features that enable reuse in C++. These features are discussed in the sections that follow.

Class Is A Unit Of Reuse In C++

The C++ *class* mechanism enables users to define a new type of data according to the needs of the problem to be solved. Classes normally are used to define concepts that don't map logically into existing or derived data types. Typically, a class is used to introduce a new data type into the program; a well-designed class can be used as easily as a predefined data type. Class identification and definition promote software reuse, as explained next.

Table 3.1   The mechanisms that enable reuse in C++.

C++ Mechanism	Use
Class	Create objects; the C++ unit of reusability.
Class derivation	Create object inheritance; adapt an existing class to a new requirement; implement polymorphism. Along with polymorphism, a major feature of creating reusable classes in C++.
Class member objects	Create object composition.
Templates	Create generic types.

To solve a problem by using OO techniques, the first step is to identify a way in which the overall program system can be partitioned into separate components. Next, you identify the classes, determining which data each instance of a class must own and which function each of these objects must perform. Some of the classes either will be reusable components from a class library or will form a new, reusable class library. This is why a class is considered a *unit of reuse* in C++.

Reusability By Class Derivation

Class derivation is the process of creating new classes from existing ones. The new class is called a *derived class, subclass,* or *child class.* The existing class is called a *base class, super class,* or *parent class.* In class derivation, each class can have a base class from which it inherits member functions and an internal structure. A class can add to the member functions that it inherits or redefine inherited member functions. However, a derived class cannot delete inherited functions. The base class is unchanged by this process.

Class derivation is one of the basic reuse features in C++. It enables programmers to assemble relevant classes into a hierarchy, with the classes at the top serving as an abstraction for the classes below. This implies that a derived class is a specialization of its base class. In other words, the derived class is a type of base class, but with more details added. For this reason, the relationship between a derived class and its base class is also referred to as an *is-a* relationship.

Class derivation can be used to serve three primary functions:

- ♦ *Promote code reuse*—Code shared by several classes can be placed in their common base class, and new classes can derive from the common base class. After a base class is written and debugged, it doesn't need to be reprogrammed or recompiled, but it can, nevertheless, be adapted to work in different situations. This is called *programming-by-difference,* because the code in the subclass defines the differences between the classes. One result of reusability is the ease of distributing class libraries and frameworks.

- ♦ *Provide a way to organize and classify classes*—Classes with the same base class are usually closely related.

- ♦ *Provide a method to implement polymorphism*—Polymorphic classes provide an identical interface, but they can be implemented to serve different specific requirements. Polymorphism makes it easier for a given object to work correctly in a wide range of new contexts.

How To Derive A Class

To derive a class, the following two supplements to the class syntax are essential:

♦ *The* class head *is modified to enable the programmer to specify a class derivation list (or base list) of classes.* A derivation list enumerates the classes from which a class derives. To derive a **CoPara** class from an existing **CoString** class, **CoPara** must be declared as follows:

```
class CoPara:public CoString
{/*...*/};
```

The colon (**:**) following **CoPara** shows that **CoPara** is being derived from one or more already defined classes. The **CoString** class is the object of the derivation; it is referred to as a *base class*. **CoPara** is referred to as a *derived class*.

♦ An additional access specifier, *denoted by the* C++ *keyword* **protected**, *is supplied to provide greater flexibility to the inheritance mechanism.* A **protected** member of a class can be accessed only by its member functions, friends, and derived classes. This is a useful way to ensure information hiding.

Class derivation enables users to access the members of a base class as if they were members of its derived class, which is where code reuse plays its major role. Here is an example:

```
class CoString
{
public:
    CoString(const char*);
    CoString(const CoString&);
    CoString();
    int getLen();
    //...

private:
    int theLength_;
    char* theString_;
};

class CoPara:public CoString
{/*...*/};
```

CoPara is allowed to access the **public** members of **CoString**:

NOTE

**Size Of A
Derived Class**

```
CoPara p;
int v=p.getLen(); //ok
```

The base class members are *inherited* by the derived class.

A derived class is always at least as big as its parent class—an instance of the derived class always inherits all the members of its base class. Programmers can't mark a base class member as *inheritable*. However, an inherited member can be made *inaccessible*. A derived class can alter or enhance its inherited members either by appending additional members or by overriding (hiding) the definition of members that were inherited.

The keyword **public** in the derivation list indicates that **CoPara** is derived publicly. Derivations can be either **public**, **protected**, or **private**—this specification affects the visibility of the inherited members within the derived class.

A derived class itself can be a base class. **CoChapter**, for example, can be derived from **CoPara**, as follows:

```
class CoChapter:public CoPara
{/*...*/};
```

CoChapter, as a consequence, inherits members from both **CoString** and **CoPara**. The further programming that is required is only for those member functions that either extend or supersede the inherited members:

```
CoChapter c;
int v=c.getLen();
```

Such an assemblage of interrelated classes is conventionally referred to as a *class hierarchy*. Such a hierarchy is generally a *tree* structure, but can also be a *graph* structure.

Compiler Resolution Rules For Inherited Names

Inheritance provides for class-scope nesting. You can consider a derived class as being enclosed by the scope of its base classes. Each member (data or function) is visible within the scope of its class.

By using derived instances to access members without the base class and scope resolution operator, the compiler resolves the name by asking the following questions:

1. Does the name have scope in the derived class? If yes, stop; otherwise, proceed to Step 2.

2. Does the name have accessible and unambiguous scope in the parent class? If yes, stop; otherwise, proceed to Step 3.

3. Does the name have accessible and unambiguous scope higher up in the hierarchy? If yes, stop; otherwise, generate a compilation error.

Similarly, a member function in a derived class resolves a name by asking the following:

1. Does the name have scope in the function itself? If yes, use it; otherwise, proceed to Step 2.

2. Does the name have accessible and unambiguous scope in the derived class? If yes, use it; otherwise, proceed to Step 3.

3. Does the name have accessible and unambiguous scope in the parent class? If yes, use it; otherwise, proceed to Step 4.

4. Does the name have accessible and unambiguous scope higher up in the hierarchy? If yes, use it; otherwise, proceed to Step 5.

5. Does the name exist at file scope? If yes, use it; otherwise generate a compilation error.

Of course, instances and member functions of the base class always refer to members from the base class, because they know nothing about members of any derived classes that can be defined in the future.

The following example demonstrates the compiler resolution rules:

```
class CoWindow
{
public:
    int getLength();
    //...
};

class CoBitMap
{/*...*/};

class CoDialogBox:public CoWindow
{/*...*/};

class CoBitMappedDialogBox:
    private CoBitMap,public CoDialogBox
{
public:
    int theLength();
    //...
};

int CoBitMappedDialogBox::theLength()
{
    return getLength();
}
```

The detection by the compiler of **getLength()** within **CoBit-MappedDialogBox::theLength()** starts the following resolution search order:

1. Is the **getLength()** function declared within the **CoBit-MappedDialogBox::theLength()** function? If yes, terminate the search. It is not.

2. Is **getLength()** declared as a class member of **CoBit-MappedDialogBox**? If yes, terminate the search. It is not.

3. Is **getLength()** inherited unambiguously from either the **CoBitMap** base class or the **CoDialogBox** base class? If yes, terminate the search. It is not.

4. Is either the **CoBitMap** or **CoDialogBox** base class also derived? Yes. Repeat the previous step.

5. At last, the reference to **getLength()** within **CoBit-MappedDialogBox::theLength()** is resolved to the inherited member **CoWindow::getLength()**.

Is Derivation A Form Of Overloading?

In the following example, the signature of the inherited **CoWindow resetColor()** member function differs from that of the **CoDialogBox resetColor(int)** member function, which raises the following question: Do the functions constitute a set of overloaded functions? The answer is no. Derivation preserves the scope of the base classes, and overloaded functions must exist in the same scope. This is explained in the following code:

```
class CoWindow
{
public:
    void resetColor(); //sets to default
    //...
};

class CoDialogBox:public CoWindow
{
public:
    void resetColor(int color);
    //...
};
```

The **CoWindow** instance of **resetColor()** is not seen by the compiler; for example, in the following statements

NOTE

A Base Class's Function Name Reuse

Reusing a base class's function name in a derived class is not a form of overloading; it is overriding.

```
CoDialogBox d;
d.resetColor(13); //ok
d.resetColor(); //error
```

the call

```
d.resetColor();
```

resolves to **CoDialogBox::resetColor(int)**. It, therefore, causes a compile-time error. The instance of **resetColor()** that is detected by the compiler demands one argument of type **int**.

How To Access A Protected Member In A Framework?

Often, a programmer needs access to a **protected** member while using a framework or a commercial class library. Listing 3.1 shows how this can be done by class derivation.

Listing 3.1 Using a protected member from a class.

```
class CoClass //commercial class library
{
public:
    CoClass(int v=0):value_(v){}

protected:
    int value_;
};

class DoClass:public CoClass //your class library
{
public:
    int& getValue()
    {
        return CoClass::value_;
    }
};

int main()
{
    DoClass w;
    cout<<w.getValue()<<endl; //prints 0
    w.getValue()=13;
    cout<<w.getValue()<<endl; //prints 13

    return 0;
}
```

White-Box Reuse: Definition

Base classes serve as extensible skeletons. A base class's application-specific behavior is usually defined by adding or overriding member functions to a derived class. Each member function added to a derived class must abide by the internal conventions of its base class. This is referred to as *white-box reuse*, because a base-class's implementation must be understood to be reused.

Note that the **DoClass::getValue()** function returns a reference to an **int** type. It enables users to modify the contents of the variable **value_**.

Polymorphism

Polymorphism is the capability of objects derived from a common class to respond differently to the same message. Classes that provide polymorphism are referred to as *polymorphic classes*. (*Polymorphic* is borrowed from the Greek term for "many forms.") C++ implements the concept of polymorphism by using **virtual** functions. Member functions whose implementation relies on subsequent derivations that are unknown at the time of the base class declarations are declared as **virtual** functions.

Virtual functions are a C++ technique to delay until runtime the selection of which member function gets called. Such a technique is called *late* (or *dynamic*) *binding*. Late binding enables the programmer to encapsulate the implementation details of the derivation hierarchy from the user. User code, no longer subject to change with each change to the hierarchy, is simpler to program and maintain. Adding a new derivation does not require the modification of existing code. A **virtual** function doesn't need to know about future derivations. Class code remains functional regardless of how the hierarchy is altered; it makes customization simplified.

Abstract Classes

An abstract class has a pure **virtual** function. Standard object interfaces are often represented by abstract classes. They declare pure **virtual** member functions that must be implemented by the subclasses. A subclass that is not abstract is *concrete*. A concrete class must provide an implementation for its abstract class.

In general, inheriting from an abstract class is better than from a concrete class. Because an abstract class doesn't have to provide a data representation, future derived classes can use any representation without a risk of conflicting with the one that they inherited. Reusing a nicely packaged abstraction is always easier than inventing one. The roots of class hierarchies are usually abstract classes. A concrete class is referred to as an *implementation* of an abstract class.

An application of abstract classes and **virtual** functions is in class libraries. A programmer can author a reusable and extensible class library that may be utilized by other programmers. Classes in the library must define the interface and components common to the entire hierarchy. Users of the class library inherit classes from the general class and then simply redefine those functions that are specific to the derived class.

An Example Of Using Polymorphism And An Abstract Class

As mentioned in Chapter 1, a base class **virtual** function is generally not intended to be invoked—it just serves as a placeholder for the still-unknown derived class types. For example, a **CoWindow** class designer may declare **show()** as a **virtual** member function that must be implemented by the subclasses. Such functions are referred to as pure **virtual** functions. For example, in the following

```
class CoWindow //standard object interface
{
public:
    virtual void show()=0; //pure virtual function
    //...
};
```

show() is a pure **virtual** function and, therefore, the **CoWindow** class is an abstract class. Thus, as demonstrated in the following example, the **CoWindow** class acts as a standard object interface for the **CoWindow** hierarchy:

```
class CoButton:public CoWindow
{
public:
    CoButton();
    void show() //overrides
    {}
    //...
};

class CoDialogBox:public CoWindow
{
public:
    CoDialogBox();
    void show() //overrides
    {}
    //...
};
```

```
void f(CoWindow* w)
{
    w->show();
}

int main()
{
    CoDialogBox * pb=new (nothrow) CoDialogBox;
    f(pb); //invokes CoDialogBox::show()

    return 0;
}
```

In this example, the **CoButton** and **CoDialogBox** classes have inherited from **CoWindow**, thus reusing the base class's code. However, the **CoWindow::show()** method does not provide any implementation. Instead, **CoButton** and **CoDialogBox** provide their own implementations. Thus, **CoWindow::show()** represents *specification reuse* rather than implementation reuse. Specification reuse is as important as implementation reuse, because specifications (polymorphic object interfaces) are the major building blocks of any OO application. This notion is discussed further in Chapter 9.

Reusability By Class Member Objects

Inheritance is often overused, because it is so powerful. Frequently, a class is made a derived class of another class when, instead, it should have had an object of that class as a member. For example, you may decide to make Car a derived class of Engine, because a Car needs the functionality of the Engine. However, the derivation relationship is not appropriate for a Car and an Engine because a Car is not a specialization of an Engine; Engine is better designated as a member of the Car.

C++'s class member object mechanism enables you to fabricate objects to form new classes. For example, you can make the Rectangle a

---

Reuse An Interface Or Implementation?

Standard object interfaces are often represented by abstract classes. They define placeholder member functions that must be implemented by the derived classes. Therefore, multiple implementations of an abstract class are possible. If you program to an implementation, you don't take advantage of dynamic binding, and, if different implementations of an abstract class exist, the program loses its flexibility. Hence, as a general rule, always program to an interface, not to an implementation.

member object of the Window. Thus, this mechanism is used as a method of reusing an object. By using this mechanism, complex classes can be created by interconnecting the existing objects with the new class. The following are the two ways to create the new class:

♦ By *delegation mechanism*—A class definition may contain an object of some other class (such an object is referred to as a *class member object*).

♦ By *acquaintance mechanism*—A class definition may contain a pointer or reference to an object of some other class (such an object is referred to as a *member class pointer* or *reference*).

Reuse-By-Delegation Mechanism

As previously mentioned, a reusable object is contained in a new class. This association between a class and an instance of another class is referred to as a *delegation* relationship (also referred to as *containership*, *has-a relationship*, or *aggregation*).

Listing 3.2 presents an example of how the delegation mechanism is implemented in C++.

Listing 3.2   Implementing delegation in C++.

```cpp
class CoRectangle
{
public:
    CoRectangle(unsigned short width, unsigned short length)
    {
        width_=width;
        length_=length;
    }

    CoRectangle()
    {
        width_=0;
        length_=0;
    }

    unsigned long area() const
    {
        return width_*length_;
    }

private:
    unsigned short width_;
    unsigned short length_;
```

```
};

class CoWindow
{
public:
    CoWindow(unsigned short width, unsigned short length);

private:
    CoRectangle x_;
};

int main()
{
    CoWindow v(13,15);
    return 0;
}
```

The definition of a **CoWindow** object invokes two constructors—its own and the constructor for its member object of the **CoRectangle** class. Now, the following two questions must be considered:

♦ What is the sequence of constructor invocations?

♦ How can the arguments be passed to the member class constructor?

A definite sequence of constructor invocation exists: The member class objects are always constructed before the containing class. This is explained later in the chapter.

Arguments can be passed to a member class constructor through a special mechanism known as the *member initialization list* (sometimes referred to as the *base initialization list*). The member initialization list follows the signature of the constructor and is separated by a colon. It consists of pairs of member class names and arguments; the pairs are separated by a comma. For example, the **CoWindow** constructor

```
CoWindow(unsigned short width, unsigned short length);
```

is defined as follows:

```
CoWindow(unsigned short width, unsigned short
length):x_(width, length)
{}
```

This is called the delegation mechanism because the **CoWindow** class can delegate messages to its member **CoRectangle** object **x_**.

For example, the **CoWindow::area()** function delegates to **CoRectangle::area()**:

```
unsigned long CoWindow::area() const
{
    return x_.area();
}
```

This way of delegating messages provides for reuse. The **CoWindow** class reuses the **CoRectangle** class. This type of reuse, however, works directly with the implementations of the reused classes, and thus can't take advantage of the dynamic binding of C++. This is obviously against the rule that dictates that you should always program to an interface, not to an implementation. This is where the acquaintance relationship—the topic of the next section—plays its role.

Reuse By Acquaintance Mechanism

A reusable object's pointer or reference can be contained in a new class. This association between a class and a pointer, or a reference of another class, is referred to as an *acquaintance* relationship (also referred to as an *association* or *using* relationship).

Here is the previous example, with minor modifications:

```
class CoWindow
{
public:
    CoWindow(CoRectangle* px):px_(px){}

private:
    CoRectangle* px_;
};

int main()
{
    CoRectangle px(13,15);
    CoWindow v(&px);
    return 0;
}
```

The **CoWindow** class now contains a pointer **px_** to **CoRectangle**. A **CoWindow** object can forward messages to its member pointer **px_**:

```
unsigned long area() const
{
    return px_->area();
}
```

This way of delegating messages provides for reuse. **CoWindow** class reuses **CoRectangle** class. Because this type of reuse works with the pointers (or references) of the reused classes, it can take advantage of the dynamic binding of C++. The pointer can be made to point to an abstract class, and you can program to an interface, and avoid using an implementation; at runtime, you can have a pointer that points to a new instance. For example, the **CoWindow** class can be modified to have another **setRectangle()** member function:

```
void CoWindow::setRectangle(CoWindow* pw)
{
    px_=pw;
}
```

Obviously, the combination of *acquaintance* and abstract classes is a very useful technique to achieve good reuse. Note that **CoWindow::setRectangle()** can be used to set a new **CoRectangle** at runtime for a **CoWindow** object. This can't be achieved in the delegation mechanism, because the delegation mechanism operates on objects rather than on pointers.

Life Cycles In Class Derivation And Object Composition

When you design frameworks, the life cycle of an object may be an important issue. Equally important is understanding how the life cycle works for class derivation and object composition.

Life Cycle In Class Derivation

In class derivation, class objects are constructed in the *base-to-derived sequence*: First, the base class subobjects are constructed, and then the derived class objects are constructed. Base class subobjects are constructed in the order of their declaration. They are destroyed in the reverse direction of the invocation of their constructors as shown in Listing 3.3.

Black-Box Reuse

The reusability inherent in the C++ programming model clearly has benefits, but the real key is to be able to focus on interface details rather than implementation details. C++'s capability to standardize interfaces and encapsulate functionality within objects does a very good job of giving you a *black-box view* of the world, which means that you can put together an application from components, without having to deal with their internal details. The interface between components can be defined by the object interface, so you need to understand only the external interface of the components. Thus, this kind of reuse is called *black-box reuse*, which is supported by object composition (acquaintance) and dynamic binding. You can compose pointers (or references) of an object, and the services from the objects can be accessed by its interface.

Clear differences exist between black-box and white-box reuse:

♦ *White-box reuse*—Represents the compile-time structure of the reusable class. The base class subobject is implicitly available to all the objects of the derived class, which is determined at compile-time.

♦ *Black-box reuse*—Represents the runtime structure of the reusable class. Any information passed to constituents of the new class must be passed explicitly.

By taking advantage of the reused classes' polymorphic behavior, you can dictate the runtime behavior of the system. On the other hand, you can't alter the base class of a derived class to get a dynamic behavior. Thus, as a general rule, you must favor object composition over inheritance while designing an OO system. However, the right combination of inheritance and composition works best in most cases.

Listing 3.3   Construction and destruction of base and derived objects.

```
class CoBase0
{
public:
    CoBase0();
};

class CoBase1
{
public:
    CoBase1();
};

class CoDerived1:public CoBase0
{
public:
    CoDerived1();
};

class CoDerived2:public CoDerived1
```

```
{
public:
    CoDerived2();
};

class CoDerived3:public CoDerived2
{
public:
    CoDerived3();
};

class CoDerived4:public CoBase0
{
public:
    CoDerived4();
};

class CoDerived5:public CoDerived4
{
public:
    CoDerived5();
};

class CoBase1_x:
    public CoBase1, public CoDerived3, public CoDerived5
{
public:
    CoBase1_x();
};

int main()
{
    CoBase1_x base1_x;
    return 0;
}
```

The constructors for **base1_x** are invoked in the following sequence. First, the base class constructor is invoked in the order of the base class declarations:

```
CoBase1();  //base class of CoBase1_x

CoBase0(); //base class of CoDerived1
CoDerived1();  //base class of CoDerived2
CoDerived2();  //base class of CoDerived3
CoDerived3();  //base class of CoBase1_x
```

```
CoBase0(); //base class of CoDerived4
CoDerived4(); //base class of CoDerived5
CoDerived5(); //base class of CoBase1_x
```

Then, the derived class constructor is invoked:

```
CoBase1_x();
```

The destructors for **base1_x** are invoked in the opposite order of the constructor invocations.

Life Cycle In Delegation

In the delegation mechanism, the life cycle of the composed objects depends on the life cycle of the container object. Whenever a container object is instantiated, the composed objects are constructed before the container object. This construction rule implies that the composed objects are destroyed after the container object. The delegation mechanism is, in fact, similar to that of the class derivation. You can think of a derived object as a container object that contains the base subobjects. However, base class subobjects are constructed before the member objects of a class as shown in Listing 3.4.

Listing 3.4   Construction and destruction of container and contained objects.

```
class CoClass1
{
public:
    CoClass1();
};

class CoClass2
{
public:
    CoClass2();
};

class CoBase0
{
public:
    CoBase0();
};

class CoBase1
{
```

```
public:
    CoBase1();
};

class CoDerived1:public CoBase0
{
public:
    CoDerived1();
};

class CoDerived2:public CoDerived1
{
public:
    CoDerived2();
};

class CoDerived3:public CoDerived2
{
public:
    CoDerived3();
};

class CoDerived4:public CoBase0
{
public:
    CoDerived4();
};

class CoDerived5:public CoDerived4
{
public:
    CoDerived5();
};

class CoBase1_x:
    public CoBase1, public CoDerived3, public CoDerived5
{
public:
    CoBase1_x();

protected:
    CoClass1 c1_;
    CoClass2 c2_;
};

int main()
```

```
{
    CoBase1_x base1_x;
    return 0;
}
```

The constructors for **base1_x** are invoked in the following sequence. First, the base class constructor is invoked in the order of the base class declarations:

```
CoBase1();  //base class of CoBase1_x

CoBase0(); //base class of CoDerived1
CoDerived1();  //base class of CoDerived2
CoDerived2();  //base class of CoDerived3
CoDerived3();  //base class of CoBase1_x

CoBase0();  //base class of CoDerived4
CoDerived4(); //base class of CoDerived5
CoDerived5();  //base class of CoBase1_x
```

Next, each member class object constructor is invoked in the order of member class declarations:

```
CoClass1();
CoClass2();
```

Finally, the derived class constructor is invoked:

```
CoBase1_x();
```

The destructors for **base1_x** are invoked in the opposite order of the constructor invocations.

Life Cycle In Acquaintance

In the acquaintance mechanism, a container object does not necessarily control the life cycle of the composed objects. The composed objects can be instantiated outside the scope of the container class and can be passed as arguments to the container's constructor or some other member functions, as shown in the previous example.

Reusability By Templates

Generic types provide a technique for reusing the functionality of code through parameters. C++ supports generic programming through its template features. (Chapter 2 discusses templates in detail.) *Templates* (also called *generic types* or *parameterized types*) are used to construct a family of related functions or classes. The following is a brief recap of these definitions:

♦ *Function templates*—Provide you with the capability to write a single function that is a skeleton, or template, for a family of similar functions.

♦ *Class templates (also called generic classes or class generators)*—Enable you to define a pattern for class definitions. Generic container classes are a good example of class templates.

C++ templates are a form of reusability, because once a template function or class is developed, it doesn't need to be reprogrammed, but can nevertheless be adapted to meet various designing or programming requirements. This is a good example of code reuse. Code reuse was a major motivation for creating the Standard Template Library (STL). STL is a significant development in C++, because it contains ready-to-use generic algorithms and components in the form of templates. The essential idea behind STL is to create components that can easily be reused in various combinations, without losing any performance. Thus, STL embodies all the major requirements that a component must possess to be called reusable.

STL is discussed extensively in Chapter 2, so the following provides a brief recap of STL's reusable components:

♦ *Container*—An object that keeps and manages a set of memory locations of arbitrary types. The container classes include **vector, list, deque, set, multiset, map, multimap, stack, queue,** and **priority queue.**

♦ *Generic algorithm*—A computational procedure that is able to work on different containers. The generic algorithms include a broad range of fundamental algorithms for the most common kinds of data manipulations, such as searching, sorting, merging, copying, and transforming.

♦ *Iterator*—An abstraction to provide a mechanism for traversing and examining the elements in a container. STL provides five categories of iterators: random access, bidirectional, forward, output, and input.

♦ *Function object*—A class that can be used like a function.

♦ *Adaptor*—A class that provides an existing component with a different interface (for example, to make a stack out of a list).

Genericity Vs. Inheritance

In general, when you need to create a set of almost-similar objects, you must consider using templates. By using class templates, you can instantiate whatever type-safe types you need. Also, no runtime overhead is imposed by this type of safety, because no derivation and **virtual** functions are involved. In other words, the structures of generic types are known at compile time, whereas in dynamic binding, function call indirections can cause runtime inefficiency. As a general rule, favor genericity over inheritance. This was a significant design criterion of the Standard Template Library (STL).

♦ *Allocator*—A class that encapsulates the information about the memory model.

Where Are The UML Notations?

The *Unified Modeling Language* (UML) provides class diagrams to show the static structure of an object model; in particular, the things that exist (such as classes and types), their internal structures, and their relationships to other things. This chapter discussed classes as reusable entities, the relationships between classes (class derivation and object composition), and templates. However, this chapter didn't show UML-based diagrams to explain the concepts. UML is the topic of the Chapter 4.

Chapter Recap

Software developers have rapidly accepted object-oriented technology as their preference for designing and implementing software systems, primarily because OOP enables *software reuse*, the process of creating software systems from predefined software components. Software reuse can cut risk, development time, and costs; thus, reuse should be practiced in virtually every software project.

By using C++, you can define reusable classes. The greater benefits of OO-based reuse are derived in conjunction with design patterns and frameworks, which provide better form and higher levels of reuse. Chapters 5 and 6 discuss reuse with design patterns and frameworks.

This chapter presented a few significant reuse notions, including the following:

♦ A reusable component should have three features: usability, generality, and adaptability.

- ◆ C++ provides a powerful springboard for developing reusable objects.

- ◆ The C++ class derivation mechanism adapts an existing class to a new requirement. Class derivation implements white-box reuse in C++.

- ◆ C++'s class-member object mechanism can be used to create object composition. Class member objects implement black-box reuse in C++.

- ◆ The C++ template mechanism enables you to create reusable generic types.

Chapter 4

Introduction To UML

The *Unified Modeling Language* (UML) is a language for specifying various attributes of an object-oriented (OO) system, such as the static and dynamic characteristics of the system. Because UML has a broad range of use and strong industry support, it has become a *de facto* industry standard and a core constituent for OO development. The Object Management Group (OMG) that defined CORBA has adopted UML into the Object Management Architecture (OMA). According to OMG, "The adoption of UML provides system architects working on Object-Oriented Analysis and Design (OOAD) with one consistent language for specifying, visualizing, constructing, and documenting the artifacts of software systems, as well as for business modeling."

UML combines the best aspects of various modeling languages, including Booch method, Object Modeling Technique (OMT), Object-Oriented Software Engineering (OOSE), and other methods, such as Hewlett Packard's Fusion. Thus, UML provides all the benefits and functions that these modeling languages provide.

This chapter's purpose is to describe only those UML concepts and their notations that are used in the book. Please note that this chapter isn't intended to be a comprehensive tutorial on UML.

UML Concepts

UML isn't an OO methodology; UML was designed and accepted as a visual modeling language. A method or process consists of a series of steps on how to perform object-oriented analysis and design, whereas UML provides a common notational vocabulary for expressing underlying object-oriented analysis and design. To build an OO system, you still need a methodology.

Why UML?

The graphical models play a significant role in OO engineering. Whenever some object or OO system needs to be developed, models must be constructed to describe the appearance of objects, interrelationships among objects, and behavior of the system. A model is also used to show a consistent view of an object or an OO system. Since models are easy to change, easy to understand, and easy to communicate to others, it is important to use them in the development of an OO system. Obviously, by employing a standard visual modeling language in a project, the overall development time is shortened.

UML is a formal language that supports visual modeling and provides all the advantages discussed in the preceding paragraph. The following are the primary goals of UML:

♦ Provide developers with a formal visual modeling language so that they can develop consistent models

♦ Help software developers to communicate (better)

♦ Be independent of a particular programming language or design methodology

♦ Be extensible and provide mechanisms for specialization to meet the modeling requirements of a very wide range of projects

UML Notations

UML provides many modeling diagrams for different purposes, such as dynamic or static system views. These diagrams depict the essential classes and their associations in an OO system. Here is a brief description of these diagrams:

♦ *Use case diagrams*—For modeling business processes; typically used to characterize the behavior of the complete OO system when interacting with one or more external actors (users)

♦ *Class diagrams*—For modeling the static structure of classes in an OO system; contain classes and their relationships

♦ *Interaction diagrams*—For modeling interactions within a system; the two types are *collaboration* diagrams and *sequence* diagrams, both of which are discussed later in the chapter

♦ *State diagrams*—For modeling the state space of an object; show the events that cause an object's transition from one state to another

- *Activity diagrams*—For analyzing use case diagrams, understanding workflow across use cases, and dealing with parallelism
- *Component diagrams*—For modeling components
- *Deployment diagrams*—For modeling the productive deployment of a system; present a visual representation of relationships among software and hardware components

This chapter presents class diagrams and the two types of interaction diagrams (collaboration diagrams and sequence diagrams), because they are the only diagrams that are used throughout the book. Other diagrams aren't in the scope of this chapter.

Class Diagram

The class and its associated concepts are presented first, before actually describing a class diagram.

Class

As mentioned in Chapter 1, a *class* is an abstraction that summarizes the objects' common properties (structure and behavior). A class can also capture its relationships with other classes. While a class is an abstraction of real-world items, *objects* are considered concrete entities that exist in space/time. Each object is always some instance of a class. You can view the world as consisting of many objects that interact with each other to produce a collective behavior. Because UML provides notations to view classes, objects, and their runtime interactions, it maps very well to OO systems.

In UML, classes are represented as three-part boxes: The top part contains the class name, the middle part contains the data members (with optional types and values), and the bottom part contains the member functions (with optional signature and return type).

A class that can be directly instantiated is referred to as a *concrete class*. The opposite of a concrete class is an *abstract class*. An abstract class's data member part (the middle part of the three-part box) is empty. For a concrete class, the data member and member function parts of the class box can be omitted, to simplify the class overview. Note that when you omit a part, you don't imply the absence of data members or member functions, whereas when you keep a part empty, you explicitly declare that no members are in that part. Figure 4.1 shows a diagram of a class **CoWindow** that has two data members and one function.

The diagram in Figure 4.1 has three parts. The top part of the diagram contains the class name (**CoWindow**), the middle part contains the

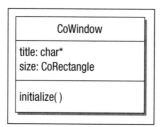

Figure 4.1
The **CoWindow** class.

data members (**title** and **size**), and the bottom part contains the member function (**initialize()**). Note that the diagram doesn't show the signature or return type of the **initialize()** member function.

Class Diagram

Class diagrams show a collection of classes and their relationships in an OO system. Class diagrams show the static structure of an OO system. A class diagram sometimes is incorrectly referred to as an *object model.* However, because a class diagram doesn't contain instantiated objects, it shouldn't be referred to as an object model. A class diagram can depict four types of relationships:

♦ *Generalization relationship*—A derivation of a class. A generalization relationship is represented as a solid line with an arrow pointing to the base class.

♦ *Composition relationship*—A form of member objects in a class. A class definition may contain an object of some other class. Composition may not be recursive. Composition is shown by a filled diamond.

♦ *Aggregation relationship*—A class definition may contain a pointer or reference to an object of some other class (such an object is referred to as a *member class pointer* or *reference*). Aggregate relationship may be recursive. An aggregate relationship is a solid line with an unfilled diamond at one end.

♦ *Association relationship*—An association represents a semantic correlation between two classes. In contrast to the preceding three relationships, associations are bidirectional. They are semantically weak, because they depict general relationships among classes. An association relationship is shown by a line. You can specify an association name to identify the type or purpose of the relationship. An association between two classes is known as a *binary association.* An association among three or more classes is known as an *N-ary* association.

Figure 4.2 shows various class relationships, using UML notations.

> **NOTE**
>
> **Class Diagram Helps Implementation**
>
> The information contained in a class diagram directly maps to the class level implementation. Therefore, a class diagram is essential for an object-oriented application.

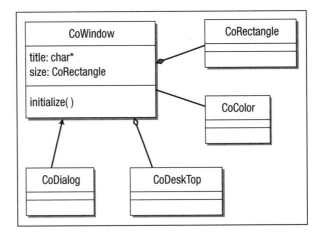

Figure 4.2
Relationships among graphical user interface (GUI) classes.

Here is a brief description of various elements of Figure 4.2:

♦ The **CoDialog** class is derived from the **CoWindow** class. This relationship is shown as a solid line with an arrow pointing to the **CoWindow** class.

♦ The **CoWindow** class definition contains an object of the **CoRectangle** class. This is the composition relationship. A filled diamond pointing to the **CoWindow** class shows composition.

♦ The **CoWindow** class definition may contain a pointer or reference to an object of type **CoDeskTop**. This is the aggregate relationship. An unfilled diamond pointing to the **CoWindow** class shows aggregation.

♦ The **CoWindow** and **CoColor** classes are joined by a line. The line shows a binary association between the classes. This is further explained in the next section.

Role

Role is the name of the specific behavior of a class that is participating in a relationship. A role can have *multiplicity specification* that indicates the number of objects participating in the given relationship. The default multiplicity is *unspecified*. Figure 4.3 shows an example of role and multiplicity of relationship.

Figure 4.3 shows that an association between the **CoWindow** class and the **CoColor** class. **CoWindow** contains a **CoColor** object. The role is tagged as *contains*, and because one **CoWindow** always contains one **CoColor** object, the multiplicity is shown as **1** at both ends of the relationship line.

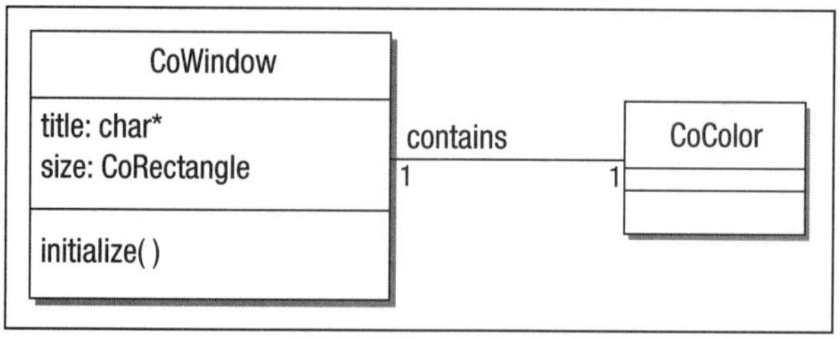

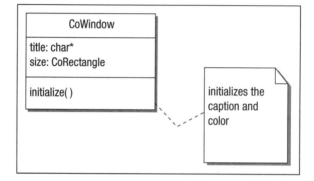

Figure 4.3
Role and multiplicity of a relationship.

Figure 4.4
A note describing a **CoWindow** member function **initialize()**.

Note

A *note* can be attached to a class, its member function, and a role in a class diagram. A note is used to provide extra information that can't be shown graphically. Figure 4.4 shows a note for the member function **CoWindow::initialize( )**.

Class Template

A *class template* (also known as *parameterized class*) is a template for creating classes that share a common behavior. A class template declares formal parameters, referred to as *type parameters*. In UML, a class template is shown as a box, and the type parameters are displayed in the dashed-line box in the upper-right corner, as shown in Figure 4.5.

A specific instance of a class template is shown as a normal class, as shown in Figure 4.6.

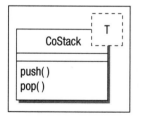

Figure 4.5
A class template **CoStack**.

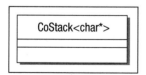

Figure 4.6
A class **CoStack<char*>**.

Interaction Diagrams

Communication between objects is done via *messages*. The receipt of a message is an *invocation of a member function*. The message-initiator object is called a *sender object*, and the target object is called a *receiver object*. The passing of a message from a sender object to a receiver object is referred to as an *object interaction*. The class of a receiver object is referred to as a *supplier class*, because it provides services that can be invoked by others. The class of the sender object that requests a service from a receiver is referred to as a *client class*.

A class diagram depicts *static behavior* of an OO system, because it doesn't show how objects interact at runtime. You must use object interaction diagrams to signify *runtime behavior* of a system, which involves message flow among objects within a particular context to achieve a particular result.

An object of a class is shown as a box with its name in one of the following formats:

```
Object name:Class name
:Class name
Object name
```

aCoWindow:CoWindow

Figure 4.7
An object **aCoWindow** of
type **CoWindow**.

You can omit the object name or class name. When you omit the object name, you need to retain the colon (**:**). Note that the names are underlined, as shown in Figure 4.7.

In UML interaction diagrams, a message is shown as an arrow from the sender object to the receiver object. UML provides two simple types of interaction diagrams:

♦ *Collaboration diagram*—A diagram that shows objects participating in an interaction, and depicts the basic relationships among objects. If you want to indicate the sequence of message flow among objects in a collaboration diagram, you can number the messages. However, this way of showing sequencing generally isn't preferred, because a sequence diagram is the right candidate for that task. Within a collaboration diagram, an object is represented as a box, and the message exchange is shown by arrows, as presented in Figure 4.8.

Figure 4.8 depicts a collaboration diagram that shows how to use a **CoMenu** object on a **CoWindow** to invoke a **CoPrintDialogBox** object. Following is a description of the steps shown in the diagram:

The Problem Of So Many Terms

The UML terms *aggregation* and *composition* create confusion. UML itself doesn't distinguish between these two concepts very strongly, except in the realm of the life-cycle of objects. In Chapter 3, *composition* was used to describe two forms of reuse—*delegation* and *acquaintance*. However, UML's definition of composition is somewhat different. It is similar to the delegation mechanism described in Chapter 3. Similarly, UML's aggregation notion is the same as the acquaintance mechanism in Chapter 3. Also, many OO engineers don't differentiate between (UML) composition and (UML) aggregation.

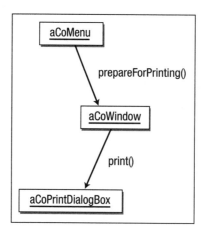

Figure 4.8
Collaboration diagram.

1. The **aCoMenu** object invokes the **prepareForPrinting()** member function on the **aCoWindow** object.

2. Then, the **aCoWindow** object invokes the **print()** member function on the **aCoPrintDialogBox** object.

♦ *Sequence diagram*—A diagram that shows object interactions and depicts the sequence of messages exchanged. Unlike a collaboration diagram, a sequence diagram doesn't indicate object relationships. Within a sequence diagram, an object is represented as a box, and the object's life (existence) is shown as a dashed vertical line. The vertical line is referred to as an object's *lifeline*. The sequence diagrams are sometimes referred to as *event-trace diagrams*. Figure 4.9 shows a sequence diagram.

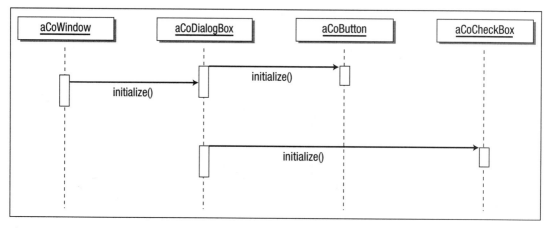

Figure 4.9
Sequence diagram.

Collaboration Diagram Vs. Sequence Diagram

One advantage of using the sequence diagram is that you can easily show the sequence of messages in an OO system. Often, it is difficult to number the message flow sequence among objects in a collaboration diagram. However, you can use a collaboration diagram to indicate how objects are related.

Figure 4.9 shows how the initialization of a **CoDialogBox** object propagates to its child controls. Following is a description of the steps shown in the diagram:

1. The **aCoWindow** object invokes the **initialize( )** member function on the **aCoDialogBox** object.

2. The **aCoDialogBox** object invokes the **initialize( )** member function on the **aCoButton** object.

3. The **aCoDialogBox** object invokes the **initialize( )** member function on the **aCoCheckBox** object.

Chapter Recap

UML isn't an OO methodology; UML is designed to provide developers with a formal visual modeling language. By using UML, developers can develop consistent models and communicate with each other better. UML is self-sufficient—it doesn't depend on a particular programming language or design methodology.

The UML notations provide a variety of diagrams for different purposes, such as dynamic or static system views. These diagrams contain the essential classes and their associations. This chapter presented class diagrams, collaboration diagrams, and sequence diagrams, including the following:

♦ Classes are represented as three-part boxes: The top contains the class name, the middle contains the data members (with optional types and values), and the bottom contains the member functions (with optional signature and return type). An object of a class is shown as a box with its name in the format **Object name:Class name**.

♦ Class diagrams show a collection of classes and their relationships in an OO system. Class diagrams show the static structure of an OO system. A class diagram can depict four types of relationships—generalization, composition, aggregation, and association relationships.

♦ A collaboration diagram shows the objects participating in an interaction and depicts the basic relationships between objects.

♦ A sequence diagram shows object interactions and depicts the sequence of messages exchanged.

Chapter 5
Introduction To Design Patterns

As Chapter 3 mentions, object-oriented (OO) technology has gained rapid acceptance among software developers and has become the preferred choice for designing and implementing software systems. The primary reason for the popularity of object-oriented programming (OOP) is that it enables *software reuse*, the process of creating software systems from predefined software components. By using OOP, you can define reusable abstract data types that package data along with the functions that are used to manipulate that data. Apart from defining reusable abstract data types, the most important benefits of OOP-based reuse come from design patterns and frameworks; they provide better forms and higher levels of reuse. This chapter focuses on design patterns and their associated concepts. A *design pattern* is an abstraction from a general design problem, which keeps recurring, in specific, nonarbitrary contexts.

This chapter builds on Chapter 3, which describes reuse concepts and C++ reuse capabilities, with accompanying examples. This chapter also uses UML notation, which is discussed in depth in Chapter 4.

Interestingly, CORBA specifications also support a few design patterns, such as the component factory, proxy, Externalization Service, Naming Service, Event Service, and so forth. These patterns are discussed in Chapter 13.

Patterns Are An Advanced Form Of Reuse

As Chapter 3 describes, almost every programmer practices reuse, by recycling old information in some ad hoc fashion. Rather than starting from scratch each time that you begin a new project, you can save time by modifying existing software programs or components to make them fit your current needs. This is referred to as an *opportunistic reuse*. However, this technique has many disadvantages—the modified components will have to address issues such as testing, configuration management, maintenance, and documentation in the same way as a new component does.

In contrast to opportunistic reuse, *systematic reuse* focuses on the use of frozen assets, or unmodified software components, which means that you don't alter the source files of the component being reused. If behavior modifications are necessary, you make them through parameter passing, generic instantiations, inheritance, or composition. This chapter (and book) focus on *systematic reuse* that has the following three levels:

♦ *Framework reuse*—Represents design and code reuse, the highest level of reuse. Framework reuse is the topic of Chapter 6.

♦ *Design pattern reuse*—Represents design reuse, an advanced level of reuse. This chapter covers design pattern reuse.

♦ *Class reuse*—Represents code reuse, the lowest level of reuse. Chapter 3 presents class reuse in depth.

The Concept Of Patterns

When you work on a new problem, do you invent a new solution, or do you prefer to adapt and apply a successful solution from a similar problem? Practicing engineers—whether they specialize in civil, mechanical, electrical, or aerospace engineering—believe in the reusability of solutions as a fundamental principle of engineering. Even in software engineering, if you apply experience from past solutions, you can help to cut risks, development time, and costs. Abstracting a new solution out of a collection of existing solutions leads to *software patterns*. Patterns exist in all levels of software design, from high-level architecture design down to smaller architectural units.

Various kinds of software patterns exist. Frank Buschmann and his co-authors for *Pattern-Oriented Software Architecture: A System of Patterns*

NOTE

**Architectural Patterns
Vs. Frameworks**

Architectural patterns
and frameworks sound
like similar concepts, but
an architectural pattern
expresses only how a
software system appears,
whereas a framework is
an implementation that
represents a software
system. A framework
may be based on a
particular architectural
pattern.

(published by John Wiley & Sons in 1996) classify patterns based on each pattern's scale or granularity, as follows:

♦ *Architectural patterns (systems design)*—Set a fundamental standard for structuring software. An architectural pattern provides a set of predefined subsystems, as well as rules and guidelines to establish the relationships between these subsystems. Architectural patterns are considered templates for concrete software architectures. Buschmann's book presents a catalog of eight architectural patterns, one of which is the *Layers* architecture, which is particularly useful for software systems in which different subtasks can be identified and attached to different levels of abstractions. The selection of a particular architectural pattern for a software system is a fundamental design decision, because the architectural pattern settles the application's basic structure.

This chapter (and book) doesn't cover architectural patterns, but instead focuses mainly on the design patterns and idioms, described next.

♦ *Design patterns*—The smaller, software architectural units that a software architecture consists of. You can use design patterns to share knowledge about the architecture. In your design activities, you encounter many problems that have previously occurred and that will occur again. You can solve a problem by applying previous, related experiences that solved a similar problem. You can reuse and possibly share the information that you learn regarding the best solution for a specific program-design problem.

♦ *Programming idioms (language-specific techniques/style)*—Deal with issues related to how a particular design should be implemented. Idioms describe how to implement particular classes and relationships between them within a specific design problem. Idioms are related to a specific programming language, and they comprise aspects of both design and implementation for a particular structure.

To summarize the concepts of patterns, architectural patterns have the highest granularity, and idioms have the lowest. Software architectures are built by following some overall structuring principles that are described by an architectural pattern. A software architecture is comprised of various smaller units, which are described by design patterns. Idioms deal with the implementation of particular design issues.

Brief History Of Patterns

The notion of a pattern is based primarily on the work of Christopher Alexander, a building architect, and his attempt to identify solutions to recurrent architectural problems. In the late 1970s, Alexander and his colleagues (also building architects) wrote two books, *The Timeless Way of Building* and *A Pattern Language*, which present the authors' views of the recurring problems they encountered while building cities, towns, neighborhoods, and buildings. Alexander describes these problems and their solutions as *patterns*. A pattern describes how to deal with a certain architectural design issue in a structured way, for example, parallel roads and a sequence of sitting spaces. Alexander's patterns start on a global level and progressively become more specific: The world is segmented by country, countries are segmented by region, and so on, all the way down to such things as the division of office connections and the placement of windows in kitchens. In *A Pattern Language*, which Oxford University Press published in 1977, Alexander presented 253 patterns, all conforming to a standard structure.

Extending Alexander's concept of patterns to software provides a new expression to the software reuse field. In 1995, Erich Gamma, Richard Helm, Ralph Johnson, and John Vlissides published *Design Patterns: Elements of Reusable Object-Oriented Software*. This is one of the most widely cited books on design patterns. It presents a catalog of 23 design patterns that were identified from numerous object-oriented systems. These patterns identify some common program-design problems—such as adapting the interface of one object to that of another object or notifying an object of a change in another object's state—and explain the best ways to solve the problems.

A Design Pattern Example

To give you an idea of what a design pattern is, this section provides a simple design example and then discusses how it can evolve into a design pattern.

Consider a computer-aided design (CAD) system for 2D and 3D modeling that enables architects to illustrate class hierarchies through the use of graphic figures. In a CAD system, users often need to build complex figures out of simpler figures. At runtime, a complex figure appears similar to a tree of objects, as shown in Figure 5.1.

In the design to solve the problem of treating simple and complex graphic figures alike, two requirements should be met:

♦ Complex figures should consist of smaller objects, to support reusability.

♦ Clients shouldn't have to worry about the types of objects that they access. Instead, clients should access simple objects and complex objects in the same way.

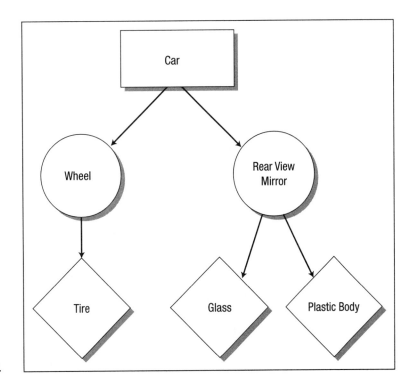

Figure 5.1
A complex figure in CAD.

The solution to the problem is to introduce an abstract class that rep-resents both the simple and complex graphic figures. For example, you can introduce a **CoPicture** class that is an abstract class and that de-clares a **paint()** member function specific to graphic objects. You can then declare a **CoCompositePicture** class, derived from **CoPicture**, that aggregates **CoPicture** objects and implements the **paint()** opera-tion to call **paint()** on its contained **CoPicture** objects. The following shows the declarations of the **CoPicture** and **CoCompositePicture** classes:

```
class CoPicture
{
public:
 virtual void paint()=0;
};

class CoCompositePicture : public CoPicture
{
```

```
public:
    typedef
    vector<CoPicture*, allocator<CoPicture*> >
    PICTURE_VECTOR;

private:
    PICTURE_VECTOR pictures;

public:
    void addImage(CoPicture* anImage);
    virtual void paint();
};
```

Because the **CoCompositePicture** interface conforms to the **CoPicture** interface, objects of the **CoCompositePicture** class can be composed of other **CoCompositePicture** objects recursively.

This mechanism, referred to as the *Composite* design pattern, composes objects into tree structures. Composite enables clients to treat individual objects and composition of objects uniformly.

The Composite design pattern isn't limited only to CAD systems. Many object-oriented applications apply the Composite design pattern to solve specific problems. The full implementation and the UML model of the Composite design pattern is presented in the "Implementing The Composite Design Pattern" and "Modeling Patterns By Using UML" sections later in this chapter.

The Composite design pattern can be applied in the following situations:

♦ In a graphical editor that handles various multimedia documents uniformly

♦ In a graphical user interface (GUI) system that manipulates all objects in a window in the same way

The preceding list shows that the Composite design pattern has broad applicability, which is why the Composite design pattern represents solutions to a particular problem that arises when developing software within a particular context.

Now that you're familiar with the design pattern concept, you are ready to review a formal definition of *design pattern*, which I'll present by using the Composite example.

Definition Of A Design Pattern

A design pattern is an abstraction from a general design problem, which keeps recurring, in specific, nonarbitrary contexts. This means that you can apply a design pattern to solve a family of design problems. For example, the Composite design pattern solves the problem of aggregating components that need to form a semantic unit.

A design pattern constitutes the following:

♦ A description of a basic scheme for structuring a software architecture's subsystems and components, as well as the interrelationships between subsystems and components.

♦ An abstraction above the level of classes and objects.

♦ A reusable building block that is application-independent.

A design pattern captures the static and dynamic structure and collaboration among key participants in software designs. For example, the Composite design pattern identifies **CoPicture** and **CoCompositePicture** as two key participants in the design. The **CoPicture** class declares the interface for the objects in the composition. For example, it contains the **paint()** member function, which is pure **virtual** and must be implemented by a class that conforms to the **CoPicture** interface. The **CoCompositePicture** class defines the behavior of a component that has children. It also implements the **CoPicture** interface. The collaboration between the **CoPicture** and **CoCompositePicture** interfaces can be defined as follows: A client uses the **CoPicture** interface to interact with objects in the composite structure. If the receiver object is *not* of type **CoCompositePicture**, the requested function is executed; otherwise, the object iterates through the contained **CoPicture** objects, to handle the request recursively.

What A Design Pattern Is Not

A design pattern may mean different things to different people. What other people call their design pattern may not agree with your concept of a design pattern. However, in this book, a design pattern is described as a *set* of classes and instances that collaborate to solve a specific kind of design problem. Thus, a single class, such as the STL **stack**, can't constitute a design pattern. The following is a list of what a design pattern is *not*:

♦ *Class*—Design patterns are bigger architectural elements than classes. The STL **stack** isn't a design pattern; it's simply a generic class. Design patterns are more specialized than classes.

- *Complete application or subsystem*—A design pattern is a set of classes and instances that collaborate to solve a specific kind of design problem; they aren't described in any programming language.

- *Framework*—A framework is the reusable design of a system, such as a set of collaborating classes. Frameworks are conceptually larger than design patterns; frameworks contain many design patterns. (A discussion of design patterns vis-à-vis frameworks appears in the "Design Patterns Vs. Frameworks" section toward the end of this chapter.)

- *Object-oriented methodology*—A design pattern is designed and accepted as a design construct. A methodology, or process, consists of a series of steps that are followed to perform object-oriented analysis and design, whereas a design pattern provides a common conceptual design for expressing underlying, low-scale object-oriented designs. To build an object-oriented system, you still need a methodology. Of course, you can use UML to model a design pattern.

Why To Use Design Patterns

Having learned the definition of a design pattern and its related concepts, you are prepared to consider the overall benefits that design patterns offer.

The biggest benefit of a design pattern is that it is a reusable design entity. Because designing is a difficult task, you should reuse existing designs whenever possible, to avoid reinventing designs. Learning and communicating complex designs is difficult, too. For example, a particular design building block may sound complex to another person, because an existing design may communicate only the "what" of the design and ignore the "why." However, communicating the reasoning that underlies a design is vital to that design's reusability (adaptability) for particular problems. Thus, you must describe designs in a manner that communicates the rationale (logic) behind your design decisions—not just the design steps. Effectively communicating this information is where a design pattern plays its role. In short, reusability and good communication are the major factors that you should consider when making a design pattern that you believe could serve as an important tool for designers.

The following sections describe a few major reasons for practicing design-pattern-based software engineering.

Help Solve Problems The OO Way

Design patterns map well to object-oriented development because they:

♦ Facilitate reuse of successful software design elements. Reuse is one of the most powerful features of OOP. Because designing software is hard, design patterns can benefit designers by enabling them to make large-scale reuse of software designs.

♦ Help partition a problem and create an object model.

♦ Define static and dynamic structure of the system.

♦ Provide a way to define and understand the framework.

♦ Raise the granularity level of designs from functions, classes, and so forth, to larger building blocks.

Solve Design Problems

Design patterns help to solve design problems by doing the following:

♦ Showing more than just the solution: They present context (when and where), rationale, and so forth.

♦ Solving recurring common design problems.

♦ Suggesting the best fit for a specific set of problem issues.

Improve Communication

Mature engineering disciplines have handbooks that catalog successful solutions to recurring problems. For example, aerospace designers don't design a spacecraft by using the basic laws of physics only; they use a spacecraft handbook to extract the required solutions.

Because they offer the following, design patterns can serve as the basis for a software engineering handbook:

♦ *A shared vocabulary for problem-solving discussions and documentation—* You can document design decisions and their rationale in terms of design patterns.

♦ *Improved communication among developers*—Design patterns are a tool to improve communication among team members. This means that you can move from team to team without relearning design vocabularies. You and your team probably already know stack and queue concepts, and after you finish this chapter, you'll also understand Composite and Factory design patterns. Design patterns also improve communication between implementers and designers, because they enable designers to communicate their ideas more easily to implementers.

Help Software Development

The following are the ways in which design patterns help in software development:

♦ Provide a technique for dealing with the complexity of software.

♦ Offer successful solutions to recurring problems, with variations.

♦ Provide solutions for those who just want the solution, not the method by which the solution was derived.

♦ Lower development costs and time, because reuse reduces and hides complexity. Standardization helps people understand the design better, thereby lowering training costs. Reuse also shortens software-development time, because a lot of the design issues have already been considered and tested, relieving you of doing those tasks.

♦ Produce higher-quality software, by enabling you to reuse well-designed structures and concentrate on improving the design quality and comprehensibility. Reusing a reviewed and quality-certified design leads to higher-quality systems.

♦ Increase software productivity, because reusing designs usually improves reliability and lowers risks.

Reuse Features Of A Design Pattern

Chapter 3 presents the properties of a reusable component. The following is a recap of those properties, in the context of a reusable design pattern:

♦ *Usability*—A design pattern should be usable. Usability is a runtime property of a reusable component. Unless a design pattern provides expected functionality, it cannot be used, and hence cannot be reused.

♦ *Generality*—A design pattern must have a broad scope of applicability. If a design pattern can be reused only once, then it isn't a reusable design pattern.

♦ *Adaptability*—A design pattern isn't used as is, because of its generality property. Its variants have to be adaptable to different architectures. Hence, a design pattern's ease of use should be an important yardstick during its development.

You should describe a design pattern in the context of the preceding properties. In fact, the common practice is to describe each object-oriented design pattern by using a standard template, to make the design pattern easier to understand. This practice makes choosing a design pattern much easier for users, because the patterns are described in a similar manner, which makes comparing them much easier. Table 5.1 shows a template that can be used to describe a design pattern. Frank Buschmann (one of the authors of *Pattern-Oriented Software Architecture: A System Of Patterns*) and Erich Gamma (one of the authors of *Design Patterns: Elements of Reusable Object-Oriented Software*) created templates to describe design patterns. The two templates are nearly identical. In general, they provide a standard description of a design pattern. Table 5.1 is similar to Buschmann's and Gamma's templates. A detailed description of the template is beyond the scope of this chapter (and book). The goal of this chapter is to provide an intuitive idea about patterns and idioms (so that you can apply them in a framework design and implementation) rather than the theoretical aspects of design patterns.

Classifying Object-Oriented Design Patterns By Their Purpose

A few different classification schemes for design patterns exist. Table 5.2 presents a classification scheme for patterns that is based on the purpose of the patterns. The table also gives an example for each pattern category. This classification may be referred to as a *C-6 classification*, because each of the categories begins with the letter C. Table 5.2 is intended to give you an idea about pattern classification. Again, this

Table 5.1   Template to describe a design pattern.

Elements	Description
Name	A pattern's popular name and classification. The name conveys the pattern's essence briefly. You can also specify other known names of the design pattern.
Intent	A pattern's rationale and intent. The intent conveys a particular design issue or problem that it addresses.
Usability	Real-world scenarios in which the pattern generally is applicable.
Generality Examples	Situations in which the design pattern can be applied. Conveys the context.
Consequences	Trade-offs and results of using the pattern. Conveys the consequences of applying the abstract structure to a system's architecture.
Collaborations	Dynamics of the design pattern. Conveys (using UML conventions) how participants collaborate to carry out their responsibilities. Participants are the classes and/or objects participating in the design pattern.
Implementation	Sample Code to illustrate how a user might implement the pattern.
Adaptability Examples	Provides examples of the pattern's adaptation in real systems.
Related Patterns	Design patterns that have a closely related intent. Conveys the important differences, and lists with which other patterns this pattern should be used.

NOTE

***A Design Pattern Is
The Rationale Behind
The Solution, Not Just
An Answer***

Design patterns capture
the aptitude and
expertise that are
invested in building
object-oriented software.
A design pattern
describes a solution to a
recurrent design problem
using a formal template
so that you get a deeper
understanding of the
design pattern. A deeper
understanding of the
design pattern enables
you to apply and
customize the design
pattern to solve your
specific problem. Hence,
a proper design pattern
explains the intent,
applicability, and
consequences of the
solution. It gives
the rationale behind
the solution, not just
an answer.

Table 5.2   C-6 Classification of object-oriented design patterns.

Category	Purpose	Example
Controller	Deal with initializing and configuring classes and objects	Factory
Composer	Deal with partitioning an object-oriented system and decoupling interface and implementation of classes and objects	Composite
Connector	Provide control access to services of other components	Proxy
Communicator	Help organize communication between components	Forwarder-receiver
Converter	Convert a class's behavior or interface into another behavior or interface	Adapter
Conductor	Deal with dynamic interactions among societies of classes and objects	Publish-subscriber

chapter doesn't present detailed descriptions of the classifications. However, a few of the design pattern examples that Table 5.2 mentions are covered in the sidebar "Catalog Of Design Patterns."

Selecting Design Patterns

The primary objective of the OO-based application design is to partition the application into a set of interconnectable collaborative objects (components). OO can help partition a complex application system into smaller, simpler objects. Similarly, you can partition a software architecture into known design patterns. You can apply many of the existing design patterns to derive good software architectures. It is, therefore, important that you apply appropriate design patterns to solve your design problems in the architecture. To achieve this you need to consider one question: What is the problem that a design pattern is going to solve? Depending on the problem that you intend to solve, you can select a pattern of a particular type. Table 5.2 presented the C-6 classification of design patterns to enable you to select an appropriate type of pattern. For example, if you are dealing with a design problem pertaining to initialing and configuring classes, you might consider using the Controller type of design patterns. One example of such a pattern is the Factory. Obviously, you need to have a catalog that presents and describes good design patterns based on the template shown in Table 5.1. The catalog together with the C-6 classification will guide you when you're searching for a suitable pattern for an architecture.

Catalog Of Design Patterns

A design pattern's catalog contains various design patterns and presents their description based on the template (refer to Table 5.1). You can use the catalog as a design pattern handbook. The handbook helps you to select a suitable design pattern for a system.

The following is an overview of a few design patterns covered in this book:

♦ *Factory*—Provides an interface to create various types of objects. This pattern is presented later in this chapter and in Chapter 13 in the realm of distributed components.

♦ *Composite*—Presents objects in a tree structure. The client can act on the individual objects and the tree uniformly. This pattern's implementation is presented later in this chapter.

♦ *Proxy*—Provides a placeholder for another object to provide access control to it. This pattern is presented in Chapter 13.

♦ *Forwarder-receiver*—Hides the communication protocol from sender and receiver objects. This pattern is presented in Chapter 13.

♦ *Adapter*—Converts a class's interface into another interface that a client can understand. This pattern is presented later in this chapter.

♦ *Publish-subscriber*—Provides a mechanism to ensure an interested component (subscriber) has a consistent view of state of another component (publisher). This pattern is presented in Chapter 13.

Modeling Patterns By Using UML

The Unified Modeling Language (UML), described in depth in Chapter 4, is used to specify various attributes of an object-oriented system, such as static and dynamic characteristics of the system. You can use UML to model design patterns. Modeling a design pattern is important, because a graphical model plays a significant role in object-oriented engineering. You can use UML to describe appearances and behaviors of design patterns and interrelationships among participants. The following are two reasons why you should use UML to model design patterns:

♦ *UML helps software developers communicate (better)*. This is also one of the prime objectives of a design pattern, as described earlier.

♦ *UML is self-sufficient and expresses no dependency on any particular programming language or design methodology*. A design pattern is also a building block that is independent of a particular programming language or design methodology.

UML provides many modeling diagrams for different purposes, such as dynamic or static system views. You can use these diagrams to depict the essential classes and their associations in a design pattern. Here is a brief recap of these diagrams in the context of design patterns:

♦ *Class diagrams*—For modeling the static structure of participants (classes) in a design pattern. A design pattern consists of at least two classes; class diagrams contain these classes and their relationships. A class diagram doesn't contain instantiated objects. A class diagram can depict four types of relationships:

   ♦ *Generalization relationship*—A derivation of a class.

   ♦ *Composition relationship*—A form of member objects in a class.

   ♦ *Aggregation relationship*—A class definition may contain a pointer or reference to an object of some other class.

   ♦ *Association relationship*—A (possibly bidirectional) association represents a semantic correlation between two classes.

♦ *Interaction diagrams*—For modeling interactions within a design pattern. A class diagram depicts only the static behavior of a design pattern, because it doesn't show how objects interact at runtime. Thus, you must use object interaction diagrams to signify the runtime behavior of a design pattern. The following are the two types of interaction diagrams:

   ♦ *Collaboration diagram*—Shows objects participating in an interaction and depicts the basic relationships among objects. You can also indicate the sequence of message flow among objects in a collaboration diagram.

   ♦ *Sequence diagram*—Shows object interactions and depicts the sequence of messages exchanged. Unlike a collaboration diagram, a sequence diagram doesn't indicate object relationships.

The Composite design pattern, discussed earlier, can be represented by using the UML notations, as shown in Figure 5.2.

Figure 5.2 shows an association between the **CoPicture** class and the **CoCompositePicture** class. The role is tagged as containing a pointer, and because one **CoCompositePicture** may contain zero or more **CoPicture** object pointers, the multiplicity is shown as **1** (near **CoPicture** class) and ***** (near **CoCompositePicture** class) at the ends of the relationship line. The symbol ***** indicates that zero or more **CoPicture** object pointers may be contained with a **CoCompositePicture** object.

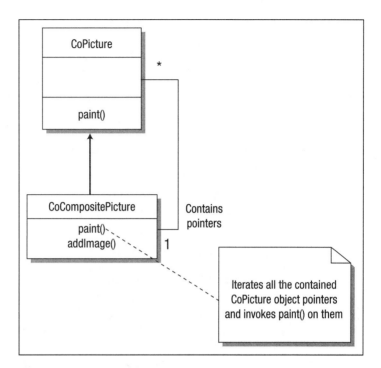

Figure 5.2
UML model of the Composite design pattern.

Implementing Object-Oriented Design Patterns Using C++

Design patterns raise the abstraction level at which people design and communicate the design of object-oriented software. However, because design patterns aren't code, they must be implemented each time that they are applied. The mechanics of implementing design patterns is left to programmers. This section discusses two broad mechanisms of C++ that are helpful in the development of object-oriented design patterns:

♦ OOP-enabling C++ features

♦ OOP-enabling C++ metapatterns

OOP-Enabling C++ Features

C++ provides features that support the OOP concepts, such as object interfaces, object inheritance, polymorphism, composition, and genericity. These five features encourage reuse in several ways. Chapters 1 and 3 present these concepts in detail, but a recap is appropriate here:

♦ *Object interface*—The specification of an object. It is a set of messages that can be sent to an object. It conveys an object's runtime behavior or functionality. A collection of well-designed object interfaces is the key to express functionality of a design pattern. C++ provides support for object interfaces through its class mechanism.

♦ *Object inheritance*—Mechanism to assemble relevant object abstractions into a hierarchy, to express hierarchical relationships among abstractions; that is, to express commonality between relevant abstractions. C++ supports object inheritance through class derivation, which can be used in three primary ways:

  ♦ To promote code reuse (also referred to as white-box reuse)

  ♦ To provide a way to organize and classify classes

  ♦ To implement polymorphism

♦ *Polymorphism*—Ability to send a message to an object without knowing the specific type of the object. A polymorphic call is easier to reuse than one that isn't polymorphic, because it will work with a wider range of objects. C++ implements the concept of polymorphism by using **virtual** functions.

♦ *Composition*—A process of combining many related abstractions into a single abstraction. Object composition is one of the most common techniques of reusing functionality in object-oriented systems. C++'s class member object mechanism enables you to fabricate objects to form new classes. Class members can be used to promote white-box reuse as well as black-box reuse.

♦ *Genericity*—A technique for reusing functionality of code through parameters. C++ supports generic programming through its template features. *Templates* (also called *generic types* or *parameterized types*) are used to construct a family of related functions or classes. Templates are discussed in detail in Chapter 2.

OOP-Enabling C++ Metapatterns

OOP features, as presented in the preceding section, are often referred to when patterns are discussed. C++ is a good language to implement design patterns, because it provides these OOP features. Using these features, C++ provides the ability to create *metapatterns*, which often are used to implement design patterns and frameworks. Metapatterns are reuse concepts that can be applied to most design patterns, to design and implement them. The following two types of metapatterns are useful:

- ◆ Hot hooks

- ◆ Frozen hooks

Hot Hooks

A hot hook is just like C++'s pure **virtual** function. A *hot hook* is used to decouple an abstraction from its implementation. A hot hook is based on the concept of acquaintance mechanism reuse (described in Chapter 3), in which an implementation's pointer or reference can be contained in a class that is visible to clients. A UML model of this concept is shown in Figure 5.3, and a corresponding example of hot hooks is provided in Listing 5.1. The example shows how different implementations of a class can be provided at runtime.

Listing 5.1   An example to demonstrate the notion of hot hooks.

```
class CoAbstractRectangle
{
public:
    virtual void draw()=0;
};

class CoRectangle
{
public:
    CoRectangle():pr_(0){}

    void attachImpl(CoAbstractRectangle* pr)
    {
        pr_=pr;
    }
```

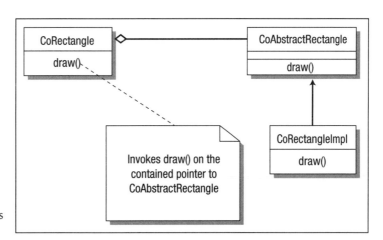

Figure 5.3
UML model to represent dynamic behavior of a class using a hot hook.

```
    void draw()
    {
        pr_->draw();
    }

private:
    CoAbstractRectangle* pr_;
};

class CoRectangleImpl1:public CoAbstractRectangle
{
public:
    virtual void draw();
};

class CoRectangleImpl2:public CoAbstractRectangle
{
public:
    virtual void draw();
};

int main()
{
    CoRectangleImpl1 r1;
    CoRectangleImpl2 r2;
    CoRectangle r;
    r.attachImpl(&r1);
    r.draw();
    r.attachImpl(&r2);
    r.draw();

    return 0;
}
```

The **draw()** member function of the **CoAbstractRectangle** class is known as a hot hook. The **CoRectangle** class provides a different implementation of **draw()** at runtime by using a member pointer of type **CoAbstractRectangle**. By using the hot hook mechanism, you can program to an interface, and avoid using an implementation. At runtime, as the preceding example shows, you attach new instances of implementations to the **CoRectangle** instance.

NOTE

Reuse By Hot Hooks

The ability to focus on interfaces rather than implementation details is the real advantage of using hot hooks. C++'s capabilities for standard-izing interfaces and encapsulating function-ality within objects does a good job of giving you a black-box view of the world. Object-composi-tion (acquaintance), together with hot hooks, supports the black-box reuse concept. You can compose pointers (or references) of an implementation to a class, and the services from the implementa-tion can be accessed through a hot hook. In this mechanism, you can dictate the runtime behavior of a class instance. The hot hook mechanism (explained further in Chapter 6) is very useful when implementing frame-works.

Frozen Hooks

A *frozen hook* is a function that consists of a series of hot hooks. Frozen hooks need not be **virtual** functions. They provide a fixed implemen-tation. However, the behavior of a frozen hook can vary at runtime, because it depends on certain hot hooks. The concept of a frozen hook is shown in Figure 5.4 and a corresponding C++ example is shown in Listing 5.2. The example presents a frozen hook that shows different behaviors at runtime, because the frozen hook consists of calls of hot hooks.

Listing 5.2   An example to implement a frozen hook.

```
class CoAbstractRectangle
{
public:
    /* virtual */ void draw()
    {
        drawBorder();
        fillColor();
    }
    virtual void drawBorder()=0;
    virtual void fillColor()=0;
};


class CoRectangleImpl1:public CoAbstractRectangle
{
public:
    virtual void drawBorder();
    virtual void fillColor();
};
```

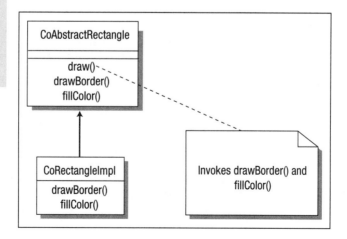

Figure 5.4
UML model to represent a frozen hook.

```
class CoRectangleImpl2:public CoAbstractRectangle
{
public:
    virtual void drawBorder();
    virtual void fillColor();
};

void draw(CoAbstractRectangle* pr)
{
    pr->draw();
}

int main()
{
    CoRectangleImpl1 r1;
    CoRectangleImpl2 r2;
    draw(&r1);
    draw(&r2);

    return 0;
}
```

The **draw()** member function of **CoAbstractRectangle** in this example is a frozen hook, because it provides a fixed implementation. However, **draw()** shows different behaviors at runtime, because it consists of calls of hot hooks, **drawBorder()** and **fillColor()**. Because the behaviors of these two hot hooks vary at runtime, the **draw()** function shows different behaviors at runtime.

Implementing The Composite Design Pattern

As mentioned earlier, a composite object consists of many different objects. The behavior of a composite object depends on the execution of polymorphic messages that pass through the tree. Listing 5.3 presents an implementation of the Composite design pattern. The example defines two classes: **CoPicture** and **CoCompositePicture**. The **CoPicture** class represents a simple picture, whereas the **CoCompositePicture** class represents a component picture.

Listing 5.3   An example of implementing the Composite design pattern.

```
#include <vector>

class CoPicture
```

```
{
public:
    virtual void paint()=0;
};

class CoCompositePicture : public CoPicture
{
public:
    typedef
    vector<CoPicture*, allocator<CoPicture*> >
    PICTURE_VECTOR;

    typedef
    PICTURE_VECTOR::iterator PICTURE_ITERATOR;

public:
    void addImage(CoPicture* anImage);
    virtual void paint();

private:
    PICTURE_VECTOR pictures_;
};

void CoCompositePicture::addImage(CoPicture* anImage)
{
    pictures_.push_back(anImage);
}

void CoCompositePicture::paint()
{
    PICTURE_ITERATOR last=pictures_.end();

    for (PICTURE_ITERATOR iter=pictures_.begin();
        iter!=last; ++iter)
    {
        (*first)->paint();
    }
}
```

Listing 5.3 shows that the hot hook **paint()** is implemented by all the participants of the Composite design pattern. When you iterate a composite object, you send the messages across the tree by using a **virtual** function. You can also implement composite objects by using a **list**, **dequeue**, or **set**, depending on your requirement.

Implementing The Factory Design Pattern

Sometimes, you need to create objects of types that aren't known at compile time. The Factory design pattern provides an interface for creating objects of various types at runtime. As an example, consider a user interface (UI) system. In a system, you should be able to work with either a character-based user interface (CUI) or a graphical user interface (GUI). If you choose to work with a CUI, all interface objects (such as windows, buttons, and so forth) should be of the CUI kind. Similarly, if you select to work with a GUI, all the objects that are created should be from the GUI hierarchy. This means that a need exists to abstract the creation of the UI object, which is where the Factory design pattern plays its role. Figure 5.5 is a partial UML model of the Factory design pattern.

Figure 5.5 clearly shows that the pattern is based on the hot hooks, such as **createWindow()** and **createButton()**. Listing 5.4 gives an implementation of the Factory design pattern based on the preceding UI example.

Listing 5.4   Example of a Factory design pattern implementation.

```
class CoUserInterface
{
public:
    virtual void repaint()=0;
};

class CoGuiWindow : public CoUserInterface
{
public:
    virtual void repaint();
```

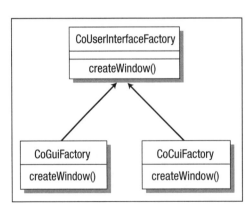

Figure 5.5
UML model of the Factory design pattern.

```cpp
};

class CoGuiButton : public CoUserInterface
{
public:
    virtual void repaint();
};

class CoCuiWindow : public CoUserInterface
{
public:
    virtual void repaint();
};

class CoCuiButton : public CoUserInterface
{
public:
    virtual void repaint();
};

class CoUserInterfaceFactory
{
public:
    virtual CoUserInterface* createWindow()=0;
    virtual CoUserInterface* createButton()=0;
};

class CoGuiFactory : public CoUserInterfaceFactory
{
public:
    virtual CoGuiWindow* createWindow()
    {
        return new CoGuiWindow;
    }
    virtual CoGuiButton* createButton()
    {
        return new CoGuiButton;
    }
};

class CoCuiFactory : public CoUserInterfaceFactory
{
public:
    virtual CoCuiWindow* createWindow()
    {
```

```
            return new CoCuiWindow;
    }
    virtual CoCuiButton* createButton()
    {
        return new CoCuiButton;
    }
};

int main()
{
    CoGuiFactory f1;
    CoCuiFactory f2;


    CoGuiWindow* pw=f1.createWindow();
    CoCuiButton* pb=f2.createButton();

    return 0;
}
```

The program defines an abstract **CoUserInterfaceFactory** class that behaves like a factory, because the class abstracts the behavior of creating different GUI objects. This class is implemented by the concrete classes **CoGuiFactory** and **CoCuiFactory**, which implement the **virtual** functions **createWindow()** and **createButton()**. The **main()** function creates instances of the **CoGuiFactory** and **CoCuiFactory** classes. When the **main()** function calls the **createWindow()** and **createButton()** functions on the instances (**f1** and **f2**) of **CoGuiFactory** and **CoCuiFactory**, the required instances of the UI objects are created.

Variation Of The Factory Pattern

The example presented in Listing 5.4 creates UI objects based on a type. The type information of the created objects comes from the function **createWindow()**. However, this isn't the only requirement to create factories. Sometimes, you can provide the type information through some identifier (such as a string) and request the factory to return an appropriate object. Listing 5.5 provides an implementation of the Factory design pattern that creates objects, given object names.

Listing 5.5   A factory based on object names.

```
#include <string>
#include <map>
#include <iostream.h>
```

```cpp
class CoAbstractRectangle
{
public:
    virtual void draw()=0;
};

class CoRectangleFactory
{
private:
    typedef CoAbstractRectangle* (*CREATE)();
    map<string, CREATE, less<string> > map_;

public:

    void addRectangle(const string& name, CREATE c)
    {
        map_[name]=c;
    }

    CoAbstractRectangle* create(const string& name)
    {
        return (map_[name])();
    }
};

class CoRectangleImpl1:public CoAbstractRectangle
{
public:
    virtual void draw();
    static CoAbstractRectangle* create()
    {
        return new CoRectangleImpl1();
    }
};

class CoRectangleImpl2:public CoAbstractRectangle
{
public:
    virtual void draw();
    static CoAbstractRectangle* create()
    {
        return new CoRectangleImpl2();
    }
};

int main()
```

```
{
    CoRectangleFactory factory;
    factory.addRectangle("r1", CoRectangleImpl1::create);
    factory.addRectangle("r2", CoRectangleImpl2::create);

    CoAbstractRectangle* r1=factory.create("r1");
    CoAbstractRectangle* r2=factory.create("r2");

    r1->draw();
    r2->draw();

    return 0;
}
```

The **CoRectangleFactory** class is the factory class to create objects of type **CoAbstractRectangle**. The **CoRectangleFactory** class has a member function **addRectangle()** that takes a name and a pointer to a callback function that can create a required instance. A *callback* is a **static** function that is registered at runtime with an object. The object then calls the function when particular events occur. When you call the **create()** function on the factory object (**factory**), the callback function (**CoRectangleImpl1::create()**, for example) is called that creates a pointer to the required implementation.

Implementing The Adapter Design Pattern

Sometimes, you have a class that does the right thing but that has the wrong interface for your purposes. The Adapter design pattern provides an existing class with a new interface. It sits between you and another class and translates the messages that you want to send into the messages that the other class wants to receive. Adapters are implemented by using the underlying operations of the existing implementation. Adapters may use class derivation to provide new functionality, by adding new member functions, or may hide the original member functions. A specific adapter is shown in Figure 5.6.

STL provides template-based adaptors to create new interfaces for containers or iterators. Container adaptors and a special adaptor, *function pointer adapter*, are presented in Chapter 2. Note that the STL adaptors are based on the object composition. For example, a **queue**-based **stack** container has an instance of type **queue**. An Adapter design pattern can be implemented by using class derivation, as shown in Listing 5.6.

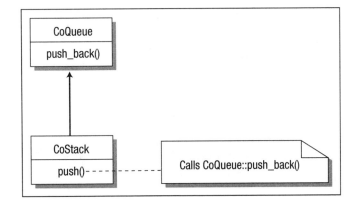

Figure 5.6
An adapter example.

Listing 5.6   An example of the Adapter design pattern.

```
template <class T>
class CoQueue
{
public:
    void push_back(const T& t);
    void pop_back();
};

template <class T>
class CoStack : protected CoQueue<T>
{
public:
    void push(const T& t)
    {
        CoQueue<T>::push_back(t);
    }
    void pop()
    {
        CoQueue<T>::pop_back();
    }
};

int main()
{
    CoStack<int> s;
    return 0;
}
```

The **CoStack** class is the adapter for the **CoQueue** class. The **CoStack** class is derived from the **CoQueue** class so that the **CoStack** class can use the functionality of the **CoQueue** class. However, an instance of the **CoStack** class can't directly invoke the member functions of the **CoQueue** class, because the derivation is a **protected** one.

The **CoStack** class provides a different interface to the **CoQueue** class by using the member functions of the **CoQueue** class. For example, the **push()** member function of the **CoStack** class uses the **push_back()** function of the **CoQueue** class.

Idioms

Idioms are the lowest-level of patterns. They are used to describe both how to implement particular classes, and the relationships of those classes to other classes in a given design. Idioms are always closely connected to a programming language. Idioms are the final link between the design phase and the implementation.

An example of a C++-specific idiom is the *reference counting idiom*, which describes how to implement reference counting in C++ to handle deallocation of multiple referenced objects. The following two idioms are presented in the sections to follow:

♦ Singleton

♦ Reference counting

Singleton

The Singleton idiom applies to the many situations in which a single instance of a class is needed in a running program (process). An important consideration in implementing this idiom is how to make this single instance easily accessible by many other objects. A singleton class will have direct control over how many instances of the class can be created, which means that when you use such a class, you don't have to worry about ensuring that only one instance of the class exists. Listing 5.7 shows how a generic Singleton idiom can be implemented.

Listing 5.7   An example of the Singleton idiom.

```
class CoSingleton
{
private:
    static CoSingleton* singleton_;

public:
    // gives back a real object!
    static CoSingleton* getInstance();
```

```
protected:
    CoSingleton(){} // constructor
};

CoSingleton* CoSingleton::singleton_ = 0;

CoSingleton* CoSingleton::getInstance()
{
    if (singleton_ == 0)
    {
        singleton_ = new CoSingleton;
    }
    return singleton_;
}
int main()
{
    CoSingleton* ps1=CoSingleton::getInstance();
    CoSingleton* ps2=CoSingleton::getInstance();
    CoSingleton* ps3=CoSingleton::getInstance();

    return 0;
}
```

The class **CoSingleton** is referred to as a singleton class. It provides a
static member function **getInstance()** that creates a new instance of
the **CoSingleton** class when called the first time. Further calls of the
getInstance() function return the same instance. The instance (**single-
ton_**) is also **static**. This mechanism makes sure that, at most, one
instance of the **CoSingleton** class exists in a process.

Reference Counting

The Reference Counting idiom makes memory management of dynamically allocated shared objects easier. It keeps a count of the number of
clients that are currently accessing the object, and doesn't allow the
object's deletion if a client still needs to access the object. Listing 5.8 is
an implementation of this idiom.

**Listing 5.8   An implementation of the Reference Counting
                idiom.**

```
#include <iostream.h>
class CoRefCount
{
private:
```

```
          unsigned long ref_; // The reference count

          // Hide copy-constructor and asignment operator
          CoRefCount(const CoRefCount&);
          void operator=(const CoRefCount&);

      public:

          CoRefCount() : ref_(1) { }
          virtual ~CoRefCount()
          {}

          // Increment reference count
          void incRef()
          {
              ++ref_;
          }

          // Decrement reference count
          void decRef()
          {
              -ref_;
          }

          // Get and set reference count
          unsigned long getRef() const
          {
              return ref_;
          }
          void setRef(unsigned long ref)
          {
              ref_ = ref;
          }
      };

      class CoWindow : public  CoRefCount
      {
      private:
          CoWindow(const CoWindow&);
          CoWindow& operator=(const CoWindow&);
          ~CoWindow(){}

      public:
          CoWindow(){}
          static inline CoWindow* duplicate(CoWindow* p)
```

```
    {
        if(p) p -> incRef(); return p;
    }

    static inline void release(CoWindow* p)
    {
        if(p)
        {
            p -> decRef();
            if (p->getRef()==0)
            {
                delete p;
                p=0;
            }
        }
    }
};

int main()
{
    CoWindow* pw=new CoWindow; //ref count=1
    cout<<pw->getRef()<<endl;

    //ref count=2
    CoWindow* pw1=CoWindow::duplicate(pw);

    //ref count=3
    CoWindow* pw2=CoWindow::duplicate(pw);
    cout<<pw->getRef()<<endl;
    //delete pw; //error: hence commented
    //CoWindow w; //error: hence commented

    CoWindow::release(pw);
    //ref count=2
    cout<<pw->getRef()<<endl;

    CoWindow::release(pw);
    //ref count=1
    cout<<pw->getRef()<<endl;

    //sets ref count=0, instance is deleted
    CoWindow::release(pw);

    cout<<pw->getRef()<<endl;
    return 0;
}
```

The **CoWindow** class provides **static** member functions, **duplicate()** and **release()**, to create and delete shared instances of the **CoWindow** type. Every call of **duplicate()** function increases the reference count of the **CoWindow** object. Every call of the **release()** function decreases the reference count of the **CoWindow** object. When the reference count goes to zero, the instance is deleted. The reference count mechanism is provided by the **CoRefCount** class that acts like a base class of the **CoWindow** class. Note that the **CoWindow** class has **private** destructor and copy operations, to make sure that the user of the **CoWindow** object can't delete the **CoWindow** object directly. Similarly, you can't directly create another instance of the **CoWindow** by using the copy constructor.

Reference counting is a popular mechanism in distributed computing, to enable multiple clients to access a shared component safely. This is explained in Chapters 9 and 13.

C++ Coding Patterns

When you use a language, you might find a few language styles or conventions that keep recurring across program files and projects. These language styles/conventions may be either idioms, or programming guidelines to make the programs consistent-looking and robust. The preceding sections explained idioms. Note that this book differentiates between idioms and programming styles/guidelines. Programming styles/guidelines are collectively referred to as *coding patterns* that you need to apply in any program that you write using that language. Other than a standard set of programming styles and guidelines, domain-related programming guidelines might help you to make the program robust and standard.

Table 5.3 provides examples of a few C++ coding patterns taken from a real project.

Table 5.3 C++ coding patterns taken from a real project.

Category	Programming Styles/Guidelines
General Coding	Check the brace-layout of the program.
	Check the class layout.
	All header files should have **#ifndef..#endif** wrapper.
	In a program, *magic numbers* should not be used.
	Variable declaration should be close to its use.

(continued)

Table 5.3   C++ coding patterns taken from a real project *(continued).*

Category	Programming Styles/Guidelines
	References should be used for passing large classes.
	A **const** reference should be used wherever possible.
	All loops (**for**, **while**, and so forth) must be terminable.
	All **switch** statements must have a **default** case appearing last.
	Check whether coding is optimized.
Pointers-Related	If you are using *no-throw form* of **new**, check the result of **new**.
	If you are using *throw form* of **new**, catch the exception **bad_alloc**.
	Before using the dereference operator (*****) on a pointer, check the pointer for zero (**0**).
	Before using the access operator (**->**) on a class or struct pointer, check the pointer for zero (**0**).
	When no longer needed, delete a dynamically allocated pointer, to avoid memory leak.
	While deallocating a dynamically allocated pointer, check for **delete[]** versus **delete**.
Class-Related	A polymorphic class must have its **virtual** destructor.
	A class must have a destructor, default constructor, copy constructor, and assignment operator.
	If objects of a class aren't supposed to have copy semantics, the class must declare a **private** copy constructor and a **private** assignment operator, and not define them.
	All member pointers of a class must be initialized to zero.
	Self copy/assignment should be checked in copy constructor and assignment operator.
	Class data members should not be **public**.
	Check whether a class derivation needs to be **virtual**.
	Check whether a class member function needs to be **virtual**.
	All class access functions should be **const**.
Exceptions-Related	Exception specification should be specified for all functions.

(continued)

NOTE

*Scope Of Coding
Patterns*

The obvious two goals of
the coding pattern
examples presented here
are to standardize source
code (naming conven-
tions, layouts, and so
forth) across programs,
and to avoid common
errors, thus making the
program more robust.
These coding patterns
may depend on a
particular project or the
experience of the person
who has decided to apply
these patterns. These
patterns don't help you
to design or use a class
library or framework. To
use a framework, you
have to use a cookbook
that contains *frameworks
adaption patterns*. This
concept is explained in
Chapter 14.

Table 5.3   C++ coding patterns taken from a real project *(continued)*.

Category	Programming Styles/Guidelines
	Check for an exception specification mismatch between the calling function and the called functions.
	Check for an exception in a loop, which will terminate the loop. If you need to continue the loop even in case of an exception, catch the exception within the loop and handle the same.
STL-Related	To insert a value in a map, use the subscript operator ([]), if you don't care whether the item is already present. If you do care, use the **map::insert()** function and check the result.
	In the STL container instances, if you need to store strings, use the standard C++ class **string** rather than **char*** or **const char***.
Domain-Related	All the date processing must be Y2K-compliant.
	Check the thread safety of the program.

The set of coding patterns presented here is just an indication of what a set of coding patterns might consist. An organization might evolve certain coding patterns to use across the projects. Apart from design patterns and idioms, coding patterns may also be a great asset for an organization.

Design Patterns Vs. Frameworks

As mentioned earlier in the chapter, the framework concept is closely related to the design pattern concept. A framework is the reusable de-sign of a system, expressed as a set of collaborating classes. Both frameworks and design patterns endeavor to reuse designs. However, frameworks are conceptually larger than design patterns, because frame-works usually contain many design patterns. Table 5.4 compares some aspects of frameworks and design patterns.

Table 5.4   Comparison between frameworks and design patterns.

Frameworks	Design Patterns
High-level design constructs	Low-level design constructs
Constitute code	Don't constitute code
Less abstract (more specialized)	More abstract (less specialized)
Cookbooks describe how the framework works and can be used	Templates describe intent, conse-quences, and so forth, of a design

Chapter Recap

Software reuse is the process of creating software systems from pre-defined software components. Using C++, you can define reusable classes. Apart from defining reusable classes, the bigger benefits of OOP-based reuse come from design patterns and frameworks; they provide better forms and higher levels of reuse. This chapter focuses on design patterns. A design pattern should have three features: usability, generality, and adaptability. Design patterns provide object-oriented solutions for recurring design problems. You can identify and partition an overall program system into separate design patterns.

Together, design patterns and frameworks help to improve key software-quality factors—reuse, extensibility, modularity, and so forth.

This chapter didn't focus on design pattern catalogs; the design pattern selection criteria or selection process; or descriptions of contexts, problems, or solutions. The chapter focused on providing information about patterns and idioms that you can apply in framework designs and C++ implementations.

Chapter 6
Concepts Of Frameworks

Improving developer productivity is one of the major benefits that object-oriented programming (OOP) provides. You can take advantage of OOP to improve productivity and to develop the leverage necessary to address the requirements of today's complex solutions. However, switching to OOP alone isn't enough. You must also exploit OOP's capabilities to increase productivity and to enhance program maintainability. Your success with OOP depends on whether you take advantage of its capabilities, such as *software reuse*, the process of creating software systems from predefined software components. Software reuse is a realistic approach to bringing about the gains in productivity and quality that the software industry needs. The success of software reuse depends on the development infrastructure. Frameworks provide an infrastructure that enables you to design and deliver systems that are more reusable and maintainable.

A *framework* is a set of prefabricated, software building blocks that you can use as a development foundation for new applications. If you use a framework as a development foundation, you don't have to start from scratch each time you design and develop an application. Frameworks make software development more productive and more innovative. For example, if you want to model a *car*, you have an advantage if you start with a car's fundamental building blocks—such as wheels, gear box, speedometer, and accelerator—with their proper interactions already established, such as pressing on the accelerator causes operations on wheels and speedometer. This cooperative and organized behavior is the result of a set of building blocks interacting under some predefined rules and conditions: a framework. Because frameworks consist of a set of classes that collaborate and express a well-defined behavior, they provide the necessary foundation for fully exploiting the promises of OOP.

By providing a framework, you present an ideal platform for creating and deploying innovative solutions. In traditional OOP, you create and deploy solutions by class libraries that consist of reusable classes. However, because class libraries don't specify default behaviors or class interactions, using a class library requires that you understand the interfaces and can determine which interfaces should be invoked and in what order. This means that you end up redeveloping most code from scratch for each new project.

Conversely, if you use a framework in a project, you get the default behavior of the framework, without writing any new code. Furthermore, because the framework is prewired to call the right functions at the right time and in the right order, you don't have to know how or when to call each function. You simply need to know where the *hooks* are (described later in the "C++ Metapatterns In Frameworks" section), so that you can specify and extend the framework's behavior and develop the hooks.

Frameworks empower you to leverage OOP's capabilities, and they provide more computing value than class libraries provide. For example, frameworks for financial domains jump-start business-application development for the banking sector. Frameworks for system-software functions, such as networking, multimedia, and database access, can also be developed.

The OOP community has adopted frameworks because of their potential to increase developer productivity significantly and encourage innovation. The future of OOP looks promising because of frameworks, which have the potential to dramatically improve the software development process. This potential is why many companies (such as Hewlett-Packard, IBM, Microsoft, and so forth) are building new application construction environments (ACEs) based on OOP and object-oriented frameworks.

With increased emphasis on distributed systems, the object metaphor appears to be the most natural one to adopt, given its emphasis on encapsulation, message passing, reuse, and extensibility. Distribut-ed computing and object-oriented frameworks can be the key players in developing solutions for various industry segments. Development that is based on frameworks and CORBA is the logical extension of OOP. CORBA, with its services and interfaces, already plays a role of a framework, which is why CORBA is one of the significant themes of this book. In this book's chapters, the following frameworks topics are discussed:

♦ Framework concepts in this chapter

♦ Framework development in Chapter 7

♦ CORBA-based frameworks in Chapter 13

♦ Documenting and using frameworks in Chapter 14

This chapter focuses on concepts related to object-oriented frameworks. Thus, it describes object-oriented frameworks and how they differ from class libraries and design patterns. This chapter also provides an abstract example that conveys the framework concept, so that you can understand the many aspects of the framework presented later in the chapter.

Levels Of Reuse

Reuse is one of the main goals of software engineering. Because OOP enables software reuse, OOP has gained rapid acceptance among software developers and has become the preferred method for designing and implementing software systems.

Reusable assets in OOP can be found in the continuous spectrum of reuse that starts from classes and proceeds to design patterns and object-oriented frameworks (this concept is shown in Figure 6.1).

As Chapter 5 mentions, the following are three levels of reuse:

♦ *Class reuse (low-level reuse)*—Reuse of a class, such as using a class derived from an abstract class. An abstract class is a small-scale design that may be reused when designing small-scale components. (Chapter 3 presents this concept.)

♦ *Design-pattern reuse (medium-level reuse)*—Reuse of classes and their interactions. Design patterns show design knowledge in terms of the behavior of object collaborations. This *isn't* code-level reuse. (Chapter 5 presents the concept of design-pattern reuse.)

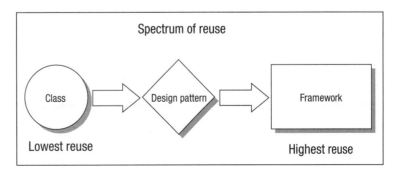

Figure 6.1
The spectrum of reuse.

♦ *Framework reuse (high-level reuse)*—An important enabling technology for reuse of design and code. A framework provides a set of classes that manifest as an abstract design for solutions to a family of related problems. Switching to framework-based development gives you the highest level of reuse in application development.

Reusing Designs And Code

Because designing software is complex, you must reuse existing designs by applying them in a systematic manner. Reuse of designs, which is the most important kind of reuse, enables you to reuse both design patterns and frameworks. As Chapter 5 explains, design patterns facilitate the reuse of successful software designs. *Design patterns* represent solutions to specific problems that arise when developing software within a particular context. Patterns capture the static and dynamic structure and collaboration among key participants in software designs.

Frameworks provide a way to reuse design and code. Because frameworks provide for reuse at the highest level, designing a framework is more difficult than designing an abstract class. Frameworks can also interact with other frameworks by sharing interfaces. Designing a framework requires a lot of experience and experimentation.

Before presenting a formal discussion of the various aspects of frameworks, the next section provides a framework example. This example proves the following points:

♦ A framework dictates the architecture of a system; a framework defines the overall structure, partitioning into objects, the key responsibilities thereof, how the objects collaborate, and the thread of control.

♦ Object-oriented features, such as object interfaces and inheritance, are key to designing object-oriented frameworks.

The example conveys the basic concept of a framework, so that you can easily understand other aspects of frameworks as they are presented in later parts of the chapter.

Example: A Business Component Framework

A *business component (BC)* is an entity that communicates with other BCs in a system to carry out a business logic or process. BCs in a design never occur in isolation. The ability of BCs to interact with each other at the semantic level is the key to a business process. The following information about BCs in a system typically is captured during design:

♦ *Static component model*—Describes the static information of the component. This model's key concepts are BCs, attributes, hierarchies, and associations between BCs.

♦ *Dynamic component model*—Adds operations to the components and describes how a BC interacts with other BCs at runtime.

Middleware (such as CORBA) provides the infrastructure for interaction among BCs. (CORBA concepts and component-development examples are presented in Chapters 8 and 9.) When you use CORBA as an application designer, you never have to worry about interoperation between components. Instead, you typically focus on relationships and collaboration among components.

This section presents a BC framework example that provides the design and development of both a static component model and a dynamic component model. The example is presented to demonstrate *horizontal framework* concepts. Horizontal frameworks (described in depth in the "Characterization Of Frameworks" section) encapsulate expertise applicable to a wide variety of programs.

Scope Of The Framework

The BC framework builds upon the following requirements and conditions:

♦ An application consists of many BCs.

♦ The BC framework should enable you to define BCs to develop applications.

♦ The BC framework controls the lifecycle of a BC. That is to say, the BC framework instantiates and deletes a BC whenever needed.

♦ The BCs of an application must be able to communicate, with the help of requests and Application Programming Interfaces (APIs) rather than via direct invocation of the member functions. The BC framework must be able to locate the target BC automatically and invoke the required member functions.

♦ A BC replies via reply messages.

♦ A request and reply carry the data between BCs.

NOTE

The Broker Architectural Pattern

Frank Buschmann and his coauthors for *Pattern-Oriented Software Architecture: A System of Patterns*, which was published by John Wiley & Sons in 1996, use the Broker architectural pattern to describe distributed software systems with decoupled components that interact by remote service invocations. CORBA is based on this pattern.

Architectural View Of The BC Framework: Application Developer's Perspective

An *architectural pattern* expresses a fundamental paradigm for structuring software. The internal structure of the BC framework can be described by the *Broker* architectural pattern, because the BC framework enables you to write decoupled BCs that interact by messages. (See "The Broker Architectural Pattern.")

Identifying the high-level structure of a framework makes describing the behavior of the framework easier and provides a starting point for designing framework interactions. Figure 6.2 presents an architectural view of the BC framework.

The BC framework has a client-server model in which the server components (BCs) register themselves with a *component manager* and make their services available to clients. Clients access the server components' services by sending requests to the components. The component manager locates and instantiates the target BC and forwards the request to that BC.

The following four participating components comprise the architecture of the BC framework:

♦ **CoComponent**—Your BC must be derived to implement the required behavior of a business entity. This class is responsible for carrying out the business processing that starts with the arrival of a message. Thus, **CoComponent** is the heart of the BC framework.

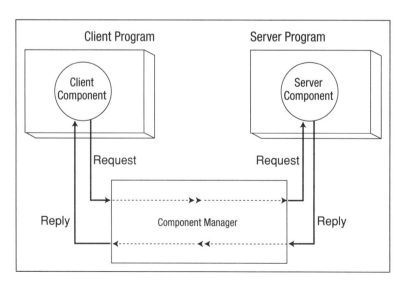

Figure 6.2
Architectural view of the BC framework.

- **CoComponentManager**—Your BC must be registered with this class, which is responsible for routing messages to a target BC.

- **CoRequest**—Dispatches requests to a target BC. A **CoRequest** can cause an alteration of the data members of the receiving BC.

- **CoReply**—Returns reply from a BC.

From the application developer's perspective, the architectural specifications for the BC framework consist of the following:

- *Static component model*—Defines BCs and responsibilities; supported by the **CoComponent** class.

- *Dynamic component model*—Identifies and describes the key patterns of interactions between BCs; supported by **CoRequest** and **CoReply** classes.

The static and dynamic component models provide an important basis for specifying components and their interactions, but these models are inherently abstract. The primary objective of the BC framework is to partition an application into a set of interconnectable, collaborative BCs. Each BC implements important aspects of the application. Access to a particular BC's application capabilities is mediated by the **CoRequest**s that it supports. **CoRequest**s are what you see when assembling BCs to construct fully functional applications. (The internal structures of the BC framework classes are not described here. Chapter 7 presents an implementation of this framework. Chapter 14 discusses how this framework can be used to develop applications.)

Why To Develop The BC Framework

The BC framework provides rich, built-in functionality, which is why it needs to be a framework. The BC framework provides a solution that requires several steps. For example, you don't have to manage the instances of a BC, because the BC framework takes care of it. The following lists the advantages that the BC framework provides:

- Construction of messages (**CoRequest** and **CoReply**) is standardized, so they can be logged generically for the purpose of *auditing*, the process of maintaining audit trails of a system to record events happening in the system. **CoRequest** and **CoReply** can carry some standard information, such as the accessor's credentials (authentication), and some business or environmental status.

- Invocation of a business operation is standardized, and this standardization is used to define security (authorization) and logging policies, to catch and record possible breaches. *Authorization* is the process of checking whether an authenticated user has access rights to a particular resource.

♦ The BC framework imposes a particular type of coding, providing for code standardization.

♦ Coding can be easily derived (and generated) from design documents, to bootstrap the application-implementation process.

The BC framework has the following general features:

♦ *Usable*—Provides expected functionality.

♦ *Broad scope of applicability*—Can be used to develop many types of applications.

♦ *Easy to adapt*—Can be easily used to develop BC-based applications.

♦ *Easy to extend to add new features*—For example, the BC framework can take advantage of the multithreaded system to process requests concurrently on a BC.

♦ *Can be made robust*—By adding a generic exception-handling policy.

Type Of The BC Framework

The BC framework addresses general functions, not any domain-specific functions. The BC framework encapsulates expertise that is applicable to a variety of programs. The BC framework encompasses a horizontal slice of functionality that can be applied to different domains. Hence, the BC framework is referred to as a *horizontal framework*.

Using The BC Framework

The following three points are important about the BC framework:

♦ A **CoComponent** implementation represents an entity of the underlying application. This includes the application data as well as business operations that the entity performs.

♦ A client of a **CoComponent** changes the **CoComponent**'s state and/or obtains application data by sending a request to the instance of the **CoComponent**. The **CoComponent** must implement the behavior of reacting to the request, which it does by registering various requests with **CoComponent**.

♦ Various **CoComponent**s are registered within a component manager instance, represented by **CoComponentManager**.

One important characteristic of a framework is that the functions that you define to tailor the framework often are called from within the framework itself, rather than from your application code.

You can adapt the BC framework in one way—you can derive new classes from the framework classes and register them with the framework in the following ways:

♦ Derive from **CoComponent** to implement the required behavior of a business entity.

♦ Derive from **CoComponentManager** and register BCs with this class.

♦ Derive from **CoRequest** to establish a relationship with member functions of the derived **CoComponent** class.

♦ Derive from **CoReply** to return a specific reply from a **CoComponent**.

The BC framework is referred to as a *white-box framework*, because its usage is based on class derivation. Chapter 7 presents the BC framework in detail. Thus, some of the BC framework details that may not be very clear from this discussion will be clarified in Chapter 7.

What Is An Object-Oriented Framework?

An *object-oriented framework* is a reusable software architecture that comprises both design and code. A framework provides a set of classes that is used as a foundation for solutions to a set of problems. The concept of frameworks is expected to raise the productivity of software engineers. You have seen that a framework tries to capture the general flow of control in an application. Frameworks typically are designed by experienced designers/developers of a particular domain and then are used by nonexperts. In this manner, a framework enables reuse of an abstract design of an entire application. Thus, a framework supports reuse at a higher level than classes support. Generic frameworks can also be developed that you can use across domains. (See "How Generic Are The Horizontal Frameworks?" later in this chapter.)

Framework Engineering

The presence of a framework influences the development process for an application because the framework represents an abstract design and implementation for the application. The following are the three significant phases in framework-centered software development:

♦ *Framework development phase*—Results in a reusable design and the implementation of a framework. (Framework development is presented in Chapter 7.)

♦ *Framework usage phase*—Results in the development of an application, using the framework as a foundation. (Also referred to as the *framework instantiation phase*.) In this phase, you adapt the framework to develop applications. (Framework usage is discussed in Chapter 14.)

♦ *Framework evolution and maintenance phase*—Fixes errors reported by framework users and adds new features to the framework. (Framework evolution and maintenance is discussed in Chapter 15.)

The framework is used as the foundation for the development of multiple applications.

Advantages Of Frameworks

Because a framework is a set of cooperating classes, by developing applications based on the framework, you completely realize the potential of design and code reuse, including reduced development requirements and maintenance, and increased robustness and efficiency.

Frameworks Improve Programming

Framework-based programming offers the following advantages:

♦ *Focuses on application requirements*—You can focus on rapidly developing and deploying the business functionality while remaining transparent to the underlying technical and application infrastructure. In other words, by using a framework, you can concentrate on developing application-specific programs and rely on the framework to solve technical and application problems. Because frameworks provide rich, built-in functionality, they provide more computing value than any other development foundation.

♦ *Captures domain knowledge*—Good software design in a particular area requires domain knowledge (such as manufacturing, accounting, or insurance). Frameworks enable domain experts to encapsulate

An Introduction To SanFrancisco

SanFrancisco is a multilayer, flexible framework-based system that is used for the development of platform-independent, distributed, and object-oriented software solutions. You can use SanFrancisco to assemble server-side business applications from existing parts, rather than build from scratch. It provides many advantages including:

♦ Provides a complete technology wrapper for a platform-independent, distributed business system.

♦ Enables you to build and modify business applications quickly.

♦ Produces robust solutions built on top of high-level reusable business frameworks that are Internet-enabled, scalable, and deployable on multiple client/server platforms.

SanFrancisco is structured using a layered architecture that shields you from the technical implementation of the system. Issues such as distributed computing, platform independence, interaction among distributed objects, and transaction integrity are transparent to you.

The complete SanFrancisco system is composed of three integrated layers:

♦ *Foundation*—Distributed computing infrastructure for SanFrancisco's middleware.

♦ *Core Business Processes (CBPs)*—Contain behavior and business objects that are particular to a business domain.

♦ *Common Business Objects (CBOs)*—Contain behavior and business objects needed for financial and general business domains.

You can get more information about SanFrancisco at **www.software.ibm.com/ad/sanfrancisco/ concepts/concepts.html**.

---

the knowledge in terms of classes that collaborate to carry out a set of responsibilities for the application or subsystem domain.

♦ *Improves consistency and compatibility*—Because frameworks encapsulate design and code expertise, a design and coding standard is automatically imposed on the developers, which means that the resulting system is well written from a developer's point of view.

♦ *Minimizes programming*—Because a framework expresses the common abstractions for the applications, the amount of code needed to implement similar applications is minimized. The framework's components are already prewired, and much of the needed functionality already exists in the framework, thereby reducing coding, testing, and debugging efforts.

♦ *Provides robust and efficient code*—Because many aspects of the software's robustness and runtime efficiency are addressed by the framework itself, you don't have to worry about them again within the application code that you develop on top of the framework. Of course, you need to address these aspects in the context of your application code.

Frameworks Enable Reuse

Because a framework represents the reusable design of a family of applications, represented as a collective set of collaborative abstract and concrete classes, the framework enables code and design reuse at a higher level than what is provided by class libraries and design-patterns. You can use a framework as a starting point to develop an application.

Frameworks Improve Software Engineering

Frameworks serve as proven solutions for a family of problems. They help software development in the context of software engineering aspects, such as quality and maintenance. The following lists the software engineering advantages that frameworks provide:

♦ *Increase software productivity*—Frameworks provide a foundation on which new applications are built. Reuse of prefabricated and prewired components enhances productivity and, usually, improves reliability and lowers risks. You can gain increased productivity through the design and code reuse provided by frameworks.

♦ *Lower development costs and time*—Frameworks reduce and hide complexity. Framework-imposed standardization helps developers to understand the application code better, thereby lowering training costs. It also shortens software development time, because a lot of component wiring is already done, so you simply reuse it.

♦ *Produce better-quality software*—Reusing pretested and quality-certified components and their collaborations improves the design quality and comprehensibility. A framework's code is already written, tested, and debugged.

♦ *Reduce maintenance*—Whenever you correct an error in the framework or add a new feature, the application automatically benefits

---

Frameworks Aren't An Object-Oriented Methodology

Frameworks are designed and accepted as an application development foundation. An object-oriented method or process consists of a series of steps on how to perform object-oriented analysis and design, whereas a framework expresses a common behavior of an underlying object-oriented application. To build an object-oriented framework or an object-oriented application using a framework, you still need a methodology. However, a particular framework usually imposes or suggests a particular methodology to develop applications. In other words, by using a framework, you are usually locked into a single methodology. Your application must conform to the framework's methodology and rules, because the framework controls the flow of the application.

due to inheritance and encapsulation. In addition, applications developed with frameworks tend to be smaller, and therefore, more easily maintained.

♦ *Integrate with application construction environment (ACE)*—An ACE for a framework can be provided that includes a variety of development tools to enable you to execute rapid application development and customization.

Design Patterns Vs. Frameworks

Frameworks promise reuse of design and code. Design patterns constitute another approach to design reuse in the object community. Design patterns help you to understand and develop the framework. A framework designer's first step to designing a framework in an object-oriented manner may be to identify a partitioning of the overall system into separate design patterns. This is why a design pattern can be considered the *unit of reuse* in a framework. (In the design pattern itself, the *class* is the unit of reuse). Levels of reuse are shown in Figure 6.3 in the realm of code reuse vis-à-vis design reuse.

Potential Weaknesses Of A Framework

Although frameworks offer great advantages, you also need to consider a few of their potential weaknesses:

♦ *Backward-compatibility*—Like other software, frameworks evolve and become mature over time. However, because applications are built on the frameworks, frameworks must ensure backward-compatibility, which can be difficult to maintain. You need experience in generic programming or in the application domain to build and maintain a good framework.

♦ *High initial learning curve*—To use a framework, you must understand the abstract design of the framework and the internal structure of its classes, so that you can adapt and extend the framework. The prewired flow of control among framework components may be nonintuitive to you. Additionally, if a framework isn't supported by the necessary "cookbooks," it likely won't be used. (Chapter 14 provides a further discussion of framework documentation.)

♦ *Generality and adaptability*—The generality and adaptability forces of a framework may not work together because very generic classes of a framework may be difficult to use. Also, generality may affect a framework's efficiency in a particular application.

♦ *Difficult debugging*—Frameworks make application debugging hard, because distinguishing bugs in the framework from bugs in the application code is difficult. A framework's bug may appear to be an application's runtime failure. Furthermore, framework bugs can't be fixed by the framework user, and verification and validation of generic components is complicated because these can be used and adapted in diversified contexts.

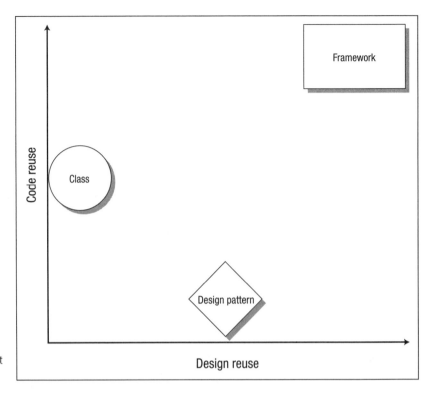

Figure 6.3
Levels of reuse with respect
to code and design.

Figure 6.3 shows that a class represents the lowest level of design reuse, whereas a design pattern represents the lowest level of code reuse. On the other hand, a framework represents the highest level of both the forms of reuse.

Design patterns and frameworks obviously are overlapping concepts, and together, design patterns and frameworks help improve key software-quality factors, such as reuse, extensibility, modularity, and so forth. However, design patterns and frameworks aren't the same thing. They differ in two ways:

♦ *Frameworks are less abstract than design patterns*—A framework is a high-level design of an integrated set of collaborating components that you express in reusable code. Conversely, design patterns are simply design constructs that contain only example code. Unlike a design pattern, a framework need not describe the intent, tradeoffs, and consequences of its usage.

♦ *Frameworks are more specialized than design patterns*—A framework can be developed that addresses a specific application domain, whereas a design pattern must be general enough to be applied in any application domain.

Class Libraries Vs. Frameworks

The integration of data and operations into objects and classes provides for reuse. The classes are packaged together into *class libraries*, sets of related classes that provide general-purpose functionality. Class libraries often consist of classes for different data structures and provide class derivations to customize existing library classes. Although class libraries provide more software reuse than procedural libraries, they don't deliver enough software reuse. You still have to develop a lot of application code yourself. The following is a list of the limitations to reusing classes and objects from class libraries:

◆ *Repetition of effort*—Because class libraries don't dictate how to reuse classes, they can be used in different ways, resulting in different solutions to the same family of problems, thereby causing code maintenance problems.

◆ *Complexity*—A system's class library may contain large and complex class hierarchies; thus, figuring out the designer's intention regarding the hierarchy can be hard.

◆ *Flow of control*—Because class libraries don't provide built-in interactions among all the objects created from the library, you are responsible for deciding the required flow of control—the order in which objects and operations have to be performed. This means that you may inadvertently introduce bugs into your application.

The preceding list of limitations can be resolved by using frameworks, because a framework outlines the main architecture for the application to be built. The following lists the main differences between a framework and a class library:

◆ *Default behavior*—Frameworks provide a way to embody application expertise, because the framework developer can provide default behavior in the framework. Therefore, you as a user of the framework don't have to know how or when to call each function—the framework is prewired to call the right functions at the right time. Thus, a framework invokes elements of your code automatically. To specify and extend a framework's behavior, you need to know only where the hooks are located. Conversely, when you use a library, you invoke the elements of the library, which typically means that you first have to determine which functions are available to call and then try to figure out which functions need to be called and in which order. This makes using and customizing the library a repetitive activity.

♦ *Adaptability*—If you use a framework, you have to understand both the abstract design of the framework and the internal structure of its classes, in order to adapt and extend them. Conversely, if you use a class library, you need to define the overall structure of its applications.

♦ *Degree of reuse*—The application's main architecture is captured by the framework. This means that the framework has a major impact on the architecture of the framework-based application. A class in a framework collaborates with other classes in the framework to solve a problem. Conversely, in a class library, a class doesn't define the application's architecture, because the classes of a class library are reused individually.

Table 6.1 summarizes the differences between a framework and a class library.

Characterization Of Frameworks

Frameworks can be characterized by the problem domains that they address, by their architectures, and by how they are used to develop applications.

Types Of Frameworks

A framework can address domain-specific functions, generic functions that are applicable to several domains, or either type of functions:

♦ *Horizontal frameworks*—Encapsulate expertise applicable to a variety of applications and domains. These frameworks provide a horizontal slice of functionality that can be applied to different domains. Borland's OWL system is one example of a framework that is horizontally oriented. Similarly, IBM's Component Broker is a horizontal framework, because it provides functionality to write distributed applications for a variety of domains. You can use such frameworks directly or modify them.

Table 6.1 Library versus framework.

Library	Framework
Set of classes instantiated by you	Provides classes for customization by subclassing
You call library functions	Calls your functions
No default behavior	Default behavior
No predefined flow of control	Predefined flow of control
No predefined object collaboration	Predefined object collaboration

How Generic Are The Horizontal Frameworks?

Horizontal frameworks are not related to a specific application domain. This means that they are generic enough to be used across domains (industry segments). However, this does not mean that horizontal frameworks are not focused on a particular type of functionality. Examples of such frameworks are GUI frameworks, distributed computing frameworks, and so forth. These frameworks don't target any particular application domain (such as a bank, tele-communications company, and so forth). However, they have a specific nature, and they can be used to build applications of that nature only. For ex-ample, you can use a GUI framework to build GUI applications (for any application domain).

The existence of horizontal frameworks means that a framework doesn't always have to be related to a specific application domain. In this respect, a horizontal framework and a design pattern are similar, because both are general and can be applied in any application domain. This is the area in which opinions may differ regarding what a design pattern is and what a basic horizontal framework is. However, the distinction is clear: A framework is always represented as code, whereas a design pattern is presented as a standard template. An implementation of a design pattern can become someone's horizontal framework.

♦ *Vertical frameworks*—Capture knowledge and expertise in a particular application domain. These frameworks encompass a vertical slice of functionality for a particular client domain, such as finance, health care, manufacturing, telecommunications, electronic commerce, or transportation. By providing a vertical framework, you provide a platform that enables creation and deployment of domain-specific solutions. IBM's *SanFrancisco* is an example of a vertical framework. It provides basic business entities, such as Customer, Address, Currency, and so forth.

♦ *Metaframeworks*—Base frameworks that are used to develop new frameworks. A metaframework can be either a vertical framework or a horizontal framework. CORBA is a good example of a horizontal metaframework. You can use CORBA to develop either specialized vertical frameworks or new horizontal frameworks. For example, the BC framework, presented earlier in this chapter, can be developed by using CORBA. (This use is shown in Chapter 13.)

Architecture Of Frameworks

An architectural pattern expresses a fundamental paradigm for structuring software. It provides a set of predefined subsystems, as well as rules and guidelines for organizing their interrelationships. The architectural pattern determines the basic structure of an application and can be thought of as a template for concrete software architectures.

If the framework's architecture is described, you may be able to comprehend its behavior more easily. You can characterize the internal structure of a framework by using architectural patterns. For example, a layered architectural pattern helps to structure frameworks that can be decomposed into groups of subtasks with different abstraction levels. The BC framework presented earlier is based on the Broker architecture pattern.

Types Of Frameworks: So Many Terms!

Some authors use the term *application framework* to mean *horizontal framework*. In this book, however, I don't use the term *application framework*, because it can be confused with *vertical framework*. Vertical frameworks are used to capture knowledge and expertise in a particular application domain—thus, the potential name confusion.

Another name for vertical framework is *domain framework*, which is a reasonable alternative. However, I prefer to use vertical framework, simply because it clearly contrasts with horizontal framework.

The two types of frameworks sometimes are referred to as *monolithic frameworks,* because each framework is used for one specific purpose.

Using A Framework

One important aspect of a framework is that it calls the functions that you define, rather than having its functions called from your application code. You do need to call a few functions to start the framework, but then the framework creates the necessary objects and calls the appropriate functions to perform a specific task (this concept is sometimes referred to as an *inversion of control* or *flip-flop of control*). In other words, a framework is like the main program that coordinates and orders the application's activities. This means that frameworks are much like extensible skeletons. Thus, for a particular application, you need to adapt the generic functions defined in the framework.

You can adapt a framework in either of two ways:

♦ Derive new classes from the framework

♦ Instantiate and compose existing classes

C++ provides object-oriented features to meet these requirements (discussed in Chapter 1). A recap of these features follows.

Framework-Enabling Object-Oriented Features

The interfaces between the components in a framework are defined in terms of the *object interface*, the set of messages that can be sent between components. An object interface conveys an object's runtime behavior or functionality. A collection of well-designed object interfaces is the key to expressing a framework's functionality. Object interfaces are often represented by *abstract classes*, which define an interface in terms of a few undefined member functions that must be implemented by the derived classes. Thus, abstract classes can be used much like program skeletons, whereby you fill in certain options, and the framework reuses the code in the skeleton. In addition to the object interface, the following concepts are important in designing and implementing a framework (these four features encourage software reuse in multiple ways):

♦ *Object inheritance*—A major strength of object orientation, because it enables programmers to assemble relevant object abstractions into a hierarchy, to express hierarchical relationships between abstractions (in other words, to express commonality between relevant abstractions). The abstraction at the top serves as a *super abstraction* for the abstraction below it, which is a specialization of its super abstraction. This implies that inheritance can be used as a method of reusing an implementation to create new abstractions. After a base abstraction is developed, it doesn't need to be reprogrammed or recompiled but can, nevertheless, be adapted to work in different situations. Other than reuse, object inheritance also helps to form the families of standard object interfaces that are so important for reuse. All the specialized objects of a particular object inherit that object's operations, so they all share its object interface. *Class derivation* is the C++ mechanism to create object inheritance. It is used to adapt an existing class to a new requirement and to implement polymorphism, discussed next. The combination of class derivation and polymorphism is a major feature for creating frameworks in C++.

♦ *Polymorphism*—Operations are performed on objects by sending them a message. Message sending causes polymorphism. A message finds the correct member function in the class of the receiver (the object to which the message is sent) and invokes that member function. With polymorphic calls, objects require less information about each other, so objects need to have only the right object interface.

♦ *Composition*—The process of combining many related abstractions into a single abstraction. Object composition is one of the most common techniques of reusing functionality in object-oriented systems. In fact, it is used as an alternative to inheritance. Whereas inheritance enables you to assemble relevant object abstractions into a hierarchy to express hierarchical relationships, composition enables you to fabricate object abstractions to form new abstractions. Thus, composition is used as a method of reusing an abstraction to create new abstractions. Using composition, complex objects can be created by interconnecting the compatible objects. The C++ class member objects mechanism supports composition in C++.

♦ *Genericity*—Generic types provide a technique for reusing function-ality of code through parameters. C++ supports generic programming via template features.

Using A Framework By Class Derivation

Class derivation is the process of creating new classes from existing ones. In class derivation, a derived class inherits operations and internal struc-tures from its base class. A derived class can either add to the operations that it inherits or redefine inherited operations. Class derivation is one of the basic reuse features in C++. One result of reusability is the ease of distributing class libraries and frameworks.

You adapt the framework by deriving new classes from the framework and overriding member functions. Frameworks that support the class derivation approach are also referred to as *white-box frameworks* (see "White-Box Vs. Black-Box Frameworks" later in this chapter), because their implementation must be understood to use them.

A problem with white-box frameworks is that every application re-quires you to create many new derived classes. Although most of these new derived classes are simple, you may end up creating many such classes, thereby making it difficult for a new programmer to learn and change the application's design. A second problem is that learning to use a white-box framework can be difficult, because you need to under-stand how it was constructed.

Using A Framework By Composition

Chapter 3 discusses the benefits of the reusability inherent in the C++ programming model. The key is to be able to focus on interfaces rather than implementation details. C++'s ability to standardize interfaces and encapsulate functionality within objects gives you a black-box view of the world, enabling you to put together an application from compo-nents without having to deal with their internals. The interface between components can be defined by an object interface, so you need to un-derstand only the external interface of the components. Thus, this kind of reuse is called *black-box reuse*. Object composition (acquaintance), together with dynamic binding, supports black-box reuse.

Some frameworks rely primarily on object composition for custom-ization. The framework defines how the objects can be combined. In other words, each of these objects must understand a particular proto-col. The interface between classes can be defined by the protocol, so you need to understand only the external interface of the classes. Thus, this kind of framework is referred to as a *black-box framework*.

Customization Of Frameworks By Templates

Generic types provide a technique for reusing functionality of code through parameters. C++ supports generic programming via templates (templates are discussed in detail in Chapter 2). *Templates* (also called *generic* or *parameterized types*) are used to construct a family of related functions or classes. C++ templates are roughly a form of reusability, because after a template function or class is developed, it doesn't need to be reprogrammed but can be adapted to meet various design or program requirements.

A framework may contain ready-to-use generic algorithms and classes in the form of templates that can easily be reused in various combinations without losing any performance. By using class templates, you can instantiate whatever type-safe types that you need. Templates can be used as a mechanism to customize a framework (as shown in Chapter 7). Templates don't impose any runtime overhead, because no derivation exists and virtual functions are involved.

C++ Metapatterns In Frameworks

Object-oriented features are often referred to when patterns and frameworks are discussed. C++ provides these features, so it is a very suitable language to implement frameworks. Using these features, C++ provides the ability to create *metapatterns*, which often are used to implement design patterns and frameworks. Metapatterns are reuse concepts that are used to define boundaries of a framework (Chapter 5 describes metapatterns). The following is a recap of the metapattern concepts in the realm of frameworks:

White-Box Vs. Black-Box Frameworks

White-box frameworks provide *generality,* whereas black-box frameworks provide *leverage*. In white-box frameworks, you tailor the framework to the application's specific needs through class derivation. For leverage, black-box frameworks must include a set of predefined classes that you can use. Thus, if the framework is too general, it won't have much added value; conversely, if a framework isn't general enough, it won't be extensible and thus, will only be usable in limited situations. In short, a black-box framework normally is easy to use, but can be limiting, whereas a white-box framework is flexible, but can be difficult to understand and use. Therefore, the combination of inheritance and composition works best in the frameworks.

A white-box framework may evolve into a black-box framework during the framework's lifecycle. The white-box approach should be seen as the beginning in the evolution of a framework. A white-box framework transforms from a loose collection of hot and frozen hooks (described later) into a concrete set of components. However, white-box frameworks are usually relatively easy to design; therefore, beginning with a white-box approach is the best design strategy. The framework can later evolve into a black-box framework with a white-box base, making the framework both extendable and easy to use.

♦ *Hot hooks*—Just like C++ pure **virtual** functions. Framework components are loosely coupled via hot hooks. Hot hooks enable you to interconnect software components that you develop, and they provide a connection-point at which generic framework objects can communicate with application objects. Hot hooks are a framework's common protocol that enables you to develop the application components. The real advantage of using hot hooks is that they enable you to focus on interfaces rather than implementation details. Hot hooks are used by both white-box and black-box frameworks. (Hot hooks are explained further in Chapter 7.)

♦ *Frozen hooks*—Functions that consist of a series of hot hooks. Frozen hooks need not be **virtual** functions. They provide a fixed implementation. However, the behavior of a frozen hook can vary at runtime, because it depends on hot hooks. A framework contains frozen hooks to provide default behavior. In fact, a framework's rich, built-in functionality is provided by frozen hooks. Frozen hooks are a framework's capability to jump-start application development. (Frozen hooks also are explained further in Chapter 7.)

♦ *Warm hooks*—If you mark a frozen hook of a framework as a hot hook by making it a **virtual** function, it becomes a *warm hook*. It is called a warm hook because it can act like either a hot hook or a frozen hook.

A Framework's Features

A reusable framework should have the features described in the following sections.

Usability

A framework must be usable. Usability is a runtime property of a framework. Unless a framework provides expected functionality, it cannot be used, and hence cannot be reused.

Generality

A framework must have a broad scope of applicability. If a framework can be reused only once, it isn't a reusable framework. Frameworks provide the highest level of reusability.

Adaptability

A reusable framework isn't used as is, due to its generality property. It has to be adapted to develop new applications. Therefore, ease of use should be an important yardstick when making a framework. A framework without a good degree of adaptability can't be used (or reused). (Chapter 14 discusses this topic in more detail.)

NOTE

Modeling Frameworks

The Unified Modeling Language (UML) can be used to specify various attributes of a framework, such as static and dynamic characteristics. Chapter 4 describes UML concepts and their notations that are used in this book. UML provides many modeling diagrams for different purposes, such as dynamic or static system views. These diagrams depict the essential classes and their associations in a framework. *Class diagrams* can be used for modeling the static structure of classes in an object-oriented system. Class diagrams contain classes and their relationships. *Interaction diagrams* can be used for modeling interactions within a system.

One major aspect of a framework is its documentation. If a framework isn't supported by proper user documentation, it likely won't be used. If the framework's documentation doesn't meet the requirements of its intended users, the framework won't be reused.

One way to adapt a framework is via an application construction environment (ACE). Framework developers can develop an ACE to allow you to interact with a framework so that you can configure and construct new applications. An ACE (also known as a *toolkit*) is a collection of high-level tools that enables you to interact with a framework. An ACE may be based on one or more frameworks.

One of the advantages of black-box frameworks is that they can easily be used with an ACE. Building a tool that lets you choose prebuilt components and connect them is easy, and a black-box framework permits most applications to be constructed that way. For white-box frameworks, you can define specialized classes by using code generators. Because frameworks have well-defined interfaces, code generators may not be very difficult to develop.

Changeability

A usable framework has a long life span, and thus may need to evolve. Obviously, a framework needs to be extensible. If you use **switch-case** within framework code and keep functions aware of the object model, the framework may possibly lose its changeability factor. Changeability also means *refactoring*, or restructuring, the framework.

Efficiency

A framework contains code, and the code impacts the speed of the application. Efficiency is a matter of both smart algorithms and the framework's overall architecture. In distributed computing, efficiency becomes an important factor in framework design. Efficiency should be one of the framework's architectural criteria, and you must avoid trying to optimize a framework as a last activity in the development phase. This is contrary to the popular belief that suggests "first run, then optimize." Efficiency and changeability are two forces that must be balanced in a framework.

Robustness

A framework must not have bugs that result in runtime failures. Because a framework acts as a foundation for many applications, it must be tested and verified for all possible runtime problems. Robustness must be the most important design and implementation yardstick for building a framework, and you shouldn't achieve efficiency at the cost of robustness.

Chapter Recap

The success of the OOP paradigm depends on reuse, and the success of reuse depends on frameworks. Frameworks empower you to leverage fully OOP's power of reuse. Frameworks provide reusable, built-in functionality to act as an application development foundation. This chapter has presented numerous framework concepts, including the following:

♦ An object-oriented framework is a development foundation designed for maximum reuse. A framework is represented as a collective set of abstract and concrete classes, with a prewired collaboration among them.

♦ Differences exist between frameworks, design patterns, and libraries.

♦ Object-oriented design patterns describe solutions to small-scale design problems in a given context, whereas frameworks address solutions to whole applications. A design pattern is more abstract than a framework, because it represents a general design solution to a problem. A framework can consist of multiple design patterns.

♦ The biggest difference between an object-oriented framework and a class library is that the framework calls the application code. Normally, the application code calls the class library.

♦ A framework generally is related to a specific application domain. Frameworks of a general nature can also be developed.

♦ Object-oriented techniques of special importance in the development of a framework are object interfaces, polymorphism, and design patterns. Development of a framework requires several design iterations to make it reusable.

♦ You can use an object-oriented framework in two ways: either derive new classes from the framework or instantiate and compose existing classes.

♦ Frameworks can be integrated with an ACE designed for OOP that includes a variety of development tools, to enable rapid application development and customization.

With frameworks, the future of object-oriented technology looks very promising. Ever-increasing development and maintenance costs of software proves that reusability is the key issue in computing. This may make frameworks a popular technology. Also, given the increasing interest in distributed computing, object-oriented-based frameworks and CORBA are going to play a crucial role in the future. CORBA, with its services and interfaces, already plays a role as a metaframework, which is why this book brings together OOP, CORBA, and frameworks. The next few chapters focus on these topics in greater detail.

Chapter 7
Framework Development

Chapter 6 explains that a *framework* is a set of prefabricated, software building blocks that you can use as a development foundation for new applications. If you use a framework as a development foundation, you don't have to start from scratch each time you design and develop an application. Recall that unlike design patterns, a framework is code and thus must be implemented. Developing a framework differs from developing a standalone application. This chapter presents a general framework development process and shows the implementation of the horizontal framework presented in Chapter 6. To implement a framework, you must first identify key abstractions, their relationships, their default behavior, and their collaborations. Then, you can implement the involved classes as defined by the architecture.

To develop a framework, you have to identify clearly the class of problem that the framework addresses. Because a framework provides solutions to a set of problems, the framework's users must understand how to adapt the framework to solve the problems. Because users have to understand how to adapt your framework to solve problems, you must follow good software design practices and be ready to go through several design iterations to make the framework more reusable and adaptable.

A successful framework provides problem-solving expertise to its users. However, the framework must be easily adaptable and must solve the problem in a natural way.

The framework example in this chapter also presents a few C++ techniques that are useful in framework implementation.

217

The General Framework Development Process

When developing a framework (as opposed to an ordinary object-oriented application), some program constructs, or design elements, are very important. Such design elements are abstract classes, object-oriented (OO) design patterns, and hot hooks. The first step in developing a framework is to identify the framework to be developed. For each framework, you take the following steps:

1. Identify the need and opportunity of the framework to be developed.

2. Identify the primary abstractions.

3. Identify the hot hooks.

4. Define the architecture by applying recurring design patterns.

5. Implement the framework.

6. Develop a few applications based on the framework. This is to test the framework. Problems encountered when using the framework in the development of these applications are captured and the framework is refined.

7. Repeat Steps 3 to 6 several times until the framework reaches an acceptable maturity level.

8. Prepare framework documentation in the form of diagrams, recipes, and sample programs.

Steps 1 to 7 are illustrated in the sections to follow (Step 8 is shown in Chapter 14).

Step 1: Identifying Frameworks

Frameworks solve architectural and programming problems that recur with variations. You don't need to develop a framework if the problem arises in only one context. Likewise, frameworks are needed only for solutions that require several steps.

You reuse a framework so that you get the capability of solving a particular type of problem without having to reinvent the solution. For example, a programmer may obtain a framework that provides a family of solutions for the banking industry; this would be a *vertical framework* because it addresses a particular domain. Similarly, a user may choose a framework that provides an infrastructure to solve problems related to distributed computing and workflow management. This must be a *horizontal framework*, because it doesn't address a particular domain. However, such a framework may be used to develop domain-specific applications and other frameworks. The business component framework (BC framework) described in Chapter 6 is a horizontal framework. A recap of the BC framework is presented in the section "Developing The Business-Component Framework."

Tips To Identify Frameworks

Frameworks can be thought of as abstractions of solutions to current and future architectural and programming problems. You can often identify opportunities for new frameworks by analyzing existing solutions. The following points are worth considering when identifying potential frameworks:

♦ If a set of applications that solve similar problems exists, then an opportunity to develop a framework exists.

♦ Look for software solutions that you build repeatedly. Identify what the solutions have in common and what is unique to each program.

♦ The common classes and algorithms across programs become the foundation for your frameworks. These common classes and algorithms form the abstractions of the frameworks.

♦ Look for class hierarchies of reusable classes. A class hierarchy may have potential to become a white-box framework (described later in the chapter).

Step 2: Identifying Abstractions

Abstraction is a key element of frameworks. Abstraction characterizes an object. It helps you to distinguish one kind of object from other kinds of objects. The use of abstractions is a good way to achieve reusability, proper use of inheritance, and utilization of dynamic binding. All of these aspects are relevant to the architecture of an object-oriented framework.

One of the objectives of framework architecture is to generalize concepts in terms of abstractions, to make the abstractions suitable for reuse in later applications. A *good* abstraction helps to avoid restructuring a framework. Frameworks must attempt to achieve a high degree of abstraction.

NOTE

Class Hierarchy Equals White-Box Framework

A class hierarchy may have the potential to emerge as a white-box framework. Sometimes, you can't draw a clear line between a white-box framework and a well-designed class hierarchy, because, like a class hierarchy, using a white-box framework also involves the mechanism of overriding virtual functions of the base classes.

Tips To Identify Abstractions

A framework doesn't need a separate methodology to identify abstractions in the problem domain. You can apply existing methodologies (such as Booch, Fusion, and so forth) to achieve the same. The following points may give you some ideas about identifying abstractions:

♦ You can discover abstractions by generalizing from a number of concrete examples. For example, you can investigate partially completed and completed projects to see whether you can discover new abstract classes. You can analyze the data structures and algorithms of the existing projects to organize them into abstractions. After you identify the abstractions, you can determine the class hierarchies and class relationships.

♦ You can discover ready-made, reusable abstractions from existing projects. You may also clean up the design of the hierarchy, to increase the reuse and adaptability value.

Step 3: Identifying The Hot Hooks

As Chapter 6 describes, a hot hook is just like a C++ pure virtual function. The framework components are loosely coupled via hot hooks. Hot hooks provide a connection point at which generic framework objects can communicate with application objects. Hot hooks are a framework's common protocol, so that you can develop the application components. Hot hooks formalize these collaborations and behavioral relationships. The following points are important:

♦ Hot hooks can be found at various levels of abstraction.

♦ Hot hooks are like contractual obligations that the framework user must maintain. The behavior of an application's participant is specified by its obligations. The application participant must support a certain external interface to meet this obligation.

♦ A hot hook's implementation may require you to call some functions as preconditions and post-conditions.

Dynamic Binding In Frameworks

Full potential of object-orientation comes with inheritance combined with dynamic binding. Dynamic binding is an essential feature for developing frameworks. If you compare a framework with a class library, you'll see the role of dynamic binding in frameworks. When a class library is used by an application, calls are made from the application to the class library only. In an object-oriented framework, however, calls also can go from the framework to the application, as depicted in Figure 7.1. Dynamic binding makes this two-way flow of control possible. The notions of abstract classes and dynamic binding are related to each other, and they play an important role in frameworks.

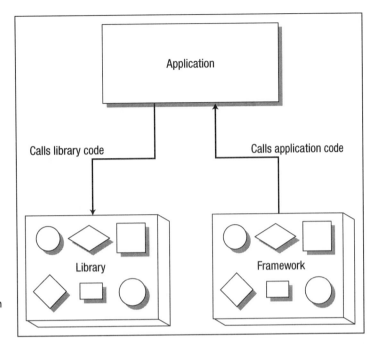

Figure 7.1
Differences in the direction of calls in traditional libraries and frameworks.

The advantages of designing hot hooks when developing object-oriented frameworks are the following:

♦ Keeps the framework flexible.

♦ Provides an object-oriented way of thinking to the application developers, because they have to think in terms of identification of application-specific classes and implementation of hot hooks. It also helps them to understand the design patterns in the framework, thereby improving the understanding of the overall framework.

♦ Establishes a well-defined vocabulary that provides the power of improved communication among application developers.

Tips To Identify Hot Hooks

Identification of hot hooks is the most significant activity in designing and developing frameworks. To identify hot hooks, you need to ask the following two questions:

♦ *What aspects differ from component to component, or application to application?* This is something like finding a variable in a design. For example, in a GUI application, the reaction to clicking an OK button is a variable, because it differs from component to component. Therefore, it is a hot hook.

♦ *What is the desired degree of flexibility?* Remember that *flexibility* and *focus* are two antithetical forces of a framework—you want to keep a framework as flexible as possible, but you also want to maintain the focus of the framework and minimize the complexity for the user. If you provide a completely flexible framework, it will be difficult for the framework users to learn, and difficult for you to support. However, you can build a highly flexible (metaframework) for your own use. From the metaframework, you derive more focused frameworks. These focused frameworks can provide the default behavior and built-in functionality, while the metaframework maintains the flexibility. For example, by using a distributed computing metaframework, you can create a framework that supports banking applications in a distributed environment. The new banking framework is focused on the banking applications, but it is not as flexible as the metaframework.

Step 4: Defining The Architecture

Of late, in the field of software engineering, the word *software architecture* is preferred over *software design*. The output of software design is software architecture. Design is an activity and architecture is the result of this activity. Software architecture expresses the subsystems and components of a system and relationships between them.

In the context of object-oriented frameworks, the concepts of design patterns are useful for the development of the architecture of the framework. Recall that design patterns capture the intent behind a design by identifying objects, how objects interact, and how responsibilities are distributed among them. Because design patterns represent abstract descriptions of solutions to common and recurring design problems, they prove to be very useful when designing frameworks. Applying design patterns facilitates an additional level of design reuse. You can also use design patterns to document the framework to make the framework easier for users to understand, apply, and customize.

Selecting Design Patterns

The primary objective of OO-based application designs is to partition the application into a set of interconnectable collaborative objects (components). Each object implements important aspects of a complete application. OOP can help to partition a complex application system into smaller, simpler objects. Similarly, you can partition a framework into known design patterns. Many design patterns exist that you can apply to derive good framework architectures. Patterns can be either generic (horizontal) or domain-specific (vertical). However, it is important that you apply an appropriate design pattern. To achieve that, you need to consider one question: What is the problem that a design pattern is going to solve?

Depending on the problem that you intend to solve, you can select a pattern of a particular type. Chapter 5 presents the C-6 classification of design patterns, to enable you to select the appropriate type of pattern. For example, if you are dealing with a design problem pertaining to initialing and configuring classes, you might consider using a *Controller* type of design pattern. One example of such a pattern is a *Factory*. Obviously, you need to have a good catalog of design patterns that contains numerous design patterns and presents their descriptions based on the template, as shown in Chapter 5. A catalog, together with the C-6 classification, serves as a guide to use when searching for a suitable pattern for the framework you are building. Of course, a catalog serves only as a guide to select design patterns, and to successfully apply design patterns to a framework, you need to have experience and understand the framework you are designing.

Architectural Guidelines For Successful Frameworks

When designing frameworks, you need to pay special attention to handling *nonfunctional* requirements; for example, exception-handling policies, efficiency, and so forth. These are called "nonfunctional" because they aren't associated with any domain-related functionality. However, a horizontal framework may exist only to address these issues. In that case, these issues can't be referred to as nonfunctional; they are purely functional properties of the framework.

For you and your framework users to get the maximum benefit from a framework, the framework should have the following features (some of these features are discussed in Chapter 6, too):

- *Usable and complete*—Usability is the yardstick to measure a framework's completeness. A framework is called *usable* only if it provides expected functionality. A framework's architecture must provide as much built-in functionality as possible. The architecture should support features needed by a wide range of users.

- *Generic*—The framework must be designed to be reusable. In other words, it should have a broad scope of applicability, because the framework must be used to develop many types of applications. In the framework architecture, however, you must strike a balance between the simplicity of the interface and the genericity of the framework. A generic interface may loose simplicity, because it needs to serve a broad range of requirements.

♦ *Adaptable*—The most important consideration when you're designing frameworks is ease of use for the users. From the users' perspective, an easy-to-use framework performs useful functions with little effort on their part. The framework must provide default implementations, where possible. For example, you can provide concrete derivations for the abstract classes in your frameworks and default member function implementations. This makes the framework easier for the users to understand, and enables them to focus on the areas that they need to customize.

The default implementation even can be simple placeholders, enabling users to apply small, incremental steps to get from the default behavior to sophisticated solutions. In addition, it is very important for a framework to impose certain usage patterns, to promote code generation. However, you shouldn't achieve this at the cost of flexibility.

♦ *Efficient*—Efficiency means response time and throughput. A framework can slow down an entire application, even if the application is designed well (the opposite is also true). Efficiency could be an important yardstick in a framework's acceptance testing. Very often, efficiency is more important than achieving extensibility. The architecture of the framework should promote this factor. You must not try to achieve the efficiency of a framework during the implementation phase, because that will be too late.

A bad architecture, bad middleware, bad data modeling, or a bad third-party product integration may damage a framework's efficiency. In such a situation, any amount of code-tuning or blaming OOP will not help.

♦ *Extensible*—A framework should be easily extensible, to add new features. This chapter shows how a logging/debugging mechanism can be added to the framework to make it more useful. A framework that follows these guidelines should be extensible:

  ♦ Keeps member functions unaware of the object model.

  ♦ Provides good encapsulation.

  ♦ Maintains separation of interface and implementation, which makes the refactoring (restructuring) of a framework easy.

  ♦ Keeps the framework platform-independent and GUI-independent, to make porting your framework easier. Designing for portability reduces the impact porting has on your users.

◆ Gives users the ability to easily add and modify the functionality of the framework. Provides hooks so that users can customize the behavior of the framework by deriving new classes.

◆ *Interactive with users*—Hot hooks are the hooks for a user to insert his/her code in the framework. This generally is done via class derivation and overriding pure virtual functions. Therefore, from a user's point of view, this whole activity must cause only minimal problems for him/her. As mentioned earlier, you need to maintain the balance between flexibility (pure virtual functions) and focus (concrete classes). You certainly must focus on minimizing the number of classes that must be derived. A system full of many derived classes will cause problems related to compilation time, maintenance, and so forth. During the design of the framework, you should also look for ways to minimize the potential for user errors. For example, if your framework's data types are too complicated to use, then design wrapper types around them to minimize user mistakes. The amount of code that has to be written by the framework user has to be reduced to a minimum, which you can achieve by doing the following:

◆ Provide concrete implementations in the framework that can be used without any kind of modification.

◆ Minimize the number of classes that have to be derived.

◆ Minimize the operations in the classes that have to be overridden; in other words, minimize the public interfaces for the framework users.

◆ *Testable*—Ascertaining whether the framework could be made more usable and proving that the framework is correct are important. The testability of a framework depends on how well the framework can detect faults at runtime. The architecture must enable you to integrate the debugging and logging components with the framework, so that you can detect faults at runtime. In addition, the framework components must exhibit weak coupling among themselves, to augment the testability. The more dependency among framework components, the more complicated the testing becomes. Many distributed systems show poor testability, simply because one instance of such a system involves many components that complicate the overall testing. (Framework testing is explained later in the chapter.)

Step 5: Implementing The Framework

This is an important step to realize the architecture of the framework. This step involves implementations of the design patterns and frozen hooks of the framework. A *frozen hook* is a function that consists of a series of hot hooks. Frozen hooks need not be virtual functions. They provide a fixed implementation. However, behavior of a frozen hook can vary at runtime, because it depends on hot hooks. A framework contains frozen hooks to provide default behavior. In fact, a framework's rich, built-in functionality is provided by frozen hooks. Therefore, frozen hooks are a framework's capability to jump-start application development. Frozen hooks should be identified during the framework design activity.

Having a good understanding of dynamic binding will help you to implement the framework. C++'s memory management, exception handling, and Standard Template Library (STL) are generally very useful for implementing successful horizontal frameworks, which is why these aspects are covered in this book.

Implementation Guidelines For A Framework

Because many applications will be developed by using your framework, you need to use the following coding guidelines to ensure the quality of the framework:

- *Robustness*—This is the system's ability to maintain both its runtime behavior per its declared functionality, and to sustain the application and external faults. Robustness should be the most important yardstick, and you must not achieve efficiency at the cost of robustness. A few coding guidelines may make an implementation robust, such as the following:

  - Check for usage of null pointers.
  - Check for memory allocation failures.
  - Check for exception handling.
  - Check for bad typecasting.
  - Check that a class provides an assignment operator and a copy constructor.
  - Check for object ownership.
  - Check for the return values and possible exceptions from functions that you use.

- *Extensibility*—Like the architecture, the implementation also must support extensibility. You must avoid using **switch-case** and **if-else** constructs to maintain the extensibility of the framework.

Follow standard coding guidelines and provide sample applications that demonstrate the use of each framework component. Using detailed style guidelines is an advantage that shows to framework users how the code has to be read and understood. Different frameworks need not differ in coding styles. Evolving a uniform coding style at organizational levels is very important.

Step 6: Testing The Framework

The Institute of Electrical and Electronics Engineers (IEEE) defines "testing" as a process that verifies that a system satisfies requirements. The testing process is used to identify bugs in a framework. In the realm of framework testing, the following definitions are important to understand:

- *Framework bug*—An undesired "feature," especially one that causes an application to break or end unexpectedly. A framework bug is also known as a *fault*. A framework bug can cause big problems for the application's developers, because determining whether a fault is a framework fault or an application fault often is difficult. You can prevent bugs by self-checking techniques, including doing a code walk-through and conducting a test before designing.

- *Developer's error*—A framework developer's actions that result in framework bugs. The activity that successfully corrects a failure is referred to as *debugging*.

- *Application failure*—Incorrect output or abnormal termination of an application. If you build an application by using a framework that has bugs, the application won't be able to perform a required service within specified limits, which is referred to as an *application failure*. The opposite, however, may not be true—an application failure may not necessarily be due to a framework bug.

Scope Of Testing

Because a framework is also software, you can test a framework under the following scopes:

- *Unit testing*—Involves the testing of the units of the framework. The *class* is the smallest natural unit for testing. Unit testing is done to verify class behavior, before it is reused or promoted into the framework. However, very often, testing a class in isolation isn't practical or possible. In such cases, groups of classes (known as *class clusters*) can be considered practical units for testing. Unit testing encounters three object-oriented issues:

♦ *Encapsulation*—Encapsulation may not cause errors, but it may be a restriction on testing. Good encapsulation makes it hard to figure out the state of the concrete and abstract objects.

♦ *Polymorphism*—Each possible binding of a polymorphic component requires a separate test, and separate tests may be hard to accomplish. Polymorphism may also complicate the integration planning process.

♦ *Inheritance*—Inheritance doesn't help to reduce the quantity of testing. Apart from all overridden and new member functions in the derived class, you need to retest all the inherited member functions of a base class in the unique context of a derived class, even if they are all tested for the base class.

♦ *Integration testing*—Combines units to evaluate the integration among them. Testing a class can verify a class in isolation. However, when untested objects of a tested class are used with other objects, the entire application must be tested before these objects can be considered tested. Still, integration testing works best when the units are stable which you can ensure in the unit testing phase. Because a framework isn't a *single application*, you need a special strategy for integration testing:

♦ Identify the slices of the framework that can be integrated and tested incrementally.

♦ Find all the possible and practical combinations of components that can be integrated for testing.

Integration testing is requirement-driven testing of the entire framework. In other words, integration testing ensures that a framework is implemented based on the functional requirements of the framework. Along with unit testing, your goal for integration testing should be extensive coverage.

♦ *System testing*—Focuses on the nonfunctional aspects of the framework. System testing doesn't include testing of the integrated components to determine the functional aspects of the framework. Instead, system testing involves stress testing, installation testing, and so forth.

Basic Testing Strategy
You can apply two kinds of testing strategies: black-box testing and white-box testing.

Black-box testing uses the requirements and specification documents to develop test cases. No knowledge about implementation details is used to develop test cases. This is also known as *functional testing*. The following questions should be answered before you start the black-box testing:

♦ What are valid and invalid message inputs, states, and message outputs?

♦ What values should be selected for test cases?

♦ Does the sequence of member-function activation matter or not?

♦ If sequence does matter, how can efficient testing sequences be selected?

The objective of black-box testing is to test, in isolation, the functionality of all framework classes/components, which ensures that, functionally, the framework performs as defined by the requirements document. Error conditions are also tested as part of black-box testing.

The objective of black-box testing is to achieve *functional coverage* of the code. The strategy used to achieve full functional coverage is to inspect all the framework headers and provide test routines for each of the interfaces/functions in the headers. Further, you can study the framework's user documentation to ensure complete functional coverage.

The scope of black-box testing is to test all the interfaces defined in the framework header files and their user documents.

White-box testing uses a framework's source code to develop test cases. This is also known as *structural testing*. White-box testing uses the notion of *coverage*, a key concept to measure test completeness. For a framework, you must achieve 100-percent statement coverage, which means that every statement of the framework has been executed by a test at least once.

The objective of white-box testing is to test, in isolation, the various paths in the framework code, without focusing on the functionality aspects. Maximizing code coverage is the main objective of these tests. Error conditions also are tested as part of white-box testing.

The scope of white-box testing is to test all the member functions of a given framework object. This involves explicitly testing all the **public**, **private**, and **protected** functions of the classes. You can use an appropriate code-coverage tool to instrument the code and measure its coverage on running all the tests. New tests can be added, as needed, to improve the coverage.

Step 7: Refining The Framework

Building a mature and reusable framework is an iterative process. The development of a good framework requires a lot of iteration between the application development and the framework development. As part of this process, you must reconsider the hot hooks from the perspective of usability and adaptability; if necessary, rearchitect and reimplement your framework, and then refine your test programs.

Tips For Refining A Framework

The following points are worth considering when you are attempting to refine your framework:

♦ You must investigate the framework's usage to determine whether you can add more default behaviors and additional ways for users to interact with the framework. For example, you may add a logging mechanism to the framework (this is demonstrated later in the chapter).

♦ Try to refine hot hooks to make a framework user's tasks easier. In some cases, you can also refine the framework to integrate it with tools such as code generators, application construction environments (ACEs), and GUI tools. Properly designed tools can make the framework's usage easier.

♦ If the framework is getting too big, try to break it down into small, focused frameworks. The new, smaller frameworks should interoperate. This set of new frameworks is designed to be very flexible and reusable in the context of other applications. For example, a framework solving workflow requirements can consist of the following, smaller frameworks:

   ♦ Distributed component management

   ♦ Resource management

   ♦ GUI support for end-user interactions

By breaking down the bigger workflow framework into a set of smaller, self-sufficient frameworks, you can adapt the resulting frameworks to develop a broad range of applications.

Metaframeworks

In the process of refining, you may even generalize your framework and create a *metaframework*, which is developed to provide a strong architectural base that enables you to create a *derived framework* that addresses a particular problem set. Derived frameworks can customize the metacomponents, or even introduce additional components and constraints that support solutions that are more specific. Derived frameworks are a way of providing default behavior for the framework users. For example, if your framework consists of a number of abstract classes, you create one or more derived frameworks that implement the abstract classes and provide supplementary built-in functionality.

Freezing The Hot Hooks And Framework

Determining when a framework should be frozen for release is a difficult task, because framework development is an iterative process. Building a *complex* framework obviously requires more iterations, and you will find it difficult to freeze. Conversely, a *simple* framework requires fewer iterations. This means that if you focus on developing smaller frameworks, you can accelerate the development process.

Your framework must reach a level of maturity before it is released. To measure the level of maturity, you may even use some degree of parallel development activity of the framework and user application. In other words, while a framework is still being refined, its beta version can be given to the users to use. Until somebody uses your framework, you can never be sure that the final framework will be usable and mature. A parallel application-development activity may provide feedback for a framework in terms of usability (functionality) and adaptability (hot hooks), which will make the framework mature. Whereas a usable and mature framework may be a great value for the application development, an evolving and "unfrozen" framework can adversely impact the application development severely. Given these two facts, it is better to maintain a balance between these two forces (that is, early release versus frozen release).

Developing The Business Component Framework

This section presents the implementation of the business component (BC) framework that is presented in Chapter 6. To recap, the BC framework is a horizontal type of framework. It builds upon the following presuppositions:

◆ An application consists of many components.

◆ The BC framework should enable application developers to define application components.

♦ A BC must have the lifecycle of creation and deletion by the BC framework.

♦ The BCs of an application must be able to communicate with each other with the help of requests and application programmers' interfaces (APIs) rather than through direct invocation of the member functions. The BC framework must be able to locate the target component automatically and invoke the required member functions.

♦ A BC will reply via reply messages.

♦ A request and reply will carry the data between components.

The BC framework has been selected to demonstrate the framework implementation example for the following reasons:

♦ It is simple to understand, and isn't domain-specific.

♦ Its architecture is interesting, because the architecture involves a few design patterns.

♦ It is extensible (examples of extensions are presented in this chapter).

Defining The Architecture Of The BC Framework

Identifying the high-level structure of the framework makes describing the behavior of the framework easier and provides a starting point for designing framework interactions. This is why the high-level architecture is thoroughly defined for the BC framework in Chapter 6. Chapter 6 explains that the internal structure of the BC framework is described by the *Broker* architectural patterns, because the BC framework enables you to write decoupled components that interact by messages. Broker architectural patterns describe software systems with decoupled components that interact via messages. (CORBA is based on this pattern.) Recall that the BC framework has a client-server model in which the server components (BCs) register themselves with a *component manager* and make their services available to clients. Clients access the server components' services by sending requests to the components. The component manager locates and instantiates the target BC and forwards the request to that BC.

Defining the framework architecture is an activity that helps to design framework components that you can reuse to develop applications. One such application is shown in the section "Using The BC Framework." The next few sections outline the foundation components of the BC framework. These components are important to understand, so that you can grasp a few other concepts that are presented later in the chapter. You will also see that the BC framework is a white-box framework, because it offers its services via class derivation. Specific information about the relationships among the components of the BC framework is presented in Chapter 14. However, examples in this chapter should give you some indication about how the components of the BC framework are interrelated.

CoComponent

As Chapter 6 mentions, your BC must be derived from the **Co-Component** class to implement the required behavior of a business entity. (An application consists of many BCs.) A **CoComponent** implementation represents a single entity within the underlying application. This includes the application data, as well as any business operations that the entity is required to perform. The **CoComponent** class is responsible for carrying out the business processing that is started by the arrival of a message. In this manner, a **CoComponent** is the heart of the BC framework. **CoComponent** is used to represent the *static component model*, which defines a particular BC and its responsibilities.

A client of a **CoComponent** changes the state of a **CoComponent** and/ or obtains application data by sending a request to the instance of the **CoComponent**. The **CoComponent** must implement the behavior of reacting to the request. This is done by registering various requests with **CoComponent**.

The **CoComponent** class declaration is shown in Listing 7.1.

Listing 7.1   The CoComponent class.

```
class CoRequest;
class CoReply;
class CoComponent;
typedef void (CoComponent::*CO_COMPONENT_FUNCTION)();

class CoComponent
{
    friend class CoComponentManager;

private:

    map<string, CO_COMPONENT_FUNCTION> functionMap_;
    CoRequest* currentRequest_;
```

```
        CoReply* currentReply_;

public:

    CoComponent();

    inline void registerService(const string& name,
        CO_COMPONENT_FUNCTION compFun);

    virtual void registerServices()=0;

    inline void setReply(CoReply* reply);
    inline CoRequest* getRequest();
};
```

The following are the important elements of the **CoComponent** class:

♦ **registerService()**—Registers a component member function with the **CoComponent** instance. The first **name** parameter is of type **string**, and the second is of type **CO_COMPONENT_ FUNCTION**. The CO_COMPONENT_FUNCTION type represents a pointer to a member function of the **CoComponent** class (the next section explains this notion). This pointer to a member function is nothing but a service provided by the **CoComponent**.

♦ **registerServices()**—A pure virtual function of the **CoComponent** class. This function is always overridden by the BC framework user. In the implementation, the user registers the derived component's services. The **registerServices()** function is automatically called by the BC framework, which is why it is the hot hook of the BC framework. The registered services are also automatically invoked by the BC framework whenever a request hits the component.

♦ **setReply()**—Enables a service to set a reply for the caller.

♦ **getRequest()**—Enables a service to access the request from the caller.

Pointers To Member Functions Of A Class

Listing 7.1 defines a very uncommon type of pointer, **CO_ COMPONENT_FUNCTION**, which points generically to a **public** member of the **CoComponent** class, not to an individual instance of the member in an object. This type of pointer is referred to as a *pointer to a class member*, which isn't identical to a typical C++ pointer; a pointer to a class member represents only its offset into an object of the class. This mechanism often is very useful while developing horizontal frameworks, which is why this section explains the concept.

A pointer to a nonmember function may not be assigned the address of a non-**static** member function, even when the return type and signature of the two agree exactly. Even a generic pointer (**void***) may not be assigned the address of a non-**static** member function. An example with a simple class (**CoClass**) is presented here:

```
typedef
int (*PF)();

class CoClass
{
public:
    int oops1();
    static int oops2();
    //...

private:

    int oops3();
};

int main()
{
    PF pfnTest1=&CoClass::oops1; //error
    PF pfnTest2=&CoClass::oops2; //ok
    void* pv1=&CoClass::oops1; //error
    void* pv2=&CoClass::oops2; //ok
    //...
}
```

Why are there errors with non-**static** functions in the preceding calls? A non-**static** member function has a supplementary-type characteristic—the class of which it is a member—which is not found in a **static** member. Thus, to assign a pointer to a function the address of a non-**static** member function, the pointer must agree exactly in three characteristics:

♦ The type and number of formal arguments; that is, its signature

♦ The return type of the function

♦ The class type of which it is a member

The declaration of a pointer to a member function calls for an augmented syntax that takes the class type into account. To account for the address of a class member function, a programmer must qualify the function name with the class name and scope resolution operator. The actual type of **CoClass::oops1()** is written as follows:

```
class CoClass; //forward declaration

typedef
int (CoClass::*CO_P_F)();
```

Now, the outcome has reversed:

```
int main()
{
    CO_P_F pfnTest1=&CoClass::oops1; //ok
    CO_P_F pfnTest2=&CoClass::oops2; //error
    //...
}
```

Note that, unlike nonmember functions, the address operator ("**&**") isn't optional for a non-**static** member function; it must be applied to the function name.

An attempt to take the address of a non-**public** class member in a section of the program without access privileges to the class results in a compile-time error:

```
CO_P_F pfnTest3=&CoClass::oops3; //error: no access
```

Because pointers to class members aren't true pointers, the *member selection operators* (**.** and **->**) cannot be applied to them. Instead, you need to use two special *pointer-to-member selection operators*:

♦ *Operator* **.***—To dereference pointers to class members

♦ *Operator* **->***—To dereference pointers to pointers to class members

The pointed members are always accessed through individual objects of the class. For example:

```
class CoClass;

typedef
void (CoClass::*CO_P_F)();

class CoClass
{
```

```
public:
    int i;

    CoClass(int v):i(v){} //constructor
    void oops()
    {
        cout<<"in oops():"<<i<<endl;
    }
};

int main()
{
    CoClass v1(13),*v2=new CoClass(169);

    CO_P_F pf=&CoClass::oops;

    (v1.*pf)(); //calls v1.oops()
    (v2->*pf)(); //calls v2->oops()

    delete v2;

    return 0;
}
```

The program generates the following output:

```
In oops():13
In oops():169
```

The calls

```
(v1.*pf)(); //calls v1.oops()
(v2->*pf)(); //calls v2->oops()
```

need the parentheses because the precedence of the function call operator, (), is higher than the precedence of the pointer-to-member selection operators.

Now that you have learned the pointer-to-member function notion, you are ready to focus on the **CoComponentManager** class.

CoComponentManager

The **CoComponentManager** class is responsible for instantiating and routing a message to a target BC, provided the BC is registered with the **CoComponentManager** instance. The class acts like a broker between a client object and the server object.

The **CoComponentManager** class shows how the architecture of the BC framework can be defined using design patterns. The **Co-ComponentManager** class must implement the following design patterns (the names of the design patterns are taken from *Design Patterns: Elements of Reusable Object-Oriented Software,* by Erich Gamma, Richard Helm, Ralph Johnson, and John Vlissides, which was published by Addison-Wesley in 1995:

♦ *Singleton*—Ensures that a class can have only one instance at runtime, and provides a single point to access that instance. Because a running process of an application (built using the BC framework) must have only one instance of the **CoComponentManager** object, the **CoComponentManager** class must be designed to be a singleton class. Chapter 5 describes a way to make a class singleton. Listing 7.2 presents another technique to make a class singleton.

♦ *Mediator*—Separates the communication between objects. Because the **CoComponentManager** object separates a client object from a server object, the **CoComponentManager** class must implement the Mediator design pattern.

♦ *Factory*—Provides a mechanism to create objects of the same type, or a family of objects. Because the **CoComponentManager** class is responsible for instantiating the requested components, it also must be a component factory.

The declaration of the **CoComponentManager** class is shown in Listing 7.2.

Listing 7.2   The CoComponentManager class.

```
class CoComponent;
class CoRequest;
class CoReply;

typedef CoComponent* (*CO_COMP_SELF_REF)();

class CoComponentManager
{
    friend class CoRequest;

private:

    map<string, CO_COMP_SELF_REF> componentMap_;
```

```
    inline static CoComponentManager& getManager();

    CoComponent* createComponent(const string& name);

    CoComponentManager(){};

    void sendMessage(const string& target,
        CoRequest* request, CoReply*& reply);
public:

    inline static void
    registerComponent(const string& name,
        CO_COMP_SELF_REF comp);
};

inline CoComponentManager& CoComponentManager::getManager()
{
    static CoComponentManager mgr;
    return mgr;
}

CoComponent*
CoComponentManager::createComponent(const string& name)
{
    return (componentMap_[name])();
}

void CoComponentManager::sendMessage(const string& target,
    CoRequest* request, CoReply*& reply)
{
    CoComponent* pc=createComponent(target);
    pc->registerServices();

    pc->currentRequest_=request;

    CO_COMPONENT_FUNCTION pf=
        pc->functionMap_[request->getName()];

    (pc->*pf)(); //invokes a service

    reply=pc->currentReply_;

    delete pc;
}
```

The following list describes the important functions of the **Co-ComponentManager** class:

- **sendMessage()**—Implements the Mediator design pattern and serves as a frozen hook of the BC framework. This is the only frozen hook of the BC framework. This function is used by **CoRequest's sendAndReceive()** function. The **sendMessage()** function calls the hot hook **CoComponent::registerServices()** function as a result of the dynamic binding. This function is a frozen hook of the BC framework, because it uses a hot hook of the BC framework. The **sendMessage()** function also invokes the desired service of the target component.

- **registerComponent()**—Registers a component's creation-pointer and name with the **CoComponentManager** class. The type of creation-pointer is **CO_COMP_SELF_REF**, which is the second parameter of the **registerComponent()** function.

- **getManager()**—Implements the **CoComponentManager** class as Singleton. This is a static member function to access the **Co-ComponentManager** class. The **getManager()** function returns a static instance of the **CoComponentManager** class. This static instance is declared within the **getManager()** function itself rather than within the **CoComponentManager** class. The **getManager()** function is private to the BC framework, and therefore, is inaccessible to the BC framework user.

- **createComponent()**—Implements the Factory design pattern to create a **CoComponent**. The functions take an argument of type **string** and return a **CoComponent***. Of course, you should already have called the **registerComponent()** function.

CoReply

A BC may need to reply to the caller. The **CoReply** class does this task. It is used to return a reply to the caller from a service of the BC. The declaration of this class is shown here:

```
class CoMessage
{
public:
    inline CoMessage(){}
    inline virtual ~CoMessage(){}
};

class CoReply : public CoMessage
{
```

```
public:
    inline CoReply()
    {
    }
    inline ~CoReply(){}
};
```

CoRequest

The **CoRequest** class is used to dispatch messages to a target BC. A **CoRequest** causes invocation of a service in the BC that receives the message. The declaration of this class follows:

```
class CoRequest : public CoMessage
{
private:

    CoString target_;

public:

    inline CoRequest(){}
    inline ~CoRequest(){}

    void sendAndReceive(const string& target,
        CoReply*& reply);

    virtual string getName()=0;
};
```

The **CoRequest** class has a pure virtual function, **getName()**, which is a hot hook of the BC framework. The function must be implemented by the derived class of the **CoRequest** class. The **getName()** function is called by the **CoComponentManager::sendMessage()** function, which is a frozen hook of the BC framework.

Using The BC Framework

The primary objective of the BC framework is to describe the partition of applications into a set of interconnectable, collaborative components. Each component implements important aspects of an application. Access to a particular component's application capabilities is mediated by the **CoRequest**s that it supports. **CoRequest**s are what the application developer sees when assembling components to construct fully functional applications. The internal structures of the BC framework classes are described in the preceding sections.

Following are the steps to develop applications using the BC framework:

1. Define requests and replies for BCs. Recall that requests are defined to invoke services of BCs.

2. Define BCs.

3. Register BCs with the component manager.

4. Develop a client to invoke the services of the BCs.

Chapter 14 discusses how the BC framework can be used to develop applications. However, a set of short examples is presented in the sections that follow to show the BC framework usage steps.

How To Define Requests And Replies

Application requests and replies are determined from base classes **CoRequest** and **CoReply**, as shown in Listing 7.3.

Listing 7.3   Example to show how to define requests and replies.

```
#include <co_component.hpp>

class openAccount : public CoRequest
{
public:

    long accountNum_;
    double money_;
    string name_;

    openAccount()
    {
    }
    openAccount(const openAccount& other)
    {
        accountNum_=other.accountNum_;
        money_=other.money_;
        name_=other.name_;
    }
    openAccount& operator=(const openAccount& other)
    {
        accountNum_=other.accountNum_;
        money_=other.money_;
```

```
            name_=other.name_;
            return *this;
        }
    string getName()
        {
            return "openAccount";
        }
};


class balanceInfo : public CoReply
{
public:
    double balance_;

    balanceInfo()
    {
    }
    balanceInfo(const balanceInfo& other)
    {
        balance_=other.balance_;
    }
    balanceInfo& operator=(const balanceInfo& r)
    {
        balance_=r.balance_;
        return *this;
    }
};
```

As Listing 7.3 shows, the derived **openAccount** request overrides the **CoRequest::getName()** function. Recall that the **CoRequest:: getName()** function is a hot hook of the BC framework, which is why the function is implemented by the derived **openAccount** request. The overridden **CoRequest::getName()** function is called by the **CoComponentManager::sendMessage()** function, which is a frozen hook of the BC framework. The next section explains how the **openAccount** and **balanceInfo** classes relate to a BC.

How To Define A Component

You derive your BC from the base **CoComponent** class, as shown in Listing 7.4.

Listing 7.4   Declaration of a derived component.

```
class account : public CoComponent
{
```

```
private:

    account()
    {
    }

    void open()
    {
        openAccount* request=
            dynamic_cast<openAccount*>(getRequest());
        cout<<request->accountNum_<<endl;
        cout<<request->money_<<endl;
        cout<<request->name_<<endl;
        balanceInfo* reply=new balanceInfo;
        reply->balance_=50.1234;

        setReply(reply);
    }

    void registerServices()
    {
        registerService("openAccount",
            CO_COMPONENT_FUNCTION(&account::open));
    }

public:

    static CoComponent* self()
    {
        return new account;
    }
};
```

The following points are important about Listing 7.4:

♦ The **account** class is derived from the **CoComponent** class and represents an account component.

♦ The **account** class has a member function, **open()**, that uses the **CoComponent::getRequest()** member to access the current request. The output of the **CoComponent::getRequest()** call is dynamically typecast to get the actual request pointer (**openAccount***).

♦ The **open()** member function uses the **CoComponent::setReply()** member to return the reply, which is of type **balanceInfo**.

- The **registerServices()** hot hook is defined by the **account** class. In the function definition, the **CoComponent::registerService()** member function is used to register the **open()** member function with the request name **"openAccount"**. When the **openAccount** request hits the **account** component, the **open()** function will be invoked. Note that the **"openAccount"** string is the same as what is being returned from the **openAccount::getName()** hot hook.

- The **self()** static function of the **account** class creates an instance of the **account** class on the heap and returns the pointer. The use of the **self()** function is shown in the next section.

How To Register A Business Component With Component Manager

Recall that the **CoComponentManager::registerComponent()** function registers a component's creation-pointer and name with the **CoComponentManager** class. You can use either this function directly in the **main()** function, or you can encapsulate the calls of this function in a class. For example, the following code defines the **model** class that uses the **CoComponentManager::registerComponent()** function to register the **account** BC:

```
class model
{
public:
    model()
    {
        CoComponentManager::registerComponent(
            "account", account::self);
    }
};
```

In the constructor of the **model** class, the **CoComponent-Manager::registerComponent()** function is called, which takes the component name (**"account"**) and a pointer to a function that creates the component on the heap (**account::self**).

How To Invoke The Business Component's Services

The following code shows how to write a client that accesses the services of the **account** component:

```
int main()
{
    model model_;
    openAccount r;

    r.accountNum_=1234;
    r.money_=13.145;
    r.name_="vishwa";

    CoReply* reply;
    r.sendAndReceive("account", reply);

    balanceInfo* rep=dynamic_cast<balanceInfo*>(reply);

    cout<<rep->balance_<<endl;

    delete reply;

}
```

The following points about the preceding code are important:

♦ The **main()** program makes an instance of the **model** class. This step causes the **account** component to be registered with Co-ComponentManager.

♦ The program instantiates the **openAccount** request, and uses the **CoRequest::sendAndReceive()** function to dispatch the request to the target component, **"account"**. The target component's name is specified as the first argument of the **CoRequest::sendAndReceive()** function. The **"account"** string is the same as what is used as the first argument of the **CoComponentManager::registerComponent()** call in the previous section.

♦ The **CoRequest::sendAndReceive()** function causes the **open()** service of the **account** component to be invoked. The **CoRequest::sendAndReceive()** call gives a pointer to **CoReply** that is stored in the variable **reply**, which then is dynamically typecast to the expected type, **balanceInfo***. Recall that the **open()** service of the **account** component uses the **setReply()** function to return a reply of the **balanceInfo** type.

Refinements In The BC Framework

The BC framework provides many built-in features, which is what makes this framework a "framework." The framework provides a solution that requires several steps. For example, you don't have to manage the instances of a BC, because the BC framework takes care of it. However, the BC framework may not be very useful in its current form. For example, the contents of requests and replies can't be logged generically. You need to know the internal structure to achieve that. Thus, the BC framework types **CoRequest**, **CoReply**, and **CoComponent** need to be refined to make them more usable.

The following lists the changes and extensions that can be incorporated into the BC framework to make it more usable:

- The structure of messages (**CoRequest** and **CoReply**) and the **CoComponent** class should be standardized. They can generically be logged for auditing and debugging purposes (*auditing* is the process of maintaining audit trails of a system, recording events happening in the system).

- **CoRequest** and **CoReply** should have additional data member to hold generic business status.

To introduce these refinements, the sections that follow suggest some code changes.

Metadata Root Type

For a framework, identification of the data type abstractions can be a very important activity. Thus, the BC framework must have all of its classes derived from the **CoType** class. The new class hierarchy is shown in Figure 7.2.

The **CoType** class defines the protocol that all subsequent classes honor. This class helps to provide a uniform view of all the classes. For example, the **CoType** class provides virtual **setName()**, **getName()**, and **getCode()** member functions to attach the metadata information for every derived class (the *metadata* is the class that provides, on request, information about itself. It is explained later in the chapter, in the context of components). The **CoType** class declaration is shown in Listing 7.5.

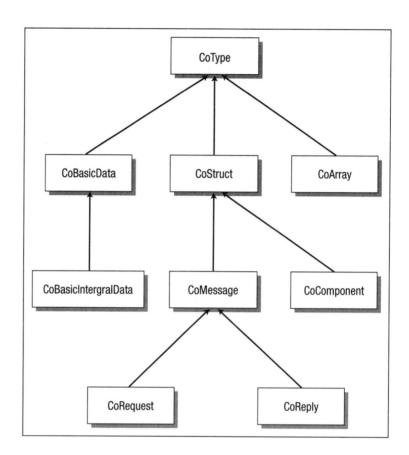

Figure 7.2
Class hierarchy of the BC framework.

Listing 7.5   The CoType class.

```
class CoType
{
    friend class CoStruct;
    template <typename T> friend class CoArray;

protected:

    string _name;

public:

    enum ECode
    {
        CO_UNKNOWN_TYPE, CO_INT_TYPE, CO_UINT_TYPE,
        CO_SHORT_TYPE, CO_USHORT_TYPE, CO_LONG_TYPE,
        CO_ULONG_TYPE, CO_FLOAT_TYPE, CO_DOUBLE_TYPE,
        CO_STRING_TYPE, CO_BOOL_TYPE, CO_CHAR_TYPE,
```

```
        CO_UCHAR_TYPE, CO_STRUCT_TYPE, CO_ARRAY_TYPE,
        CO_REQUEST_TYPE, CO_REPLY_TYPE, CO_COMPONENT_TYPE
    };

    virtual void setName(const string& name);
    virtual const string& getName() const;

    virtual bool isEqual(const CoType& t) const;

    virtual CoType::ECode getCode() const = 0;
    virtual void makeNull()= 0;
    virtual string asString() const;

protected:

    CoType();
    virtual ~CoType();
};
```

The following describes the member functions of the **CoType** class:

♦ **setName()**—Sets a name for an instance of the **CoType**.

♦ **getName()**—Gets a name of an instance of the **CoType**.

♦ **isEqual()**—Determines whether two instances of type **CoType** are of the same value and type at runtime.

♦ **getCode()**—Gets the code of a **CoType**.

♦ **makeNull()**—Makes the value of a **CoType** zero.

♦ **asString()**—Returns values of a **CoType** as a string, which is a very useful function that can be used to debug and log various values in the BC framework. Because this is a pure virtual function, all types in the BC framework will implement it. Hence, given a **CoType** pointer, you can print its value.

Simple Data Types

Listing 7.6 shows a class, **CoBasicData**, that is a template class derived from the **CoType**. Also note that a class, **CO_DATA_MODULE**, is defined, which is a collection of the nested **typedef**s. These **typedef**s serve as portable data types. You can change the **typedef**s on different machines to represent different word sizes. This kind of approach is also taken by CORBA (CORBA concepts are presented in Chapter 8).

Listing 7.6 The CoBasicData class.

```
class CO_DATA_MODULE
{
public:

    typedef int Int;
    typedef unsigned int UInt;
    typedef long Long;
    typedef unsigned long ULong;
    typedef short Short;
    typedef unsigned short UShort;
    typedef char Char;
    typedef unsigned char UChar;
    typedef float Float;
    typedef double Double;
    typedef bool Boolean;
    typedef string string;
};


template <typename T>
class CoBasicData : public CoType
{
protected:

    T _t;

public:

    //user can access raw-data type
    typedef T type;

    inline CoBasicData();
    inline CoBasicData(T val);
    inline CoBasicData(const CoBasicData<T>& val);

    inline CoBasicData<T>&
        operator=(const CoBasicData<T>& rhs);

    inline void operator=(const T& rhs);
    inline operator T() const;
    inline T operator+() const;
    inline T operator-() const;
    inline double operator/(T t);
    inline bool operator!() const;
    inline bool operator==(T t) const;
```

```
    inline bool operator!=(T t) const;
    inline bool operator<(T t) const;
    inline bool operator>(T t) const;

    //...
    //other operators

    inline void makeNull();
    virtual string asString() const;

    virtual CoType::ECode getCode() const
    {
        return CO_UNKNOWN_TYPE;
    }
};

inline CoType::ECode
CoBasicData<CO_DATA_MODULE::Float>::getCode() const
{
    return CO_FLOAT_TYPE;
}

inline CoType::ECode
CoBasicData<CO_DATA_MODULE::Double>::getCode() const
{
    return CO_DOUBLE_TYPE;
}
```

The **CoBasicData** is a class template that represents nonintegral value types (**float** and **double**). The **getCode()** member function is specialized for the types **CO_DATA_MODULE::Double** and **CO_DATA_MODULE::Float**.

Listing 7.7 presents the **CoBasicIntegralData** class that represents integral value types (**int**, **short**, **long**, and so forth).

Listing 7.7 The CoBasicIntegralData class.

```
template <typename T>
class CoBasicIntergralData : public CoBasicData<T>
{
public:

    inline CoBasicIntergralData();
    inline CoBasicIntergralData(T val);
```

```
        inline CoBasicIntergralData
            (const CoBasicIntergralData<T>& val);

        inline CoBasicIntergralData<T>& operator=
            (const CoBasicIntergralData<T>& rhs);

        inline void operator=(const T& rhs);
        inline T operator%(const T& t);
        inline void operator%=(const T& t);

        virtual CoType::ECode getCode() const;
};

inline CoType::ECode
CoBasicIntergralData<CO_DATA_MODULE::Int>::getCode() const
{
    return CO_INT_TYPE;
}

inline CoType::ECode
CoBasicIntergralData<CO_DATA_MODULE::UInt>::getCode() const
{
    return CO_UINT_TYPE;
}

inline CoType::ECode
CoBasicIntergralData<CO_DATA_MODULE::Short>::getCode() const
{
    return CO_SHORT_TYPE;
}

inline CoType::ECode
CoBasicIntergralData<CO_DATA_MODULE::UShort>::getCode()
const
{
    return CO_USHORT_TYPE;
}

inline CoType::ECode
CoBasicIntergralData<CO_DATA_MODULE::Long>::getCode() const
{
    return CO_LONG_TYPE;
}

inline CoType::ECode
```

```
CoBasicIntergralData<CO_DATA_MODULE::ULong>::getCode() const
{
    return CO_ULONG_TYPE;
}

inline CoType::ECode
CoBasicIntergralData<CO_DATA_MODULE::Boolean>::getCode()
const
{
    return CO_BOOL_TYPE;
}

inline CoType::ECode
CoBasicIntergralData<CO_DATA_MODULE::Char>::getCode() const
{
    return CO_CHAR_TYPE;
}

inline CoType::ECode
CoBasicIntergralData<CO_DATA_MODULE::UChar>::getCode() const
{
    return CO_UCHAR_TYPE;
}
```

CoBasicIntergralData is a class template that is derived from **Co-BasicData**. The **getCode()** member function is specialized for the types **CO_DATA_MODULE::Int, CO_DATA_MODULE::Long,** and so forth. The **CoBasicIntergralData** class provides the following additional functions:

```
inline T operator%(const T& t);
inline void operator%=(const T& t);
```

Listing 7.8 presents the **CoString** class that is derived from the standard **string** class, and the root **CoType** type.

Listing 7.8   The CoString class.

```
class CoString : public CoType, public string
{
    friend inline ostream& operator<<(
        ostream &os, const CoString& s);

public:

    typedef string type;
```

```
    inline CoString();
    inline CoString(const char* val);
    inline CoString(const string& val);
    inline CoString(const CoString& val);

    inline CoString& operator=(const char* s);
    inline CoString& operator=(const string& s);
    inline CoString& operator=(const CoString& s);

    void makeNull();
    inline CoType::ECode getCode() const;
};

inline CoType::ECode CoString::getCode() const
{
    return CO_STRING_TYPE;
}
```

As you can see in the preceding code, the **CoString** class is derived multiple times from the **CoType** and **string** classes.

Basic Types' Typedefs

The following **typedefs** are provided to the BC framework user, to make using the data types easier:

```
typedef
CoBasicData<CO_DATA_MODULE::Float> CoFloat;

typedef
CoBasicData<CO_DATA_MODULE::Double> CoDouble;

typedef
CoBasicIntergralData<CO_DATA_MODULE::Int> CoInt;

typedef
CoBasicIntergralData<CO_DATA_MODULE::UInt> CoUInt;

typedef
CoBasicIntergralData<CO_DATA_MODULE::Short> CoShort;

typedef
CoBasicIntergralData<CO_DATA_MODULE::UShort> CoUShort;

typedef
CoBasicIntergralData<CO_DATA_MODULE::Long> CoLong;
```

```
typedef
CoBasicIntergralData<CO_DATA_MODULE::ULong> CoULong;

typedef
CoBasicIntergralData<CO_DATA_MODULE::Char> CoChar;

typedef
CoBasicIntergralData<CO_DATA_MODULE::Boolean> CoBoolean;
```

User-Defined Types (UDT)

The classes presented in the preceding list are just the basic types. Although the constructed types can be used to construct UDTs, such as structures and arrays, they will not be part of the **CoType**'s hierarchy. Therefore, UDTs need to be represented using **CoType**, which is done by the **CoStruct** and **CoArray** classes.

The *CoStruct* Type

The **CoStruct** class must be able to assemble simple and composite objects in a tree form, and provide a uniform interface to operate on the objects. This means the **CoStruct** must implement the Composite design pattern, which is described and implemented in Chapter 5. Listing 7.9 presents the declarations of the **CoStruct** class.

Listing 7.9   The CoStruct class.

```
typedef CO_DATA_MODULE::Long CoDataStatus;
class CoStruct : public CoType
{
private:

    typedef vector<CoType*> CO_STRUCT_VECTOR;
    CO_STRUCT_VECTOR _vector;
    CoLong _dataStatus;

public:

    virtual void registerMembers() = 0;
    inline size_t size() const;

    inline const CoLong& getStatus() const;
    inline void setStatus(const CoLong& dataStatus);

    inline CoType::ECode getCode() const;

    virtual void makeNull();
```

```
        virtual string asString() const;

    protected:

        inline CoStruct();

        inline void registerAttribute(const string& name,
            CoType* pt);

        inline void registerAttribute(CoType* pt);

    private:

        //not to be implemented
        CoStruct(const CoStruct& s);

        //not to be implemented
        CoStruct& operator=(const CoStruct&);

        //not to be implemented
        bool operator==(const CoStruct&);
    };
```

The following list describes some of the member functions of the **CoStruct** class (some member functions of the **CoStruct** class are intuitive and self-descriptive, and thus, aren't described here):

♦ **registerAttribute()**—Registers an element of type **CoType*** with the **CoStruct** instance. The element can be either a basic type, a **CoString** type, or another **CoStruct** value. This enables you to form a tree of values. The function is overloaded, so you can register an element either with or without a name.

♦ **registerMembers()**—A pure virtual function that you will override. In the implementation, you call the function **registerAttribute()** for all the data members of the structure.

Note that **CoStruct** also implements the **CoType::asString()** pure virtual function. Obviously, the **CoStruct::asString()** function recursively calls the **asString()** function on each of its registered attributes.

The **CoStruct** class has a data member, **_dataStatus**. This variable can be used to represent some business status of the derived structure from **CoStruct**, which is done via the member functions **getStatus()** and **setStatus()**.

The *CoArray* Type

Whereas the **CoStruct** class can be used to create a collection of different types, the **CoArray** type is used to represent a collection of the same type. Listing 7.10 gives the declaration of the **CoArray** class.

Listing 7.10   The CoArray class.

```
template <typename T>
class CoArray : public CoType
{
private:

    vector<T> _vector;

public:

    inline CoArray();
    inline CoArray(const CoArray<T>& va);

    inline CoArray<T>& operator= (const CoArray<T>& va);
    inline T& operator[](size_t n);
    inline const T& operator[](size_t n) const;
    inline size_t size() const;
    inline void clear();
    inline void add(const T& t);
    inline virtual void makeNull();
    virtual string asString() const;
    inline CoType::ECode getCode() const;

private:

    //not to be implemented
    bool operator==(const CoArray<T>&);
};
```

The member function of the **CoArray** class is intuitive and self-descriptive. Hence, no description is provided here.

Reimplementing CoRequest And CoReply

Listing 7.11 shows the redeclarations of the **CoMessage**, **CoRequest**, and **CoReply** classes. These classes are more or less the same as previous declarations except that the **getCode()** function is added in each class, and the base **CoMessage** class is derived from the **CoStruct** class. As a result of the derivation from the **CoStruct** class, the **CoRequest**

Architecture Vs. Implementation

Designing software is an important activity in the lifecycle of software development. However, after you finish this activity and produce the architecture, you aren't necessarily finished with the design process, because the implementation activity can influence the architecture of the framework. For example, implementation of root data types, such as **CoType** and **CoStruct**, can make the redesign of these classes necessary. Such changes are possible in the entire class hierarchy, which means that you need to be ready to redesign and reimplement certain components of the framework during its implementation phase. This also means that if parallel development activities of a framework and user application are occurring, users are likely to face many problems including compilation errors, inconsistent binaries, and incorrect results.

---

and **CoReply** classes are able to carry any complex data types in a uniform way. This uniformity helps in logging the messages. Logging is shown in Listing 7.12.

Listing 7.11   Redeclarations of the CoMessage, CoRequest, and CoReply classes.

```cpp
#include <co_complex_data_types.hpp>

class CoMessage : public CoStruct
{
public:
    inline CoMessage(){}
    inline virtual ~CoMessage(){}
};

class CoReply : public CoMessage
{
public:
    inline CoReply()
    {
    }
    inline ~CoReply(){}

    virtual CoType::ECode getCode() const;
};

class CoRequest : public CoMessage
{
private:

    CoString target_;

public:
```

```
inline CoRequest()
{
}
inline ~CoRequest(){}

void sendAndReceive(const string& target,
    CoReply*& reply);

    virtual CoType::ECode getCode() const;
};
```

In the **CoRequest** class, the **getName()** function declaration is not needed because the function declaration is available in the base **CoType** class.

Reimplementing CoComponent

The following is the new declaration of the **CoComponent** class:

```
#include <co_message.hpp>
#include <co_component_mgr.hpp>

class CoComponent;
typedef void (CoComponent::*CO_COMPONENT_FUNCTION)();

class CoComponent : public CoStruct
{
    friend class CoComponentManager;

private:

    map<string, CO_COMPONENT_FUNCTION> functionMap_;
    CoRequest* currentRequest_;
    CoReply* currentReply_;

public:

    void getServices(vector<string>& services) const;
    virtual CoType::ECode getCode() const;

protected:

    CoComponent();
    inline void registerService(const string& name,
        CO_COMPONENT_FUNCTION compFun);
```

```
    inline void setReply(CoReply* reply);
    inline CoRequest* getRequest();

private:

    virtual void registerServices()=0;
};
```

The **CoComponent** class is derived from the **CoStruct** class. In addition, the **CoComponent** class provides one supplementary **getServices()** member function, which returns the list of services that a component supports in an attempt to make the **CoComponent** type a metatype. Using the **getServices()** member function, you can query a BC's capabilities at runtime. A BC's capabilities are represented by the set of services it supports. Two similar functions are also provided in the **CoComponentManager** class, which is described in the following section.

Reimplementing CoComponentManager

Listing 7.12 presents the modified declaration of the **Co-ComponentManager** class.

Listing 7.12   Redeclaration of the CoComponentManager class.

```
typedef CoComponent* (*CO_COMP_SELF_REF)();

class CoComponentManager
{
    friend class CoRequest;

private:

    map<string, CO_COMP_SELF_REF> componentMap_;
    inline static CoComponentManager& getManager();

    CoComponentManager(){};
    void sendMessage(const string& target,
        CoRequest* request, CoReply*& reply);

public:

    inline static void registerComponent(const string& name,
        CO_COMP_SELF_REF comp);
```

```
        void getComponents(vector<string>& components) const;

        void getServices(const string& component,
            vector<string>& services) const;
};

void CoComponentManager::sendMessage(const string& target,
    CoRequest* request, CoReply*& reply)
{
    CoComponent* pc=(componentMap_[target])();
    pc->registerServices();

    pc->currentRequest_=request;

    cout<<"Incoming request:"<<request->asString()<<endl;
    cout<<"Target:"<<target<<endl;
    cout<<"Component data before invocation:"<<
        pc->asString()<<endl;

    CO_COMPONENT_FUNCTION pf=
        pc->functionMap_[request->getName()];

    (pc->*pf)();

    cout<<"Component data after invocation:"<<
        pc->asString()<<endl;

    reply=pc->currentReply_;

    cout<<"Outgoing reply:"<<reply->asString()<<endl;

    delete pc;
}
```

The **CoComponentManager** class redefines the **sendMessage()** member function. The new **sendMessage()** function uses the **asString()** function in four places to print logging/debugging information (as shown in the highlighted code in listing 7.12).

The **CoComponentManager** class provides two additional functions:

♦ **getComponents()**—Provides a list of the components that the singleton instance of the **CoComponentManager** class supports.

♦ **getServices()**—Provides a list of the services that a particular component registered with the instance of the **CoComponentManager** class supports.

Simplifying The Framework By Using Templates

Generic types provide a technique for reusing functionality of code through parameters. C++ supports the generic-programming-by-template feature. Templates are discussed in detail in Chapter 2. *Templates* (also called *generic* or *parameterized types*) are used to construct a family of related functions or classes. A C++ template is roughly a form of reusability, because after a template function or class is developed, it doesn't need to be modified again, but can nevertheless be used to meet various design or program requirements.

A framework may contain *ready-to-use* generic algorithms and classes, in the form of templates that can easily be reused in various combinations without any performance loss. By using class templates, you can instantiate whatever type-safe types you need. Templates can be used as a mechanism to customize a framework, which is shown in this section. Templates don't impose any runtime overheads, because no derivation occurs and no virtual functions are involved.

A previous section, "How To Define A Component," mentioned that a component developer must provide a static **self()** member function which creates the component on the heap (free storage), as follows:

```
static CoComponent* self()
{
    return new account;
}
```

Imposing such a requirement on the framework user is perfectly acceptable, because every framework defines certain rules and constraints under which it can be used. However, recall that one of the architectural guidelines for a framework is the ease of use; if you can minimize user interactions with the framework somehow, you will add value for the framework user.

CoFactory is a class that simplifies the code that the user has to write for the **self()** function:

```
#include <string>
#include <co_component_mgr.hpp>

template <typename T>
class CoFactory
```

```
{
public:
    inline CoFactory(const string& name);
    inline static CoComponent* create();
};

template <typename T>
inline CoFactory<T>::CoFactory(const string& name)
{
    CoComponentManager::registerComponent(
        name, CoFactory<T>::create);
}

template <typename T>
inline CoComponent* CoFactory<T>::create()
{
    return new T;
}
```

The **CoFactory** class is a class template that has a static member function **create()** that creates an instance of the **T** type on the heap. The constructor of the **CoFactory** registers this pointer with the **CoComponentManager** instance, even if you create a temporary instance of the **CoFactory** class. An example is shown in Listing 7.13.

The Framework Usage Example (Redeveloped)

Listing 7.13 redevelops the set of examples presented in the section "Using The BC Framework." Listing 7.13 shows how to use the reimplemented classes that were shown in the preceding sections.

Listing 7.13   An example of using the BC framework.

```
#include <co_component.hpp>
#include <co_factory.hpp>

class openAccount : public CoRequest
{
public:

    CoLong accountNum_;
    CoDouble money_;
    CoString name_;
```

```
        openAccount()
        {
            registerMembers();
            setName("openAccount");
        }
        openAccount(const openAccount& other)
        {
            accountNum_=other.accountNum_;
            money_=other.money_;
            name_=other.name_;
            registerMembers();
        }
        openAccount& operator=(const openAccount& other)
        {
            accountNum_=other.accountNum_;
            money_=other.money_;
            name_=other.name_;
            return *this;
        }

private:

        void registerMembers()
        {
            registerAttribute("accountNum_", &accountNum_);
            registerAttribute("money_", &money_);
            registerAttribute("name_", &name_);
        }
};

class balanceInfo : public CoReply
{
public:

        CoDouble balance_;

        balanceInfo()
        {
            registerMembers();
            setName("balanceInfo");
        }
        balanceInfo(const balanceInfo& other)
        {
            balance_=other.balance_;
            registerMembers();
        }
```

```
    balanceInfo& operator=(const balanceInfo& r)
    {
        balance_=r.balance_;
        return *this;
    }

private:

    void registerMembers()
    {
        registerAttribute("balance_", &balance_);
    }
};

class account : public CoComponent
{
public:

    account()
    {
    }

private:

    void open()
    {
        cout<<"open():"<<getRequest()->asString()<<endl;

        openAccount* request=
            dynamic_cast<openAccount*>(getRequest());

        balanceInfo* reply=new balanceInfo;
        reply->balance_=50.1234;

        reply->setStatus(12345);

        setReply(reply);
    }

    void registerServices()
    {
        registerService("openAccount",
            CO_COMPONENT_FUNCTION(&account::open));
    }

    void registerMembers()
```

```
    {
    }
};

class model
{
public:
    model()
    {
        CoFactory<account>("account");
    }
};

int main()
{
    model model_;
    openAccount r;

    r.accountNum_=1234;
    r.money_=13.145;
    r.name_="vishwa";

    CoReply* reply;
    r.sendAndReceive("account", reply);

    balanceInfo* rep=dynamic_cast<balanceInfo*>(reply);

    cout<<reply->asString()<<endl;

    delete reply;
}
```

Listing 7.13 is similar to the examples provided in the section "Using The BC Framework." However, the differences between the examples are shown by the highlighted statements. Listing 7.13 uses the **asString()** function to display the contents of the request and reply. Recall that **asString()** is a pure virtual function of the **CoType** class, and all types in the BC framework implement the **asString()** function.

Note that Listing 7.13 doesn't give examples of using the **CoStruct** and **CoArray** types; Chapter 14 covers them.

Simplify The User Interactions With Macros

Macros can be very handy in simplifying user interactions with a framework. For example, a construct such as

```
CoFactory<account>("account");
```

can be replaced by a simple macro call

```
CO_REGISTER_COMPONENT(account);
```

where the macro **CO_REGISTER_COMPONENT()** is defined as follows:

```
#define CO_REGISTER_COMPONENT(component)
CoFactory<component>(#component);
```

The **CO_REGISTER_COMPONENT()** macro relieves the BC framework user from having to pass the component name to the **CoFactory** instance.

Clearly, the combination of the **CoFactory** class template and the **CO_REGISTER_COMPONENT()** macro is much better than having a **self()** function in each component and using that to register with the **CoComponentManager** instance.

Exception Handling Model

A service of a BC may need to throw an exception when something goes wrong. However, the implementation of the BC framework presented so far doesn't suggest how business exceptions can be added to a component. One way to implement this would be to define a class **CoException** deriving from the **CoStruct** class. Derived objects from this class can be thrown from any service of a BC. This ensures the *exception protocol*; in other words, all the services of a component will be able to throw derived objects from a generic exception class.

You may have noticed that the BC framework code presented so far neither throws any exceptions nor does much to ensure robustness. For example, various functions of the BC framework don't check for null pointers and other potential failure cases, such as when the **CoComponentManager::sendMessage()** function uses the **componentMap_** data member (of type **map**)—no check occurs to determine whether the map contains data for the requested key.

Obviously, if such checks are implemented, you need to log the error and indicate the failure to the caller. This can be done via an exception-handling mechanism, which means that you have to define exception specifications for various member functions of the BC framework. Alternatively, you can choose to use the **CoException** class in the entire framework code, which maintains uniformity in the exception specifications of various functions within the BC framework.

Having exception specifications for functions is always advantageous, because it ensures robustness of the framework. An even bigger advantage of using uniform exception specifications for functions is that you can log the exceptions generically, and handle the exceptions without having a big sequence of **catch** blocks. You get all the advantages of having hierarchical exceptions (refer to Chapter 1 for information about hierarchical exceptions and exception specifications).

Chapter Recap

Developing a framework differs from developing a standalone application. This chapter has presented several framework development concepts. Development of a framework requires multiple design iterations to make it reusable. Design elements of special importance in the development of a framework are abstract classes, hot hooks, and design patterns.

The chapter has also described the following steps to develop a framework:

1. *Identify the need and opportunity of the framework to be developed.* A programmer reuses a framework to get the capability of solving a particular problem without having to develop the solution independently. You often can identify opportunities for new frameworks by analyzing existing solutions. To determine what frameworks you need, think in terms of families of applications rather than individual programs.

2. *Identify the primary abstractions.* The use of abstract classes is a good way to achieve reusability, proper use of inheritance, and utilization of dynamic binding. All of those aspects are relevant to the architecture of an object-oriented framework. A framework doesn't need a separate methodology to identify abstractions in the problem domain. You can apply existing methodologies (such as Booch, Fusion, and so forth) to achieve the same result.

3. *Identify the hot hooks.* Hot hooks are a framework's common protocol, enabling you to develop the application's components. Hot hooks formalize these collaborations and behavioral relationships.

Identification of hot hooks is the most significant activity in developing a framework, and the actual development of the framework can start only after the initial hot hooks are identified.

4. *Define the architecture by applying recurring design patterns.* Defining the framework architecture is an activity that involves designing components that can be reused in the development of applications.

5. *Implement the framework.* Implementation of a framework involves implementation of the design patterns and frozen hooks of the framework. A frozen hook is a function that consists of a series of hot hooks. A good understanding of dynamic binding helps in the implementation of the framework.

6. *Test the framework.* Develop a few applications based on the framework. This is the testing activity of the framework. Capture any problems that occur when using the framework to develop the applications, and then refine the framework.

7. *Repeat Steps 3 to 6.* Repeat several times until the framework reaches an acceptable maturity level.

8. *Prepare framework documentation.* Documentation includes diagrams, recipes, and sample programs.

This chapter has presented the implementation of the horizontal framework (business component framework) presented in Chapter 6. For information about the issue of framework documentation, see Chapter 14. The notion of metadata is covered in Chapter 13.

Chapter 8
CORBA Concepts

The Common Object Request Broker Architecture (CORBA) is a mechanism to create, deploy, and manage objects in a distributed environment. These objects are generally referred to as *distributed components* or CORBA *components*. This chapter introduces you to the fundamental concepts of CORBA. It also introduces the Object Management Group (OMG), the organization that is responsible for defining the *Object Management Architecture* (OMA), the key to creating distributed components. This chapter presents various features of OMA. It also presents a section on the *Interface Definition Language* (IDL), which enables you to create specifications for a component. You can encapsulate application data and business logic within a component that can be instantiated and used in a distributed environment.

In addition to providing the capability to write application components, OMA provides several CORBA services and facilities to handle components at runtime, enabling you to do such tasks as locate a component, manage its life cycle, and so forth. This chapter discusses these services and facilities briefly; however, Chapters 12 and 13 present them in depth, because they are critical to creating component frameworks. Furthermore, this chapter doesn't focus on the development of CORBA components, which is covered in Chapter 9.

Why To Choose CORBA

Today, the business world is driven by information—perhaps the most important asset of any organization. Information must be accurate and it must be accessible across offices, departments, and organizations, whether an organization is in one building or dispersed globally. This means that an organization's computing infrastructure must be closely linked to a *common network* and must be capable of information transmission and reception. As a result, an organization may have a large computing infrastructure that consists of many operating systems (OSs) and a variety of underlying networks and protocols connecting those operating systems.

Theoretically, the different blends of operating systems and networking schemes that are available should enable an organization to deploy the best hardware/software combination for its needs with relative ease. In reality, however, this isn't an easy task. Defining and applying the right standards for interoperability and portability necessary to deal with the information requirements of an organization can be a complex and difficult task. The time and money needed to develop, integrate, deploy, maintain, enhance, and configure the software components in a distributed environment can be costly.

To address such problems, a mechanism is needed that can broadly provide the following features:

♦ *Platform independence*—Distributed components can be developed and deployed on any supported platform.

♦ *Language independence*—Distributed components and clients can be implemented in any programming language. A client can communicate with other components irrespective of the language that is used to implement them. A *client* of a component is a program that uses the component's services. The program that contains component instances is called a *server*. A component's service corresponds to one of the component's member functions. In CORBA, a component's member function is also referred to as an *operation*.

♦ *Contracts between components*—A standard mechanism to define contracts between components and translate the contracts into an implementation, using any supported language.

♦ *Standard services*—A standard set of services, such as event services and transaction services, so that developers can focus on application development.

♦ *Component interaction*—A standard mechanism that enables various components to communicate with each other regardless of the underlying networking protocols.

CORBA, as defined by OMG, provides all of these features. You learn how CORBA supports these features later in the chapter, as well as in Chapters 9 and 12. The next section provides a brief introduction to OMG.

Object Management Group (OMG)

To address the problems of distributed components, the Object Management Group was formed in 1989. As a result, OMG provided a new paradigm of computing—*distributed computing with CORBA*. OMG's ongoing objective is to help reduce complexity, lower costs, and accelerate the deployment of new software applications in a distributed software system. OMG is an 800-plus member consortium that develops the CORBA standards and specifications. Its headquarters are in Framingham, Massachusetts, and it has marketing offices in Frankfurt, Germany; Tokyo, Japan; and Hounslow, England. Unlike the Open Software Foundation (OSF), OMG does not develop software—OMG only defines an *architectural framework* with supporting object-oriented (OO) interfaces. OMG's standards and specifications are created by using ideas and technology solicited from OMG members, who respond to Requests For Information (RFI) and Requests For Proposals (RFP) issued by OMG.

What Is A CORBA Component?

The OMG-specified architecture is appropriate for defining, developing, and deploying flexible, distributed systems. OMG makes it possible to encapsulate application data and the business logic within objects that can be used in a distributed environment. These objects are generally referred to as *distributed components*. The term *component* means different things to different people, but in this book, the term *CORBA component* refers to a distributed CORBA object. A component represents a significant portion of an overall application system, yet is small enough to enable efficient and flexible assembly with other components to form full-fledged applications. Interaction among components is referred to as *component collaboration*.

The principle of "divide and conquer" can be applied to designing component-based applications. Applying this principle is similar to applying OO techniques. The primary objective of the CORBA-based application designer is to partition the application into a set of interconnectable collaborative components. Each component implements important aspects of a complete application. OO can help partition a complex application system into smaller, simpler components.

Component Interface

Access to a particular component's application capabilities is mediated by the *remotable interface* that the component supports. A component interface represents a potential point of integration and interoperation between a component and its client. A program that uses a component's implementation is referred to as its *client*. The component interface "hides" the underlying implementation from its client. Clients can be developed independently of an implementation. A component that implements a particular behavior represents its capabilities via its interface. For example, an **Account** component supports the interface that allows operations such as **withdraw_money()** and **deposit_money()** to be performed. In other words, a component's application behavior is exposed to its client through the interface. In the CORBA architecture, a *component interface* is a set of semantically related operations that a component's client can use to access the component's capabilities. The component interface is described in detail in the "Interface Definition Language (IDL)" section later in this chapter.

Expressing Interactions Among Components

The following list describes the five key concepts regarding the interaction of components:

- *Interoperable object reference (IOR)*—The basis of all communication between components in CORBA. Accessibility of a component is provided through its IOR, which a client must first obtain to access a component's services. The client uses the IOR to invoke operations on the component. An IOR is analogous to a C++ pointer that reliably denotes a component in a distributed environment. A component may be denoted by multiple, distinct IORs.

- *Request*—Used by a client to make a request for services on an IOR, resulting in an operation call on the target component.

- *Operation*—An identifiable entity that denotes a component service that can be requested by a client. An operation is just like a C++ member function in a class. Optionally, an operation can specify its exception specification that may be raised by the corresponding implementation in the component.

- *Client*—An application that uses the services of a CORBA component; that is, an application that invokes operations on other components by using the component's IOR. Because the client isn't

Elements Of An IOR

An IOR encapsulates the following elements:

◆ *Hostname*—The name of the host on which the server is running. If you run the server on a new host, the previously published IOR of a component gets invalidated.

◆ *Port number*—The port number on which the server listens for incoming requests. If you rerun a server, the previously published IOR may become invalid.

◆ *Object key*—A unique key for a particular instance of a component.

If any of these elements change and you attempt to use a published IOR, you will get an exception stating that you have attempted to use an invalid object reference.

aware of a component's implementation details, the component's implementation changes are transparent to the client.

◆ *Server*—An application that creates CORBA components, publishes the IORs of the components, and provides services to clients. A server has a component implementation that provides the definitions of the data and services. A variety of component implementations can be supported. Figure 8.1 shows a component receiving a request through an IOR.

Why Componentization Is So Significant

Mapping abstractions and real-world entities into a CORBA component is referred to as *componentization*. Like a classical C++ object, a CORBA component is a reusable entity, through inheritance, encapsulation, and polymorphism. However, unlike a classical C++ object, a CORBA component is capable of efficiently communicating with other components across networks, operating systems, and languages. Figure 8.2 shows a typical component interaction. Four different components, written in different languages and running on different platforms, are collaborating by using CORBA.

The following properties explain why CORBA components are much smarter than classical C++ objects, and why a component-based application development approach is so effective:

◆ *Independent development*—Components can be developed independently of other components. Interfaces between components define the contract between them that enables independent development (as long as the contracts are respected).

Figure 8.1
A component receiving a request.

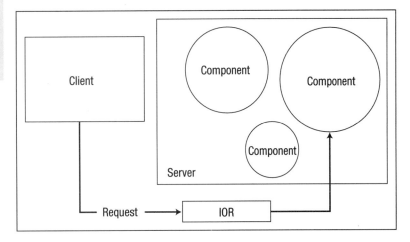

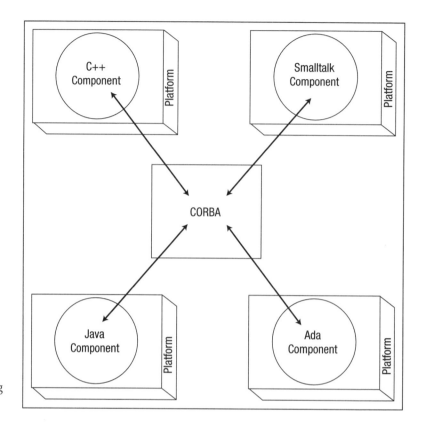

Figure 8.2
Components collaborating
by using CORBA.

- *Independent business entity*—The componentization approach is to partition a complex application system into smaller, simpler pieces that are self-contained business entities.

- *Packagable*—Components can be packaged in a variety of ways, which provides great flexibility for deployment. (This is discussed in depth in Chapters 9 and 13).

- *Buildable*—A variety of tools, technologies, and design methods can be employed to design and implement components.

- *Rapid development*—Application developers can focus on rapidly developing and deploying the business functionality, while remaining transparent to the underlying infrastructure. Components can be used in unpredictable combinations to form applications.

- *Extensible*—New components with new capabilities can be added to an existing system in a modular and organized manner.

- *Configurable*—Different implementations of the same logical component can be readily interchanged at runtime, enabling you to provide the capabilities that you need without redesigning applications.

♦ *Scalable*—Components can be physically distributed or alternatively located on a single machine, depending on the system load and computing infrastructure.

♦ *Flexible*—Components can communicate with other components across networks, operating systems, and languages.

♦ *Extended objects*—A component may support many properties, such as transactions, persistence, security, events, and so forth.

The preceding list highlights the many benefits provided through componentization, the essential element for developing, integrating, and deploying true distributed applications. Componentization not only saves time and money in performing these tasks, it also reduces the complexity associated with maintaining, enhancing, and configuring a typical distributed environment.

Object Management Architecture (OMA)

To develop, integrate, and deploy components as described in the previous section, a mechanism is required that can both define the semantics for externally visible characteristics of components and characterize interactions between components. Fortunately, the OMG Object Management Architecture defines various elements that are necessary for component-based distributed computing.

The following two concepts constitute OMA:

♦ The object model

♦ The reference model

The Object Model

The OMG object model is much like a classical object model, in which a client interacts with a component, and the component provides services to the client. The object model describes a component's behavior. The object model also makes transparent to clients the representation of a component's internal data and the implementation of its behavior. The following are two core elements of the OMA object model:

♦ *Object semantics*—Defines or characterizes components to help distinguish one component from other components. Object semantics represents the "outside view" of a component, defining it as an identifiable, encapsulated entity that provides one or more services that can be requested by a client through its interface. In short, object semantics is used to specify three characteristics of a component—its type, the set of services that it supports, and its data representation. Object semantics also specifies a component's life cycle—components can be created and destroyed as an outcome of their clients' requests.

♦ *Object implementation*—The "inside view" of a component, which gives a mechanism to define a component's state and services. When a client issues a request on a component, a member funciton of the target component is called. The execution of a service is called a *method activation*.

The Reference Model

The reference model characterizes interactions between distributed components, as opposed to the object model, which defines common semantics to characterize components. The reference model consists of four major elements:

♦ *Object Request Broker (ORB)*—Defines the middleware to carry out component collaboration in a distributed environment. ORB is also referred to as an *object-bus*.

♦ *Object services*—Defines domain-independent horizontal interfaces that are used in distributed applications.

♦ *Common facility*—Defines horizontal and vertical interfaces that are used in most distributed applications.

♦ *Application objects*—The business objects that are used to form applications.

ORB

ORB enables clients to communicate with a remote component in a distributed environment. In other words, ORB provides transparency of a component's location, activation, communication, and implementation. Thus, ORB is essential for building and packaging distributed components. ORB sometimes is referred to as an *object-bus*, because it carries a client's requests to the target components. ORB encapsulates some aspects of the underlying OS and the networking layer.

Marshaling And Unmarshaling

Marshaling is the process in which the input and output parameters of an operation are mapped into a platform-independent format that can be transmitted over a network. *Unmarshaling* is the process in which the marshaled parameters are converted back to the actual parameters. Because ORB takes care of marshaling and unmarshaling of data between components, the communication between components is automatically platform-independent. For example, you can run a client on an NT platform and invoke an operation on a server running on an HP-UX system. This means that ORB not only provides OS-independence, but it also takes care of differences in hardware, word size, and so on.

Whereas the marshaling process converts data into a platform-independent format (as per the CORBA specification), the unmarshaling process converts the received format into a *platform-specific* format.

You don't have to write any extra code to make the entire marshaling/unmarshaling process happen. Your client application simply invokes the remote method on a target component and, in return, receives either the requested results or an exception, whichever the case may be.

Another important service provided by ORB is the marshaling and unmarshaling of parameters and return values to and from remote method invocations.

The use of ORB provides platform independence to distributed CORBA components. The specifications to interface with ORB are defined in CORBA.

ORB is one of the cornerstones of CORBA. ORB must run on both the client side and the server side. The ORB process on the client side is referred to as *client-ORB*, and the ORB process on the server side is referred to as *server-ORB*. The following summarizes the purpose of ORB and the responsibilities that it carries out automatically and transparently:

1. Client-ORB locates a component implementation on behalf of the client, when given an IOR by the client. A component can be located in a number of ways; this is demonstrated in Chapters 9 and 12.

2. When the server is located, server-ORB prepares the server to receive the request. For example, server-ORB can launch the server if it is not running.

3. Client-ORB accepts the input parameters from the client and marshals the parameters.

4. Server-ORB unmarshals the input parameters.

CORBA's IDL specification provides langauge and OS platform independence. An IDL data type's language mapping depends on the language and the OS platform. For example, the IDL **long** type is a 32-bit integral type that maps to **long** in C++ on HP-UX, and **int** in Java.

5. Server-ORB invokes the requested operation on the target component.

6. Server-ORB marshals the return parameters or exception.

7. Client-ORB unmarshals the return parameters or exception.

The following section shows how ORB makes component collaboration possible in a distributed environment.

Interface Definition Language (IDL)

An important part of CORBA is its use of the *Interface Definition Language*, which specifies interfaces between CORBA components. IDL facilitates CORBA's language independence—because interfaces described in IDL can be mapped to any supported programming language, CORBA applications are independent of the language(s) used to implement them. For example, a client written in C++ can communicate with a server written in Java, which in turn can communicate with another server written in Smalltalk, and so forth. IDL isn't an implementation language—you can't write applications in IDL. The sole purpose of IDL is to define interfaces that you can implement using a programming language.

A component that needs to provide remote services must specify its interface in an IDL. Recall that an interface consists of a set of operations, and that access to a particular component's services is provided by the interface that the component supports. Actually, IDL defines a component's object model as defined by OMG. IDL also makes transparent to clients the representation of a component's internal data and the implementation of its behavior.

Figure 8.3 shows that IDL and ORB, together, make component collaboration possible in a distributed environment.

OMG IDL obeys the same lexical rules as C++; it provides basic data types (such as **short**, **long**, **float**, **double**, and **boolean**) and user-defined types (such as **struct**, **union**, and **sequence**). These are used in operation declarations to define arguments' types and return types.

IDL And OO

IDL reinforces OO. IDLs focus on interfaces rather than implementation details. Because an IDL defines an interface and a component's functionality is encapsulated within component implementations, a client of the component gets a black-box view of the component. Thus, IDL reinforces the notions of encapsulation, one of the core elements of OO. IDL also supports the notion of reuse, which is covered in the "How Does CORBA Support Reusability" section later in this chapter.

NOTE

CORBA Client And Server

In CORBA, a component can act both as a client and a server. A component is always a *server*, because it provides an implementation to an IDL specification. However, you call a component a *client* if it makes remote calls to another component. At runtime, a component is referred to as either a server or a client, depending on whether it is providing services or accessing services, respectively.

The following example creates the specification for the **Account** component by using the IDL syntax:

```
module CoBank
{
    interface Account
    {
        void deposit(in double money);
        boolean withdraw(in double money);
    };
};
```

In this example, an **Account** interface has been declared within the module **CoBank**. The module provides a sort of namespace for different interfaces. The **Account** interface has two operations: **deposit()** and **withdraw()**.

If an **Account** component that implements these operations is registered with ORB, it can be remotely accessed by any client through these operations. ORB provides a function for registering a component; this is demonstrated in Chapter 9.

Like a C++ class, an interface can be derived from another interface, which is then called a *base* interface of the derived interface. A derived interface, like all interfaces, may declare new elements (constants, types, attributes, exceptions, and operations), for example:

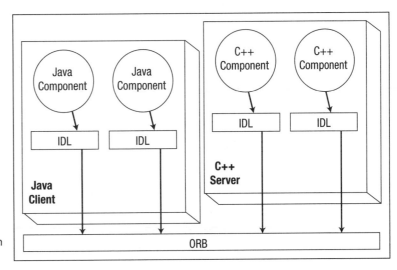

Figure 8.3
IDL and ORB performing component collaboration in a distributed environment.

```
module CoBank
{
    interface Account
    {
        void deposit(in double money);
        boolean withdraw(in double money);
    };

    interface CurrentAccount : Account
    {
        readonly attribute double overdraft_limit;
    };
};
```

Interface derivation is an important feature of OMG IDL interfaces, because it enables you to reuse existing interfaces when defining new services. For example, a **CurrentAccount** component can be used anywhere that an **Account** component is expected, because a **CurrentAccount** supports all **Account** operations. The new capabilities of a **CurrentAccount** component thus can be added to the system without requiring changes to the existing applications that use the **Account** interface. This example shows the polymorphic nature of interfaces, which plays an important role in developing OO applications using CORBA. Also, because CORBA IDL is just a declarative language, the separation of interface and implementation is automatically imposed—and that is a good thing. Another good thing about IDL is that it supports only *interface* inheritance, not *implementation* inheritance. By inheriting a base interface, a component of a derived interface promises to support that interface. The new component, however, can alter the implementation by using the C++ mechanism of overriding virtual functions.

IDL language-mapping standards determine how OMG IDL features are mapped to a specific programming language. OMG has standardized many language mappings, including C, C++, Smalltalk, Java, and Ada 95. C++ maps very naturally to IDL, for example:

♦ Modules map to C++ namespaces (or to nested classes for C++ compilers that don't yet support namespaces)

♦ OMG IDL interfaces map to C++ classes

♦ Operations map to member functions of those classes

♦ All operations are effectively **virtual**

Because mapping of OMG IDL to C++ is a standard, it should be the same for all CORBA implementations. An IDL compiler that is provided with CORBA products supports this requirement. An IDL compiler (described in the next section) is basically a code-generator that maps an IDL into a few source code files of the programming language of your choice.

An IDL compiler typically generates the following C++ mapping for the **CoBank** module and the **Account** interface:

```
Class CoBank
{
public:
    class Account: public virtual CORBA::Object
    {
    public:
        Account ();
        virtual void deposit (CORBA::Double money) = 0;
        virtual CORBA::Boolean
            withdraw (CORBA::Double money) =0;
    };
}
```

You must derive an implementation class from the **CoBank::Account** class to implement virtual member functions. The new class can be given any name (**CoBank_AccountImpl**, for example). The **CoBank_AccountImpl** class is actually called a *component implementation* for the **CoBank::Account** interface. You can create many different component implementations for the **CoBank::Account** interface.

Note that the C++ mapping shown in the previous example is only an approximate mapping. Chapter 9 provides a more detailed discussion on IDL and IDL-to-C++ mapping.

Now that you know about IDL, you are ready to focus on the anatomy of ORB, as represented in Figure 8.4.

Stubs And Skeletons

As mentioned in the previous section, after you define an IDL in a file, you use a CORBA-compliant IDL compiler to compile it. This process generates source code into whichever programming language you choose. The generated files typically are referred to as *IDL-generated files*.

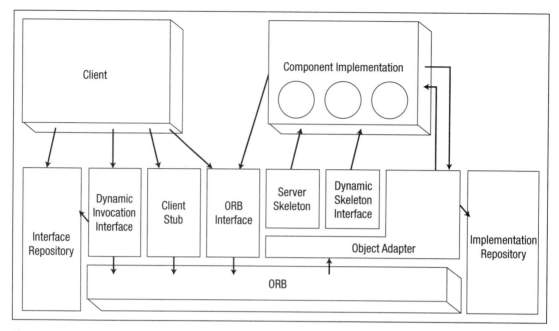

Figure 8.4
The anatomy of ORB.

When an IDL is compiled, the following two types of files are generated:

♦ *Client stub*—An IDL-generated code that allows a client component to access services of a server component (a client stub is also referred to as a *surrogate* or a *proxy*). A stub represents the same set of operations that its IDL contains. A stub is compiled and linked with client code and is used to issue requests. This means that a stub is the client-side mechanism for communicating with ORB, and that a stub basically marshals and unmarshals input/output (I/O) parameters of operations.

♦ *Server skeleton*—An IDL-generated code that allows a component implementation to receive requests of a client. A skeleton represents the same set of operations that its IDL contains. You adapt a skeleton to implement a server component. A skeleton is compiled and linked with component code, and works with the server-ORB to unmarshal the request and dispatch it to the component instance.

IDL Compilers Reinforce Standards

IDL compilers standardize the translation of IDLs into programming language code. This process eliminates inconsistencies in the stubs and skeletons that may result from hand-coding. In addition, IDL compilers map the IDL data types into the desired language and OS platform-specific data types. This ensures that the components in a distributed environment don't use incompatible data types.

NOTE

Stubs Vs. Component Distribution

Stubs make a distributed component's location (local or remote) transparent. In other words, when a client requests a service from a component, the client is unaware that it is dealing with a compo-nent that is running on a remote machine. A distributed component may become unreach-able due to a server program crash, network outage, and so on. A client must be informed when such a scenario happens. Fortunately, a client receives an exception when a remote operation can't be invoked. This process is explained in detail in Chapter 9.

Because the IDL compiler generates stubs and skeletons from OMG IDL specifications, they both have complete knowledge of the IDL interfaces—which is why dispatching through stubs and skeletons is often called *static invocation*.

To recap the discussion on stubs and skeletons:

1. The stub interacts with the client-ORB to issue and marshal the request.

2. The skeleton interacts with the server-ORB to unmarshal and dis-patch the request.

3. After the component implementation completes the requested execution, the skeleton and server-ORB marshal the reply and send it to the client.

4. On the client side, the stub unmarshals the reply.

Object Adapter (OA)

Object adapters provide a way to connect component implementations to ORB to receive requests. An OA acts as an intermediary between a component implementation and ORB, providing the mechanism that enables a component implementation to access services provided by ORB. Without an OA, component implementations would have to connect themselves directly to ORB to receive requests. Figure 8.5 shows

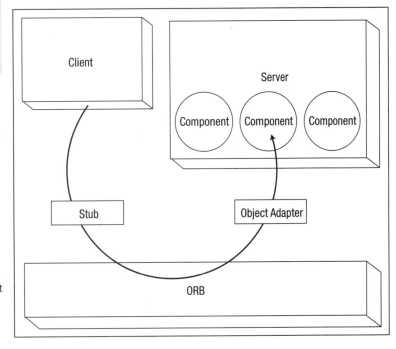

Figure 8.5

Interaction between a client and a component imple-mentation, using stub, ORB, and OA.

a typical interaction between a client and a component implementation, using stub, ORB, and OA.

Services provided by ORB through an OA include:

♦ *Generation and interpretation of IORs*—OAs generate IORs for CORBA components.

♦ *Object registration*—OAs supply operations that enable components to be registered with ORB.

♦ *Object and server activation*—OAs activate registered components if they are inactive when a request is dispatched to them. Also, if necessary, an OA launches server processes in which components can be activated (mentioned in the next section). Note that a *server process* is a running program that instantiates components to serve clients. Sometimes, the terms *server process* and *server* are used interchangeably. However, you can differentiate them in the following way: A server is the *logical* entity that constitutes a program containing components; a server process is the *physical* entity that is running on the machine under an OS.

♦ *Method invocation*—OAs dispatch requests to registered components.

A CORBA implementation may provide many OAs. Without OAs, CORBA couldn't easily support diverse component granularities, lifetimes, and implementation styles. However, a special OA, called the *basic object adapter* (BOA), is the most commonly used OA. According to the CORBA specification, BOA should be available in every ORB implementation.

BOA And Server Activation Policies

BOA defines how a component is activated, either by launching another server process, by starting another thread within the same server process, or by reusing a thread in the same server process. This means that many ways exist to activate a component implementation.

BOA provides the following four types of activation policies for server implementations. *Activation policies* indicate how application components are to be initialized. This is a very important and useful feature of BOA.

♦ *Shared server policy*—A single server process contains multiple component implementations. When a client request is sent to one of the components in the server, BOA launches the server process. The server then notifies BOA, by calling **BOA::impl_is_ready()**, that it is ready to accept client requests. Any further requests on any of the components will not cause BOA to launch another server process. The server process remains active until you call **BOA::deactivate_impl()**. Examples using the **BOA::impl_is_ready()** call are shown in Chapter 9.

◆ *Unshared server policy*—A server contains only one component implementation. When a client request is sent to the components in the server, BOA launches the server process. The server then notifies BOA that it is ready to accept client requests, by calling **BOA::object_is_ready()**. Any further requests on the same component will not cause BOA to launch another server process. However, any requests on another component (same or different type) will produce another launch of the server process. The server process remains active until you call **BOA::deactivate_obj()**.

◆ *Server-per-method policy*—A new server is always launched when a request on a component is sent. The server exits when the member function returns.

◆ *Persistent server policy*—The server is not launched by BOA; it may be launched by a system daemon, an external agent, and so forth. The rest of the mechanism is similar to the shared server policy.

Interface Repository (IR)

The *interface repository* is a CORBA component. It provides persistent storage of module, interface, and type definitions. Given an IOR, you can query about an interface's details and all the information associated with that interface by calling services provided by the IR.

First, you have to make a standard **get_interface()** call on an IOR without knowing the type of the IOR. This operation returns an IOR of the IR that is called **InterfaceDef**, which provides a set of operations that describes the particular IOR's interface.

The primary utilization of the IR is to provide the runtime-type information (RTTI) of an interface. In other words, the IR provides runtime-type information so that you can issue requests using the *dynamic invocation interface* (DII), which is described in the next section.

IR can play a very important role for some tools, such as object browsers and case tools. Using IR, you can discover existing CORBA interfaces in a system and present the information to the user. Chapters 11 and 13 present information about the usage and applications of IR.

Dynamic Invocation Interface (DII)

The compilation and linking of IDL-generated stubs with a client enables the client to invoke operations on known components by using the component's IOR. Most of the time, stub definitions are available to write clients. However, occasionally you may encounter a situation in which a client needs to make calls on components without having compile-time knowledge of their interfaces. This procedure is supported by the *dynamic invocation interface*. DII enables requests to be constructed at runtime. Using DII, clients can specify the target IOR, the operation/attribute name, and the parameters to be passed. You can use IR services to obtain information about the operation to be performed and the types of the parameters to be passed. A detailed description of DII is provided in Chapter 11.

Dynamic Skeleton Interface (DSI)

Similar to DII, the *dynamic skeleton interface* is the server-side mechanism to handle dynamic object invocations. DSI does not require the server to be compiled and linked with the skeleton code for an interface to accept client requests. You can use services of the IR to obtain the parameters. The implementation code must provide to ORB the descriptions of all the operation parameters. ORB, in turn, provides the values of any input parameters to use in performing the operation. DSIs may be invoked both through client stubs and through DII.

One typical application of DSI is to build a generic bridge between different ORBs.

Implementation Repository

The *implementation repository* contains information that enables ORB to locate and launch implementations of components. An implementation repository may typically maintain a mapping from a server's name to the executable's name that is used to launch the server. A server must be registered with the implementation repository. The server is then automatically activated by ORB when an operation invocation is made to any component whose IOR names that particular server.

ORB-To-ORB Interaction

One of the goals of CORBA is to provide interoperability among distributed components, which it achieves by means of IDL. Internally, an ORB implementation is used at runtime to facilitate the interaction among components. What happens if a client based on a particular CORBA implementation wants to talk to a component that is running on another ORB implementation? A standard protocol is needed through which various ORB implementations can communicate with each other—OMG has defined the standard for such a protocol, known as the *Internet Inter-ORB Protocol* (IIOP). IIOP is basically based on TCP/IP. Using IIOP, a CORBA ORB from one vendor can communicate with an ORB from another vendor. A CORBA-compliant product must implement IIOP. (Actually, a CORBA 2-compliant product that was adopted after December 1994). IIOP guarantees interoperability among CORBA products, which means that your CORBA application is vendor-independent, if you are using a CORBA 2-compliant product.

Other protocols for inter-ORB communication also exist, but IIOP is fast becoming the most popular, because it is the standard, and because it is based on TCP/IP (the networking protocols used by the Internet).

CORBA Services And Facilities

ORB enables you to write *application interfaces* to represent those components that implement specific tasks for an application. Three points must be noted:

♦ One component may support many interfaces.

♦ One application is typically composed of many components.

♦ New application components can be built by modifying existing components.

Recall that ORB allows components to communicate with each other. Because everything runs and depends on ORB, ORB is essential to creating distributed applications. Unfortunately, ORB alone isn't enough to create distributed applications: You typically need services to locate components and manage their life cycles; you may need system management services to observe the health of the system; and you may even need domain-specific interfaces and frameworks to help you do rapid development. OMA thus provides additional capabilities in the form of services and facilities that provide both horizontal and vertical capabilities. *Horizontal services* generally are useful to all industries, whereas *vertical services* are designed to meet specific industries' needs. These services are discussed briefly in the following sections. A more substantive description of horizontal services is provided in Chapter 13.

Object Services

Object services are domain-independent horizontal interfaces that are used in most distributed applications. They are available in the form of

CORBA interfaces and come with implementations. Without object services, writing distributed applications wouldn't be easy. Object services are collectively called *CORBAservices*.

CORBA provides 15 types of object services, each of which is described briefly in the following list:

♦ *Naming service*—Provides a client with the capability to obtain an IOR of another component anywhere on the bus. Also allows a component to bind its name to a *naming context,* an object that contains a set of name bindings in which each name is unique. (This service is discussed further in Chapter 12.)

♦ *Event service*—Supports asynchronous event notifications and event delivery. Allows components to register dynamically their interest in an event. The design of this service is scalable and is suitable for distributed environments. (This service is examined in depth in Chapter 13).

♦ *Life cycle service*—Defines operations to create, copy, move, and remove components on ORB.

♦ *Persistent object service (POS)*—Provides a set of generic interfaces for storing and managing the persistent state of components. The component ultimately has the responsibility of managing its state, but it can use or delegate to POS for the actual work. A major characteristic of POS is its openness—it allows a variety of different clients and implementations of POS to work together.

♦ *Transaction service*—Supports a two-phase commit protocol between components. Supports two transaction models—the flat and nested models.

♦ *Concurrency control service*—Enables multiple clients to coordinate their access to shared resources. This service is useful for keeping a resource in a consistent state when multiple, concurrent clients access it.

♦ *Relationship service*—Allows components to form dynamic relationships (links) between each other. This service defines two new kinds of objects: *relationships* and *roles*. A role represents a CORBA component in a relationship. One potential use of this service is to create workflow managers.

♦ *Externalization service*—Defines protocols for externalizing and internalizing component data. This service enables a component to externalize its state in a stream of data (in memory, on a disk file, or across the network) and then internalize into a new instance of the component in the same or a different server process.

- *Licensing service*—Enables component vendors to control the use of their intellectual property. This service doesn't impose any business policy or practice—vendors can implement the licensing service according to their own requirements, and the requirements of their customers.

- *Query service*—Enables a component to invoke queries on collections of other components. The queries can be used to invoke arbitrary operations.

- *Property service*—Provides a mechanism to associate properties (named values) dynamically with components. This service defines operations to create and manipulate sets of name-value pairs. (This service is demonstrated in Chapter 13.)

- *Security service*—Ensures secure communication between components by providing authentication, authorization, auditing, non-repudiation, and administration (for example, a security policy).

- *Time service*—Enables the user to obtain current time in a distributed environment. The service can be used to determine the order in which events occurred, and compute the interval between two events.

- *Collections service*—Provides a uniform way to create and manipulate the most common collections of components.

- *Trader service*—Enables a client to obtain an IOR of another component on ORB based on some *component properties*. (Note that "properties" has nothing to do with the property service.)

Common Facilities

Like object services, *common facilities* are interfaces. Printing facilities, database facilities, system management facilities, and email facilities are some examples of common facilities that are horizontally oriented. OMG also provides *domain interfaces*, which are vertically oriented interfaces for application domains, such as finance, health care, manufacturing, telecom, electronic commerce, and transportation. Common facilities are collectively called *CORBAfacilities*.

Developing Component Frameworks

The interfaces for using services and facilities are standardized by OMG in terms of IDLs, which means that you can use them transparently in any language and platform. Generally, an application combines application components with the set of services and common facilities. You can also create *component frameworks*, by combining interfaces for application, common facility, and object services. Component frameworks

CORBA Implementations

CORBA-compliant products are not required to implement all the services and facilities; they need to support only the CORBA core functionality. Before designing an application or framework that might depend on certain services, you should do some research on various CORBA products to find out whether they provide the services you are looking for.

Various commercial and free CORBA implementations are available. Two of the more popular commercial products include IONA Technologies' Orbix and Visigenic Software's VisiBroker. The examples in this book are developed using ORBacus, a free implementation from Object Oriented Concepts, Inc. ORBacus can be found at **www.ooc.com/ob/**. Because ORBacus supports only naming, events, and property services, this book doesn't include examples of other services. The examples have been compiled using Visual C++ 5. The examples may work on other CORBA products and compilers with no or few changes.

are reusable designs with predefined component interactions that provide functionality of direct interest to end users in an application or infrastructure domain. Chapter 13 presents more information about this topic.

How Does CORBA Support Reusability?

CORBA is an object-oriented architecture. CORBA components exhibit many C++ features, including interface inheritance, polymorphism, and reuse. CORBA-based designs must focus on interfaces rather than implementation details. This is supported by IDLs. Because an IDL standardizes interfaces, and a component's functionality is encapsulated within component implementations, you get a black-box view of the component. This black-box view means that a developer can combine various application components to form the actual application, without having to deal with components' internals.

The CORBA component model and C++ together form a powerful springboard for software reuse in two ways:

♦ *Abstraction reuse*—CORBA provides the capability to reorganize application modules within various layers of the application. CORBA's interoperability and cross-platform portability make this possible in an easy way.

♦ *Real reuse*—The whole component concept is absolutely important for reuse producers and reuse consumers. This concept gives reuse producers the power to create reusable components, and gives reuse consumers the power to leverage components with greater flexibility. When you start a project that has a significant portion of the application and infrastructure already done, and you are able to reuse that portion, you can deliver a solution in less time.

Reuse is discussed in Chapter 9 in greater detail.

Chapter Recap

OMG's CORBA can be used to implement real-life components that can run in distributed applications and collaborate with each other. Also, CORBA enables new applications to work seamlessly with existing components, irrespective of the OS on which they run and the implementation language that is used to implement them. Because component specifications are defined by using IDL, application designers can design their applications in terms of interacting components. This enables designers to apply OO software development techniques.

CORBA is expected to drive the software industry toward component-based software development. This seems possible, because most of the major players in the commercial distributed and OO fields are among the several hundred OMG members.

This chapter presented a few significant CORBA concepts and features, including the following:

♦ CORBA isn't a language; it is an environment for deploying interoperable, reusable, and portable software components.

♦ CORBA is an object-oriented architecture. It focuses on interfaces rather than implementation details.

♦ The Object Request Broker is central to the CORBA architecture. ORB manages the intercommunication of CORBA components.

♦ The Interface Definition Language defines the application component interfaces upon which CORBA applications are built. Chapter 9 discusses IDL and the development of CORBA applications in more depth.

♦ Compiling IDL definitions creates client stubs and server skeletons, which in turn are used to implement CORBA clients and servers.

♦ CORBAservices and CORBAfacilities provide additional functionality to CORBA applications. They can be used to create component frameworks.

Chapter 9
Developing CORBA Components

Key Topics:

- *Details of IDL syntax*

- *Mapping of IDL types to C++ code*

- *Componentization using CORBA*

- *Developing a component factory*

- *CORBA and reuse*

- *CORBA design issues*

Chapter 8 discussed the details of the CORBA architecture, one important feature of which is the use of the Interface Definition Language (IDL) to describe the interfaces between CORBA components. This chapter gives you more details about IDL and how to use it to describe components' interfaces. Then, the chapter introduces the development of a simple CORBA application.

This chapter is logically divided into two parts: the details of IDL and developing components by using CORBA. The end of the chapter presents a discussion of CORBA application design and development issues.

Examples in this book have been tested by using ORBacus (version 3.1) on Windows NT and Visual C++ 5. ORBacus, from Object-Oriented Concepts, is a CORBA implementation that is compliant with the CORBA 2 specification. ORBacus includes the following features:

- Full CORBA IDL support
- Complete CORBA IDL-to-C++ mapping
- Complete CORBA IDL-to-Java mapping
- Naming, event, and property services
- Full support for dynamic programming: Dynamic Invocation Interface, Dynamic Skeleton Interface, Interface Repository, and DynAny

Interface Definition Language

Chapter 8 provided an introduction to IDL and IDL compilers. This section presents more syntactic details about IDL, the language used to

NOTE

Experimentation Is The Key

This chapter is full of technical terminology, IDL syntax, IDL-generated code, and hand-coded implementation source code, as well as client and server source files. The best way to understand this chapter is to experiment with CORBA by using C++ and ORBacus. ORBacus is freely available for noncommercial use. Information on ORBacus, as well as a downloadable copy, is available on Object-Oriented Concepts' Web site at **www.ooc.com/ ob/.** Experimentation is very important to understanding and learning all the nuts and bolts of CORBA.

NOTE

Operation Vs. Method

What the Object Management Group (OMG) refers to as *operations* are also referred to as *methods*, *member functions,* and *requests.* Throughout this book, the term *operation* is used to refer to an IDL function.

specify a component's interface. IDL obeys the same lexical rules as C++:

♦ IDL provides basic data types (such as **short** and **long**) and constructed types (such as **struct** and **sequence**). These types are used in operation declarations, to define argument types and return types.

♦ In IDL, identifiers (such as names of interfaces and operations) are case-sensitive. IDL imposes another restriction—the names of identifiers in the same scope (for instance, two interfaces in the same module, or two operations in the same interface) cannot differ in case only. For example, within the **CoObject** interface, the **anOperation** and **anOPERATION** operations can't coexist.

♦ All definitions in IDL are terminated by a semicolon (**;**). Definitions that enclose other definitions do so with braces (**{}**), again like C++. When a closing brace appears at the end of a definition, it is followed by a semicolon (**;**).

♦ IDL has two comment delimiters: the comment pair (**/*...*/**) and the double slash (**//**). The comment pair is the same as is used in C, and the double slash is the same as used in C++. IDLs typically receive a blend of both comment forms. Multiline commentaries generally are placed between comment pairs. Half-line and single-line notes more often are outlined by double slashes.

♦ Preprocessing directives allow macro substitution, conditional compilation, and source file inclusion. One IDL file can be included in another IDL file by using **#include**. The preprocessor resolves macros, processes directives such as **#ifdef...#endif**, and performs substitutions of **#define**d symbols. IDL uses a C++ preprocessor to process constructs, such as macro definitions and conditional compilation.

The first step to writing a CORBA application is to write an interface in IDL. Hence, a detailed description on IDL syntax and its mapping to C++ code is provided in the next few sections.

IDL Types

Like most programming languages, IDL features a variety of basic types and complex types. Complex types are known as user-defined types (UDT).

Basic Types

IDL basic types store simple values, such as integral numbers, floating-point numbers, character strings, and so on. IDLs support the following data types that are similar to C++ data types:

- **void**—Analogous to the **void** type of C++. You can't have a variable of type **void**, but the type is used for operations that don't return any value.

- **long** (**signed** and **unsigned**)—32-bit integral types.

- **long long** (**signed** and **unsigned**)—64-bit integral types.

- **short** (**signed** and **unsigned**)—16-bit integral types.

- **float**—Single-precision floating-point numbers as defined by Institute of Electrical and Electronics Engineers (IEEE).

- **double**—IEEE double-precision floating-point numbers.

- **long double**—Represents an IEEE double-extended floating-point value, having an exponent of at least 15 bits and a signed fraction of at least 64 bits.

- **char**—Represents character type. The **char** type in IDL (analogous to the **char** type in C++) stores a single character value. The **char** data type is an 8-bit quantity.

- **wchar**—A wide character type that has an implementation-dependent width.

- **boolean**—A Boolean type taking the values true and false.

- **octet**—An 8-bit value, guaranteed not to undergo any conversion during transfer between components. Because this type has no direct counterpart in C++, **unsigned char** type is used by ORBacus to represent this type.

Note that IDL doesn't define a plain **int** type; it defines only **short** and **long** integer types.

Complex Types

IDL supports the following complex types in an IDL:

- **struct**—Similar to the C++ structure. Structures are used in IDL as a mechanism to achieve pass-by-value effect. On the other hand, CORBA components (which are represented by interfaces) are passed by reference rather than by value.

- **union**—A discriminated union type, consisting of a discriminator followed by an instance of a type appropriate to the discriminator value.

- **string**—Consists of a variable-length array of characters; the length of the string is available at runtime.

- **sequence**—Consists of a variable-length array of a single type; the length of the sequence is available at runtime.

- **array**—Consists of a multidimensional fixed-length array of a single type.

- **interface**—Specifies the set of operations that an instance of that type must support. An **interface** declares the services that your application components will provide.

- **enum**—Enumerated types consisting of an ordered sequence of identifiers. IDL doesn't specify the ordinal numbering for the identifiers. Therefore, comparing **enum** values to integral values might not be safe.

- **any**—Can represent any possible basic or constructed type (the **any** type is explained in the next section).

The following is an example that shows how a **struct** data type is defined in an IDL:

```
struct CoPerson
{
    string name;
    short age;
};
```

The **struct CoPerson** has two data members: **name** of type **string** and **age** of type **short**. Note that you can't have **struct** derivation in an IDL, as you do in C++. A **struct** derivation introduces complications in your programs. For example, you can represent a derived **struct** using its base **struct**, and in some cases, you probably would be required to typecast a base **struct** into a derived **struct**.

Any

The **any** type, which is very similar to **void*** in C++, can be used to pass or return a value of an arbitrary IDL type in an operation. Just like **void*** usage, an operation that accepts an **any** as an input parameter determines the type of value being passed before the operation can manipulate the object. Here is an example:

```
interface CoTest
{
    void op(in any a);
};
```

A client can construct an **any** that can contain a value of any IDL type. The client can pass the **any** value by calling the **op()** operation. An application that receives an **any** value first determines what type of value that it contains and then reads the value.

Note that the IDL **union** mechanism can also be used to represent a value of an arbitrary IDL type. When you use **union**, the types of the parameters are fixed. However, this isn't true for an **any** type: an **any** parameter can contain any IDL type.

The *TypeCode* Pseudotype

CORBA provides a special type, known as **CORBA_TypeCode**, to provide type information to a CORBA application. **CORBA_ TypeCode** acts as a sort of runtime-type information (RTTI) for CORBA applications. The **CORBA_TypeCode** type generally is used when querying the type of an instance of **any**. The IDL **any** type is represented as a **CORBA_Any** class in C++. The **CORBA_Any** class has a **public** member function, **type()**, which has a return type of **CORBA_TypeCode_ptr**. This return type can be queried at runtime to determine the type of the value contained in the **CORBA_Any**.

Use of **CORBA_Any** and **CORBA_TypeCode** is demonstrated in Chapter 10.

Interface Declaration

An IDL interface provides a description of the functionality that is provided by a component. An interface definition provides all the information needed to develop clients that use the interface. An interface definition typically specifies the attributes and operations belonging to that interface, as well as the parameters of each operation. Defining the interfaces between components is the most important aspect of distributed system design.

Consider a simple banking application that manages bank accounts. A user of an **Account** component will want to make deposits and withdrawals. The following is an example **bank.idl** interface:

```
//bank.idl
interface CoAccount
{
    void deposit(in float amount);
    void withdraw(in float amount);
};
```

This example creates the specification for the **CoAccount** component by using the IDL syntax. A **CoAccount** interface has been declared. **CoAccount** has two operations:

- ◆ deposit()
- ◆ withdraw()

If a **CoAccount** component that implements these operations is registered with the Object Request Broker (ORB), **CoAccount** can be remotely accessed by any client through these operations.

The syntax for an interface definition is very similar to the syntax used in C++. The body of the interface contains operation signatures and attribute declarations, in no particular order.

Two operations are provided in the **CoAccount** interface: **deposit()** and **withdraw()**. Each has one parameter of type **float**. Each parameter must specify its passing mode. The possible parameter passing modes are as follows:

♦ **in**—The parameter is passed from the caller (client) to the target component.

♦ **out**—The parameter is passed from the target component to the caller.

♦ **inout**—The parameter is passed in both directions.

In the preceding bank example, **amount** is passed as an **in** parameter to both operations. The parameter passing mode must be specified for each parameter.

Module Of An Interface

IDL provides the **module** keyword to use to group together IDL definitions that share a common purpose. The use of the **module** construct is simple: A **module** declaration specifies the module name and encloses its members in braces.

A module is used to serve three purposes:

♦ An interface can be defined within a module; this allows interfaces and other IDL type definitions to be grouped in logical units.

♦ Modules provide you with a way to solve a problem in an OO way. You can identify a partitioning of the overall program system into separate modules and interfaces.

♦ The module provides a sort of namespace for different interfaces. Names defined within a module don't clash with names defined outside the module, which enables sensible names for interfaces and other definitions to be chosen without clashing with other names.

The following example illustrates the use of a module—the **Account** interface is defined within a module, **CoBank**:

```
module CoBank
{
    interface Account
    {
        void deposit(in float amount);
        void withdraw(in float amount);
    };
};
```

In this example, the **Account** interface is declared in the **CoBank** module. The name **CoBank** provides a namespace to the **Account** interface.

Attributes Of An Interface

An *attribute* of an IDL interface is similar to a data member of a C++ class. The only difference is that IDL attributes always have public visibility. In fact, an IDL interface doesn't provide the notion of nonpublic members.

Other than defining **withdraw()** and **deposit()** operations, an **Account** component needs to hold the balance of the account and the name of the account's owner. For example:

```
module CoBank
{
    interface Account
    {
        attribute float balance;
        attribute string holder;

        void deposit(in float amount);
        void withdraw(in float amount);
    };
};
```

The **Account** interface defines **balance** and **holder** attributes, which are properties of an **Account** component. The **balance** attribute takes values of type **float**. The **holder** attribute is of type **string**.

Readonly Attributes Of An Interface

IDL provides the **readonly** modifier for an attribute. This modifier is used to specify that a particular attribute is for accessing only; its value cannot be modified directly by an external client. In fact, in the preceding example, **balance** and **holder** must be **readonly** attributes, so that they can't be directly modified by an external client. For example:

```
module CoBank
{
    interface Account
    {
        readonly attribute float balance;
        readolny attribute string holder;
        //...
    };
};
```

Exceptions

An IDL operation may raise an *exception*, to indicate that an application error has occurred. Like C++, IDL supports user-defined exceptions. CORBA also provides predefined standard exceptions. When a component throws an exception, the server-side ORB marshals that exception and passes it back to the client-side ORB, which then unmarshals the exception and rethrows it to the client. In this way, the C++ exception handling mechanism is extended to CORBA.

To illustrate exceptions, the following code extends the example banking interface by providing an exception:

```
module CoBank
{
    interface Account
    {
        readonly attribute float balance;
        readonly attribute string holder;

        exception NoMoney{};

        void deposit(in float amount);
        void withdraw(in float amount) raises (NoMoney);
    };
};
```

The **withdraw()** operation can raise the **NoMoney** exception. Exceptions provide a clean way to enable an operation to raise an error to a caller rather than return error codes. You can specify more than one exception for an operation. As you can see, the definition for an exception type also resembles the **struct** definition; it can contain various data members of IDL types. An exception can't have operations and it doesn't support inheritance. The preceding example demonstrates that an exception can be an empty declaration. It can act as an error type.

Standard Exceptions

A set of standard exceptions is defined by CORBA. These exceptions are thrown when standard runtime errors occur during the execution of an operation. They are referred to as *system exceptions*. In an IDL operation, you don't have to declare explicitly that the operation can raise a system exception; rather, these exceptions are raised implicitly by ORB.

The Array

IDL provides multidimensional fixed-size arrays to hold lists of elements of the same type. The size of each dimension should be specified in the definition. An IDL array corresponds directly to the array constructs in C++. For example,

```
module CoArray
{
    interface test
    {
    };

    typedef test testArray[5];
    typedef long longArray[5][3];
};
```

defines two array types: **testArray** and **longArray**. You need to use **typedef** before you can declare a variable of the required array type. Note that, like C++, IDL supports the notion of **typedef** to create user-defined type names. Fundamental and derived types can be given new symbolic names by the **typedef** mechanism, such as,

```
typedef T U;
```

where **T** is some type, and **U** is the new data type name for **T**.

Oneway Operations

When a client makes an operation call on a remote component, the client is blocked while the call is being executed by the target component. However, an IDL operation can be defined to be *oneway*, so that the client isn't blocked and continues processing while the target component executes the remote operation. For example, you could provide a oneway operation in **bank.idl** on the **Account** interface to print its monthly statement (to be posted later):

NOTE

Oneway Vs. Normal Operations

A oneway call isn't guaranteed to execute successfully. As a result, the client has no way to determine whether the oneway call invoked was executed successfully. On the other hand, calls to the normal operation will block until the operation has been carried out. Therefore, oneway operations are useful only to communicate with a remote component, without waiting for a reply. You must use a oneway operation if the call is not important and you don't expect a response. Note that a normal operation with a **void** return type isn't automatically considered to be oneway.

```
module CoBank
{
    interface Account
    {
        readonly attribute float balance;
        readonly attribute string holder;

        exception NoMoney{};

        void deposit(in float amount);
        void withdraw(in float amount) raises (NoMoney);
        oneway void print_monthly_statement();
    };
};
```

In this example, the selected IDL statement shows the syntax for a oneway **print_monthly_statement()** call. The advantage of declaring **print_monthly_statement()** oneway is that the client can continue to work rather than wait for the **print_monthly_statement()** call to complete. However, two limitations are associated with this approach:

♦ Because the operation invocation returns before the operation execution is completed, the operation cannot return a value. Therefore, a oneway operation must specify a **void** return type and can't have **out** or **inout** parameters.

♦ A oneway operation can't raise any exceptions.

The const Modifier

Like C++, IDL allows constant values to be specified. This is done by using the **const** modifier, which is used to make a variable value unmodifiable. For example,

```
const short aShortConstant = 13;
```

defines **aShortConstant** to be a symbolic constant initialized with the value **13**. Any attempt to change the value from within the program will result in a compile-time error.

Forward Declarations

In cases where an interface definition has not been discovered, a forward declaration of the interface can be supplied. A *forward declaration* permits an interface to be passed/returned as a data type in operations. This mechanism is useful when two interfaces need to reference each other. This problem is known as a *circular reference*. For example:

```
module CoTest
{
    interface I1; //forward declaration
    interface I2; //forward declaration

    interface I1
    {
        void op(in I2 i);
    };

    interface I2
    {
        void op(in I1 i);
    };
};
```

In this example, the **I1** and **I2** interfaces are forward declarations, because **I1::op()** uses **I2**, and **I2::op()** uses **I1**.

There are no issues involved with circular references. This is also used when one interface is contained within another interface, and they need to expose each other's object reference. For example,

```
interface Container; //forward declaration

interface Contained
{
    readonly attribute Container defined_in;
};

typedef sequence<Contained> ContainedSeq;

interface Container
{
    readonly attribute ContainedSeq contents;
};
```

In the preceding example, the **Container** interface contains instances of the **Contained** interface. Obviously, both the interfaces are required to have attributes to denote this relationship. This can be done only by using forward declarations. (The **Container** and **Contained** interfaces are the part of the **CORBA** module and are discussed in Chapter 11.)

A forward declaration can be used to increase readability. For example:

```
module CosNaming
{
    typedef string Istring;

    struct NameComponent
    {
        Istring id;
        Istring kind;
    };

    typedef sequence<NameComponent> Name;
    enum BindingType {nobject, ncontext};

    struct Binding
    {
        Name binding_name;
        BindingType binding_type;
    };

    interface BindingIterator; //forward declaration
    interface NamingContext
    {
        void list(in unsigned long how_many,
            out BindingList bl, out BindingIterator bi);
    };

    interface BindingIterator
    {
        //...
    };

    //...
};
```

In the preceding **CosNaming** module, the **BindingIterator** interface has its forward declaration before the **NamingContext** interface is declared. This forward declaration was not needed. You could have declared the **BindingIterator** interface before the **NamingContext** interface because the **BindingIterator** interface doesn't depend on the **NamingContext** interface. However, because the **NamingContext** is the significant interface of the **CosNaming** module, it makes sense to declare the **NamingContext** interface before the secondary

BindingIterator interface. Hence, the **BindingIterator** interface has its forward declaration before the **NamingContext** interface. (The **CosNaming** module is one of standard modules defined by OMG and is discussed in Chapter 12).

IDL To C++ Mappings

IDL language mappings determine how IDL features are mapped to the facilities of a particular programming language. The OMG has standardized many language mappings, including C, C++, Java, Smalltalk, and Ada 95. C++ maps very naturally to IDL. Mapping of an OMG IDL to C++ should be the same for all ORB implementations. This is ensured by an *IDL compiler* that is provided with a CORBA product. An IDL compiler is used to produce a C++ class corresponding to each IDL interface; that is, the IDL compiler translates from IDL to C++ declarations. This step is required before the interface can be implemented or used by a client. The following sections explain how the mapping of interfaces and various other IDL constructs is done in C++.

Mapping Of IDL Data Types To C++ Code

The IDL data types (such as **long, char**, and so fourth) map to certain types in C++ that are defined in various ORBacus header files. Table 9.1 shows the mapping of IDL types to C++ types in ORBacus.

As Table 9.1 shows, some IDL types (**long long, unsigned long long, long double**, and **wchar**) are not supported by ORBacus, and they should not be used in an IDL.

Mapping Of IDL Complex Data Types To C++ Code

Mappings of types **string, union, struct, sequence**, and **array** are shown in the next few sections.

Mapping Of IDL *Structs* To C++ Code
IDL **structs** are like C++ **structs**. The IDL

```
module CoStruct
{
    struct Person
    {
```

Table 9.1 Mapping of IDL data types to C++ types in ORBacus.

IDL Types	C++ Types
void	void
long	CORBA_Long
unsigned long	CORBA_ULong
long long	Not available in ORBacus
unsigned long long	Not available in ORBacus
short	CORBA_Short
unsigned short	CORBA_UShort
float	CORBA_Float
double	CORBA_Double
long double	Not available in ORBacus
char	CORBA_Char
wchar	Not available in ORBacus
boolean	CORBA_Boolean
octet	CORBA_Octet
enum	enum

```
        string name;
        short age;
    };
};
```

maps to the following C++ code:

```
struct CoStruct_Person
{
    CoStruct_Person();
    CoStruct_Person(const CoStruct_Person&);
    ~CoStruct_Person();
    CoStruct_Person& operator=(const CoStruct_Person&);

    CORBA_String_var name;
    CORBA_Short age;
};

typedef OBVarVar< CoStruct_Person > CoStruct_Person_var;
```

The variable **name** of type **string** maps to a **CORBA_String_var** class, which is a wrapper class for type **char***. It is very close to standard string classes. Similarly, the **CoStruct_Person_var** class is a wrapper class for the type **CoStruct_Person***. It is similar to a smart pointer.

The preceding example shows the following:

♦ An IDL module name provides a kind of namespace. The name of a module is attached with names of types defined within a module. (IDL modules may be mapped either to C++ classes or to C++ namespaces if the C++ compiler supports their use.)

♦ An IDL **struct** maps to a C++ **struct** type.

♦ A **struct**'s data members are generated as **public** data members of the **struct** in C++.

♦ A corresponding **_var** for the **struct** type is generated.

The following example shows a case in which a **struct** instance is a member of another **struct**:

```
module CoStruct
{
    struct Address
    {
        short doorNumber;
        string street;
    };

    struct Person
    {
        string name;
        short age;
        Address address;
    };
};
```

The generated code for the preceding example is shown in Listing 9.1.

Listing 9.1   Generated code for an IDL struct.

```
struct CoStruct_Address
{
    CoStruct_Address();
    CoStruct_Address(const CoStruct_Address&);
    ~CoStruct_Address();
    CoStruct_Address& operator=
        (const CoStruct_Address&);

    CORBA_Short doorNumber;
    CORBA_String_var street;
};
```

```
typedef
    OBVarVar< CoStruct_Address > CoStruct_Address_var;

struct CoStruct_Person
{
    CoStruct_Person();
    CoStruct_Person(const CoStruct_Person&);
    ~CoStruct_Person() { }
    CoStruct_Person& operator=(const CoStruct_Person&);

    CORBA_String_var name;
    CORBA_Short age;
    CoStruct_Address address;
};


typedef OBVarVar< CoStruct_Person > CoStruct_Person_var;
```

This example shows that a corresponding **_var** type is always generated for a **struct** definition. For example, the **CoStruct_Person_var** type is defined for the **struct CoStruct_Person**.

Mapping Of Unions To C++ Code

The IDL **union** type, like a **struct**, represents values of different types. The IDL **union** type provides a space-saving type, whereby the amount of storage required for a **union** is the amount necessary to store its largest element. A tag field is used to specify which member of a **union** instance is currently assigned a value. For example:

```
module UnionExperiment
{
    enum Selection
    {
        E_APPLE, E_FOOTBALL, E_COMPUTER
    };

    struct Apple
    {
        short color;
    };

    struct Football
    {
        float weight;
    };

    struct Computer
```

```
    {
        boolean is_super;
    };

    union MixedSelection switch (Selection)
    {
        case E_APPLE: Apple apple;
        case E_FOOTBALL: Football football;
        case E_COMPUTER: Computer computer;
    };

};
```

In this code, the **MixedSelection** identifier following the **union** keyword defines a new legal type. IDL unions are discriminated: The **union** header specifies the tag field **Selection** that determines which **union** member is assigned a value. A default case can also appear (at most, once) in a **union** declaration.

In the preceding example, a variable of type **MixedSelection** might have either an **Apple**, **Football**, or **Computer** value, depending on the value of the parameter when the **union** is used in an operation call (the parameter is known as a *discriminator*). Here, **Selection** is the discriminator. In the example, an **enum** was used for the discriminator; other types can be used also, including **long** (including **unsigned**), **long long** (including **unsigned**), **short** (including **unsigned**), **char**, or **boolean**. The constant values in the case statements must match the discriminator's type.

Listing 9.2 shows the code that is generated when the previous example is compiled using the ORBacus IDL compiler.

Listing 9.2   Generated code for a union.

```
enum UnionExperiment_Selection
{
    UnionExperiment_E_APPLE,
    UnionExperiment_E_FOOTBALL,
    UnionExperiment_E_COMPUTER
};

struct UnionExperiment_Apple
{
    CORBA_Short color;
};
```

```
struct UnionExperiment_Football
{
    CORBA_Float weight;
};

struct UnionExperiment_Computer
{
    CORBA_Boolean is_super;
};

class UnionExperiment_MixedSelection
{
    union
    {
        UnionExperiment_Apple apple;
        UnionExperiment_Football football;
        UnionExperiment_Computer computer;
    } _ob_v_;

    UnionExperiment_Selection _ob_d_;

public:

    void _d(UnionExperiment_Selection);
    UnionExperiment_Selection _d() const;

    void apple(const UnionExperiment_Apple&);
    const UnionExperiment_Apple& apple() const;
    UnionExperiment_Apple& apple();

    void football(const UnionExperiment_Football&);
    const UnionExperiment_Football& football() const;
    UnionExperiment_Football& football();

    void computer(const UnionExperiment_Computer&);
    const UnionExperiment_Computer& computer() const;
    UnionExperiment_Computer& computer();
};
```

The following points must be noted about the generated C++ code:

♦ The **union** maps to a **class**.

♦ The **union** members are mapped to accessor and mutator functions. As mentioned in Chapter 1, *accessor functions* provide access to the data members of a class whereas *mutator functions* are functions that change the data members of a class.

◆ The **union** has two special overloaded **_d()** member functions that set and return the current value of the discriminator.

In practice, IDL unions don't seem to be too useful. However, they are useful to create metadata types in framework development (this is shown in Chapter 13).

Mapping Of Sequences To C++ Code

An IDL *sequence* is simply a dynamically sizable array of values. An IDL sequence data type allows lists of items to be passed between components. All values of a sequence must be of the same type or derived from the same type. A sequence may be bounded or unbounded, depending on whether the maximum size is specified. For example:

```
module SequenceExperiment
{
    typedef sequence<short> SeqShort;
    typedef sequence<short, 10> Seq10Short;
};
```

The **SeqShort** type is an unbounded sequence, and the **Seq10Short** type is a bounded sequence because it specifies the maximum number of values that it can hold.

When the preceding IDL is compiled using the ORBacus IDL compiler, the following code is generated:

```
typedef
OBFixSeq< CORBA_Short >
    SequenceExperiment_SeqShort;

typedef
OBSeqVar< OBFixSeq< CORBA_Short > >
    SequenceExperiment_SeqShort_var;

typedef
OBBndFixSeq< CORBA_Short, 10 >
    SequenceExperiment_Seq10Short;

typedef
OBSeqVar< OBBndFixSeq< CORBA_Short, 10 > >
    SequenceExperiment_Seq10Short_var;
```

The **OBFixSeq** class is a class template that is defined by ORBacus. Its declaration is shown in Listing 9.3.

Listing 9.3   Declaration of the OBFixSeq class.

```
template<class T>
class OBFixSeq
{
    CORBA_ULong max_;
    CORBA_ULong len_;
    CORBA_ULong off_;
    CORBA_Boolean rel_;
    T* data_;

public:

    static T* allocbuf(CORBA_ULong n)
    {
        return new T[n];
    }
    static void freebuf(T* p)
    {
        delete [] p;
    }

    OBFixSeq();
    OBFixSeq(CORBA_ULong);
    OBFixSeq(CORBA_ULong, CORBA_ULong, T*,
        CORBA_Boolean = false);
    OBFixSeq(const OBFixSeq<T>&);
    ~OBFixSeq();

    OBFixSeq<T>& operator=(const OBFixSeq<T>&);

    CORBA_ULong maximum() const;

    void length(CORBA_ULong);
    CORBA_ULong length() const;

    T& operator[](CORBA_ULong idx);
    const T& operator[](CORBA_ULong idx) const;
};
```

As you can see, the **OBFixSeq** class is similar to the **vector** class (defined by STL).

The **OBBndFixSeq** class is also a class template that is defined by ORBacus. Its declaration is shown in Listing 9.4.

Listing 9.4   Declaration of the OBBndFixSeq class.

```
template<class T, CORBA_ULong max>
class OBBndFixSeq
{
    CORBA_ULong len_;
    CORBA_Boolean rel_;
    T* data_;

public:

    static T* allocbuf(CORBA_ULong n)
    {
        return new T[n];
    }
    static void freebuf(T* p)
    {
        delete [] p;
    }

    OBBndFixSeq();
    OBBndFixSeq(CORBA_ULong, T*, CORBA_Boolean = false);
    OBBndFixSeq(const OBBndFixSeq<T, max>&);
    ~OBBndFixSeq();

    OBBndFixSeq<T, max>& operator=
        (const OBBndFixSeq<T, max>&);

    void length(CORBA_ULong);
    CORBA_ULong length() const { return len_; }

    T& operator[](CORBA_ULong idx);
    const T& operator[](CORBA_ULong idx) const
};
```

As this listing demonstrates, the **OBBndFixSeq** class is also similar to an STL vector.

Mapping Of Array To C++ Code

When the IDL

```
module CoArray
{
    typedef long longArray[5];
};
```

is compiled by using the ORBacus compiler, a few types and functions are generated, as shown in Listing 9.5.

Listing 9.5   IDL-generated code for an array of length 5.

```
typedef CORBA_Long CoArray_longArray[5];
typedef CORBA_Long CoArray_longArray_slice;

inline CoArray_longArray_slice*
CoArray_longArray_alloc()
{
    return new CORBA_Long[5];
}

inline CoArray_longArray_slice*
CoArray_longArray_dup(const CoArray_longArray_slice* s)
{
    CoArray_longArray_slice* to = new CORBA_Long[5];
    memcpy(to, s, 5 * sizeof(CORBA_Long));
    return to;
}

inline void
CoArray_longArray_copy(const CoArray_longArray_slice* s,
CoArray_longArray_slice* to)
{
    memcpy(to, s, 5 * sizeof(CORBA_Long));
}

inline void
CoArray_longArray_free(CoArray_longArray_slice* s)
{
    delete [] s;
}
```

Mapping Of An Interface To C++ Code

When the module

```
module CoBank
{
    interface Account
    {
        void deposit(in float amount);
        void withdraw(in float amount);
    };
};
```

is compiled by using the ORBacus IDL compiler, the C++ code shown
in Listing 9.6 is generated.

Listing 9.6   IDL-generated code for the CoBank module.

```
class CoBank_Account;
typedef CoBank_Account* CoBank_Account_ptr;
typedef CoBank_Account* CoBank_AccountRef;
typedef OBObjVar< CoBank_Account > CoBank_Account_var;

class CoBank_Account : virtual public CORBA_Object
{
    CoBank_Account(const CoBank_Account&);
    void operator=(const CoBank_Account&);

protected:

    CoBank_Account() { }

public:

    virtual void deposit(CORBA_Float amount);
    virtual void withdraw(CORBA_Float amount);
};

class CoBank_Account_skel :
    virtual public CoBank_Account,
    virtual public CORBA_Object_skel
{
    CoBank_Account_skel(const CoBank_Account_skel&);
    void operator=(const CoBank_Account_skel&);

public:
    CoBank_Account_skel();
    virtual void deposit(CORBA_Float amount) = 0;
    virtual void withdraw(CORBA_Float amount) = 0;
    //...
};
```

The following points should be noted in Listing 9.6:

♦ IDL interfaces are mapped to C++ classes, with model name attached. The **CoBank_Account** class is the stub used by a client; the
  CoBank_Account_skel class is the skeleton used by a server.

♦ Interface operations are mapped to pure virtual member functions
  in the **CoBank_Account_skel** class. These functions have to be

implemented by a developer of the **Account** component (as explained later in the "Step 3: Implement The Interface Of The Component" section).

Types **CORBA_Object** and **CORBA_Object_skel** are standard types defined in one of the CORBA header files. The **CORBA_Object_skel** class is derived from the **CORBA_Object** class.

Mapping Of Attributes

In C++, attributes of a class generally are declared to be non-**public**, and accessor and mutator member functions are provided to access them. IDL follows that same practice. IDL attributes map to accessor and mutator operations when the IDL is compiled. For instance, in the following definition

```
module CoBank
{
    interface Account
    {
        attribute float balance;
        attribute string holder;
        //...
    };
};
```

the **balance** and **holder** attributes map to the following accessor/mutator operations in the **CoBank_Account** and **CoBank_Account_skel** classes:

```
virtual CORBA_Float balance(); //accessor operation
virtual void balance(CORBA_Float); //mutator operation

virtual char* holder(); //accessor operation
virtual void holder(const char*);  //mutator operation
```

A **readonly** maps to an accessor operation only. For example, when the IDL

```
module CoBank
{
    interface Account
    {
        readonly attribute float balance;
        readonly attribute string holder;
```

NOTE

Exceptions By Attributes

The accessor/mutator operations—corresponding to the attributes of interfaces—can't raise user-defined exceptions. However, at runtime, they can raise system exceptions.

```
        //...
    };
};
```

is compiled, the **readonly** attributes **balance** and **holder** map to the following accessor operations in the **CoBank_Account** and **CoBank_Account_skel** classes:

```
virtual CORBA_Float balance();//accessor operation
virtual char* holder();//accessor operation
```

Note that the type **string** maps to **char*** and not **CORBA_String_var**. The **CORBA_String_var** class is just a smart-pointer class for the **char*** type and is only used within programs for automatic memory management for the **char*** type.

Mapping Of Operation Parameters

Table 9.2 shows how **in** and **out** parameters of an operation are mapped.

Table 9.3 shows how **inout** and **return** parameters of an operation are mapped.

Table 9.2. **Mapping of in and out parameters.**

Type	in	out
long	CORBA_Long	CORBA_Long&
unsigned long	CORBA_Ulong	CORBA_Ulong&
short	CORBA_Short	CORBA_Short&
unsigned short	CORBA_Ushort	CORBA_UShort&
float	CORBA_Float	CORBA_Float&
double	CORBA_Double	CORBA_Double&
char	CORBA_Char	CORBA_Char&
boolean	CORBA_Boolean	CORBA_Boolean&
octet	CORBA_Octet	CORBA_Octet&
string	const char*	char*&
enum (E)	E	E&
struct (S1)	const S1&	S1&
struct (S2)	const S2&	S2*&
array (A)	const A	A
sequence (Q)	const Q&	Q*&
interface (I)	I_ptr	I_ptr&

NOTE

C++ Mappings Of The struct Type

As Tables 9.2 and 9.3 show, **struct** has two kinds of mappings. The first mapping (**S1**) is applied when the **struct** has only fixed-size data, such as **float**, **short**, and so forth. The second mapping (**S2**) is applied when the **struct** has at least one variable-length data array, such as a **string**, **sequence**, and so forth.

Table 9.3. Mapping of inout and return parameters.

Type	inout	return
long	CORBA_Long&	CORBA_Long
unsigned long	CORBA_Ulong&	CORBA_Ulong
short	CORBA_Short&	CORBA_Short
unsigned short	CORBA_UShort&	CORBA_UShort
float	CORBA_Float&	CORBA_Float
double	CORBA_Double&	CORBA_Double
char	CORBA_Char&	CORBA_Char
boolean	CORBA_Boolean&	CORBA_Boolean
octet	CORBA_Octet&	CORBA_Octet
string	char*&	char*
enum (E)	E&	E
struct (S1)	S1&	S1
struct (S2)	S2&	S2*
array (A)	A	A_slice*
sequence (Q)	Q&	Q*
interface (I)	I_ptr&	I_ptr

A detailed description of **in**, **out**, **inout**, and **return** parameters is not within the scope of this book.

Mapping Of Exceptions

Mapping of IDL exceptions is very similar to the mapping of a **struct**. Here is an example:

```
module CoBank
{
    interface Account
    {
        exception NoMoney
        {
            float balance;
        };

        //...
    };
};
```

When the preceding IDL is compiled using the ORBacus IDL compiler, C++ code is generated, as shown in Listing 9.7.

Listing 9.7   IDL-generated code for an exception.

```
class CoBank_Account;
typedef CoBank_Account* CoBank_Account_ptr;
typedef CoBank_Account* CoBank_AccountRef;
typedef OBObjVar< CoBank_Account > CoBank_Account_var;

class CoBank_Account : virtual public CORBA_Object
{
    CoBank_Account(const CoBank_Account&);
    void operator=(const CoBank_Account&);

protected:

    CoBank_Account() { }

public:

    struct NoMoney : public CORBA_UserException
    {
        NoMoney();
        NoMoney(const NoMoney&);
        NoMoney(CORBA_Float);
        virtual ~NoMoney() { }
        NoMoney& operator=(const NoMoney&);

        CORBA_Float balance;
    };

    //...
};
```

The preceding example shows the following:

♦ An IDL **exception** type maps to a C++ **struct** type that is derived from a standard **CORBA_UserException** class.

♦ An **exception**'s data members are generated as **public** data members of the corresponding **struct** in C++.

♦ A corresponding **_var** for the **exception** type is not generated because exception pointers are not used anywhere within the generated code.

Componentization Using CORBA

This section introduces the development of a simple CORBA application. Before presenting that information, however, the following list provides a recap of important concepts from Chapter 8 that are used in developing this application:

♦ *Distributed component*—OMG enables application data and business logic to be encapsulated within *objects* (generally referred to as *distributed components*) that can be instantiated and interacted with from anywhere. Access to a particular component's application capabilities is mediated by the *object interface* that it supports. An object reference is analogous to a C++ pointer that reliably denotes a component in a distributed environment. A component may be denoted by multiple, distinct object references. A component interface represents a potential point of integration and interoperation between a component and its client. The component interface "hides" the underlying implementation. Clients can be developed independently of an implementation.

♦ *OMA object model*—Similar to a classical object model, in which a client interacts with a component, and the component provides services. An object model describes a component's behavior and presents the mechanism by which clients are isolated from the component data representations and behavior implementation. Two core elements of the object management architecture (OMA) object model are the following:

  ♦ *Object semantics*—Used to specify a component's type, the services that it supports, and its data representation. As Chapter 8 explains, object semantics represents the "outside view" of a component. Object semantics defines a component as an identifiable, encapsulated entity that provides one or more services that can be requested by a client through its interface.

  ♦ *Object implementation*—Typically gives a mechanism that can be used to define the state and services of a component. As Chapter 8 explains, object implementation represents the "inside view" of a component.

♦ *Stubs and skeletons*—When an IDL is compiled, IDL language compilers generate client-side stubs and server-side skeletons. A *stub* (also referred to as a *surrogate* or *proxy*) is used to create and issue requests on behalf of a client, whereas a *skeleton* is required to deliver requests to the component. IDL stubs and skeletons are linked directly to the client application and the component implementation, respectively.

Business Components

Business components in a design never occur in isolation—they communicate with other components to carry a business logic or process. Because CORBA provides the required infrastructure for component interaction, application designers never have to worry about inter-operation between components. Instead, they typically focus on the relationships and collaboration between components. The components' ability to interact with each other at the semantic level is the key to a business process. Most of the popular object-oriented analysis and design (OOAD) methodology tools are able to capture and describe component relationships and interactions—designers can use, for example, Ivar Jacobson's *use cases* or Fusion's *object interaction diagrams*. The following information about components in a system typically is captured:

◆ *Static component model*—Describes the static information of the component. It is more like an object model, as used in an OOAD. Its key concepts are interfaces, attributes, hierarchies, and associations between interfaces.

◆ *Dynamic component model*—Adds operations to the interface and describes how a component interacts with other components at runtime.

Because CORBA components support late binding and well-defined interfaces, designers can apply traditional C++ design concepts (such as reusability by inheritance and composition) and design patterns (such as factories). Reuse by inheritance and composition is described in Chapter 3, and the concept of the factory design pattern is presented in Chapter 5.

Also, by using CORBA services such as transactions and events, components that act like real-world components can be implemented.

Other key aspects of *componentization* are development, packaging, and testing. A simple but concrete example that demonstrates how to write a component in C++ is presented in this section.

Developing An Account Component

Up to this point, this chapter has presented IDL syntax and its mapping to C++. IDL is used to define modules; within a module, you can define interfaces, exceptions, structs, and so forth. This section demonstrates how to write an **Account** component by using ORBacus, from defining object interfaces to running the server.

Why An *Account* Component

For a class to be understood by CORBA and accessed remotely, it must have an interface that is expressed in IDL. A bank account class has to be accessed remotely by using an ATM or credit card. Hence, the bank account class must be expressed by using an IDL, and thus becomes a distributed component. This is the simplest way to decide whether a class should be based on an IDL.

An **Account** component can be implemented in C++ and installed in a server that is responsible to instantiate as well as manage the component instance within the server.

Steps To Developing An *Account* Component

To build a CORBA application, you typically need to define the interfaces (which in turn define the capabilities that will be made available by the server, and how those capabilities are accessed), implement those interfaces, and then compile and run the server. You'll encounter a few issues along the way, which are discussed later in the "CORBA Design Issues" section.

The following programming steps are required to write the distributed **Account** component in C++:

1. Define the **Account** interface, using the standard IDL.

2. Compile the interface by using the IDL compiler.

3. Implement the interface of the component in C++.

4. Write a **CoBank** server, which instantiates the **Account** component and informs ORB when initialization is done and the server is ready to accept requests.

5. Write a client to connect to the **CoBank** server and use the **Account** component.

Step 1: Define The *Account* Interface

The first step in writing a CORBA program is to define the IDL interface. The interface to your **Account** component can be defined in IDL (**bank.idl**) as follows:

```
//File: bank.idl
#ifndef __BANK_IDL__
#define __BANK_IDL__

module CoBank
{
```

```
struct Person
{
    string name;
    short age;
};

interface Account
{
    readonly attribute float balance;
    readonly attribute Person holder;

    exception NoMoney
    {
        float balance;
    };

    void deposit(in float amount);
    void withdraw(in float amount) raises (NoMoney);
};
};

#endif
```

Here is the description of each element in the preceding **bank.idl** file:

♦ The module **CoBank** provides a **Person** structure and the **Account** interface.

♦ **Account** provides two attributes, **balance** and **holder**, which define the basic characteristics of the **Account** component. Because these attributes are labeled **readonly**, they can't be directly modified.

♦ **Account** specifies a **NoMoney** exception that has the **Account** balance as its data member.

♦ The **Account** interface has two operations: **deposit()**, which allows the **Account** owner to deposit money, and **withdraw()**, which withdraws money for the owner. The parameters to the operations are labeled as **in**, which means that they are being passed from the client to the server. The **deposit()** operation can throw the **NoMoney** exception when not enough money is available to make the withdrawal.

Step 2: Compile The Interface
The IDL specification must be compiled, both to check the specification and to map it into C++ so that it can be implemented and used.

The **bank.idl** file can be compiled by using the IDL compiler supplied with ORBacus. The IDL compiler produces four C++ files:

♦ **bank.h**—A stub header file that declares proxy for **Account**.

♦ **bank.cpp**—A source file to be compiled and linked into the clients of the **Account** component.

♦ **bank_skel.h**—A header file to be included in the implementation of the **Account** component.

♦ **bank_skel.cpp**—A skeleton source file to be compiled and linked into the implementation of the **Account**.

Figure 9.1 shows the IDL-generated files.

The following two sections describe the **bank.h** and **bank_skel.h** files. The **bank.cpp** and **bank_skel.cpp** files are not described because they present definitions of only a few functions declared in the **bank.h** and **bank_skel.h** files.

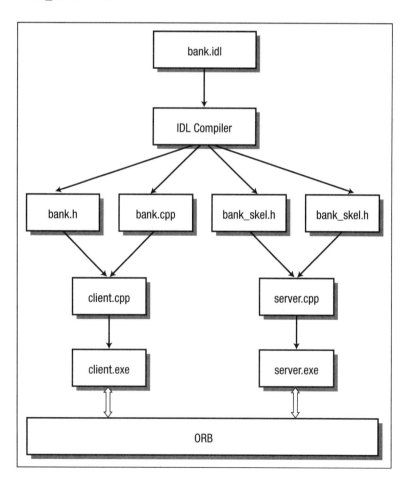

Figure 9.1
Generation of C++ files using IDL.

The *bank.h* File

The **bank.h** file is a stub header file that declares proxy for the **Account** type. The **bank.h** file contains the declarations shown in Listing 9.8.

Listing 9.8   Declaration for stub of the Account interface.

```
class CoBank_Account;
typedef CoBank_Account* CoBank_Account_ptr;
typedef OBObjVar< CoBank_Account > CoBank_Account_var;

struct CoBank_Person
{
    CoBank_Person();
    CoBank_Person(const CoBank_Person&);
    ~CoBank_Person() { }
    CoBank_Person& operator=(const CoBank_Person&);

    CORBA_String_var name;
    CORBA_Short age;
};

typedef OBVarVar< CoBank_Person > CoBank_Person_var;

class CoBank_Account : virtual public CORBA_Object
{
    CoBank_Account(const CoBank_Account&);
    void operator=(const CoBank_Account&);

protected:

    CoBank_Account() { }

public:

    virtual CORBA_Float balance();
    virtual CoBank_Person* holder();
    struct NoMoney : public CORBA_UserException
    {
        NoMoney();
        NoMoney(const NoMoney&);
        NoMoney(CORBA_Float);
        virtual ~NoMoney() { }
        NoMoney& operator=(const NoMoney&);

        CORBA_Float balance;
    };
```

```
        virtual void deposit(CORBA_Float amount);

        virtual void withdraw(CORBA_Float amount);
};
```

The **CoBank_Account** class acts as the proxy for the **Account** component. The **CoBank_Account** class has **balance()**, **holder()**, **deposit()**,
and **withdraw()** operations that are defined in the **bank.cpp** file. These
operations allow a client to call remote operations on an object reference of the type **CoBank_Account**.

Note that the **CoBank_Account** class doesn't have a **public** constructor. Hence, this class can't be directly instantiated. An instance of the
object reference is represented by either **CoBank_Account_ptr** or
CoBank_Account_var (shown in the client program in the "Step 5:
Write A Client" section). The **CoBank_Account_var** class is the smart
pointer for the **CoBank_Account** class.

The *bank_skel.h* File

The **bank_skel.h** header file should be included in the implementation of the **Account** component. The **bank_skel.h** file contains the
declarations, as follows:

```
#include <bank.h>

class CoBank_Account_skel :
    virtual public CoBank_Account,
    virtual public CORBA_Object_skel
{
    CoBank_Account_skel(const CoBank_Account_skel&);
    void operator=(const CoBank_Account_skel&);

public:

    CoBank_Account_skel() { }

    virtual CORBA_Float balance() = 0;
    virtual CoBank_Person* holder() = 0;
    virtual void deposit(CORBA_Float amount) = 0;
    virtual void withdraw(CORBA_Float amount) = 0;
};
```

The **CoBank_Account_skel** class contains the same function names
that the IDL contains. However, **CoBank_Account_skel** functions are

pure virtual functions. They are implemented by the **Account** component via class derivation. The two **readonly** attributes, **balance**
and **holder**, have been replaced with access functions. The
CoBank_Account_skel class inherits from the **CoBank_Account** and
CORBA_Object_skel classes. The **CORBA_Object_skel** class is itself a derived class from the **CORBA_Object** class. A detailed
description of the **CORBA_Object_skel** and **CORBA_Object** classes
is not within the scope of this book.

Step 3: Implement The Interface Of The Component

To implement the **Account** interface, a class must be implemented that
defines the pure virtual functions listed in the **CoBank_Account_skel**
class. The implementation class is called **CoBank_AccountImpl**. It implements the **CoBank_Account** interface by means of derivation. The
declaration is shown next as the **bank_impl.h** file:

```
//File: bank_impl.h

#ifndef __BANK_IMPL_H__
#define __BANK_IMPL_H__

#include <bank_skel.h>

class CoBank_AccountImpl: public CoBank_Account_skel
{
private:

    CORBA_Float _balance;
    CoBank_Person _person;

public:

    CoBank_AccountImpl(const CORBA_Float& balance,
                       const CoBank_Person& person);

    virtual CORBA_Float balance();

    virtual CoBank_Person* holder();

    virtual void deposit(CORBA_Float amount);

    virtual void withdraw(CORBA_Float amount);
};

#endif
```

The elements of the **CoBank_AccountImpl** class are as follows:

♦ The **CoBank_AccountImpl** implementation class is inherited from the IDL-generated **CoBank_Account_skel** class. The name of the implementation class has the following format: **<the module name>_<interface name>Impl**.

♦ The **CoBank_AccountImpl** class overrides each of the **balance()**, **holder()**, **deposit()**, and **withdraw()** functions of the base class.

♦ The **CoBank_AccountImpl** class adds data members **_person** and **_balance**, and a constructor. The data members represent the interface attributes.

♦ The constructor of the **CoBank_AccountImpl** class is user-defined and can take any form.

Listing 9.9 shows a simple definition of the **CoBank_AccountImpl** class.

Listing 9.9   Definition of the CoBank_AccountImpl class.

```
//File: bank_impl.cpp
#include <OB/CORBA.h>
#include <bank_impl.h>

CoBank_AccountImpl::CoBank_AccountImpl(
    const CORBA_Float& balance,
    const CoBank_Person& person):
    _person(person), _balance(balance)
{
    cout<<"Creating account for "<<person.name<<"
    with initial balance "<<balance<<endl;
}


CORBA_Float CoBank_AccountImpl::balance ()
{
    cout<<"In CoBank_AccountImpl::balance()"<<endl;
    return _balance;
}


CoBank_Person* CoBank_AccountImpl::holder ()
{
    cout<<"In CoBank_AccountImpl::holder()"<<endl;
    CoBank_Person* pp=new CoBank_Person(_person);
    return pp;
}
```

```
void CoBank_AccountImpl::deposit (CORBA_Float amount)
{
    cout<<
    "In CoBank_AccountImpl::deposit(). Depositing: "<<
    amount<<endl;
    _balance+=amount;
}

void CoBank_AccountImpl::withdraw (CORBA_Float amount)
{
    cout<<
    "In CoBank_AccountImpl::withdraw(). Withdrawing: "<<
    amount<<endl;

    if (_balance<amount)
    {
        throw CoBank_Account::NoMoney(_balance);
    }
    _balance-=amount;
}
```

NOTE

Another Approach To Implementation

The interface implementation approach as defined earlier in "Step 3: Implement The Interface Of The Component" is not the only way to implement an interface. CORBA provides another approach to implement an interface. You can implement the **Account** interface in a class that does not inherit from the **CoBank_Account_skel** class. In this case, IDL compiler generates classes for delegate-based interface implementations. This approach is referred to as the _tie-approach_. This approach is described in Chapter 16.

Two points must be noted about the preceding code:

♦ The **AccountImpl::holder()** function returns a new copy of the member **_holder**. A pointer that is returned by a CORBA operation must always be a new copy on heap. (Refer to Chapter 1 to get information about memory allocation on heap.) ORB takes the ownership of the pointer and deallocates after marshalling.

♦ The **withdraw()** function can throw only the **NoMoney** exception. The **balance()**, **holder()**, and **deposit()** functions don't throw any user-defined exception. Any attempt to throw unexpected exceptions from these functions will terminate the server.

The class, such as **CoBank_AccountImpl**, is referred to as an _implementation_ of the **Account** interface. It is also called a _component_, because it can live anywhere on the ORB and it can be communicated with through its well-defined interface.

Step 4: Write A **CoBank** Server

After you develop the **Account** component, you need to write a server program that instantiates the component and makes its services available to a client. The client needs to obtain the object reference of the component that will use the services provided by the component. Recall that an object reference is analogous to a C++ pointer that reliably denotes a component in a distributed environment. Using CORBA,

A stringified object reference is the simplest way of establishing the first contact with a server. However, this mechanism isn't the only method for bootstrapping an object reference. The CORBA specification provides a standard way to bootstrap an object reference—it is done through a set of initial services. You can obtain object references for the initial services by using the **resolve_initial_references()** operation on the **ORB** interface. This mechanism is described in Chapter 12.

the client can obtain the object reference of a component in many ways. One of the most common ways is by receiving an object reference through a file. The server program first publishes a component's object reference into a well-known file, and subsequently, the client can resolve that. To do this, the CORBA specification defines two operations on the **ORB** interface in the **CORBA** module:

```
module CORBA
{
    interface ORB
    {
        string object_to_string(in Object obj);
        Object string_to_object(in string ref);
    };
    //...
};
```

The **object_to_string()** operation converts the **obj** argument into a string. The converted value is referred to as a *stringified object reference*. The **string_to_object()** operation converts a stringified object reference back to an object reference. All of the examples described in this chapter involve the publication of an object reference in the stringified form.

Listing 9.10 shows the **server.cpp** file that creates an instance of the **Account** component, and uses the **object_to_string()** operation to publish **Account**'s object reference into a well-known file (**CoAccount.ref**).

Listing 9.10   Server for the Account interface.
```
#include <OB/CORBA.h>
#include <OB/Util.h>
#include <bank_impl.h>
#include <stdlib.h>
#include <errno.h>
#ifdef HAVE_FSTREAM
#    include <fstream>
#else
#    include <fstream.h>
#endif

int main(int argc, char* argv[], char*[])
{
    try
    {
        // Create ORB and BOA
        CORBA_ORB_var orb =
```

```
        CORBA_ORB_init(argc, argv);
    CORBA_BOA_var boa =
        orb -> BOA_init(argc, argv);

    // Create implementation component
    CoBank_Person person;
    person.name=(const char*)"vishwa";
    person.age=29;

    CoBank_Account_var p =
        new CoBank_AccountImpl(100, person);

    // Save reference
    CORBA_String_var s =
        orb -> object_to_string(p);

    const char* refFile = "CoAccount.ref";
    ofstream out(refFile);
    if(out.fail())
    {
        cerr << argv[0] << ": can't open " <<
        refFile << ": "<< strerror(errno) << endl;
        return 1;
    }

    out << s << endl;
    out.close();

    // Run implementation
    boa ->impl_is_ready(
        CORBA_ImplementationDef::_nil());
    }
catch(CORBA_SystemException& ex)
{
    OBPrintException(ex);
    return 1;
}

    return 0;
}
```

The following discusses selected code in the preceding program:

♦ The bank server program must initialize the ORB before doing anything else. The **CORBA_ORB_init()** call does that task. The call returns a pointer to ORB that is stored in the variable, **orb** of type **CORBA_ORB_var.**

♦ The server then initializes the basic object adapter (BOA) by calling **BOA_init()** on the **orb** pointer. The call returns a pointer to BOA that is stored in the **boa** pointer of the type **CORBA_ BOA_var**. Recall that BOA defines how a component is activated. BOA can do this by launching another server process, starting another thread within the same server process, or reusing a thread in the same server process.

♦ The server program **server.cpp** instantiates a **CoBank_AccountImpl** instance on heap by using its constructor. It provides initial data. The pointer is stored in variable **p** of type **CoBank_Account_var**. Note that **CoBank_Account_var** represents the object reference for **CoBank_AccountImpl**.

♦ The server needs to *export* the object reference **p** that can be used by the bank client. This is done in a very simple manner. First, the object reference is stringified by using an ORB **object_to_string()** function. Then, the stringified object reference is written to the **CoAccount.ref** file that the bank client can read.

♦ The program indicates to ORBacus that the server's initialization has completed, by calling **impl_is_ready()**. This function must be called when a server wants to start processing network requests. The parameter to **impl_is_ready()** can be ignored for the time being.

♦ The program handles the **CORBA_SystemException** and prints its contents by calling **OBPrintException()**. The exception can be thrown by the **CORBA_ORB_init()** and **BOA_init()** calls.

Step 5: Write A Client

After you develop the server program, you need to write a client program to access the services from the **Account** component. The client program that uses **Account** is shown in Listing 9.11.

Listing 9.11   Client for the Account interface.

```
//File: client.cpp
#include <OB/CORBA.h>
#include <OB/Util.h>
#include <bank.h>
#include <stdlib.h>
#include <errno.h>
#ifdef HAVE_FSTREAM
#    include <fstream>
#else
#    include <fstream.h>
#endif
int main(int argc, char* argv[], char*[])
```

```
{
    try
    {
        // Create ORB
        CORBA_ORB_var orb = CORBA_ORB_init(argc, argv);

        const char* refFile = "CoAccount.ref";
        ifstream in;
        in.open(refFile);
        if(in.fail())
        {
            cerr << argv[0] <<
                ": can't open " << refFile << ": "
                << strerror(errno) << endl;
            return 1;
        }

        char s[1000];
        in >> s;

        CORBA_Object_var obj =
            orb -> string_to_object(s);
        assert(!CORBA_is_nil(obj));

        CoBank_Account_var account =
            CoBank_Account::_narrow(obj);

        assert(!CORBA_is_nil(account));

        cout<<"Intial balance:"<<
        account->balance()<<endl;
        account->deposit(50);
        cout<<"Balance:"<<account->balance()<<endl;
        account->withdraw(50);
        cout<<"Balance:"<<account->balance()<<endl;

        CoBank_Person_var person=account->holder();

        cout<<"Name:"<<person->name<<endl;
        cout<<"Age:"<<person->age<<endl;
        account->withdraw(1000);
    }
    catch(CORBA_SystemException& ex)
    {
        OBPrintException(ex);
        return 1;
    }
```

```
  catch(const CoBank_Account::NoMoney& nm)
{
    cout<<"No money. Current balance:"<<
    nm.balance<<endl;
}
catch(...)
{
    cerr << "Unexpected exception " << endl;
    exit(1);
}
return 0;
}
```

Before the bank client can invoke the operations of an **Account** interface, it must get the object reference for that interface. Recall that the object reference uniquely identifies an **Account** component on ORB. The following list discusses the important aspects of this program:

♦ The client opens the **CoAccount.ref** file. First, the program reads the object reference to a **char** array. Recall that the server saved the object reference in a stringified form. Then, the program converts the stringified reference to an object reference by calling the **string_to_object()** function on the **orb** pointer. The returned value is stored in **CORBA_Object_var**.

♦ The returned object reference is checked for **null** by using a **CORBA_is_nil()** function.

♦ The base **CORBA_Object_var** object reference is typecast to the object reference of type **Account_var** by calling an IDL-generated static function **CoBank_Account::_narrow()**. The returned value is stored in the **account** variable. Recall that **CORBA_Object** is a base class of **CoBank_Account**. If you know that a reference of type **CORBA_Object_var** object actually references a **CoBank_Account** object, then narrowing the **CORBA_Object_var** object reference to a **CoBank_Account_var** reference is legal.

♦ The program uses the arrow (**->**) operator on the **account** variable to invoke operations on the **Account** component.

♦ The program handles the **CORBA_SystemException** and **CoBank_Account::NoMoney** exceptions. The **CORBA_SystemException** exception generally is raised by ORB when the server either isn't running, doesn't have the required instance of the implementation, or has become unreachable due to a network fault.

NOTE

Using ORBacus To Build And Run Programs

This book doesn't give information about makefiles, the ORBacus runtime environment, and ORBacus configuration files to build and run CORBA programs. These topics are not within the scope of the book. This information can be found in the ORBacus manual that can be downloaded from **www.ooc.com/ob/ download.html**.

Running The Server And Client

When you run the server program, you initially see the following messages on the screen:

```
Creating account for vishwa with initial balance 100
```

As a result of running the client, the following messages appear on the server-side screen:

```
In CoBank_AccountImpl::balance()
In CoBank_AccountImpl::deposit(). Depositing: 50
In CoBank_AccountImpl::balance()
In CoBank_AccountImpl::withdraw(). Withdrawing: 50
In CoBank_AccountImpl::balance()
In CoBank_AccountImpl::holder()
In CoBank_AccountImpl::withdraw(). Withdrawing: 1000
```

And, the client-side screen will have the following messages:

```
Intial balance:100
Balance:150
Balance:100
Name:vishwa
Age:29
No money. Current balance:100
```

The last output shows that the **CoBank_Account::NoMoney** exception is raised by the server program because not enough money exists to perform the withdraw of amount **100**.

Managing The Life Cycle Of The **Account** Component

The server program just developed has one problem—the **Account** component is always running, even if the client isn't accessing. Therefore, you need a mechanism that can control the life cycle of your **Account** component. This mechanism must ensure that an **Account** is instantiated when it is needed, and destroyed when it isn't needed. You can address this issue by applying a *factory*, a special component that can provide a mechanism to manage other components' instances. You can have a factory that manages the life cycles of a variety of components. However, this section develops a simple factory that manages the instances of the **Account** component. In this example, you add an **AccountFactory** component that will be responsible for managing instances of **Account**. It requires an **AccountFactory** interface to be added to the **CoBank** module. The new module is shown in Listing 9.12.

Listing 9.12 The AccountFactory interface.

```
#ifndef __BANK_IDL__
#define __BANK_IDL__

module CoBank
{
    struct Person
    {
        string name;
        short age;
    };

    interface Account
    {
        readonly attribute float balance;
        readonly attribute Person holder;

        exception NoMoney
        {
            float balance;
        };

        void deposit(in float amount);
        void withdraw(in float amount)
        raises (NoMoney);
    };

    interface AccountFactory
    {
        Account create(in Person person,
        in float balance);

        void destroy();
    };
};

#endif
```

The **AccountFactory** interface has two operations: **create()** and **destroy()**. A call to **create()** instantiates the **Account** component in the server and returns its object reference, so that the client can operate on it. The **destroy()** operation removes the **Account** instance. The **AccountFactory** interface must be compiled by the IDL compiler before you can start implementing the **AccountFactory** component.

The following code, produced by the ORBacus IDL compiler, is the declaration of the **AccountFactory** component in the **bank_impl.h** file:

```
class CoBank_AccountFactoryImpl:
    public CoBank_AccountFactory_skel
{
private:

    CoBank_Account_ptr _account;

public:

    CoBank_AccountFactoryImpl();
    virtual CoBank_Account_ptr create(
        CORBA_Float balance,
        const CoBank_Person& person);
    virtual void destroy();
};
```

The **CoBank_AccountFactoryImpl** class maintains a private variable **_account** of type **CoBankAccount_ptr**. Recall that the type **CoBank_Account_ptr** represents an **Account** reference.

Listing 9.13 presents the implementation of the **AccountFactory** component in the **bank_impl.cpp** file.

Listing 9.13   The implementation for the AccountFactory interface.

```
//In file: bank_impl.cpp
CoBank_AccountFactoryImpl::CoBank_AccountFactoryImpl()
{
    _account=CoBank_Account::_nil();
    cout<<"creating factory object"<<endl;
}


CoBank_Account_ptr CoBank_AccountFactoryImpl::create
        (CORBA_Float balance, const CoBank_Person& person)
{
    cout<<"Creating account for "<<person.name<<
    " with initial balance "<<balance<<endl;
    _account=new CoBank_AccountImpl(balance, person);
    return CoBank_Account::_duplicate(_account);
}


void CoBank_AccountFactoryImpl::destroy()
{
    cout<<"Destroying account"<<endl;
    CORBA_release(_account);
    CORBA_release(_account);
}
```

This list discusses the preceding implementation:

♦ The constructor initializes the data member **_account** to **null** by calling an IDL-generated static **CoBank_Account::_nil()** function.

♦ The **create()** operation instantiates the **CoBank_AccountImpl** on heap and stores the returned values in **_account**. Before _account is returned from the **create()** operation, an IDL-generated static function **CoBank_Account::_duplicate()** is called. An object reference that is returned by a CORBA operation must always be duplicated. ORBacus maintains a reference count for each reference to determine whether it should destroy the component. The *reference count* of a component is the number of pointers to the object that exist within the same address space. The initial reference count for a component is always one. A call to **_duplicate()** increments the reference count by one. After the call to **create()**, the reference count for **CoBank_Account** is two.

♦ In the **destroy()** operation, the **CoBank_AccountImpl** instance must be deallocated. However, you can't delete the instance unless the reference count is zero. Therefore, the **CORBA_release()** function is called twice. This function reduces the object reference count by one, and destroys the object if the reference count is zero. To deallocate a reference, don't call **delete**. Instead, call the **CORBA_release()** function, as shown in the preceding example.

The preceding discussion presents an important notion of ORB—the reference count mechanism. ORB uses reference counting to manage the lifetime of distributed components. To recap: An object reference is duplicated (its reference count is incremented) when the reference is passed to a client). Similarly, when the server is finished using the component instance, it releases the object reference (decrements the reference count). When the reference count reaches zero, the instance is automatically destroyed.

Listing 9.14 shows the rewritten server program (from Listing 9.10) that uses the **AccountFactory** component that was just developed.

Listing 9.14   The server for the Account and AccountFactory interfaces.

```
#include <OB/CORBA.h>
#include <OB/Util.h>
#include <bank_impl.h>
#include <stdlib.h>
#include <errno.h>
```

```cpp
#ifdef HAVE_FSTREAM
#   include <fstream>
#else
#   include <fstream.h>
#endif

int main(int argc, char* argv[], char*[])
{
    try
    {
        // Create ORB and BOA
        CORBA_ORB_var orb = CORBA_ORB_init(argc, argv);
        CORBA_BOA_var boa = orb -> BOA_init(argc, argv);

        // Create implementation object

        CoBank_AccountFactory_var p =
        new CoBank_AccountFactoryImpl;

        // Save reference
        CORBA_String_var s = orb -> object_to_string(p);

        const char* refFile = "CoAccount.ref";
        ofstream out(refFile);
        if(out.fail())
        {
            cerr << argv[0] << ": can't open " <<
            refFile << ": "<< strerror(errno) << endl;
            return 1;
        }

        out << s << endl;
        out.close();

        // Run implementation
        boa -> impl_is_ready(
            CORBA_ImplementationDef::_nil());
    }
    catch(CORBA_SystemException& ex)
    {
        OBPrintException(ex);
        return 1;
    }

    return 0;
}
```

This server simply instantiates the **AccountFactory** component and then informs BOA that the server's initialization has completed, by calling **impl_is_ready()**.

The client program also needs modifications to use the **AccountFactory** reference. The new client program is shown in Listing 9.15.

Listing 9.15 The client for the Account and AccountFactory interfaces.

```cpp
#include <OB/CORBA.h>
#include <OB/Util.h>
#include <bank.h>
#include <stdlib.h>
#include <errno.h>
#ifdef HAVE_FSTREAM
#   include <fstream>
#else
#   include <fstream.h>
#endif

int main(int argc, char* argv[], char*[])
{
    CoBank_AccountFactory_var accountFactory;

    try
    {
        // Create ORB
        CORBA_ORB_var orb = CORBA_ORB_init(argc, argv);

        // Get "Account" object
        const char* refFile = "CoAccount.ref";
        ifstream in;
        in.open(refFile);
        if(in.fail())
        {
            cerr << argv[0] << ": can't open " <<
            refFile <<":"<< strerror(errno) << endl;
            return 1;
        }

        char s[1000];
        in >> s;

        CORBA_Object_var obj =
            orb -> string_to_object(s);
        assert(!CORBA_is_nil(obj));
```

```
        accountFactory =
            CoBank_AccountFactory::_narrow(obj);

        assert(!CORBA_is_nil(accountFactory));

        CoBank_Person person;
        person.name=(const char*)"vishwa";
        person.age=29;

        CoBank_Account_var account =
        accountFactory->create(100, person);

        assert(!CORBA_is_nil(account));

        cout<<"Intial balance:"<<
        account->balance()<<endl;

        account->deposit(50);
        cout<<"Balance:"<<account->balance()<<endl;

        account->withdraw(50);
        cout<<"Balance:"<<account->balance()<<endl;

        cout<<"destroying"<<endl;
        accountFactory->destroy();

        cout<<
        "trying to call withdraw() on destroyed account"<<
        endl;
        account->withdraw(50);
    }
    catch(CORBA_SystemException& ex)
    {
        OBPrintException(ex);
        return 1;
    }
    catch(const CoBank_Account::NoMoney& nm)
    {
        cout<<"No money. Current balance:"<<
        nm.balance<<endl;
    }
    catch(...)
    {
        cerr << "Unexpected exception " << endl
        exit(1);
    }
```

```
        return 0;
}
```

In the preceding listing, the object reference **accountFactory** is bound to the **AccountFactory** component running in the server. A **create()** call returns the CORBA reference to the **Account** component. The client program further uses this reference to invoke operations on the **Account** component. When the client is done with the **Account** component, it calls **destroy()** to remove the instance of the **Account** component. This ensures that the server doesn't have **Account** instances running all the time.

When the server runs, it shows the following initial output:

```
creating factory object
```

When the client runs, the server shows the following output:

```
Creating account for vishwa with initial balance 100
In CoBank_Account::balance()
In CoBank_Account::deposit(). Depositing: 50
In CoBank_Account::balance()
In CoBank_Account::withdraw(). Withdrawing: 50
In CoBank_Account::balance()
Destroying account
in destructor of CoBank_AccountImpl
Warning: Servant method raised a non-CORBA exception
Client receives this exception as CORBA::UNKNOWN
```

And, the client shows the following output:

```
Intial balance:100
Balance:150
Balance:100
destroying
trying to call withdraw() on destroyed account
System exception 'UNKNOWN'
Completed: no
Minor code: 0
```

The exception statements shown in the server and client outputs are caused by the client's attempt to call the **withdraw()** operation after the **Account** component was destroyed by calling **destroy()**. In this case, the client received a system exception. The content of the exception is displayed by using the **OBPrintException()** function. The full description and interpretation of a system exception is not within the scope of this book.

CORBA Design Issues

This section discusses a few significant design issues related to a CORBA architecture and application. This isn't a comprehensive list of issues. However, these are very generic issues, and thus, are important to understand.

Writing Real-World Components

The **Account** component shown in the previous sections is a light-weight application component. The real applications' components may use CORBA services (such as transaction services, security services, events services, and so forth) to provide the required application functionality. Similarly, the **AccountFactory** component is a minimal factory implementation. The real-life factories may support more than one type of application component; they will maintain a data structure to handle various types. The mechanism to read an object reference from a file shown in the previous examples is also a simple mechanism. The applications generally use CORBA naming and trader services to locate other components. (CORBA services are described in Chapter 12.)

Packaging And Deployment Of Components

CORBA provides the required infrastructure for *component inter-operation*—and as an application designer, you typically focus on component relationships and their collaboration, which is the core of an application design. An application design is actually the process of combining components to form a desired application. *Component packaging*, on the other hand, is the process of creating a platform from which the components can collaborate with other components, based on the application design. Component factories generally provide such platforms. Because components can exist independently, they provide great flexibility in packaging. The following are some issues and policies regarding component packaging:

♦ Factories can either launch new components when they are demanded, or recycle those components that are no longer used by the application. This mostly becomes an issue of factory design.

- You may want to package *many* components or *few* components in a factory. A factory runs as a process, and when this process crashes, it causes all the running component instances to crash. If high availability is an application-design criteria, you may only want to package a few components in each factory. This sort of packaging is mostly a configuration issue of factories. The factory designer must take care of designing configurable factories that can control how many instances of a component can coexist at runtime.

- Because components can run anywhere, it is important that they support the internationalization (I18N). You can't package a French component along with a component that works only with English. Configuring a factory to run in a particular locale generally is a good idea, so that all packaged components also share the same locale. Components requiring a different locale must run in a different process; otherwise, the functionality and performance of the application may be affected.

- Performance may be a critical parameter when deciding whether to package a particular component in a particular factory. If the application consists of many vertical slices of interacting components, packaging each of these slices in a factory may help. In other words, the components that interact frequently with each other may be packaged in the same factories.

- A factory itself may introduce performance problems by creating a bottleneck. If a factory is expected to receive frequent calls to process a component, you need to scale the factory and make it multithreaded.

- The functionality of a component may generally give a good indication of how it should be packaged. Components that need to check authentication may be packaged in factories that run closer to firewalls and authentication agents. Similarly, components that provide persistence may be packaged in factories that run closer to databases.

Although deciding component packaging during application design is possible, it generally becomes an iterative process and may not get finalized until system testing. Bad packaging may lead to repackaging of the component from one factory to another. Though transparent repackaging is supported by CORBA, the changed factories need to be compiled and retested before they can be redeployed in the system. A good factory design is an important element in good component packaging.

CORBA And Reusability

The CORBA components support the notion of reuse. CORBA provides the power to leverage components with great flexibility. As described in Chapter 3, a reusable component should have the following three properties:

♦ *Usability*—A runtime property of a reusable component. Unless a CORBA component provides the expected functionality and efficiency, it can't be leveraged, and hence can't be reused.

♦ *Generality*—A reusable component must have a broad scope of applicability. If a CORBA component can be reused only once, it isn't a reusable component. Because information domains have fuzzy, changing boundaries, you need to understand that reusable components undergo evolutionary changes. You need to manage this process to ensure that a component's generality never declines. This management includes protecting existing reuses of that component from the effects of subsequent evolutionary change.

♦ *Adaptability*—A reusable component isn't used as-is, because of its generality property. It has to be modified via proper programming. *Adaptability* means ease of reuse, an important yardstick in making a reusable component. Often, other reusable components automate the adaptation of a particular component to suit a particular context, making the adaptability problem trivial in those cases.

The CORBA component model and C++ together provide a strong platform for software reuse across two dimensions:

♦ Reuse across projects (white-box reuse)

♦ Specification reuse (black-box reuse)

Reuse Across Projects

Reuse across projects refers to the ability of a developer to leverage CORBA components from one project into the next. This is also referred to as *white-box reuse*, because you are effectively using the code or implementation of a component in another place. This sort of reuse is no different from the C++ way of reusing a class. A component is generally reused and adapted via *component derivation*, the process of creating new component implementations from existing ones. (It is the same as class derivation.) Recall that a component's implementation is just a C++ class.

In component derivation, the derived component inherits the implementations of IDL operations and the internal structure of the base component. The new implementation can either add to the IDL operations that it inherits or redefine inherited IDL operations. Component derivation enables programmers to assemble relevant components into a hierarchy. This sort of reuse promotes *code reuse*. Polymorphism enables a particular object reference to work correctly in a wide range of new contexts.

Specification Reuse

CORBA and C++ together provide a good platform for promoting software reuse. You can achieve a higher degree of reuse only if components are properly designed for reusability. Code reuse is one design technique that makes reusability possible. Another design technique is *IDL reuse*, which is widely used within the CORBA community. IDL reuse is referred to as *specification* or *black-box* reuse. Recall that IDL is the expression for a component's external specification. Because creating a specification is a tough and iterative process, specification reuse provides a huge advantage to the software community.

As Chapter 3 explains, the key to reuse is the ability to focus on interfaces rather than implementation details. CORBA's ability to standardize interfaces and encapsulate functionality within C++ objects does a very good job of giving you a black-box view of the world. This black-box view means that you can put together an application from components, without having to deal with their internals.

IDL reuse is supported by IDL inheritance. Like a C++ class, an interface can be derived from another interface, which is then called a *base* interface of the derived interface. A derived interface, like all interfaces, may declare new elements (constants, types, attributes, exceptions, and operations). The derived interface can also be substituted anywhere that its base interface is expected. This notion is illustrated by the following example, which builds on the previous bank example.

A banking application may need many types of bank accounts, such as checking accounts and savings accounts. Both checking and savings accounts are, in fact, special types of accounts that share the properties of an account and respond to the same operations with different behaviors. The new account types can also have additional properties and operations.

New accounts can be described by interface inheritance. **Checking-Account** and **SavingsAccount** can be derived from **Account**. The **Account** interface is called a *base interface* of **CheckingAccount** and **SavingsAccount**. The **CheckingAccount** and **SavingsAccount** interfaces are referred to as *derived interfaces* of the **Account** interface. This is shown in Listing 9.16.

Listing 9.16   IDL with inheritance.

```
module CoBank
{
    struct Person
    {
        string name;
        short age;
    };

    interface Account
    {
        readonly attribute float balance;
        readonly attribute Person holder;

        exception NoMoney
        {
            float balance;
        };

        void deposit(in float amount);

        void withdraw(in float amount)
        raises (NoMoney);
    };

    interface CheckingAccount : Account
    {
        readonly attribute float overdraft_limit;
        float transfer_money(
            in Account acc, in float money);
    };

    interface SavingsAccount : Account
    {
    };
};
```

The **CheckingAccount** interface defines one attribute, **overdraft_limit**, and inherits the **balance** and **holder** attributes defined in its base **Account** interface. The **CheckingAccount** interface also inherits the **deposit()** and **withdraw()** operations from **Account**, and defines a new **transfer_money()** operation. Similarly, the **SavingsAccount** interface inherits members **balance, holder, deposit()**, and **withdraw()** from **Account**, but defines no additional operations. However, the implementation for **SavingsAccount** can provide new definitions for the **deposit()** and **withdraw()** operations.

Specification reuse is an important feature of OMG IDL interfaces because it makes reusing existing interfaces possible when defining new services. In other words, IDLs support polymorphism. For example, a **SavingsAccount** component can be used anywhere that an **Account** component is expected, because a **SavingsAccount** supports all **Account** operations. The new capabilities of the **SavingsAccount** component can therefore be added to the system, without requiring changes to the existing applications that use the **Account** interface. This shows the polymorphic nature of interfaces and plays an important role in developing object-oriented applications using CORBA.

Note that IDL provides the separation of interface and implementation, and doesn't support implementation inheritance. This is very important in developing true OO applications.

IDLs Everywhere

For a client to use a class, the class interface must be expressed in CORBA IDL. If an interface operation needs to pass a class's pointer, the passed class must also be expressed in an IDL. As a result, an application system quite possibly may be full of CORBA interfaces. Because CORBA's current implementations don't provide the mechanism to pass objects by value, your design of an application may be affected. Though nothing is wrong with converting classes into IDLs, you must

Reuse By CORBA In Applications

CORBA has the ability to deliver superior software reuse. However, using CORBA alone may not address all the issues related to OO and software reuse. Corporate commitment, good planning, and application of proper processes and design techniques make reuse more successful. One of the simplest design techniques is partitioning the potential solution into discrete modules, which minimizes the effect of code changes from each other.

An application architecture typically has three software packages: the user interface, the business logic, and the data source. The user interface package makes CORBA calls to the business logic package, which, in turn, sends requests to the data source code. The data source package makes calls to a database system to read and write data. Of course, your application might have security, event notification, transactions, logging, and so forth. Some of these items may be reused in various applications. If you are developing your application by using a higher-level framework than CORBA, you may get these features as part of the framework.

make sure that frequently and heavily used interfaces have their IDL specification frozen much earlier; otherwise, their fluidity of interfaces may cause very high impact on the system design.

Pass-By-Value Mechanism

CORBA's current implementations don't support the mechanism of passing components by value, which means that you always get an object reference of a component to invoke operations remotely on that component. In terms of runtime efficiency, invoking operations remotely may not be a good idea. In other words, if a client needs to operate on a reference many times, the runtime performance of your system may be affected. Because CORBA doesn't support this notion yet, you have to either continue to use the existing pass-by-reference mechanism or use CORBA **struct**s to achieve pass-by-value effect. Note that a **struct** is always passed by value. You can bundle all the attributes of a CORBA interface that need to be passed by value into a **struct**. The **struct** itself is defined as an attribute of the interface. Then, you can pass the **struct** rather than pass the interface. The disadvantage of this approach is that CORBA **struct**s can't express the interface inheritance, because they don't express the inheritance relationship.

Another approach for a client is to link with an implementation of the required interface and store its attributes on the local instance. This approach, however, may not be very suitable, because it may kill the motivation of using CORBA to distribute application logic in various layers of the architecture.

Multiple Interfaces

The previous bank example shows that the **CheckingAccount** component supports two interfaces: the **Account** interface and the **CheckingAccount** interface. A component may be required to support multiple interfaces, which can be done by multiple inheritance, as shown in Listing 9.17.

Listing 9.17   IDL with multiple interfaces.

```
module CoBank
{
    struct Person
    {
        string name;
        short age;
    };
```

```
interface Account
{
    readonly attribute float balance;
    readonly attribute Person holder;

    exception NoMoney
    {
        float balance;
    };

    void deposit(in float amount);

    void withdraw(in float amount)
    raises (NoMoney);
};

interface CheckingAccount : Account
{
    readonly attribute float overdraft_limit;
    void order_chequebook();
};

interface SavingsAccount : Account
{
    float calculate_interest();
};

interface CheckingSavingsAccount :
    CheckingAccount, SavingsAccount
{
};

};
```

The **CheckingSavingsAccount** component supports three interfaces: **CheckingAccount**, **SavingsAccount**, and **CheckingSavingsAccount**. This way of providing multiple interfaces on a component may look like an easy task, but it has a disadvantage: After the IDL is frozen, you can't add any more interfaces on the component. This means, the component has static interfaces. However, by using C++ and CORBA techniques, you can provide interfaces dynamically on a component. This can be achieved by using the containment mechanism in the component implementation that enables a component to have many interfaces, and the interfaces can be exposed through some query mechanism, which itself will be based on some CORBA interface. (This is demonstrated in Chapter 13.)

Testing Of Components

A component is the smallest natural unit of an application; therefore, verifying its behavior before it is (re)used in an application is important. A component is a proper candidate for unit testing.

Component testing can be a difficult activity, due to the following two facts:

♦ *A component is an entity that is built using object-oriented concepts.* Hence, all the testing issues that apply on an OO entity also apply on a CORBA component. Three issues generally are related to OO testing:

  ♦ *Encapsulation*—Doesn't cause runtime defects, but may be a restriction to testing—good encapsulation makes it hard to provide reporting on the state of a component.

  ♦ *Polymorphism*—Each possible binding of a polymorphic component requires a separate test, which is hard to do and may complicate integration testing.

  ♦ *Inheritance*—Doesn't significantly reduce the amount of testing. A tester needs to retest all the inherited operations of a base component in the unique context of a derived component, even if they are all tested for the base component. Also, a deep and multiple hierarchy may lead to many runtime defects.

To test a component, you can apply the white-box testing strategy, which uses the implementation to develop test cases. You may apply the statement coverage to measure the test completeness. Non-**public** local member functions of a component can be tested at the server side by providing a **friend** driver function. A *friend driver function* is a **friend** function of a component that invokes a component's private functions to test them.

♦ *A CORBA component is a distributed object.* Therefore, creating a test environment and simulating yet-to-be-developed components can be a difficult task. In the context of distribution, a component can be tested by using the black-box testing strategy, which uses IDL interfaces and requirements to develop test cases. No knowledge about implementation details is used to develop test cases. A client program can act like a component's test driver. It can fire IDL calls in a well-defined sequence and determine whether the component behavior is as expected.

If an IDL operation doesn't return any value, the behavior of the component has to be captured and verified in the component's implementation, which means that you need to mix the black-box testing strategy with white-box testing. This is referred to as *gray-box testing*.

Chapter Recap

OMG's CORBA can be used to implement real-life distributed components that can collaborate with each other by using IDL interfaces. Chapter 8 provided an introduction to IDL and IDL compilers. This chapter presented more syntactic details about IDL, the language used to specify a component's interface. IDL obeys the same lexical rules as C++. IDL basic types store simple values, such as integral numbers, floating-point numbers, character strings, and so on. IDL supports basic data types that are similar to C++ data types. IDL also supports many complex types in an IDL: **struct, union, array, string, sequence, interface, enum,** and **any**.

IDL doesn't have many complex features. An IDL interface provides a description of the functionality that is provided by a component. An interface definition provides all the information that is needed to develop clients that use the interface. An interface definition typically specifies the attributes and operations belonging to that interface, as well as the parameters of each operation. An IDL operation can throw user-defined exceptions.

The chapter presented mapping of various IDL features to C++ code. This mapping is generated by an IDL compiler. An interface's attributes are mapped to accessor functions.

This chapter presented the following programming steps to write a distributed **Account** component in C++:

1. Define the **Account** interface, using the standard IDL.

2. Compile the interface by using the IDL compiler.

3. Implement the interface of the component in C++.

4. Write a **CoBank** server, which instantiates the **Account** component and informs ORB when initialization has been done and the server is ready to accept requests.

5. Write a client to connect to the **CoBank** server and to use the **Account** component.

By using a factory component, you can control the life cycle of a component. This mechanism ensures that a component comes up when it is needed, and goes down when it isn't needed.

CORBA supports two types of software reuse: code reuse, which is the same as class derivation, and specification reuse, which is supported by interface derivation. This is an important feature of OMG IDL interfaces, because it enables you to reuse existing interfaces when defining new services. This shows the polymorphic nature of interfaces and plays an important role in developing OO applications using CORBA. Also, because CORBA IDL is just a declarative language, the separation of interface and implementation is automatically imposed—which is a good thing. Another good thing about IDL is that it supports only interface inheritance, as opposed to implementation inheritance.

## Chapter 10

Dynamic Type Identification In CORBA

CORBA provides full support for dynamic type identification. CORBA enables you to build powerful and flexible dynamic applications. CORBA's **Any** data type is essential to dynamic programming. An object of type **Any** can contain any type of object. An **Any** consists of a **TypeCode** (describing the type of the **Any**) and the value itself. This chapter presents detailed descriptions of both **Any** and **TypeCode**. The Interface Repository (IR) depends a lot on **Any** and **TypeCode**. IR is presented in Chapter 11.

Expressions Of Dynamic Type Identification In CORBA

CORBA provides support for dynamic type identification through the following features:

♦ **Any**

♦ **TypeCode**

♦ **DynAny**

The subsequent sections describe these features, except for **DynAny**. **DynAny** is not covered in this book.

The Any Type

This section gives the details of the Interface Definition Language (IDL) type **Any** and the corresponding C++ class **CORBA_Any**. You can use type **Any** to pass a value of an arbitrary type as a parameter to an operation or to a return value from an operation.

Parameter Vs. Argument

The words *parameter* and *argument* are often used interchangeably. However, a difference exists between the two words that you must understand. The following definitions should make the differentiation clear:

♦ *Argument*—An expression in the comma-separated list that is bounded by the parentheses in a function call. An argument is known as an *actual parameter*. The operands of **throw**, **typeid**, or a template name in the comma-separated list that is bounded by the angle brackets in a template instantiation are also arguments.

♦ *Parameter*—An object or reference that is declared as part of a function declaration or definition. A parameter is known as a *formal argument*. Also, parameters are an object or reference in the **catch** clause of an exception handler, and a template-parameter.

Consider the following interface:

```
module CoAnyExample
{
    struct Person
    {
        string name;
        short age;
    };

    interface Test
    {
        void op(in any a);
    };
};
```

The **Test** interface has an operation **op()** that accepts a parameter of type **any**. Thus, in a client program, you can construct an **any** containing any type of value that can be specified in IDL, and then pass this **any** in a call to the **op()** operation. The implementation of the **op()** operation must resolve the type of value that the argument **any** contains, and then extract the value. Several ways exist to construct and interpret an **any**, and these are introduced in the next few sections.

The IDL type **any** maps to the C++ **CORBA_Any** class. The class declaration of **CORBA_Any** is shown in Listing 10.1.

Listing 10.1   Declaration of the CORBA_Any class.
```
class CORBA_Any
{
CORBA_TypeCode_var type_;
    void* value_;
```

```
public:

    CORBA_Any();
    CORBA_Any(const CORBA_Any&);
    CORBA_Any(CORBA_TypeCode_ptr, void*,
              CORBA_Boolean = false);
    ~CORBA_Any();

    CORBA_Any& operator=(const CORBA_Any&);

    void operator<<=(CORBA_Short);
    void operator<<=(CORBA_UShort);
    void operator<<=(CORBA_Long);
    void operator<<=(CORBA_ULong);
    void operator<<=(CORBA_Float);
    void operator<<=(CORBA_Double);
    void operator<<=(const char*);
    void operator<<=(const CORBA_Any&);
    void operator<<=(CORBA_Any*);
    void operator<<=(CORBA_TypeCode_ptr);
    void operator<<=(CORBA_TypeCode_ptr*);
    void operator<<=(CORBA_Object_ptr);
    void operator<<=(CORBA_Object_ptr*);

    CORBA_Boolean operator>>=(CORBA_Short&) const;
    CORBA_Boolean operator>>=(CORBA_UShort&) const;
    CORBA_Boolean operator>>=(CORBA_Long&) const;
    CORBA_Boolean operator>>=(CORBA_ULong&) const;
    CORBA_Boolean operator>>=(CORBA_Float&) const;
    CORBA_Boolean operator>>=(CORBA_Double&) const;
    CORBA_Boolean operator>>=(char*&) const;
    CORBA_Boolean operator>>=(CORBA_Any*&) const;
    CORBA_Boolean operator>>=(CORBA_TypeCode_ptr&) const;
    CORBA_Boolean operator>>=(CORBA_Object_ptr&) const;

    void replace(CORBA_TypeCode_ptr, void*,
                 CORBA_Boolean = false);
    CORBA_TypeCode_ptr type() const;
    const void* value() const;
};
```

As Listing 10.1 shows, the **CORBA_Any** class contains the private data member **value_** of type **void*** to store the value of **Any**. **CORBA_Any** also contains a data member **type_** of type **CORBA_ TypeCode** to store the type of **value_**. The sections that follow describe and give examples of using member functions of the **CORBA_Any** class. The **CORBA_TypeCode** type is described in the "TypeCode" section later in this chapter.

Inserting In An Any

The **CORBA_Any** class overloads a number of left-shift assign operators (**<<=**) to assign a value to a **CORBA_Any**. An overloaded **operator<<=()** is provided for each of the basic IDL types, such as **long**, **short**, **float**, **double**, **string**, and so forth.

In the previous IDL definition (**CoAnyExample** module), if you need to pass an **Any** containing an IDL **long** (or, in C++, a **CORBA_Long**) as the argument to the **op()** operation, you can use the corresponding operator, as shown in the following code:

```
int main(int argc, char* argv[], char*[])
{
    CoAnyExample_Test_var p = new CoAnyExample_TestImpl();

    CORBA_Any any;

    CORBA_Long L;
    L=13;

    any<<=L; //inserting in Any using <<=()
    p->op(any);

    return 0;
}
```

This example instantiates a **CORBA_Any** by using its default constructor, and uses the **operator<<()** member function to insert a **CORBA_Long** value of **13** in the **CORBA_Any** object. This value must be extracted somehow at the receiving end of the **op()** operation. The way in which this is accomplished is shown in the next section.

Extracting From An Any

The **CORBA_Any** class overloads a number of right-shift assign operators (**>>=**) to extract value from a **CORBA_Any**. These operators correspond to the basic IDL types, such as **long**, **unsigned long**, **float**, **double**, **string**, and so on. The following example illustrates use of the **operator>>()** function:

```
void CoAnyExample_TestImpl::op(const CORBA_Any& a)
{
    CORBA_Long L;
    if (a>>=L)
    {
        cout<<"Value is any is:"<<L<<endl;
    }
    else
    {
        cout<<"Any doesn't have CORBA_Long type"<<endl;
    }
}
```

This example implements the **op()** operation to interpret the incoming **CORBA_Any** argument. If you attempt to extract a wrong type from **CORBA_Any**, the **operator>>=()** function returns 0.

Inserting A User-Defined Data Type

In addition to basic IDL types, you can insert in a **CORBA_Any** instance a user-defined data type (UDT) that appears in an IDL. Recall that the **CoAnyExample** module, as defined in the "The **Any** Type" section, has a user-defined type **Person** that is a **struct**. If you need to pass an instance of **Person**, you can use the following operators that are generated by the IDL compiler:

```
void operator<<=(CORBA_Any&, CoAnyExample_Person*);
void operator<<=(CORBA_Any&, const CoAnyExample_Person&);
```

Therefore, a typical client code looks like this:

```
CoAnyExample_Test_var p = new CoAnyExample_TestImpl();

CoAnyExample_Person person;
person.name=(const char*)"vishwa";
person.age=29;

CORBA_Any any;
any<<=person;

p->op(any);
```

This example instantiates an object **person** of type **CoAny Example_Person**, populates **person** with proper values, and uses the generated **operator<<()** function to insert **person** in a **CORBA_Any** object **any**.

Example Of Extracting A UDT

In addition to basic IDL types, you can extract from a **CORBA_Any** instance a UDT that appears in an IDL. The **Person** UDT can be extracted by using the following operator that is generated by the IDL compiler:

```
CORBA_Boolean
    operator>>=(const CORBA_Any&, CoAnyExample_Person*&);
```

You can extract a **Person** from a **CORBA_Any** as follows:

```
void CoAnyExample_TestImpl::op(const CORBA_Any& a)
{
    CoAnyExample_Person* person;
    if (a>>=person)
    {
        cout<<"person.name="<<person->name<<endl;
        cout<<"person.age="<<person->age<<endl;
    }
    else
    {
        cout<<"Any doesn't have CoAnyExample_Person type"<<
            endl;
    }
}
```

This example declares a pointer **person** of type **CoAnyExample_Person**, and then uses the generated **operator>>()** function to populate **person** from the incoming **CORBA_Any** object a.

Memory Management For Pointers Returned By Any

As the preceding example shows, the generated **>>=** operator for UDTs takes a pointer to the UDT as the right-hand parameter. If the call to the operator is successful, **CORBA_Any** allocates and manages the memory for the returned pointer. Therefore, you should remember the following three rules:

♦ You should not deallocate a pointer returned by a generated **>>=** operator for UDTs.

♦ You should not extract the returned pointer into a **_var** variable. Note that a **_var** variable assumes ownership of the memory and deallocates the pointer when a **_var** variable goes out of scope.

♦ You should not attempt to access the storage associated with a **CORBA_Any** after the **CORBA_Any** variable has gone out of scope.

Also, remember that each left-shift assign operator makes a copy of the value being inserted. For example, when you insert an object reference, **_duplicate()** is used. The operators release the previous **CORBA_TypeCode** and deallocate the storage previously associated with the value, if necessary.

NOTE

Other Ways To Use Any

Note that the notion of insertion and extraction member operators is the key to providing a type-safe mechanism to use **CORBA_Any**. The C++ overloading mechanism makes sure that the correct operator is called, based on the type of the value being inserted. If you attempt to insert/extract a value that has no corresponding IDL type, a compile-time error results. Therefore, the **operator <<=()** and **operator >>=()** functions should be used whenever you use **CORBA_Any**. However, you can write a program without using these operators. The following overloaded **CORBA_Any** constructor is a way to create a **CORBA_Any**:

```
CORBA_Any(CORBA_TypeCode_ptr tc, void* value,
          CORBA_Boolean release= false);
```

Using the **CORBA_Any** constructor means that, instead of creating a **CORBA_Any** variable by using the default constructor, and then inserting a value by using **operator<<=()**, you can specify the type and value when the **CORBA_Any** is being instantiated.

The first parameter **tc** in the **CORBA_Any** constructor is a **CORBA_TypeCode_ptr**. The second parameter is a pointer to the value to be inserted into the **CORBA_Any**. The type of this value should match the type specified by **tc**. The third parameter **release** specifies which code assumes ownership of the memory occupied by the value in the **CORBA_Any** variable. If **release** is 1, **CORBA_Any** assumes ownership of the storage pointed to by the value parameter. If **release** is 0, you should manage the memory associated with **value**.

Here is an example that constructs a **CORBA_Any** variable by using the overloaded constructor to contain a bounded string:

```
//IDL
typedef string<15> string15; //bounded string

//IDL generated code
typedef char* CoAnyExample_string15;
typedef CORBA_String_var CoAnyExample_string15_var;
extern OBTypeCodeConst CoAnyExample__tc_string15;

//C++ program (client)
CoAnyExample_Test_var p = new CoAnyExample_TestImpl();
```

Using The Overloaded Constructor

The overloaded constructor for **CORBA_Any** is more difficult to use than **operator<<=()**. Furthermore, the constructor isn't type safe, because the **tc** and **value** arguments may not match. Because the type of **value** is **void***, a mismatch can't be detected at compile time and this will show up as runtime faults.

However, you do have to use the overloaded constructor in one particular situation. Because both bounded and unbounded IDL strings map to **char*** in C++, you can't use **operator<<=()** for both of the types. This operator is used to insert unbounded strings, whereas the bounded strings use the overloaded constructor.

```
CoAnyExample_string15 str=CORBA_string_dup("vishwa");
CORBA_Any any(CoAnyExample__tc_string15, &str, 0);
p->op(any);

CORBA_string_free(str); //okay to do this
```

In this example, the **CoAnyExample__tc_string15** constant (generated by the IDL compiler) is passed as a first argument in the **any** object.
The second argument is the address of the **str** variable of type
CoAnyExample_string15. Because the third argument is 0, the constructed **CORBA_Any** doesn't assume ownership of the memory
associated with **str**. You are required to deallocate this memory that
was allocated using the **CORBA_string_dup()** function. As the example shows, when constructing **CORBA_Any**s for **string** types, the
second parameter is of type **char****.

As Listing 10.1 showed earlier in the chapter, class **CORBA_Any** provides three member functions:

```
void replace(CORBA_TypeCode_ptr, void*,
             CORBA_Boolean = false);
CORBA_TypeCode_ptr type() const;
const void* value() const;
```

Here is a brief description of each of the three member functions:

♦ **replace()**—Similar to the overloaded constructor that was just introduced, and is intended for use only with types that can't use the
type-safe operator interface (such as bounded strings). The **replace()**
function can be used at any time after construction of a
CORBA_Any to replace the existing contents of **CORBA_Any**
(**CORBA_TypeCode** and value). Note that, like the left-shift assign operators, **replace()** releases the previous **CORBA_TypeCode**
and deallocates the storage previously associated with the value, if
necessary.

♦ **type()**—Returns an object reference for a **CORBA_TypeCode** that
describes the type of the **CORBA_Any**. You can assign the returned
reference to a **CORBA_TypeCode_var** variable for automatic
memory management.

♦ **value()**—Returns a pointer to the data that is stored in the
CORBA_Any. The **value()** value returns the null pointer if no value
is stored. The returned value must be cast to the appropriate C++
type, depending on the **CORBA_Any**'s **CORBA_TypeCode**.

NOTE

**CORBA_Any
Containing An
Object Reference**

If the **CORBA_Any**
contains an object
reference, the **type()**
function returns a
reference for a
CORBA_TypeCode
object that is equal
to the **_tc_object**
TypeCode constant. The
value() function will
return a **void*** that
can be typecast to a
CORBA_Object_ptr*.

The following is an example to illustrate the use of the **value()** member function:

```
void CoAnyExample_TestImpl::op(const CORBA_Any& a)
{
    CoAnyExample_string15* str=
        (CoAnyExample_string15*)(a.value());
    if (str)
    {
        cout<<"string="<<*str<<endl;
    }
    else
    {
        cout<<"Any contained some other type"<<endl;
    }
}
```

This example calls **value()** on the **CORBA_Any** object (**a**) and typecasts the returned value into the pointer to **CoAnyExample_string15**. If the typecast value **str** is non-null, the string data is displayed by dereferencing **str**.

Any With Array Types

Recall that IDL arrays are mapped to regular C++ arrays, which means that you can't use **CORBA_Any**'s operators to insert or extract arrays of different lengths. To solve this problem, the IDL compiler generates a distinct C++ type for each IDL array type. The IDL compiler also generates insertion and extraction operations for the new generated type. The name of this type is the name of the array, followed by the suffix **_forany**. For example, for the IDL type

```
//IDL
typedef short short_array[16];
```

the following code is generated:

```
//IDL generated code
typedef OBFixArrayForAny< CORBA_Short, CORBA_Short, 16 >
CoAnyExample_short_array_forany;

void operator<<=(CORBA_Any&,
                const CoAnyExample_short_array_forany&);
```

```
CORBA_Boolean
operator>>=(const CORBA_Any&,
           CoAnyExample_short_array_forany &);
```

The preceding code shows that you can now perform type-safe manipulation of arrays with **CORBA_Any**.

Partial declaration of the **OBFixArrayForAny** class is shown in Listing 10.2.

Listing 10.2   Declaration of the OBFixArrayForAny class.

```
template<class T_slice, class T, CORBA_ULong n>
class OBFixArrayForAny
{
    T_slice* ptr_;
    CORBA_Boolean nocopy_;

public:

    OBFixArrayForAny() : ptr_(0), nocopy_(false) { }
    OBFixArrayForAny(T_slice* p, CORBA_Boolean nc = false)
        : ptr_(p), nocopy_(nc) { };
    OBFixArrayForAny(
        const OBFixArrayForAny<T_slice, T, n>& r,
        CORBA_Boolean nc = false)
        : ptr_(r.ptr_), nocopy_(nc) { };

    OBFixArrayForAny<T_slice, T, n>&
    operator=(T_slice* p)
    { ptr_ = p; return *this; }

    OBFixArrayForAny<T_slice, T, n>&
    operator=(const OBFixArrayForAny<T_slice,
              T, n>& r)
    { ptr_ = r.ptr_; return *this; }

    T_slice& operator[](unsigned long idx)
    { return ptr_[idx]; }
    const T_slice& operator[](unsigned long idx) const
    { return ((const T_slice*)ptr_)[idx]; }

    operator T_slice*() const { return ptr_; }
    operator const T_slice*() const { return ptr_; }
    //...
};
```

Note that, unlike an array **_var** type, the **_forany** type doesn't have a destructor to deallocate its storage, because a **_forany** instance doesn't restrict how the memory for an array should be allocated.

Here is an example that shows how to insert a **_forany** in an **Any** instance:

```
int main(int argc, char* argv[], char*[])
{
    CoAnyExample_Test_var p = new CoAnyExample_TestImpl();

    CORBA_Any any;

    CoAnyExample_short_array sa;

    for (CORBA_Short s=0; s<16; ++s)
    {
        sa[s]=s;
    }

    CoAnyExample_short_array_forany short_array(sa);
    any<<=short_array;
    p->op(any);
}
```

The preceding code uses stack memory (**sa**) to initialize the variable **short_array** of type **CoAnyExample_short_array_forany**.

The extraction is done as follows:

```
void CoAnyExample_TestImpl::op(const CORBA_Any& a)
{
    CoAnyExample_short_array_forany short_array;
    if (a>>=short_array)
    {
        for (CORBA_Short s=0; s<16; ++s)
        {
            cout<<short_array[s]<<endl;
        }
    }
}
```

Note that the **CORBA_Any** variable (**a**) performs the memory management for **short_array**.

Any With CORBA_Boolean, CORBA_Octet, And CORBA_Char

The overloaded right-shift and left-shift assignment member operators of the **CORBA_Any** class are resolved based on the type of the right-hand argument. This means that inserting and extracting types **boolean**, **char**, and **octet** isn't possible using the functions **operator<<=()** and **operator>>=()**, because these types all map to the **unsigned char** in ORBacus. This is shown here:

```
typedef unsigned char OBUnsignedChar;
typedef OBUnsignedChar CORBA_Boolean;
typedef OBUnsignedChar CORBA_Char;
typedef OBUnsignedChar CORBA_Octet;
```

To resolve this problem, ORBacus provides additional types to work with **CORBA_Any**. These types are **struct**s defined with the **CORBA_Any** class. Listing 10.3 presents the declarations of these **struct**s.

Listing 10.3   Additional types in the CORBA_Any class to enable insertion/extraction of the types boolean, char, and octet.

```
Class CORBA_Any
{
private:

    void operator<<=(unsigned char);
    CORBA_Boolean operator>>=(unsigned char&) const;

public:
    //...
    struct from_boolean
    {
        CORBA_Boolean val;

        from_boolean(CORBA_Boolean v) : val(v) {};
        from_boolean(const from_boolean& v) : val(v.val) {};
    };

    struct from_octet
    {
        CORBA_Octet val;

        from_octet(CORBA_Octet v) : val(v) {};
```

```
        from_octet(const from_octet& v) : val(v.val) {};
    };

    struct from_char
    {
        CORBA_Char val;

        from_char(CORBA_Char v) : val(v) {};
        from_char(const from_char& v) : val(v.val) {};
    };

    void operator<<=(from_boolean);
    void operator<<=(from_octet);
    void operator<<=(from_char);

    struct to_boolean
    {
        CORBA_Boolean& val;

        to_boolean(CORBA_Boolean& v) : val(v) {};
        to_boolean(const to_boolean& v) : val(v.val) {};
    };

    struct to_octet
    {
        CORBA_Octet& val;

        to_octet(CORBA_Octet& v) : val(v) {};
        to_octet(const to_octet& v) : val(v.val) {};
    };

    struct to_char
    {
        CORBA_Char& val;

        to_char(CORBA_Char& v) : val(v) {};
        to_char(const to_char& v) : val(v.val) {};
    };

    CORBA_Boolean operator>>=(to_boolean) const;
    CORBA_Boolean operator>>=(to_octet) const;
    CORBA_Boolean operator>>=(to_char) const;
};
```

The **CORBA_Any** provides six additional nested types: **from_boolean**, **from_octet**, **from_char**, **to_boolean**, **to_octet**, and **to_char**. Left-shift

NOTE

Using unsigned char With CORBA_Any

The **CORBA_Any** class provides the following two **private** operators:

♦ **void operator<<= (unsigned char);**

♦ **CORBA_Boolean operator>>=(unsigned char&) const;**

These are provided to detect the attempts to insert or extract an **unsigned char** by using a **CORBA_Any** object.

and right-shift assignment operators are provided for each of these nested types. Listing 10.4 shows how to use the **CORBA_Any::from_char** type.

Listing 10.4   Using CORBA_Any::from_char.

```
//client: inserting in a CORBA_Any::from_char
CoAnyExample_Test_var p = new CoAnyExample_TestImpl();

CORBA_Any any;

CORBA_Any::from_char fromChar('v');
any<<=fromChar;
p->op(any);

//server: extracting from a CORBA_Any::from_char
void CoAnyExample_TestImpl::op(const CORBA_Any& a)
{
    CORBA_Char c;
    CORBA_Any::to_char toChar(c);
    if (a>>=toChar)
    {
        cout<<"value of char="<<c<<endl;
    }
    else
    {
        cout<<"Any doesn't have a char type"<<endl;
    }
}
```

The client program instantiates a **CORBA_Any::from_char** and initializes that with value '**v**'. Then, the program uses the **operator<<=()** member function to insert the value. The server program instantiates a variable **toChar** of type **CORBA_Any::to_char** by using a constructor that accepts a **CORBA_Char** argument (**c**) by reference. As a result of the **operator>>=()** call, the variable **c** gets the value from the incoming **CORBA_Any** (**a**).

Any As Return Value And Out Parameter

The examples presented so far have used **any** as an **in** parameter in an IDL operation. The **any** type also can be used as a return value and **out** parameter. The IDL operation

```
// IDL
any op(in any a1, out any a2, inout any a3);
```

maps to:

```
// IDL compiler generated code (C++)
CORBA_Any* op(const CORBA_Any& a1, CORBA_Any*& a2,
              CORBA_Any& a3);
```

As the generated code shows, both the return value and **out** parameter map to pointers to **CORBA_Any**. When you use the **op()** operation, you can use the **CORBA_Any_var** class for automatic memory management for the **CORBA_Any** pointer.

TypeCode

This section describes the C++ **CORBA_TypeCode** class, which is used to describe arbitrary complex IDL types at runtime. **CORBA_TypeCode** is used for two purposes in a program:

♦ As an element of the **CORBA_Any** class.

♦ As a parameter to some of the functions of the Interface Repository, as explained later in the chapter.

You can use the **CORBA_TypeCode** class to find out the type of an instance of **CORBA_Any**. Recall that **CORBA_Any** has a public member function, **type()**, which has a return type of **CORBA_TypeCode_ptr** that can be queried at runtime to resolve the type of the value contained in the **CORBA_Any**.

Declaration of the **CORBA_TypeCode** class is presented in Listing 10.5.

Listing 10.5   Declaration of the CORBA_TypeCode class.
```
class CORBA_TypeCode : public OBRefCount
{
    CORBA_TCKind kind_;

    //CORBA_tk_objref, CORBA_tk_struct, CORBA_tk_union,
    //CORBA_tk_enum, CORBA_tk_alias, CORBA_tk_except
    CORBA_String_var id_;
    CORBA_String_var name_;

    //CORBA_tk_struct, CORBA_tk_union, CORBA_tk_enum,
    //CORBA_tk_except
    OBStrSeq memberNames_;

    //CORBA_tk_struct, CORBA_tk_union, CORBA_tk_except
    OBObjSeq< CORBA_TypeCode > memberTypes_;
```

```
                //CORBA_tk_union
                OBVarSeq< CORBA_Any > labels_;

                //CORBA_tk_union
                CORBA_TypeCode_var discriminatorType_;

                //CORBA_tk_string, CORBA_tk_sequence, CORBA_tk_array
                CORBA_ULong length_;

                //CORBA_tk_sequence, CORBA_tk_array, CORBA_tk_alias
                CORBA_TypeCode_var contentType_;

                //Hide copy-constructor and asignment operator
                CORBA_TypeCode(const CORBA_TypeCode&);
                void operator=(const CORBA_TypeCode&);

        protected:

                CORBA_TypeCode();
                virtual ~CORBA_TypeCode();

        public:

                class Bounds { };
                class BadKind { };

                CORBA_Boolean equal(CORBA_TypeCode_ptr) const;
                CORBA_TCKind kind() const;

                const char* id() const throw(BadKind);
                const char* name() const throw(BadKind);

                CORBA_ULong member_count() const
                throw(BadKind);

                const char* member_name(CORBA_ULong index) const
                throw(BadKind, Bounds);

                CORBA_TypeCode_ptr member_type(CORBA_ULong index) const
                throw(BadKind, Bounds);

                CORBA_Any* member_label(CORBA_ULong index) const
                throw(BadKind, Bounds);

                CORBA_TypeCode_ptr discriminator_type() const
                throw(BadKind);
```

```
    CORBA_Long default_index() const
    throw(BadKind);

    CORBA_ULong length() const
    throw(BadKind);

    CORBA_TypeCode_ptr content_type() const
    throw(BadKind);
    //...
};
```

As Listing 10.5 shows, each **CORBA_TypeCode** instance consists of a **kind_** data member and a set of other data members (for example, **id_**, **name_**, and so forth). The **kind_** data member categorizes a **CORBA_TypeCode**. Type of **kind_** is the **enum CORBA_TCKind** that is declared as follows:

```
enum CORBA_TCKind
{
    CORBA_tk_null,
    CORBA_tk_void,
    CORBA_tk_short,
    CORBA_tk_long,
    CORBA_tk_ushort,
    CORBA_tk_ulong,
    CORBA_tk_float,
    CORBA_tk_double,
    CORBA_tk_boolean,
    CORBA_tk_char,
    CORBA_tk_octet,
    CORBA_tk_any,
    CORBA_tk_TypeCode,
    CORBA_tk_Principal,
    CORBA_tk_objref,
    CORBA_tk_struct,
    CORBA_tk_union,
    CORBA_tk_enum,
    CORBA_tk_string,
    CORBA_tk_sequence,
    CORBA_tk_array,
    CORBA_tk_alias,
    CORBA_tk_except
};
```

CORBA_TCKind categories a **TypeCode** instance; that is, whether a **TypeCode** is a basic type, a **struct**, a sequence, and so on.

Predefined **CORBA_TypeCode** object reference constants are provided to enable you to access **TypeCode**s for all standard types that are listed in the declaration of **CORBA_TCKind**. For example, **CORBA__tc_float** is an object reference for a **float TypeCode**, **CORBA__tc_string** is an object reference for a **string TypeCode**, and so forth.

TypeCode For UDTs

In addition to basic IDL types, you have a **CORBA_TypeCode_ptr** for a UDT that appears in an IDL. The IDL compiler generates a **CORBA_TypeCode_ptr** for each UDT that is defined in an IDL file. The **CORBA_TypeCode_ptr** will point to a **TypeCode** constant generated by the IDL compiler. These constants have names of the form **_tc_<T>**, where **<T>** is the UDT. For example, given the following IDL file:

```
module CoAnyExample
{
    struct Person
    {
        string name;
        short age;
    };

    typedef string<15> string15;
    typedef short short_array[16];

    interface Test
    {
        void op(in any a);
    };
};
```

the following **CORBA_TypeCode_ptr** constants are generated:

```
CoAnyExample__tc_Person
CoAnyExample__tc_string15
CoAnyExample__tc_short_array
CoAnyExample__tc_Test
```

Getting TypeCode From An Any

Using the IDL specified in the previous section, a client program can be developed that invokes **op()**:

```
CoAnyExample_Test_var p = new CoAnyExample_TestImpl();

CoAnyExample_Person person;
person.name=(const char*)"vishwa";
person.age=29;

CORBA_Any any;
any<<=person;
p->op(any);
```

At the server side, you can query the actual type of the parameter to **op()** through the **type()** function of **CORBA_Any**. For example:

```
void CoAnyExample_TestImpl::op(const CORBA_Any& a)
{
    CORBA_TypeCode_var t=a.type();
    if (t->equal(CoAnyExample__tc_Person))
    {
        cout<<"Type is Person"<<endl;
    }
    else
    {
        cout<<"Type is not Person"<<endl;
    }
}
```

This example gets the type information from a **CORBA_Any** by using **CORBA_Any**'s member function **type()**. The **type()** function returns a **CORBA_TypeCode_ptr**. On the returned pointer, the **equal()** member function is invoked to determine whether the incoming **CORBA_Any** argument is a **CoAnyExample__tc_Person**. This is one of the most common uses of **TypeCode**s.

A brief description of other member functions of the **CORBA_TypeCode** class is presented in the next section.

TypeCode Member Functions

The **CORBA_TypeCode** member functions are useful when using the Interface Repository (IR) functions. For example, while using IR, you can determine the number of parameters of an operation and the **TypeCode** of each parameter. You can invoke the **kind()** member function and other member functions on each **TypeCode** to determine further details of the type of each parameter. (See Chapter 11 for more information about IR.)

Except for the member functions **kind()** and **equal()**, all the member functions are not valid for all the **TypeCode**s. Table 10.1 describes the valid operations that can be applied on various IDL types. Listing 10.6 will present an example that covers the applications of the various member functions of the **CORBA_TypeCode** class.

The following list describes each of the functions listed in Table 10.1:

♦ **equal()**—Can be invoked on any **TypeCode**. Two **TypeCode**s are equal if the IDL type specifications from which they are compiled denote equal types.

♦ **kind()**—Can be invoked on any **TypeCode**. Returns the **CORBA_TCKind** enum value that determines what is **TypeCode**'s IDL type and, therefore, what other functions can be invoked on the **TypeCode**.

♦ **id()**—Valid for object reference, structure, union, enumeration, alias, and exception **TypeCode**s. Returns the **RepositoryId** that is their global type identity. You should not free the returned string.

♦ **name()**—Valid for object reference, structure, union, enumeration, alias, and exception **TypeCode**s. Returns the simple name identifying the type within its enclosing scope. You should not free the returned string.

Table 10.1   List of valid TypeCode member functions and the IDL types of the corresponding TypeCodes.

Legal Operations	IDL Type Of The TypeCode
Id()	CORBA_tk_objref, CORBA_tk_struct, CORBA_tk_union, CORBA_tk_enum, CORBA_tk_alias, CORBA_tk_except
name()	CORBA_tk_objref, CORBA_tk_struct, CORBA_tk_union, CORBA_tk_enum, CORBA_tk_alias, CORBA_tk_except
member_name()	CORBA_tk_struct, CORBA_tk_union, CORBA_tk_enum, CORBA_tk_except
member_count()	CORBA_tk_struct, CORBA_tk_union, CORBA_tk_enum, CORBA_tk_except
member_type()	CORBA_tk_struct, CORBA_tk_union, CORBA_tk_except
member_label ()	CORBA_tk_union
discriminator_type()	CORBA_tk_union
default_index()	CORBA_tk_union
length()	CORBA_tk_string, CORBA_tk_sequence, CORBA_tk_array
content_type()	CORBA_tk_sequence, CORBA_tk_array, CORBA_tk_alias

- **member_count()**—Valid for structure, union, and enumeration **TypeCode**s. Returns the number of members in the type.

- **member_name()**—Valid for structure, union, and enumeration **TypeCode**s. Takes an **unsigned long** as a parameter. Returns the simple name of the member identified by the **index** parameter. Raises **Bounds** if the **index** argument is greater than or equal to the number of members forming the type. You should not free the returned string.

- **member_type()**—Valid for structure and union **TypeCode**s. Takes an **unsigned long** as a parameter. Returns the **TypeCode** describing the type of the member identified by the **index** parameter. Raises **Bounds** if the **index** parameter is greater than or equal to the number of members declared in the type.

- **member_label()**—Valid for union **TypeCode**s. Takes an **unsigned long** as a parameter. Returns the label of the union member identified by the **index** parameter (for the default member, the label is the zero octet). Raises **Bounds** if the **index** parameter is greater than or equal to the number of members forming the type.

- **discriminator_type()**—Valid for union **TypeCode**s. Returns the **TypeCode** describing the type of the discriminator.

- **default_index()**—Valid for union **TypeCode**s. Returns the index of the default member, or **-1** if the default member doesn't exist.

- **content_type()**—Valid for sequence, array, and alias **TypeCode**s. Returns the **TypeCode** describing the type of the element for sequences and arrays; returns the original type for aliases. An array **TypeCode** describes only a single dimension of an array. Multidimensional arrays call for nesting **TypeCode**s, one per dimension. The outermost **TypeCode** describes the leftmost array index of the array as defined in IDL. Its **content_type()** describes the next index. The innermost nested **TypeCode** describes the rightmost index and the array element type.

- **length()**—Valid for string, sequence, and array **TypeCode**s. Returns the bound for strings and sequences; returns **0** for unbound strings and sequences; returns the number of elements in the array for arrays.

If you invoke an invalid function on a **TypeCode**, exception **BadKind** is thrown.

A Detailed TypeCode Example

This section presents a detailed example that shows how to use various member functions of the **CORBA_TypeCode** class. The example demonstrates how to:

♦ Show the applications of valid member functions on a **CORBA_TypeCode** instance.

♦ Find out the type information of various types defined in an IDL.

♦ Show the recursion involved while invoking member functions on a **CORBA_TypeCode** instance.

Consider the IDL declaration in Listing 10.6.

Listing 10.6   IDL declaration for the TypeCode example.

```
module CoAnyExample
{
    struct Person
    {
        string name;
        short age;
    };

    typedef string<15> string15;
    typedef short short_array[16];

    enum Type
    {
        E_APPLE, E_FOOTBALL, E_COMPUTER
    };

    struct Apple
    {
        short color;
    };

    struct Football
    {
        float weight;
    };

    struct Computer
    {
        boolean is_super;
    };

    union MixedType switch (Type)
```

```
    {
        case E_APPLE: Apple apple;
        case E_FOOTBALL: Football football;
        case E_COMPUTER: Computer computer;
    };
};
```

Listing 10.7 presents a function **showNameOfTypeCode()** that applies various member functions on **TypeCode**. The purpose of the **showNameOfTypeCode()** function is to display the name of a **CORBA_TypeCode_ptr** that is passed to the function.

Listing 10.7   Application of various member functions of TypeCode to display the name of a CORBA_TypeCode_ptr.

```
#include <OB/CORBA.h>
#include <OB/Util.h>
#include <stdlib.h>
#include <errno.h>
static const char* names [] =
{
    "null", "void", "short", "long",
    "unsigned short", "unsigned long", "float",
    "double", "boolean", "char",
    "octet", "any", "TypeCode", "Principal",
    "objref", "struct", "union",
    "enum", "string", "sequence", "array", "alias",
    "exception"
};

void showNameOfTypeCode(CORBA_TypeCode_ptr tc)
{
    CORBA_TCKind kind = tc->kind();

    switch ( kind ) {
    case CORBA_tk_objref:
    case CORBA_tk_enum:
    case CORBA_tk_union:
    case CORBA_tk_struct:
    case CORBA_tk_except:
    case CORBA_tk_alias:
        cout << tc->name();
        break;

    case CORBA_tk_string: {
        cout << "string";
        CORBA_ULong length = tc->length();
```

```
            if (length != 0)
                cout << '<' << length << '>';
        } break;

    case CORBA_tk_sequence: {
        cout << "sequence<";
        CORBA_TypeCode_var content_type =
            tc->content_type();
        showNameOfTypeCode(content_type); //recursive call
        CORBA_ULong length = tc->length();
        if (length != 0)
            cout << ", " << length;
            cout << '>';
        } break;

    case CORBA_tk_array: {
        CORBA_TypeCode_var content_type =
            tc->content_type();
        showNameOfTypeCode(content_type); //recursive call
        cout << '[' << tc->length() << ']';
        } break;

    default:
        cout << names [kind];
        break;
    }
}
```

Note the recursion of the **showNameOfTypeCode()** function in Listing 10.7 in the following code segment:

```
CORBA_TypeCode_var content_type =
    tc->content_type();
showNameOfTypeCode(content_type); //recursive call
```

Because the **content_type()** member function returns a **CORBA_TypeCode_var** instance, you can invoke the **showNameOfTypeCode()** function recursively to operate on the returned **CORBA_TypeCode_var** instance.

Listing 10.8 presents a function **showIDLTypeCode()** that displays the name of the IDL type of a **CORBA_TypeCode_ptr**.

Listing 10.8   Displaying the name of the IDL type of a CORBA_TypeCode_ptr.

```
void showIDLTypeCode(CORBA_TypeCode_ptr tc)
{
    CORBA_ULong i;
    CORBA_TCKind kind = tc->kind();

    switch ( kind ) {
    case CORBA_tk_objref:
        cout << "interface " << tc->name() << ';';
        break;

    case CORBA_tk_struct:
    case CORBA_tk_except: {
        cout << names[kind] << ' ' << tc->name() <<
            " {" << endl;

        for (i=0; i<tc->member_count(); i++) {
            cout;
            CORBA_TypeCode_var member_type =
                tc->member_type(i);
            showNameOfTypeCode(member_type);
            cout << ' ' << tc->member_name(i) <<
            ';' << endl;
        }
        cout << "};";
    } break;

    case CORBA_tk_union: {
        cout << "union " << tc->name() <<
        " switch(";
        CORBA_TypeCode_var discriminator_type =
            tc->discriminator_type();
        showNameOfTypeCode(discriminator_type);
        cout << ") {" << endl;

        for (i=0 ; i<tc->member_count(); i++)
        {
            CORBA_Any_var any_member_label =
                tc->member_label(i);
            CORBA_TypeCode_var type_label =
                any_member_label->type();
            if ( type_label->kind() == CORBA_tk_octet)
            {
                cout << "default";
```

```
            }
            else
            {
                cout << "case ";
            }
            cout << ": ";
            CORBA_TypeCode_var member_type =
                tc->member_type(i);
            showNameOfTypeCode(member_type);
            cout << ' ' << tc->member_name(i) <<
            ';' << endl;
        }
        cout << "};";
    } break;

    case CORBA_tk_enum:
        cout  << "enum " << tc->name() << " {";
        for (i=0; i<tc->member_count(); i++) {
            if ( i != 0 ) cout << ", ";
            cout << tc->member_name(i);
        }
        cout << "};";
        break;

    case CORBA_tk_string:
    {
        cout << "string";
        CORBA_ULong length = tc->length();
        if (length != 0)
        cout << '<' << length << '>';
    }
    break;

    case CORBA_tk_sequence: {
        cout << "sequence<";
        CORBA_TypeCode_var content_type =
            tc->content_type();
        showNameOfTypeCode(content_type);
        CORBA_ULong length = tc->length();
        if (length != 0) cout << ", " << length;
        cout << '>';
    } break;

    case CORBA_tk_array: {
        cout;
```

```
        CORBA_TypeCode_var content_type =
            tc->content_type();
        showNameOfTypeCode(content_type);
        cout << '[' << tc->length() << ']';
    } break;

    case CORBA_tk_alias: {
        cout << "typedef ";
        CORBA_TypeCode_var content_type =
            tc->content_type();
        showNameOfTypeCode(content_type);
        cout << ' ' << tc->name() << ';';
    } break;

    default:
        cout << names [kind];
            break;
    }
    cout << endl;
}
```

Note that the global **showIDLTypeCode()** function from Listing 10.8 uses the **showNameOfTypeCode()** function that is defined in Listing 10.7. The **showIDLTypeCode()** function performs the following tasks:

♦ Finds the IDL type of the **tc** parameter and displays the name of the IDL type of **tc**.

♦ Invokes the **showNameOfTypeCode()** function on UDTs (such as **struct**, **union**, and so forth) to display the information about the elements within the UDTs.

Listing 10.9 presents the **main()** function that invokes the **showIDLTypeCode()** function.

Listing 10.9   Invoking the showIDLTypeCode() function.

```
int main(int argc, char* argv[], char*[])
{
    CoAnyExample_Person person;

    CORBA_Any any1;
    any1<<=person;

    CORBA_TypeCode_var typeCode1=any1.type();
    cout<<"---------------------------"<<endl;
    cout<<"Test# 1"<<endl;
    cout<<"---------------------------"<<endl;
```

```
    showIDLTypeCode(typeCode1);

CORBA_Any any2;

CoAnyExample_short_array sa;
CoAnyExample_short_array_forany short_array(sa);

any2<<=short_array;

CORBA_TypeCode_var typeCode2=any2.type();
cout<<"-------------------------"<<endl;
cout<<"Test# 2"<<endl;
cout<<"-------------------------"<<endl;
showIDLTypeCode(typeCode2);

CORBA_Any any3;
CoAnyExample_Type Type;
any3<<=Type;

CORBA_TypeCode_var typeCode3=any3.type();
cout<<"-------------------------"<<endl;
cout<<"Test# 3"<<endl;
cout<<"-------------------------"<<endl;
showIDLTypeCode(typeCode3);

CORBA_Any any4;
CoAnyExample_MixedType m;
CoAnyExample_Apple a;
a.color=0;
m.apple(a);
any4<<=m;

CORBA_TypeCode_var typeCode4=any4.type();
cout<<"-------------------------"<<endl;
cout<<"Test# 4"<<endl;
cout<<"-------------------------"<<endl;
showIDLTypeCode(typeCode4);

return 0;
}
```

The **main()** function instantiates four **CORBA_Any** objects (**any1**, **any2**, **any3**, and **any4**) and fills them with values of four different types (**CoAnyExample_Person**, **CoAnyExample_short_array**, **CoAnyExample_Type** and **CoAnyExample_MixedType**). The **main()**

function invokes the global **showIDLTypeCode()** function that produces the following output:

```
- - - - - - - - - - - - - - - - - - - - - - - - - -
Test# 1
- - - - - - - - - - - - - - - - - - - - - - - - - -
struct Person {
string name;
short age;
};
- - - - - - - - - - - - - - - - - - - - - - - - - -
Test# 2
- - - - - - - - - - - - - - - - - - - - - - - - - -
short[16]
- - - - - - - - - - - - - - - - - - - - - - - - - -
Test# 3
- - - - - - - - - - - - - - - - - - - - - - - - - -
enum Type {E_APPLE, E_FOOTBALL, E_COMPUTER};
- - - - - - - - - - - - - - - - - - - - - - - - - -
Test# 4
- - - - - - - - - - - - - - - - - - - - - - - - - -
union MixedType switch(Type) {
case : Apple apple;
case : Football football;
case : Computer computer;
};
```

Note that Listing 10.9 doesn't show all the possible test cases. It just gives four test cases—**struct**, **short[16]**, **enum**, and **union**. You need to study this example carefully to understand how to apply various functions of the **TypeCode** class. Most of the function calls are intuitive.

Chapter Recap

CORBA provides support for dynamic type identification and construction. CORBA enables you to build powerful, flexible dynamic applications. This chapter presented a few significant CORBA notions and features, including the following:

♦ **Any**—IDL has a generic data type **any**, whose corresponding C++ class is **CORBA_Any**. Type **any** is used to indicate that a value of an arbitrary type can be passed as a parameter or a return value of an operation.

♦ TypeCode—**CORBA_TypeCode**, which is a component of **CORBA_Any**, is used to describe arbitrary complex IDL types at runtime. **CORBA_TypeCode** is used as a parameter to some of the functions of the Interface Repository.

CORBA supports dynamic typing through **DynAny**, too, but this chapter didn't present the type **DynAny**.

## Chapter 11

Dynamic Programming In CORBA

C ORBA provides full support for dynamic type identification and programming. CORBA enables you to build powerful and flexible dynamic applications. CORBA's **Any** data type is essential to dynamic programming. (**Any** is described in depth in Chapter 10.) Recall that an object of type **Any** can contain any type of object; a **TypeCode** is an object that describes an object's type. An Object Request Broker (ORB) provides distributed access to a collection of components by using the components' publicly defined interfaces, specified in an Interface Definition Language (IDL). The *Interface Repository (IR)* provides for the storage, distribution, and management of a collection of related objects' interface definitions.

Dynamic Invocation Interface (DII) is another way to invoke operations on remote CORBA components. Recall that the other operation invocation mechanism is the static invocation. DII is presented in this chapter by using simple examples. Compared to the traditional method of static invocation, the DII mechanism has advantages and disadvantages, which also are explained in this chapter.

Expressions Of Dynamic Programming In CORBA

CORBA provides support for dynamic programming through the following features:

♦ Interface Repository (IR)

♦ Dynamic Invocation Interface (DII)

♦ Dynamic Skeleton Interface (DSI)

Subsequent sections describe IR and DII. This book doesn't cover DSI.

Interface Repository

An ORB provides distributed access to a collection of objects by using a component's interface, which is specified in an IDL. IR provides this access. Clients can use the information maintained in IR to determine at runtime the component's type and all information about that type. In other words, you can consult IR to find out the runtime type identification (RTTI) of a component. IR maintains interface definitions as a set of objects that are accessible through a set of IDL-specified interface definitions. IR essentially is used to get RTTI about components, so that requests can be issued using DII. (DII is explained in "The Dynamic Invocation Interface" later in this chapter.) IR is also useful as a mechanism in developing tools such as browsers.

The following are three basic ideas that are important to understanding IR:

♦ *Scoped names and repository identifiers*—Names in IR are always relative to an explicit or implicit module. Interface definitions are considered explicit modules. Scoped names are used to uniquely identify modules, interfaces, constants, typedefs, exceptions, attributes, and operations in IR. Repository identifiers are used to globally identify modules, interfaces, constants, typedefs, exceptions, attributes, and operations.

♦ *Types and typecodes*—IR stores information about types that aren't interfaces in **TypeCode**s (**TypeCode** is covered in Chapter 10). **TypeCode** is the key to determining the complete structure of a given type.

♦ *Interface objects*—IR is composed of objects that represent IDL definitions. These objects, referred to as *interface objects*, are queried to determine their definitions. The next section provides detailed information about interface objects.

Query Using Interface Objects

Information about an IDL definition that has been processed by the IDL compiler goes into IR and can be browsed by clients through interface objects. A program can browse IR to get the set of modules and interfaces, determining the name of each module, the name of each interface, and the full definition of that interface. For example, if you have an object reference (**CORBA_Object_ptr**) of a component, you can determine the IDL specification of the component to which the object reference points. Typically you want to determine:

◆ The module in which the interface was defined, if any.

◆ The name of the interface.

◆ The interface's attributes, and the attributes' definitions.

◆ The interface's operations, and the operations' full definitions, including parameter and exception definitions.

◆ The inheritance hierarchy of the interface.

Interface objects are nested according to the IDL interface. For example, an interface's constant, typedef, exception, attribute, and operation definitions are contained in an interface object representing an interface. The conceptual nesting of IR is as follows:

◆ Module, constant, typedef, exception, and interface definitions can appear outside of any module.

◆ A module can contain module, constant, typedef, exception, and interface definitions.

◆ An interface can contain constant, typedef, attribute, operation, and exception definitions.

◆ An operation can contain parameters and exception definitions.

Clearly, interface objects must be structured the same way that definitions are structured in the corresponding IDL. The interface objects are represented by the **Repository**, **ModuleDef**, **InterfaceDef**, **ConstantDef**, **TypedefDef**, **ExceptionDef**, **AttributeDef**, and **OperationDef** types. These are types defined by IR. Given an object of any of these types, full information on that definition can be determined. The following list provides a short description of these types:

◆ **Repository**—The outermost object of IR. **Repository** is the global root of IR. The **Repository** object contains the **ConstantDef**, **TypedefDef**, **ExceptionDef**, **InterfaceDef**, and **ModuleDef** types that are defined outside the scope of a module.

◆ **ModuleDef**—A set of interfaces. **ModuleDef** contains the **ConstantDef**, **TypedefDef**, **ExceptionDef**, **InterfaceDef**, and **ModuleDef** types that are defined within the scope of the module.

◆ **InterfaceDef**—An interface definition. **InterfaceDef** contains the **ConstantDef**, **TypedefDef**, **ExceptionDef**, **AttributeDef**, and **OperationDef** types that are defined within or inherited by the interface.

◆ **AttributeDef**—The definition of an attribute of the interface.

- **OperationDef**—The definition of an operation on the interface. **OperationDef** contains parameters and exceptions raised by this operation.

- **TypedefDef**—The definition of named types that aren't interfaces.

- **ConstantDef**—The definition of a named constant.

- **ExceptionDef**—The definition of an exception that can be raised by an operation.

Clearly, there is a containment relationship among IR interfaces. Figure 11.1 shows the IR containment hierarchy.

A full description of IR interfaces is beyond the scope of this book. However, the following interfaces are explained later in this chapter:

- **Repository**
- **ExceptionDef**
- **AttributeDef**
- **OperationDef**
- **InterfaceDef**

These interfaces depend on four other interfaces:

- **IRObject**
- **IDLType**

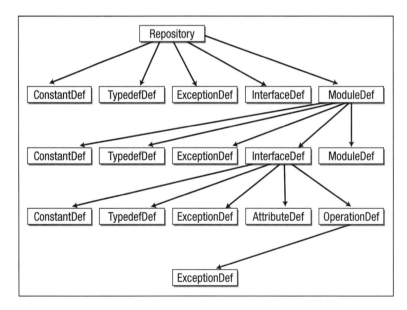

Figure 11.1
IR containment hierarchy.

♦ **Contained**

♦ **Container**

These four interfaces are presented in the sections that follow. Note that all the attributes and operations of the interfaces aren't shown—only the important and relevant ones are presented.

IRObject

The **IRObject** interface is the most generic interface, and it represents the base interface for all other IR interfaces. The **IRObject** interface provides an attribute for identifying the actual type of the object:

```
enum DefinitionKind
{
    dk_none,
    dk_all,
    dk_Attribute,
    dk_Constant,
    dk_Exception,
    dk_Interface,
    dk_Module,
    dk_Operation,
    dk_Typedef,
    dk_Alias,
    dk_Struct,
    dk_Union,
    dk_Enum,
    dk_Primitive,
    dk_String,
    dk_Sequence,
    dk_Array,
    dk_Repository
};

interface IRObject
{
    readonly attribute DefinitionKind def_kind;
};
```

The **def_kind** attribute of the **IRObject** interface identifies the type of the definition.

IDLType

The **IDLType** interface represents the base interface for IDL types. **IDLType** describes the type defined by a derived interface for which **IDLType** acts as a base interface:

```
interface IDLType : IRObject
{
    readonly attribute TypeCode type;
};
```

The **type** attribute describes the type of a definition.

Contained

The **Contained** interface is the base interface for IR interfaces that are contained by other IR objects:

```
interface Container;
typedef string Identifier, RepositoryId,
    VersionSpec, ScopedName;

interface Contained : IRObject
{
    attribute RepositoryId id;
    attribute Identifier name;
    attribute VersionSpec version;

    readonly attribute Container defined_in;
    readonly attribute ScopedName absolute_name;
    readonly attribute Repository containing_repository;

    struct Description
    {
        DefinitionKind kind;
        any value;
    };

    Description describe();
};
```

The following is a description of the attributes and operations of the **Contained** interface:

♦ **id**—Attribute that identifies a **Contained** component uniquely and globally. The type of **id** is **RepositoryId**, which is defined as **string**.

- **name**—Attribute that identifies a **Contained** component uniquely within the enclosing **Container** object. The **name** attribute is of type **Identifier** that is defined as **string**.

- **version**—Attribute that distinguishes **Contained** components from other object versions with the same name.

- **defined_in**—Attribute that identifies a **Container** component within which the **Contained** component is contained. An inherited component is also of type **Contained** (for example, an operation of a base interface is contained by a derived interface). If a component is contained through inheritance, the **defined_in** attribute identifies the **Container** from which the component is inherited.

- **absolute_name**—Attribute that represents an absolute name that identifies a **Contained** component uniquely within its enclosing **Repository** component. An *absolute name* is a name formed by one or more **Identifier**s separated by the characters "::". It conforms to the IDL's scoped names and unambiguously identifies a definition in a **Repository**. For example, if a component's **defined_in** attribute is **Repository**, the value of **absolute_name** becomes a concatenation of "::" and the component's **name** attribute. Otherwise, the **absolute_name** is a concatenation of the **absolute_name** attribute of the component's **defined_in** attribute, "::", and the component's **name** attribute.

- **containing_repository**—Attribute that identifies a particular **Repository**, the root of IR. Note that **containing_repository** can also be reached by recursively applying the **defined_in** attribute.

- **describe()**—Operation that returns a structure of type **Description** that contains information about the interface. For example, if you invoke the **describe()** operation on an attribute object, you will find that **kind**'s value is **dk_Attribute** and that the **value** member contains an **Any** having the **AttributeDescription** structure.

Container

The **Container** interface, as the name suggests, expresses the con-tainment hierarchy in IR. A **Container** can contain any number of **Contained**'s derivations. Declaration of **Container** is shown in Listing 11.1.

Listing 11.1 The Container interface.

```
typedef sequence<Contained> ContainedSeq;
interface Container : IRObject
{
```

```
ContainedSeq contents(
    in DefinitionKind limit_type,
    in boolean exclude_inherited);

ContainedSeq lookup_name(
    in Identifier search_name,
    in long levels_to_search,
    in DefinitionKind limit_type,
    in boolean exclude_inherited);

struct Description
{
    Contained contained_object;
    DefinitionKind kind;
    any value;
};

typedef sequence<Description> DescriptionSeq;

DescriptionSeq describe_contents(
    in DefinitionKind limit_type,
    in boolean exclude_inherited,
    in long max_returned_objs);
};
```

The following is a description of the operations of the **Container** interface:

♦ **contents()**—Returns the list of objects directly contained by or inherited into the object. You can use this operation to navigate through the hierarchy of objects. For example, you can start with the **Repository** object and enumerate all the objects contained by the **Repository**, all the objects contained by the modules within the **Repository**, all the interfaces within a specific module, and so on. If you set **limit_type** to be **dk_all**, you get objects of all interface types. However, if **limit_type** is set to **dk_Attribute**, only attribute objects are returned. If **exclude_inherited** is set to **1**, the operation doesn't return inherited objects. Otherwise, all contained objects including inherited ones are returned.

♦ **lookup_name()**—Used to locate an object by name contained within a **Container**. The **search_name** parameter specifies the name that is to be looked up. The **levels_to_search** parameter controls whether **lookup_name()** searches just the object on which the operation is invoked, or searches recursively (iterating objects contained by the object). If you set **levels_to_search** to **-1**, the current object and all contained objects are looked up. To search only the current object, you should set **levels_to_search** to **1**. The remaining two parameters of **lookup_name()** are the same as those of the **contents()** operation.

♦ **describe_contents()**—A combination of the **contents()** operation and the **Contained::describe()** operation. The **Contained::describe()** operation is invoked on each object returned by the **contents()** operation. The **max_returned_objs** parameter limits the number of objects to be returned. You can set the parameter to **-1** to return all contained objects. The remaining two parameters of **lookup_name()** are the same as those of the **contents()** operation.

Repository

The **Repository** object provides global access to IR, and can contain constants, typedefs, exceptions, interfaces, and modules. **Repository** is derived from **Container** and, therefore, **Repository** can be used to look up any definition by name or **RepositoryId**:

```
interface Repository : Container
{
    Contained lookup_id(in RepositoryId search_id);
};
```

The **lookup_id()** operation of the **Repository** interface is used to look up an object in a **Repository**, given its **RepositoryId**. If the lookup fails, a nil object reference is returned.

ExceptionDef

The **ExceptionDef** interface represents the information that defines an exception:

```
struct ExceptionDescription
{
    Identifier name;
    RepositoryId id;
    RepositoryId defined_in;
    VersionSpec version;
    TypeCode type;
};

struct StructMember
{
```

```
        Identifier name;
        TypeCode type;
        IDLType type_def;
};


typedef sequence<StructMember> StructMemberSeq;

interface ExceptionDef : Contained
{
    readonly attribute TypeCode type;
    attribute StructMemberSeq members;
};
```

The following list describes the **ExceptionDef** interface:

+ **type**—Attribute that is a **tk_except TypeCode** describing the exception.

+ **members**—Attribute that is a **StructMemberSeq** describing exception members.

+ **Contained::describe()**—Inherited operation that, when invoked on an **ExceptionDef** object, returns an **ExceptionDescription** object. Recall that the **Contained::describe()** operation is a member of the **Contained** interface and returns **Description**. In this case, in the **Description** structure, the value of **kind** is **dk_Exception** and the **value** member contains an object of type **Any** having the **ExceptionDescription** structure.

AttributeDef

The **AttributeDef** interface represents a definition of an attribute of an interface:

```
enum AttributeMode
{
    ATTR_NORMAL,
    ATTR_READONLY
};

interface AttributeDef : Contained
{
    readonly attribute TypeCode type;
    attribute IDLType type_def;
    attribute AttributeMode mode;
};
```

The following is a description of the attributes of **AttributeDef**:

♦ **type**—A **TypeCode** that describes the type of the attribute.

♦ **type_def**—Identifies the object defining the type of the attribute.

♦ **mode**—Specifies whether the mode of attribute is read-only or read/write.

OperationDef

The **OperationDef** interface, as shown in Listing 11.2, represents an operation of an interface.

Listing 11.2   The OperationDef interface.

```
enum OperationMode
{
    OP_NORMAL,
    OP_ONEWAY
};

enum ParameterMode
{
    PARAM_IN,
    PARAM_OUT,
    PARAM_INOUT
};

struct ParameterDescription
{
    Identifier name;
    TypeCode type;
    IDLType type_def;
    ParameterMode mode;
};

typedef sequence<ParameterDescription> ParDescriptionSeq;
typedef sequence<ExceptionDef> ExceptionDefSeq;
typedef sequence<ExceptionDescription> ExcDescriptionSeq;

interface OperationDef : Contained
{
    readonly attribute TypeCode result;
    attribute IDLType result_def;
    attribute ParDescriptionSeq params;
    attribute OperationMode mode;
    attribute ExceptionDefSeq exceptions;
    //...
};
```

The following describes the attributes and operations of **OperationDef**:

♦ **result**—Attribute that identifies the type of the value returned by the operation.

♦ **result_def**—Attribute that represents the definition of the returned type.

♦ **params**—Attribute that describes the parameters of the operation. The **params** attribute is a sequence of **ParameterDescription** structures. The **name** member of each structure identifies the parameter name. The type of the parameter is identified by the **type** member. The **type_def** member represents the definition of the type of the parameter. The **mode** member identifies the mode of a parameter; that is, whether the parameter is an **in**, **out**, or **inout** parameter. Note that the order of the **ParameterDescription**s in the sequence is important.

♦ **mode**—Attribute that specifies whether the operation is **oneway** or normal.

♦ **exceptions**—Attribute that specifies all the possible exception types that the operation can throw.

♦ **Contained::describe()**—Inherited operation that, when invoked on an **OperationDef** object, returns an **OperationDescription**.

InterfaceDef

The **InterfaceDef** interface describes an IDL interface. An **InterfaceDef** interface, as shown in Listing 11.3, represents an interface definition. **InterfaceDef** can contain constants, typedefs, exceptions, operations, and attributes.

Listing 11.3   The InterfaceDef interface.

```
interface InterfaceDef;

typedef sequence<InterfaceDef> InterfaceDefSeq;

struct AttributeDescription
{
    Identifier name;
    RepositoryId id;
    RepositoryId defined_in;
    VersionSpec version;
    TypeCode type;
    AttributeMode mode;
};
```

```
struct OperationDescription
{
    Identifier name;
    RepositoryId id;
    RepositoryId defined_in;
    VersionSpec version;
    TypeCode result;
    OperationMode mode;
    ContextIdSeq contexts;
    ParDescriptionSeq parameters;
    ExcDescriptionSeq exceptions;
};

typedef sequence<RepositoryId> RepositoryIdSeq;
typedef sequence<OperationDescription> OpDescriptionSeq;
typedef sequence<AttributeDescription> AttrDescriptionSeq;

interface InterfaceDef : Container, Contained, IDLType
{
    attribute InterfaceDefSeq base_interfaces;
    boolean is_a (in RepositoryId interface_id);

    struct FullInterfaceDescription
    {
        Identifier name;
        RepositoryId id;
        RepositoryId defined_in;
        VersionSpec version;
        OpDescriptionSeq operations;
        AttrDescriptionSeq attributes;
        RepositoryIdSeq base_interfaces;
        TypeCode type;
    };

    FullInterfaceDescription describe_interface();
};
```

The attributes and operations of **InterfaceDef** are explained as follows:

◆ **base_interfaces**—Attribute that represents the sequence of base interfaces of this interface.

◆ **is_a()**—Operation that determines whether this interface is identical to or inherits, directly or indirectly, from the interface identified by its **interface_id** parameter. The **is_a()** operation returns 1 if the interfaces are identical; otherwise, **is_a()** returns 0.

♦ **describe_interface()**—Operation that provides information about an interface. This operation is used to determine an interface's operations and attributes.

♦ **Contained::describe()**—Inherited operation that returns an **InterfaceDescription**.

Using InterfaceDef

The base **CORBA_Object** class provides the **_get_interface()** operation that returns a pointer to **InterfaceDef** within Interface Repository:

```
virtual CORBA_InterfaceDef_ptr _get_interface();
```

You can invoke this operation on an interface to get an **InterfaceDef** pointer that can be used to retrieve information about that interface. This section presents an example that uses the **InterfaceDef** interface and other types that have been described in preceding sections. The example covers the following operations:

♦ **CORBA_Object::_get_interface()**

♦ **InterfaceDef::describe_interface()**

♦ **InterfaceDef::lookup_name()**

♦ **CORBA_OperationDef::params()**

A client program uses these operations to determine information about an interface. Consider the following IDL:

```
module CoRepTest
{
    interface Base1 { };
    interface Base2 { };
    interface Base3 { };

    interface TestInterface : Base1, Base2, Base3
    {
        attribute short attr1;
        attribute short attr2;
        attribute short attr3;

        void op1();
        void op2();
        void op3();
    };
};
```

IR can be used by a client to determine **TestInterface**'s base interfaces, attributes, and operations.

A dummy implementation of the **TestInterface** interface can be defined as follows:

```
class CoRepTest_TestInterface_impl :
    public CoRepTest_TestInterface_skel
{
public:

    CoRepTest_TestInterface_impl() { }

    virtual void op1() { }
    virtual void op2() { }
    virtual void op3() { }

    virtual void attr1(CORBA_Short) { }
    virtual void attr2(CORBA_Short) { }
    virtual void attr3(CORBA_Short) { }

    virtual CORBA_Short attr1() { return 0; }
    virtual CORBA_Short attr2() { return 0; }
    virtual CORBA_Short attr3() { return 0; }
};
```

Listing 11.4 represents a minimal server program that instantiates a **CoRepTest_TestInterface_impl** and writes its interoperable object reference (IOR) to a file. The client program, shown in Listing 11.5, reads the IOR and invokes the **_get_interface()** operation.

Listing 11.4   A server program writing an IOR in a file.
```
int main(int argc, char* argv[], char*[])
{
    try
    {
        CORBA_ORB_var orb = CORBA_ORB_init(argc, argv);
        CORBA_BOA_var boa = orb -> BOA_init(argc, argv);

        CoRepTest_TestInterface_var p =
            new CoRepTest_TestInterface_impl();

        CORBA_String_var s = orb -> object_to_string(p);
```

```
                      const char* refFile = "Interface.ref";
                      ofstream out(refFile);
                      if(out.fail())
                      {
                          cerr << argv[0] << ": can't open `" <<
                              refFile << "': "
                              << strerror(errno) << endl;
                          return 1;
                      }

                      out << s << endl;
                      out.close();

                      boa -> impl_is_ready(
                          CORBA_ImplementationDef::_nil());
                  }
                  catch(CORBA_SystemException& ex)
                  {
                      OBPrintException(ex);
                      return 1;
                  }


                  return 0;
              }
```

Listing 11.5 presents a client program that uses the function
_get_interface() and retrieves information about the **TestInterface**
interface.

Listing 11.5   A client program using IR.

```
int main(int argc, char* argv[], char*[])
{
    try
    {
        CORBA_ORB_var orb = CORBA_ORB_init(argc, argv);

        // Get "interface" object
        const char* refFile = "Interface.ref";
        ifstream in;
        in.open(refFile);
        if(in.fail())
        {
            cerr << argv[0] << ": can't open `" <<
                refFile << "': "
                << strerror(errno) << endl;
```

```
        return 1;
    }

    char s[1000];
    in >> s;

    CORBA_Object_var obj = orb -> string_to_object(s);
    assert(!CORBA_is_nil(obj));

    CORBA_InterfaceDef_var idef =
        obj -> _get_interface();
    if(CORBA_is_nil(idef))
    {
        cerr << argv[0] <<
            ": no interface repository available" <<
            endl;
        return 1;
    }
    else
    {
        CORBA_InterfaceDef::FullInterfaceDescription_var
            desc =idef -> describe_interface();

        CORBA_ULong i;

        cout << "name = " << desc -> name << endl;
        cout << "id = " << desc -> id << endl;
        cout << "defined_in = " <<
            desc -> defined_in << endl;
        cout << "version = " << desc -> version << endl;
        cout << "operations:" << endl;
        for(i = 0 ; i < desc -> operations.length() ;
            i++)
        {
            cout << i << ": " <<
                desc -> operations[i].name << endl;
        }
        cout << "attributes:" << endl;
        for(i = 0 ; i < desc -> attributes.length() ;
            i++)
        {
            cout << i << ": " <<
                desc -> attributes[i].name << endl;
        }
        cout << "base_interfaces:" << endl;
    for(i = 0 ; i < desc -> base_interfaces.length() ;
```

```
                                i++)
                    {
                        cout << i << ": " <<
                            desc -> base_interfaces[i] << endl;
                    }
                }
            }
            catch(CORBA_SystemException& ex)
            {
                OBPrintException(ex);
                return 1;
            }

            return 0;
        }
```

Here is the discussion about this program:

♦ The program gets the object reference for the **TestInterface** interface and stores the object reference into a variable **obj**. Recall that an object reference uniquely identifies a component instance in a distributed environment.

♦ The program invokes the **_get_interface()** operation on the **obj** variable. The returned value is stored in a variable **idef** of type **CORBA_InterfaceDef**.

♦ The program invokes the **describe_interface()** operation on **idef** and stores the returned values in a variable **desc** of type **CORBA_InterfaceDef::FullInterfaceDescription_var**.

♦ The **desc** variable is used to find out details about the **TestInterface** interface.

The client program produces the following output:

```
name = TestInterface
id = IDL:CoRepTest/TestInterface:1.0
defined_in = IDL:CoRepTest:1.0
version = 1.0
operations:
0: op1
1: op2
2: op3
3: op4
attributes:
0: attr1
1: attr2
```

```
2: attr3
base_interfaces:
0: IDL:CoRepTest/Base1:1.0
1: IDL:CoRepTest/Base2:1.0
2: IDL:CoRepTest/Base3:1.0
```

The program outputs the list of operation names and attribute names defined on the **TestInterface** interface.

Now, assume that you add an **ex** exception and an **op4()** operation on the same IDL definition:

```
exception ex
{
    string str;
};


short op4(in long longParam, in short shortParam)
    raises (ex);
```

You can find information about this operation by using the **lookup_name()** operation defined on the **Container** interface. The client program, as shown in Listing 11.5, can be modified as follows to use the **lookup_name()** operation:

```
// Look up the operation op4() on the interface:
CORBA_ContainedSeq_var operations;
cout << "Looking up operation op4()" << endl;
operations = idef->
    lookup_name("op4", 1, CORBA_dk_Operation, 1);

if (operations->length() != 1)
{
    cout << "Incorrect result lookup_name()";
    exit(1);
}
else
{
    //Narrow the result to be an OperationDef
    CORBA_OperationDef_var op4Var =
    CORBA_OperationDef::_narrow(operations[0]);
    CORBA_ParDescriptionSeq_var parDescriptionSeq=
        op4Var->params();

    for (CORBA_ULong i=0; i<parDescriptionSeq->length();
        i++)
```

```
{
    cout<<"Parameter name ["<<i<<"] :"<<
        parDescriptionSeq[i].name<<endl;
}
}
```

This following occurs in this program:

◆ The program uses the **lookup_name()** operation and stores the returned value in a variable **operations** of type **CORBA_ContainedSeq**. Recall that the first parameter **"op4"** to **lookup_name()** is the name of the entity to be searched. The second parameter **(1)** limits the search to the current object only. The third parameter **CORBA_dk_Operation** determines that an interface of type **CORBA_OperationDef** is to be searched. The last parameter **1** means that inherited entities are to be excluded.

◆ The first element of the **operations** is narrowed into the **CORBA_OperationDef** interface and the result is stored in a variable **op4Var**.

◆ The **params()** operation is invoked on the **op4Var** variable and the result is stored in a variable **parDescriptionSeq** of type **CORBA_ParDescriptionSeq_var**.

◆ The **parDescriptionSeq** variable is used to find parameter names of the **op4()** operation.

This part of the client program produces the following output:

```
Looking up operation op4()
Parameter name [0] :longParam
Parameter name [1] :shortParam
```

The output shows the names of arguments to the **op4()** operation. You can modify the program to display more information about **op4()** by using the contents of **CORBA_ParDescription** that is returned as a result of calling the subscript operator on the **CORBA_ParDescriptionSeq_var**.

The Dynamic Invocation Interface (DII)

For an object to be understood by CORBA and accessed remotely, it must have an interface, and that interface must be expressed in IDL. Consequently, when a client invokes operations on a component, the client application already knows about the interface of the component. However, a situation may arise in which a client needs to invoke

NOTE

Interface Inheritance Isn't DII

You need to understand that, although the mechanism of interface inheritance coupled with polymorphism offers a way to invoke operations on an implementation that is not known at compile time, this mechanism works only for those operations that are at least declared in the base interface. To invoke operations specific to the derived interface, you still need to know the stub.

operations on components without knowing their interfaces. CORBA provides this feature through the Dynamic Invocation Interface. DII allows dynamic creation and invocation of requests to remote components. A client application using DII can be compiled with no client stubs at all, thus having no prior knowledge of the target component. Note that the component receiving DII provides the same semantics as the component receiving the operation invocation through the stubs generated from the IDL definition. In other words, the DII mechanism is used only for clients—a server implementation has no knowledge of whether an operation was invoked as a result of DII calls or as a result of stub calls. This concept is shown in Figure 11.2.

The Request Object

The mechanism of invoking operations through DII differs from issuing a static stub invocation (SSI). The mechanism of DII is implemented through *request objects* (also referred to as *requests*). A request consists of an object reference, an operation, and a list of parameters. As mentioned earlier, DII allows dynamic requests to be constructed by specifying the target component reference, the operation name, and the parameters to be passed. The parameters in a request are supplied as elements of a list. Each element is an instance of a type **NamedValue** (described later in the chapter). Parameters supplied to a request are subjected to runtime type checking. The order in which parameters are passed is significant.

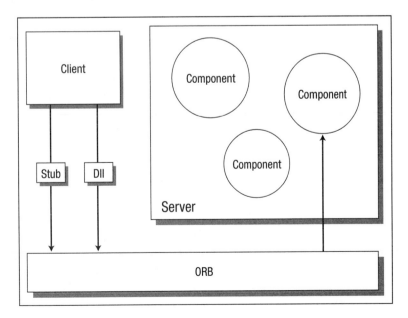

Figure 11.2

A component receiving a call.

The **Request** class is declared as follows:

```
class CORBA_Request;
typedef CORBA_Request* CORBA_Request_ptr;
typedef OBObjVar< CORBA_Request > CORBA_Request_var;

class CORBA_Request : public OBRefCount
{
    // Hide copy-constructor and asignment operator
    CORBA_Request(const CORBA_Request&);
    void operator=(const CORBA_Request&);

public:

    CORBA_Status invoke();
    CORBA_Status send_oneway();
    CORBA_Status send_deferred();
    CORBA_Boolean poll_response();
    CORBA_Status get_response();

    CORBA_Environment_ptr env();
    CORBA_NamedValue_ptr result();
    CORBA_NVList_ptr arguments();
    //...
};
```

The following are the operations of **CORBA_Request**:

♦ **invoke()**—Represents the normal call (non-**oneway**) on a remote target. Note that the returned type **CORBA_Status** is **typedef**ed to **void**.

♦ **send_oneway()**—Represents the **oneway** operation in the IDL definition.

♦ **send_deferred()**—Represents an invocation that returns immediately.

♦ **poll_response()**—Function to periodically check for a response from the **send_deferred()** operation invocation.

♦ **get_response()**—Function to be invoked after **poll_response()** notifies that the result has been received. The client can also use this function if it wants to block other requests while waiting for the result. This function is used after using the **send_deferred()** function. If you use the **send_oneway()** function, no return result exists, and thus, you don't call any function to get the result.

♦ **env()**—Function to check whether an exception was raised.

♦ **result()**—Function to obtain the **CORBA_NamedValue_ptr** that contains the results of the operation invocation. Use this function if you invoked the function by using the **invoke()** function on the **CORBA_Request** object.

♦ **arguments()**—Function to get **CORBA_NVList_ptr** that represents the parameter list. This is shown in an example presented later in the chapter.

As the preceding description indicates, the **CORBA_NamedValue** and **CORBA_NVList** structures are used in the **CORBA_Request** member functions to describe the return and argument values. The types **CORBA_NamedValue** and **CORBA_NVList** are defined as shown in Listing 11.6.

Listing 11.6   Partial declarations of the CORBA_NamedValue and CORBA_NVList classes.

```
typedef CORBA_Long CORBA_Flags;
class CORBA_NamedValue : public OBRefCount
{
    CORBA_String_var name_;
    mutable CORBA_Any_var value_;
    CORBA_Flags flags_;

    // Hide copy-constructor and asignment operator
    CORBA_NamedValue(const CORBA_NamedValue&);
    void operator=(const CORBA_NamedValue&);

public:

    const char* name() const;
    CORBA_Any* value() const;
    //...
};

class CORBA_NVList : public OBRefCount
{
    OBObjSeq<CORBA_NamedValue> namedValueSeq_;

    // Hide copy-constructor and asignment operator
    CORBA_NVList(const CORBA_NVList&);
    void operator=(const CORBA_NVList&);

public:
```

```
        CORBA_NamedValue_ptr add_value(const char*,
            const CORBA_Any&, CORBA_Flags);
        //...
};
```

The member functions of the **CORBA_NamedValue** class are described as follows:

♦ **name()**—Returns the name of a **CORBA_NamedValue** object.

♦ **value()**—Returns the value of a **CORBA_NamedValue** object in the form of **Any**.

By using the **add_value()** member function of the **CORBA_NVList** class, you can populate the arguments for an operation to be invoked using DII. The first parameter is the name of the argument, the second parameter takes the value of the argument in the form of **Any**, and the last argument represents the mode of the parameter passing. This is used in an example presented later in the chapter.

Using DII To Invoke An Operation

This section presents a simple example that shows how to combine various functions necessary to use DII. The typical steps involved in a DII example are as follows:

1. Obtain the object reference for the target component.

2. Instantiate a **Request** object by using the target component's object reference.

3. Populate the Request object with arguments using the **arguments()** member function of the Request object.

4. Populate the **Request** object with return types, and exceptions, using the **result()** member function of the **Request** object.

5. Invoke the desired operation (using one of the member functions of the **Request** object).

6. Retrieve the result of the operation invocation.

The first five steps are demonstrated in this section. However, Step 6 is covered in the "Using DII To Read An Attribute" section.

Consider the **Account** IDL that was presented in Chapter 9:

```
//IDL
module CoBank
{
```

```
struct Person
{
    string name;
    short age;
};

interface Account
{
    readonly attribute float balance;
    readonly attribute Person holder;

    exception NoMoney
    {
        float balance;
    };

    void deposit(in float amount);
    void withdraw(in float amount) raises (NoMoney);
};
};
```

The following code segment of the client shows a simple way to obtain the object reference for the target component (Step 1):

```
// Create ORB

CORBA_ORB_var orb = CORBA_ORB_init(argc, argv);

// Get "Account" object
const char* refFile = "CoAccount.ref";
ifstream in;
in.open(refFile);
if(in.fail())
{
    cerr << argv[0] << ": can't open `" << refFile <<
    "': "<< strerror(errno) << endl;
    return 1;
}

char s[1000];
in >> s;

CORBA_Object_var obj = orb -> string_to_object(s);
assert(!CORBA_is_nil(obj));
```

In this example, the **obj** reference is initialized from a stringified IOR. This is one of the simplest ways to find an IOR. CORBA's Naming Service provides a better way to locate a component in a distributed environment. (Naming Service is covered in Chapter 12.)

Now, you need to set up a request to be sent to the **obj** reference as Step 2. The **CORBA_Object** class provides the following declaration to create a **Request** object:

```
CORBA_Request_ptr _request(const char* operation);
```

The **_request()** member function is always performed on the target component. The **operation** parameter is the name of the operation to be invoked, as shown here (Steps 2 and 3):

```
CORBA_Request_var request=obj->_request("deposit");
CORBA_NVList_ptr arguments = request->arguments();
CORBA_Any amount;
amount<<=CORBA_Float(13.169);
arguments->add_value("amount", amount, CORBA_ARG_IN );
```

Here is the explanation of the preceding code segment:

1. The client creates a **Request** object on the target **obj** component by calling the **_request()** operation. The name of the operation that the client wants to invoke on the **Account** component is the **deposit()** operation, which is used as the parameter to the **_request()** operation.

2. The client gets a parameter list (**CORBA_NVList_ptr**) from the **request** variable by using the **arguments()** member function.

3. The client populates the **arguments** by using the **add_value()** member function of the **CORBA_NVList** class. Recall that the **deposit()** operation takes a **CORBA_Float** as an **in** parameter. This is why the argument **amount** to the **add_value()** member function is inserted as a value **13.169** of the type **CORBA_Float**, and the last argument to **add_value()** is **CORBA_ARG_IN**.

Now, you need to define the result type from the **deposit()** call that is done as follows (Step 4):

```
CORBA_NamedValue_ptr result=request->result();
CORBA_Any* value=result->value();
value->replace(CORBA__tc_void, &result);
```

NOTE

Using User-Defined Types (UDT) In DII

The previous example uses the **CORBA_Float** data type to invoke an operation through DII. If you need to pass a UDT (such as **struct**, **union**, **sequence**, and so forth), you can't use the mechanism presented in the example. To achieve passing a UDT, you need to use the **DynAny** (Dynamic Any) data type that is defined in the **CORBA_DynAny** class in ORBacus. **CORBA_DynAny** is a construct that enables you to parse through a type **Any** and extract or insert values, given the typecode, which can be extracted from IR. **DynAny** wasn't included in the CORBA 2.1 specification, but has been formally accepted in the CORBA 2.2 specification. This book doesn't cover **CORBA_DynAny**.

The following explains the preceding code segment:

1. The client calls **result()** on the **request** object. The returned value is stored in a variable **result** of type **CORBA_NamedValue_ptr**. Recall that **result()** is a member function of the **CORBA_Request** class. The **result()** member function is used to obtain the **CORBA_NamedValue_ptr** that contains the results of the operation invocation.

2. The client calls **value()** on the **result** variable. The **value()** function returns the value of the **result** variable in the form of **Any**.

3. The program calls **replace()** to specify the expected return type for the operation. Because the **deposit()** operation returns a **void**, the **TypeCode** for this **void** (**CORBA__tc_void**) is inserted into the result.

Now, you invoke the request as follows (Step 5):

```
request->invoke();
CORBA_Environment_ptr env = request->env();
if (env->exception())
{
    cout << "An exception occurred"<<endl;
}
```

Here is a description of the preceding code segment:

1. The client calls the **invoke()** operation on the **Request** object, which in turn, invokes the **deposit()** operation on the **obj** reference.

2. The client calls **env()** and **exception()** on the **request** and **env** objects, respectively, to check for any exceptions that were raised by the **deposit()** operation. If an exception was raised by the operation call, **exception()** returns a non-**NULL** result.

The example just discussed doesn't handle any exceptions. You must, however, handle **CORBA_SystemException** and use the *catch-all* construct (**...**). This is shown is the next section.

Using DII To Read An Attribute

The previous DII example shows how to invoke an operation on an IDL interface. DII can also be used to read and write attributes of an interface. To read/write an attribute **A**, the operation name should be set to one of the following:

◆ **_get_A()**—To read the attribute.

◆ **_set_A()**—To write the attribute.

For example, to read the attribute **balance** from the **Account** interface, the operation name should be set to **_get_balance**. The rest of the programming remains the same. However, because **balance()** returns a **CORBA_Float**, you need to capture that value as shown in Listing 11.7.

Listing 11.7   Reading an attribute by using DII.

```
try
{
    CORBA_Request_var request=obj->
        _request("_get_balance");

    CORBA_NamedValue_ptr result=request->result();
    CORBA_Any* value=result->value();
    value->replace(CORBA__tc_float, &result);
    request->invoke();
    CORBA_Environment_ptr env = request->env();

    if (env->exception())
    {
        cout << "An exception occurred"<<endl;
    }
    else
    {
        cout<<"balance is:"<<*(CORBA_Float*)value->value();
    }
}
catch(CORBA_SystemException& ex)
{
    OBPrintException(ex);
    return 1;
}
catch(...)
{
    cerr << "Unexpected exception " << endl;
    exit(1);
}
```

The client calls the **value()** function on the **Any** pointer (**value**) that is returned by the **result()** function. The returned value (**void***) is cast to a **CORBA_Float** pointer. This corresponds to Step 6 mentioned earlier in the "Using DII To Invoke An Operation" section.

Static Interfaces Vs. DII

You generally won't need to use DII, because DII isn't useful for most applications and typically only adds unnecessary complexity to most applications.

DII, however, offers two advantages:

♦ A client need not be aware of server interfaces at compile time. In fact, you can develop a client even when the interface definition for a server component doesn't exist. This provides great flexibility to write clients.

♦ A client can invoke an operation by using the **send_oneway()** operation (even if the interface's IDL didn't declare the operation as **oneway**). Although this may not be advisable, it provides flexibility.

However, the following are some disadvantages associated with using DII:

♦ Applications using DII are more complex than those using SSI.

♦ SSI provides static type checking, which doesn't exist for DII. Therefore, you may write a program that compiles without any problem, but then exhibits runtime faults.

♦ Because arguments to an operation are inserted one at a time, additional overhead is incurred in each DII function call.

♦ The DII examples presented so far assume the types of the interfaces and operations being invoked. In practice, you need to interact with IR (as explained earlier in the chapter) to get information about the operation to be performed, and the types of the parameters to be passed. This causes additional overhead associated in using DII.

Note that the preceding code uses the catch-all construct (...). It is a good programming practice to use the catch-all construct as an exception handler.

Use Of IR And DII In Frameworks

Compared to SSI, you can see that DII is much more complex to write and understand. This is why you generally won't use IR and DII in application development. However, if you're creating development frameworks, testing tools, and system management tools, you may find IR and DII effective, because you need to work with unknown CORBA objects in a generic way. A discussion on this topic is presented in Chapter 13.

Chapter Recap

CORBA provides support for dynamic programming and enables you to build powerful, flexible dynamic applications. This chapter presented a few significant CORBA notions and features, including the following:

♦ *Interface Repository*—IR maintains information about IDL type definitions, allowing information about a component's type to be determined at runtime by calling functions defined by IR. The primary function of IR is to provide the type information necessary to issue requests using DII.

♦ *Dynamic Invocation Interface*—DII is a new way to invoke operations on remote CORBA components. DII allows requests to be constructed by specifying at runtime the target component reference, the operation name, and the parameters to be passed. Compared to the static invocation, the DII mechanism has advantages and disadvantages. Note that DII depends a lot on **Any**, **TypeCode**, and IR.

CORBA also provides DSI to support dynamic programming. This book, however, doesn't cover DSI.

Chapter 12

Introduction To CORBA Object Services

C hapters 9, 10, and 11 present information about how to develop distributed object-oriented applications. Recall that object request broker (ORB) allows components to communicate with each other. Because everything runs and depends on ORB, ORB is key to creating distributed applications. However, ORB alone isn't enough to create robust and enterprise-distributed applications. Thus, the Object Management Group (OMG) provides additional capabilities in the form of object services. OMG created specifications for several object services that are useful to applications in general. CORBA *object services* (COS) basically consists of domain-independent generic interfaces that are likely to be used in a distributed application, regardless of the industry. Object services are reusable basic building blocks to create distributed object-oriented applications. Object services are collectively called *CORBAservices*.

This chapter presents an overview of all the CORBA object services and describes the Naming Service concepts, including examples. Naming Service provides a mechanism with which you can register a component and locate a component by name. This chapter doesn't provide a complete description of Naming Service, but it does provide an overview that will get you started.

Overview Of CORBA Object Services

OMG defines 15 object services to meet industry requirements for creating distributed applications. Service interfaces are designed to allow a wide range of implementation approaches, which depend on the characteristics of the service required in any particular environment. OMG provides only the specifications of the services, in the form of interfaces, and doesn't offer implementations of those specifications. However, OMG did consider the following design principles while defining object services:

♦ *Services should be generic*—Services don't depend on the type of the client or a participating component.

♦ *Services should be flexible*—Services can be combined to produce new, powerful services and frameworks. For example, Event Service and Relationship Service can be combined to create workflow frameworks.

♦ *Services should follow CORBA's philosophy*—Services are based on CORBA concepts. Because OMG provides only interfaces, the separation of interface and implementation is automatically imposed—a good thing. CORBA services promote specification reuse, because some of the services use the interface inheritance concept to extend, evolve, and customize the functionality of the service being used.

♦ *Services should not be monolithic*—Services typically are partitioned into several distinct interfaces to simplify the way in which a particular client uses a service. A particular service implementation can support the constituent interfaces either as a single CORBA object or as a collection of distinct objects.

Brief Description Of CORBA Object Services

As described in Chapter 8, CORBA provides 15 types of object services. Chapter 8 presents brief information about the services. Table 12.1 gives an overview of the services.

The following sections present more information about each of the object services and show how some of the services relate to other services.

Event Service

Typically, an *event* is a communication between two components in which one of the components needs to inform the other about its change of state. This requires that the two components know about each other's interests in events. Event Service does the following:

Table 12.1   Overview of CORBA object services.

Service	Description
Event Service	Supports asynchronous event notifications and event delivery.
Security Service	Ensures secure communication between components.
Licensing Service	Enables component vendors to control the use of their intellectual property.
Naming Service	Provides a client with the capability to locate a component by name.
Relationship Service	Allows components to form dynamic relationships (links) between each other.
Life Cycle Service	Defines operations to create, copy, move, and remove components on ORB.
Object Trader Service	Enables a client to locate a component using some component properties.
Externalization Service	Defines protocols for externalizing and internalizing component data.
Persistent Object Service	Provides interfaces for storing and managing the persistent state of components.
Time Service	Enables a user to obtain current time in a distributed environment.
Concurrency Control Service	Enables multiple clients to coordinate their access to shared resources.
Object Transaction Service	Supports a two-phase commit protocol between components.
Object Query Service	Enables a component to invoke queries on collections of other components.
Object Collections Service	Provides a uniform way to create and manipulate collections of components.
Object Property Service	Associates properties (named values) dynamically with components.

♦ Enables components to register interest in an event dynamically.

♦ Supports asynchronous event notifications and event delivery.

♦ Supports two kinds of event delivery models: *push* and *pull*. Using push and pull models, components can either request events or be notified of events, depending on the application requirements. The event-generating components are *suppliers*, and the event-receiving components are *consumers*. Suppliers can generate events without knowing the identities of the consumers. This is made possible by inserting a component, referred to as an *event channel*, between the consumers and the suppliers.

Note that the Event Service design is scalable and is suitable for distributed environments. Event Service is described in more detail in Chapter 13.

Security Service

Security Service presents a model by which you can ensure secure communication between components. Security Service specifies the interfaces to meet the following security-related requirements:

♦ *Identification and authentication of users*—Verifies that a user, also referred to as a *principal*, is who he or she claims to be.

♦ *Authorization and access control*—Determines which users are permitted access to which services or components.

♦ *Security auditing*—Provides records of users' actions.

♦ *Security of communication*—Authenticates users to services (and vice versa) and protects the confidentiality of the users.

♦ *Nonrepudiation*—Prevents a receiver/sender from falsely denying the receiving or sending of data. It provides proof of the origin of data sent to the recipient, or proof of the receipt of data to the sender.

Licensing Service (LS)

Component providers may need to control the use of their services, and LS enables them to achieve that. LS itself doesn't define any business policy or practice—vendors can define and implement LS to meet their own requirements and the requirements of their customers. A license in LS consists of the following three types of attributes that enable producers to apply license controls flexibly:

♦ *Time*—Enables a license to set a start date, an expiration date, and the duration of the license.

♦ *Value mapping*—Enables licensing based on units (allocation, consumption, and so on).

♦ *Consumer*—Enables a license to be engaged or reserved for specific entities; for example, a license could be restricted to a particular machine.

Naming Service

Naming Service gives a component the capability to locate another component by name. Naming Service enables a component to bind its name to a *naming context*, an object that contains a set of name bindings in which each name is unique. *Resolving* a name refers to the process of determining the object associated with the name in a given context. (Name resolution is described later in the chapter, along with an example.)

Relationship Service

Distributed components cannot exist in isolation. They collaborate with each other and may need to form relationships. Relationship Service enables you to form dynamic relationships (links) among components. Relationship Service defines two new kinds of objects: *relationships* and *roles*. A role represents a CORBA component in a relationship. A set of related objects forms an *object graph*. The edges of the graph represent relationships. One potential use of this service is to create workflow managers.

Life Cycle Service

A CORBA component's life starts from its creation, and the component remains available until it is destroyed. Between the creation and the destruction, a component may be cloned or moved to another location. This is accomplished by Life Cycle Service, which defines operations to create, copy, move, and remove components. Life Cycle Service also supports the notion of an *object factory*, which is a CORBA component that creates other CORBA components. Chapter 9 presents a simple factory implementation to explain the notion of a factory. A component factory is, in fact, a design pattern that Chapter 5 explains and Chapter 13 discusses further, within the realm of distributed components.

Object Trader Service

Object Trader Service essentially is a better Naming Service that enables a component to locate another component by providing some properties or capabilities instead of names. In effect, Object Trader Service provides a matchmaking service for objects. The service provider registers the availability of the service by invoking an export operation on the trader, passing as parameters the information about the offered service and the object reference of the component being registered.

Object Trader Service in a single trading domain may be distributed over multiple trader objects. Traders in different domains may be federated, which enables systems in different domains to negotiate the sharing of services without losing control of their own policies and services.

NOTE

**Naming Service Vs.
Object Trader Service**

Naming Service and
Object Trader Service
are used for the same
purpose—locating a
particular component on
ORB. However, they are
defined as different
services because they
depend on different
inputs. Object Trader
Service simulates the
Yellow Pages, in which
you discover a compo-
nent based on its
location, service, or
name. Naming Service,
on the other hand,
resembles the White
Pages, in which you
locate a particular
component if you know
its exact name.

Externalization Service

Sometimes, you need to stream out (externalize) a component's state
and later stream the component's state back (internalize) to its original state. Externalization Service defines interfaces for externalizing
and internalizing a component's state. By using Externalization Service, you can externalize a component state in a stream of data (in
memory, on a disk file, or across the network). Externalization Service
enables you to internalize the stream into a new instance of the component in the same or a different process. Externalization Service can
be used as a device to implement a pass-by-value mechanism for
CORBA objects.

Persistent Object Service (POS)

It is a natural requirement for a system to manage and store persistent
data. In a CORBA-based system, *persistent data* means the persistent
state of a component. POS provides a set of generic interfaces for storing and managing the persistent state of a CORBA component.
Although a component defines, manipulates, and manages its state, it
still can delegate POS to perform the actual work related to persistency. POS is an open architecture, enabling a variety of different clients
and implementations of POS to work together.

Time Service

Time Service enables a component to obtain the current time. You can
also use Time Service to determine the order in which events occurred
and to compute the interval between two events. Time Service also
generates time-based events that are based on timers and alarms.

Concurrency Control Service (CCS)

In a distributed environment, multiple, concurrent clients may need
to coordinate shared resources by reconciling any conflicting actions
by the resources. This ensures that the resource remains in a consistent
state. CCS enables this by using *locks*.

Each lock is associated with a single resource and a single client. A
locking mechanism prevents multiple clients from concurrently pos-
sessing the same resource. Thus, a client must acquire an appropriate
lock before approaching a shared resource. CCS defines several lock
modes. For example, providing different modes for reading and writing
enables multiple, concurrent clients to perform read-only transactions.

Object Transaction Service (OTS)

A client may need to operate a component that is participating in a transaction. The client can be the originator of the transaction and may make a decision to commit the transaction. OTS supports a two-phase commit protocol between components. OTS supports two transaction models:

♦ *Flat transaction model*—Has a *begin transaction*, followed by one or more steps and then issues a *commit transaction* or an *abort transaction*. In this model, all the work done is at the same level.

♦ *Nested transaction model*—Allows subtransactions to occur within a transaction. Subtransactions may nest to any arbitrary level. This mechanism enables you to define hierarchical transactions. In this mechanism, a subtransaction's effect becomes permanent after it issues a local commit and all its ancestors commit. If a parent transaction aborts, all its descendent transactions abort—regardless of whether they issued local commits.

An OTS implementation must provide the flat model; the nested model is optional.

Implementing OTS in a transaction processing monitor (TP monitor) environment enables you to execute multiple transactions concurrently and run clients, servers, and transaction services in separate processes.

Object Query Service (OQS)

Sometimes, you need query capability on a CORBA component or a collection of components. The result of the query may be a single component or collections of components. OQS allows a component to invoke queries on another component or on collections of components.

A CORBA query not only lets you find components, but also lets you invoke arbitrary operations on components. Queries can specify target components to act upon, based on some search criteria. Thus, query capability provides database-like semantics to CORBA components.

Object Collections Service

Collections are groups of components that provide some operations and display collection-specific behaviors (rather than component-specific behaviors). Examples of collections are sets, queues, stacks, lists, and binary trees. Object Collections Service provides a uniform way to create and manipulate the generic collections of components.

Object Property Service (OPS)

You occasionally may need to associate runtime attributes with a component. OPS provides a mechanism to associate properties (named values) with components dynamically. OPS defines operations to create, delete, and manipulate properties. The names (of named values) are simple interface definition language (IDL) strings. The values are IDL **any**s. (Chapter 13 details OPS further and provides examples of OPS scenarios.)

Resolving A CORBA Service

Using CORBA, you can obtain an object reference of a component in various ways. One of the simplest ways is to convert a stringified object reference into an object reference, as the examples in Chapter 9 demonstrate. To recap, the CORBA specification defines two operations (**object_to_string()** and **string_to_object()**) on the **ORB** interface in the **CORBA** module for converting object references to and from strings:

```
module CORBA
{
    interface ORB
    {
        string object_to_string(in Object obj);
        Object string_to_object(in string ref);
    };
};
```

A stringified object reference is the simplest way of establishing the first contact to a server. However, this mechanism isn't the only method to bootstrap an object reference. The CORBA specification provides a standard way to bootstrap an object reference—through a set of initial services. You can obtain object references of the initial services by using the **resolve_initial_references()** operation on the **ORB** interface, which is defined as follows:

```
// IDL
module CORBA
{
    interface ORB
    {
        typedef string ObjectId;
        exception InvalidName {};
```

```
Object resolve_initial_references(in ObjectId identifier)
     raises(InvalidName);
   };
};
```

The operation **resolve_initial_references()** takes a standard name and returns an object reference. OMG has standardized the names for some of the CORBA services. For example, Naming Service has the name **"NameService"**, Trader Service has the name **"TradingService"**, and Event Service has the name **"EventService"**. Listing 12.1 presents an example in which the ORB is queried for a Naming Service object reference by using the **resolve_initial_references()** operation on the **ORB** reference (**orb**).

Listing 12.1   Resolving an initial reference of Naming Service.

```
int main(int argc, char* argv[], char*[])
{
    try
    {
        // Create ORB
        CORBA_ORB_var orb =
            CORBA_ORB_init(argc, argv);

        // Get naming service
        CORBA_Object_var obj;

        try
        {
            obj = orb ->
                resolve_initial_references("NameService");
        }
        catch(const CORBA_ORB::InvalidName&)
        {
            cerr << argv[0] <<
            ": can't resolve `NameService'" << endl;
            return 1;
        }

        if(CORBA_is_nil(obj))
        {
            cerr << argv[0] <<
            ": `NameService' is a nil object "
            << endl;
            return 1;
        }
```

```
        CosNaming_NamingContext_var nc =
            CosNaming_NamingContext::_narrow(obj);

        if(CORBA_is_nil(nc))
        {
            cerr << argv[0]
            << ": `NamingContext' is a nil object"
            << endl;
            return 1;
        }
    }
    catch(CORBA_SystemException& ex)
    {
        OBPrintException(ex);
        return 1;
    }

    return 0;
}
```

Here is a short description of the selected statements in Listing 12.1:

♦ The program tries to resolve Naming Service through the **resolve_initial_references()** operation and stores the returned object in a variable, **obj**.

♦ The program narrows the **obj** object reference to the **CosNaming_NamingContext** interface. Note that the interface **NamingContext** is defined in the **CosNaming** module. This is explained in the next section.

♦ If ORB can't resolve a service, an **InvalidName** exception is thrown.

Expressions Of Naming Service

As mentioned earlier in the chapter, Naming Service enables a component to locate another component by name. This process involves steps that are executed by the server and the client programs. This section presents an overview of the fundamental concepts of Naming Service.

Name Binding

Referencing a component in a distributed environment by its component name is more natural than using a stringified object reference. This core feature of Naming Service enables you to attach a name to a component at runtime. This name-to-object association is referred to as *name binding*. The name is later used by a client to locate the component.

Naming Context

A name binding is always defined relative to a scope, or *naming context*. Different names can be bound to an object simultaneously in the same or different naming contexts. To bind a name is to create a name binding in a given context.

Name Resolution

Naming Service gives a component the capability to resolve another component by name. *Resolving a name* means to locate the component associated with the name in a particular context. A name is always resolved relative to a context—no absolute names exist.

Naming Graphs

A naming context is an object that contains a set of name bindings, in which each name is unique. Because a context is an object, it can also be bound to a name in another naming context. Binding contexts in other contexts creates a tree that is referred to as a *naming graph*. This means that you can create some sort of relationship among components at runtime. Given a context in a naming graph, a sequence of names can reference an object. This sequence of names (called a *compound name*) defines a path in the naming graph to navigate the resolution process. Figure 12.1 shows an example of a naming graph.

The tree in Figure 12.1 shows that a compound name, Palo Alto, consists of the four naming contexts: World, North America, USA, and CA. This example demonstrates that in a naming graph, the intermediate nodes are naming contexts, and the leaf nodes are compound names. Therefore, to resolve the name Palo Alto, you have to traverse the naming graph, starting from World, which is the root of the naming graph.

The Name Of A Component

Naming Service is defined by a module called **CosNaming**, which consists of the structures and interfaces that are necessary to register and locate a component. Components are registered with a unique name, which can later be used to resolve its associated object reference. Object references registered with Naming Service are maintained in a hierarchical structure,

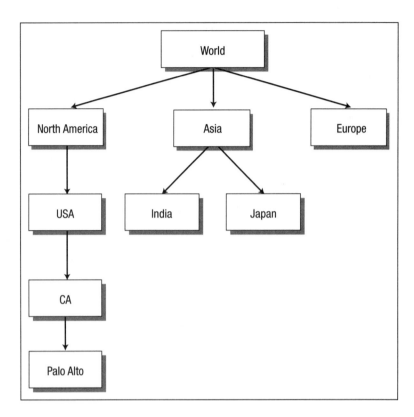

Figure 12.1
A naming graph.

as previously shown in Figure 12.1. The names stored in Naming Service are called *bindings*. A binding consists of a component's name and its type, as defined in the **CosNaming** module:

```
typedef string Istring;

struct NameComponent
{
    Istring id;
    Istring kind;
};


typedef sequence<NameComponent> Name;
```

As you can see, a **Name** instance consists of one or more **Name-Components**. Each name component consists of two strings: **id** and **kind**. The **id** string denotes the name associated with a distributed component. The **kind** string is used to classify the component, if needed (see the sidebar "Names In Naming Service").

NOTE

Naming Graphs Provides Scalability

Naming graphs can be supported in a distributed, federated fashion. Federation enables name servers across the network to work in conjunction with each other. This is possible because the naming graph concept provides a scalable design that supports the distributed, heterogeneous implementation and administration of names and naming contexts. Federated naming servers are used by applications in highly distributed systems.

Naming Service Interfaces

The **CosNaming** module provides two Naming Service interfaces:

- **NamingContext**—Provides the mechanism to create and resolve name graphs.

- **BindingIterator**—Provides the mechanism to iterate all components registered with Naming Service.

Because the **NamingContext** and the **BindingIterator** are both CORBA interfaces, they are accessed via object references.

The *NamingContext* Interface

The **NamingContext** interface is declared as shown in Listing 12.2.

Listing 12.2   The NamingContext interface.

```
interface NamingContext
{
    enum NotFoundReason
    {
        missing_node,
        not_context,
        not_object
    };

    exception NotFound
    {
        NotFoundReason why;
        Name rest_of_name;
    };

    exception CannotProceed
    {
        NamingContext ctx;
```

Names In Naming Service

Naming Service design assumes no semantics or interpretation of the names; this is up to the implementations. Naming Service provides only a structural convention for names, such as compound names.

The **id** attribute of the **NameComponent** structure is used to denote the name of a component that is to be located, whereas the **kind** attribute can be used to characterize a name. For example, **kind** can be used to facilitate application localization. The naming system doesn't interpret, assign, or manage user values of **kind** in any way. You may make policies about the use and management of these values.

```
        Name rest_of_name;
    };

    exception InvalidName { };
    exception AlreadyBound { };
    exception NotEmpty { };

    void bind(in Name n, in Object obj)
    raises(NotFound, CannotProceed, InvalidName,
        AlreadyBound);

    void rebind(in Name n, in Object obj)
    raises(NotFound, CannotProceed, InvalidName);

    void bind_context(in Name n, in NamingContext nc)
    raises(NotFound, CannotProceed, InvalidName,
        AlreadyBound);

    void rebind_context(in Name n, in NamingContext nc)
    raises(NotFound, CannotProceed, InvalidName);

    NamingContext new_context();

    NamingContext bind_new_context(in Name n)
    raises(NotFound, AlreadyBound, CannotProceed,
        InvalidName);

    Object resolve (in Name n)
    raises(NotFound, CannotProceed, InvalidName);

    void unbind(in Name n)
    raises(NotFound, CannotProceed, InvalidName);

    void destroy() raises(NotEmpty);
};
```

Here is a brief description of each of the operations of the **Naming-Context** interface shown in Listing 12.2:

♦ **bind()**—Registers a new component with Naming Service. Naming contexts that are bound using **bind()** aren't considered in name resolution when compound names are passed to be resolved.

♦ **rebind()**—Creates a binding of a name and a component in the naming context, even if the name is already bound in the context. Naming contexts that are bound using **rebind()** aren't considered in name resolution when compound names are passed to be resolved.

- **bind_context()**—Registers a new context. Naming contexts that are bound using **bind_context()** are considered in name resolution when compound names are passed to be resolved.

- **rebind_context()**—Creates a binding of a name and a naming context in the naming context even if the name is already bound in the context. Naming contexts that are bound using **rebind_context()** are considered in name resolution when compound names are passed to be resolved.

- **new_context()**—Creates a new naming context object.

- **bind_new_context()**—Returns a bound naming context object.

- **resolve()**—Retrieves a component bound to a name in a given context.

- **unbind()**—Deletes a particular binding.

- **destroy()**—Deletes a naming context.

Table 12.2 explains the exceptions thrown by the operations of the **NamingContext** interface.

The *BindingIterator* Interface

To use the **resolve()** operation of the **NamingContext**, you should know the name of the desired component in advance. Sometimes, you need to ask for a list of all bindings registered with a particular naming context. Thus, the **NamingContext** interface provides one operation, **list()**, to return a list of bindings. Here is another code segment from the **CosNaming** module:

```
enum BindingType {nobject, ncontext};

struct Binding
{
    Name binding_name;
    BindingType binding_type;
};
```

Table 12.2 Exceptions raised by binding operations.

Exception	Description
NotFound	Indicates that the name does not identify a binding.
CannotProceed	Indicates that the implementation has given up for some reason.
InvalidName	Indicates that the name is invalid (such as null string).
AlreadyBound	Indicates that a component is already bound to the specified name.
NotEmpty	Indicates that the naming context contains bindings.

```
typedef sequence<Binding> BindingList;

interface BindingIterator;

interface NamingContext
{
    void list(in unsigned long how_many, out BindingList bl,
        out BindingIterator bi);
    //...
};

interface BindingIterator
{
    boolean next_one(out Binding b);
    boolean next_n(in unsigned long how_many,
        out BindingList bl);
    void destroy();
};
```

The following describes the operations shown in the preceding code segment:

- **list()**—Allows a client to iterate through a set of bindings in a naming context. The **list()** operation returns the maximum number of **how_many** bindings in **BindingList**. If the naming context contains additional bindings, the **list()** operation returns a **BindingIterator** with the additional bindings. If the naming context doesn't contain additional bindings, the returned **BindingIterator** object reference is **nil**.

- **next_one()**—Returns the next binding. If no more bindings exist, zero is returned.

- **next_n()**—Returns the maximum number of **how_many** bindings.

- **destroy()**—Destroys the iterator.

Writing A Server Using Naming Service

Determining where to apply Naming Service is easy: Naming Service is a service to locate a component, thereby replacing the use of the stringified object reference mechanism. Chapter 9 presents an **Account** example that applied the stringified object reference mechanism. The **Account** IDL is shown in Listing 12.3.

Listing 12.3   The interface for the Account component.

```
module CoBank
{
    struct Person
    {
        string name;
        short age;
    };

    interface Account
    {
        readonly attribute float balance;
        readonly attribute Person holder;

        exception NoMoney
        {
            float balance;
        };

        void deposit(in float amount);
        void withdraw(in float amount) raises (NoMoney);
    };
};
```

To use Naming Service with the **Account** interface, you don't have to change the implementation of **Account**. The only changes required are in the server and client programs. Listing 12.4 presents the modifications needed in the server program to make the server program register an **Account** component with Naming Service. Listing 12.4 assumes that you already have determined the **boa**, **orb**, and Naming Context object (**nc**), as shown in Listing 12.1.

Listing 12.4   Registering an Account component with Naming Service.

```
// Creates Accout implementation
CoBank_Person person;
person.name=(const char*)"vishwa";
person.age=29;

CoBank_Account_var account =
    new CoBank_CoAccountImpl(0,person);

try
{
    // Bind name with Naming Service
    CosNaming_Name aName;
```

```
        aName.length(1);
        aName[0].id = (const char*)"account";
        aName[0].kind = (const char*)"";
        nc -> bind(aName, account);
        // Run implementation
        boa -> impl_is_ready(CORBA_ImplementationDef::_nil());
        // Unregister names with Naming Service
        nc -> unbind(aName);
    }
catch(const CosNaming_NamingContext::NotFound& ex)
{
        cerr << argv[0] << ": Got a `NotFound' exception (";
        switch(ex.why)
        {
            case CosNaming_NamingContext::missing_node:
                cerr << "missing node";
                break;
            case CosNaming_NamingContext::not_context:
                cerr << "not context";
                break;
            case CosNaming_NamingContext::not_object:
                cerr << "not object";
                break;
        }
        cerr << ")" << endl;
        return 1;
}
catch(const CosNaming_NamingContext::CannotProceed&)
{
        cerr << argv[0] <<
        ": Got a `CannotProceed' exception" << endl;
        return 1;
}
catch(const CosNaming_NamingContext::InvalidName&)
{
        cerr << argv[0] <<
        ": Got an `InvalidName' exception" << endl;
        return 1;
}
catch(const CosNaming_NamingContext::AlreadyBound&)
{
        cerr << argv[0] <<
        ": Got an `AlreadyBound' exception" << endl;
        return 1;
}
catch(const CosNaming_NamingContext::NotEmpty&)
```

```
{
    cerr << argv[0] <<
    ": Got a `NotEmpty' exception" << endl;
    return 1;
}
```

The following describes the highlighted segments of the program in Listing 12.4:

1. The **Account** instance **account** is created to bind to Naming Service. The example uses the same implementation that is presented in Listing 9.9 in Chapter 9.

2. A **CosNaming_Name** variable **aName** is instantiated, and **aName**'s **id** is assigned the name **"account"**. The **kind** part is kept empty.

3. The server program binds **account** to a Naming Context by using the **bind()** operation.

4. The server goes to listen mode to obtain requests by calling **impl_is_ready()** on the **boa** variable.

5. Before exiting, the program should unbound all the bindings by using the **unbind()** operation.

6. You might encounter various Naming Service exceptions. For example, if a name already exists while calling **bind()**, an **Already Bound** exception is thrown. The **IllegalName** exception is thrown if an empty string was provided as part of a **NameComponent**.

Writing A Client Using Naming Service

One advantage of using Naming Service is that a client doesn't depend on the location or the implementation of a participating component in a distributed environment. Listing 12.5 presents a client program segment that uses Naming Service to locate the **Account** component that was registered in Listing 12.4. Listing 12.5 assumes that you already have resolved the **boa**, **orb**, and Naming Context object (**nc**), as shown in Listing 12.1.

Listing 12.5   A client program segment using Naming Service to access the Account component.

```
// Get objects by name
try
{
    // Resolve name with Naming Service
```

```
        CosNaming_Name aName;
        aName.length(1);
        aName[0].id = CORBA_string_dup("account");
        aName[0].kind = CORBA_string_dup("");
        CORBA_Object_var aObj = nc -> resolve(aName);
        CoBank_Account_var account =
            CoBank_Account::_narrow(aObj);

        assert(!CORBA_is_nil(account));

        cout << "Resolved account" << endl;
        account->deposit(100);
    }
catch(const CosNaming_NamingContext::NotFound& ex)
    {
        cerr << argv[0] << ": Got a `NotFound' exception (";
        switch(ex.why)
        {
            case CosNaming_NamingContext::missing_node:
                cerr << "missing node";
                break;

            case CosNaming_NamingContext::not_context:
                cerr << "not context";
                break;

            case CosNaming_NamingContext::not_object:
                cerr << "not object";
                break;
        }
        cerr << ")" << endl;
        return 1;
    }
catch(const CosNaming_NamingContext::CannotProceed&)
    {
        cerr << argv[0] <<
        ": Got a `CannotProceed' exception" << endl;
        return 1;
    }
catch(const CosNaming_NamingContext::InvalidName&)
    {
        cerr << argv[0] <<
        ": Got an `InvalidName' exception" << endl;
        return 1;
    }
```

NOTE

***Running The
Programs***

The examples presented
in Listings 12.4 and 12.5
expect a Naming Service
server to be running
already. You should refer
to the ORBacus docu-
mentation to find more
information about how
to configure and run a
Naming Service server.

The client program uses the Naming Context reference (**nc**) to resolve
an **Account** by the name "account". The following describes the highlighted parts of the program in Listing 12.5:

1. The client program fills a **CosNaming_Name** instance **aName**.
   The **id** part is assigned with the value **"account"**. Recall that the
   server program used the same name in Listing 12.4.

2. The program calls **resolve()** on the Naming Context reference **nc**.

3. The program then narrows down the returned reference to the
   Account interface type.

4. The program invokes a **deposit()** operation on the **Account** component.

5. The program handles various exceptions.

Chapter Recap

This chapter presented an overview of CORBA object services (COS)
specified by OMG. COS can be used to implement real-life components that can run in heterogeneous, distributed applications and
collaborate with each other. COS specifications are expected to drive
the software industry toward interoperable, reusable, portable software-
component development.

CORBA services are generic and can be combined to create frameworks. Each of the object services is based on CORBA concepts.
CORBA services promote specification reuse, because some of the services use the interface inheritance concept to extend, evolve, and
customize the functionality of the service being used. Services typically are partitioned into several distinct interfaces that provide different
views for different kinds of clients of the service.

The chapter didn't present how to use and extend all the services for
an application. However, this chapter presented Naming Service concepts, including the following:

♦ A CORBA service can be obtained by using the **resolve_
   initial_references()** operation on the ORB object.

♦ Naming Service provides the capability to register a component and
   locate a component by name.

♦ Naming Service enables you to create name graphs, to create runtime
   relationships among CORBA components.

Chapter 13 presents a discussion on how to enhance the **Account** application by using various object services. Chapter 13 also gives more details about Event Service and Object Property Service in the realm of creating a CORBA-based framework.

Chapter 13

CORBA's Generic Business Object Framework

Key Topics:

- *CORBA design patterns/idioms*

- *CORBA metadata*

- *Event and property services*

- *Introducing business objects*

- *Introducing a CORBA-based metaframework*

An important requirement for distributed applications is simplification. Today, most IT organizations have a difficult time designing and implementing these applications, despite the many reasons for doing so. The Object Request Broker (ORB) provides transparent connectivity and integrated object services that can be used to develop component frameworks. Component frameworks can provide distributed architectures that are efficient and easy to program, because of their inherent reusability and adaptability features. Component frameworks should make development of distributed applications more predictable and feasible. Application design and generation tools that can be integrated with such frameworks will improve the adaptability of these frameworks even further.

As Chapters 8 and 9 explain and demonstrate, CORBA is a mechanism to create, deploy, and deal with object-oriented components in a distributed environment. These chapters introduce you to the fundamental concepts of CORBA and the Object Management Architecture (OMA). OMA is the key to creating distributed components. The CORBA architecture defines an interface definition language (IDL) that enables you to create specifications for a component. You can encapsulate application data along with business logic into a component that can be instantiated and interacted with from anywhere.

You must understand that CORBA only *acts* like a collection of infrastructure frameworks; it doesn't impose any application architecture that is built using CORBA. CORBA provides only low-level request/response communication for making requests to a component and for the component to respond to the application that's making the request. In addition to providing you with the capability to write application components, OMA provides several additional services and facilities to handle a component at runtime, such as locating a component, managing the lifecycle of a component, and so forth. These services are required by every application, regardless of the application's nature. These services are defined in the CORBA IDL. CORBA vendors implement the service with varying degrees of robustness.

Note that OMA and CORBA services and facilities exhibit framework-like behavior, and these services and facilities are critical for creating generic, business object frameworks.

This chapter builds on the content and concepts presented in previous CORBA chapters. However, this chapter gives you a broader information about CORBA and its framework capabilities. This chapter also provides an architecture for a generic, business object metaframework.

CORBA-Based Applications

Whereas CORBA provides a way of thinking about and describing enterprise architectures for application systems, CORBA doesn't actually prescribe a particular architecture or technology.

Although many possible ways exist to design application systems that can be described using CORBA, this chapter lays the foundation for the particular approach that leads to a *business object metaframework (BOM)*. This approach has its basis in an object-oriented partition of application and application system capabilities into a set of software components. Each component embodies a significant portion of an overall application or system of applications. Complete applications and application systems are formed when the relevant components are interconnected so that they can collaborate to provide the desired functionality.

Because the complete application is defined in terms of components, components that implement the functionality represented by each of the application aspects will need to be specified. Although each of these components serves a distinct role, the core concepts that are common to all components must be specified, which is possible using the metaframework. By using the metaframework, you can create a framework that has common specifications, enabling you to provide specification reuse. The component architecture specified in this chapter describes a general way of thinking about distributed components, and it prescribes a particular way to express their specific capabilities.

CORBA-Based Object-Oriented Components

Chapter 8 describes the architecture specified by the Object Management Group (OMG) that is used to define, develop, and deploy flexible distributed systems. OMG makes it possible to encapsulate application data and the business logic within objects that can be instantiated and interacted with from anywhere. These objects are generally referred to as *distributed components*. A component is an object-oriented entity and is central to creating and using CORBA frameworks.

Access to a particular component's application capabilities is mediated by the *object interface* that the component supports. A component interface represents a potential point of integration and interoperation between a component and its client. The component interface "hides" the underlying implementation. Clients can be developed independently of an implementation.

A *component* represents a significant portion of an overall application system, but it's small enough to enable efficient and flexible composition with other components to form full-fledged applications. Components need to be complete and independent.

Components are based on the OMG *object model*, which is similar to a classical object model, in which a client interacts with a component, and the component provides services to the client. The object model describes a component's behavior. The object model also presents the mechanism by which a component's internal data can be represented and its behavior implemented transparent to clients. Two core elements of the OMA object model are the following:

♦ *Object semantics*—Defines, or characterizes, components, enabling you to distinguish one component from other kinds of components. It represents the "outside view" of a component, defining a component as an identifiable, encapsulated entity that provides one or more services that can be requested by a client through its interface. In short, object semantics is used to specify three characteristics about a component—its type, the set of services it supports, and its data representation. Object semantics also specifies a component's lifecycle, which means that a component can be created and destroyed as an outcome of its clients' requests.

♦ *Object implementation*—Represents the "inside view" of a component. Object implementation gives a mechanism to define a component's state and services. When a client issues a request on a component, a method of the target component is called. The execution of a service is called a *method activation*.

Whereas the OMG object model defines common semantics to characterize components, the *reference model* defines the ORB. The ORB enables clients to communicate with a remote component in a distributed environment. In other words, the ORB provides transparency of component location, activation, communication, and implementation. Thus, ORB is the key for building and packaging distributed components and frameworks.

Componentization

Components in a design never occur in isolation. They interact with other components to perform a business logic or process. Interaction among components is referred to as *component collaboration*. Because CORBA provides you the required infrastructure for component collaboration, application designers never have to worry about interoperation between components. Instead, they typically focus on relationships and collaboration among components. The ability of components to interact with each other at the semantic level is the key to a business process.

The principle of divide and conquer can be applied when designing component-based applications, which is similar to applying object-oriented techniques. The primary objective of the CORBA-based application designer is to partition the application into a set of interconnectable, collaborative components, each of which implements important aspects of a complete application. Object-oriented programming (OOP) techniques can help you to partition a complex application system into smaller, simpler components.

Component collaboration can be captured and described by using most of the popular object-oriented analysis and design (OOAD) methodologies—a designer can use Ivar Jacobson's methodology or Fusion's methodology. The following information about components in a system will typically be captured:

♦ *Static component model*—Describes the static information of the component. It is more like an object model used in an OOAD. This model's key concepts are interfaces, attributes, hierarchies, and associations between interfaces.

♦ *Dynamic component model*—Adds operations to the interface, and describes how a component interacts with other components at runtime.

Because CORBA components support late binding and well-defined interfaces, designers can apply both traditional C++ design concepts—such as reusability by inheritance and composition—and design patterns, such as factories. Some of the characteristics of a distributed component include the following:

♦ *Simplification*—Components can make the approach to partitioning a complex application system into smaller, simpler pieces that are apparent and precise.

♦ *Replaceability*—Existing components can be readily replaced with new implementations, as long as the new component supports the same interfaces as the component it replaces.

♦ *Extensibility*—New components with new capabilities can be added to an existing system in a modular manner. In addition, new capabilities that are added to existing components can be represented by new component interfaces, without requiring changes to existing interfaces.

♦ *Independence*—The interfaces between components define the "contract" between components that can enable independent development—as long as the contracts are respected.

♦ *Scalability*—Components can either be physically distributed or co-located, depending upon the computing infrastructure available and the desired performance goal.

The Reusability Of Components

CORBA components are object-oriented entities. CORBA components exhibit many C++ features, including interface inheritance, polymorphism, and reuse. CORBA-based design focuses on interfaces rather than implementation details. This is supported by IDLs. Because an IDL standardizes interfaces, and the component's functionality is encapsulated within component implementations, you get a black-box view of the component. This black-box view means that a developer can combine various application components to form the actual application, without having to deal with the components' internals.

As Chapter 9 describes, you can achieve two levels of reuse in the context of components:

♦ Reuse across projects (white-box reuse)

♦ Specification reuse (black-box reuse)

Reuse Across Projects

Reuse across projects refers to the ability of a developer to leverage CORBA components from one project into the next. This is also referred to as *white-box reuse*, because you are effectively using the code or implementation of a component in another place. This sort of reuse is no different from the C++ way of reusing a class. A component generally is reused and adapted via component derivation. This sort of reuse promotes *code reuse*.

Specification Reuse

An interface can define a contract that is applicable to different types of components, enabling a common semantic behavior to be specified across different components using a single interface definition. Even though the underlying component implementations may be different, they appear to behave in a manner that is consistent with semantics implied by the interface. This is referred to as *interface polymorphism*, and forms an important principle for reusing an interface.

Interface polymorphism enables interfaces to serve as conceptual building blocks that can be reused throughout a system. Although this reuse doesn't necessarily imply that the underlying component implementations of the interfaces are also reused, interface polymorphism does provide a form of reuse. This form of reuse can be thought of as *specification reuse* (also referred to as *IDL reuse*, *interface reuse*, or *black-box reuse*) rather than code reuse. Interface reuse is widely used within the CORBA community. Recall that an interface is the expression for a component's external specification. Because creating a specification is a complicated and iterative process, specification reuse provides a huge advantage to object-oriented practitioners.

Specification reuse is supported by IDL inheritance. Like a C++ class, an interface can be derived from another interface, which is then called a *base interface* of the derived interface. A derived interface, like all interfaces, may declare new elements (constants, types, attributes, exceptions, and operations). The new, or derived, interface is essentially the union of the operations defined for the base interface plus all the operations specifically defined for the new interface. A derived interface can have more than one base interface, which is referred to as *multiple inheritance*. The derived interface can also be substituted anywhere that its base interface is expected. This notion is illustrated by the following banking example.

A banking application may need many types of bank accounts, such as checking accounts and savings accounts, both of which are, in fact, special types of accounts that share the properties of an account and respond to the same operations with different behaviors. The new account types can also have additional properties and operations.

New accounts can be described by interface inheritance. **Checking Account** and **SavingsAccount** can be derived from **Account**. The **Account** interface is called a base interface of **CheckingAccount** and **SavingsAccount**. Interfaces **CheckingAccount** and **SavingsAccount** are referred to as the *derived interfaces* of the **Account** interface. This is shown in Listing 13.1.

Listing 13.1   IDL with inheritance.

```
module CoBank
{
    struct Person
    {
        string name;
        short age;
    };

    interface Account
    {
        readonly attribute float balance;
        readonly attribute Person holder;

        exception NoMoney
        {
            float balance;
        };

        void deposit(in float amount);

        void withdraw(in float amount)
        raises (NoMoney);
    };

    interface CheckingAccount : Account
    {
        readonly attribute float overdraft_limit;
```

NOTE

Reuse By Interface Composition

Inheritance is one way of achieving reuse. Interface composition is another technique that enables you to reuse an interface. This can be achieved by using the *delegation mechanism* in the component implementation that allows a component to have many interfaces, and they can be exposed through some query mechanism, which will be based on some CORBA interface. This concept is implemented later in the chapter, in the section "Overcoming The Complexity Of Distributed Computing."

```
        float transfer_money(in Account acc,
            in float money);
    };

    interface SavingsAccount : Account
    {
    };
};
```

The **CheckingAccount** interface defines one new attribute, **overdraft_limit**, and inherits the attributes **balance** and **holder** defined in its base **Account** interface. Similarly, the **CheckingAccount** interface inherits the **deposit()** and **withdraw()** operations from **Account**, and defines a new operation, **transfer_money()**. Similarly, the **SavingsAccount** interface inherits **balance**, **holder**, **deposit()**, and **withdraw()** members from **Account**, but defines no additional operations. However, the implementation for **SavingsAccount** can provide new definitions for the **deposit()** and **withdraw()** operations.

Specification reuse is an important feature of OMG IDL interfaces, because it enables existing interfaces to be reused when defining new services. For example, a **CheckingAccount** component can be used anywhere that an **Account** component is expected, because a **CheckingAccount** component supports all **Account** operations. The new capabilities of the **CheckingAccount** component, therefore, can be added to the system without requiring changes to the existing applications that use the **Account** interface. This supports the polymorphic nature of interfaces, and plays an important role in developing object-oriented applications by using CORBA.

Foundation For CORBA Frameworks

Now that you have learned about CORBA components, componentization, and reuse mechanisms, you are prepared to read more about CORBA features in the realm of frameworks.

Imagine the CORBA-based component architecture as a three-dimensional space. One dimension represents the design patterns/idioms, the second dimension represents the metadata, and the third dimension represents the services and facilities. This three-dimensional space can be referred to as the *foundation for generic BOM*, because it enables you to develop component frameworks using CORBA. This chapter provides interesting information about these dimensions of CORBA, some of which have been covered briefly in previous chapters. This chapter adds another way to conceptualize these ideas.

After covering the foundation and related concepts for BOM, this chapter proposes a small implementation of BOM.

First Dimension: CORBA Design Patterns And Idioms

Abstracting a new solution out of a collection of existing solutions leads to *software patterns*. As Chapter 5 points out, the following are the three types of patterns:

◆ *Architectural patterns (systems designs)*—Express a fundamental paradigm for structuring software, by providing a set of predefined subsystems as well as rules and guidelines for organizing the relationships between the subsystems. CORBA is based on the Broker architectural pattern (described in the upcoming section "Networking Patterns: Broker, Proxy, And Forwarder-Receiver Patterns").

◆ *Design patterns*—An abstraction from a general design problem that keeps recurring in specific, nonarbitrary contexts. Design patterns describe the smaller software architectural units of which a software architecture consists.

◆ *Programming idioms (language-specific techniques/style)*—The lowest granularity level, idioms deal with realization and implementation of particular design issues.

Clear evidence of patterns exists in all levels of CORBA, from high-level CORBA architectures down to detailed designs. Table 13.1 presents a common set of design patterns and idioms that you can discover in the CORBA architecture and while using CORBA. The design patterns described in Table 13.1 are presented in more depth in the sections that follow.

Table 13.1   A subset of CORBA design patterns and idioms.

Design Pattern	Description
Proxy	Provides a placeholder for a component to provide access control to it.
Externalization Service	Defines protocols for externalizing and internalizing component data.
Factory	Provides an interface to create various types of components. Components can be packaged (by factory) in a variety of ways, which provides great flexibility for deployment.
Forwarder-receiver	Hides the communication protocol from sender and receiver components.
Publisher-subscriber	Provides a mechanism to ensure an interested component (subscriber) has a consistent view of state of another component (publisher).
Reference counting	Keeps track of the number of connections to a particular remote component.

Stubs And Skeletons

When an IDL is compiled, IDL language compilers generate client-side *stubs* and server-side *skeletons*. A stub is used to create and issue requests on behalf of a client; IDL stubs are linked directly into the client application.

A server skeleton is an IDL-generated code that allows a component implementation to receive requests from a client. A skeleton represents the same set of operations that its IDL contains. You adapt a skeleton to implement a server component. Skeletons are compiled and linked with component code.

Networking Patterns: Broker, Proxy, And Forwarder-Receiver

CORBA is based on the Broker architectural pattern. *Broker* describes distributed software systems with decoupled components that interact using remote service invocations. The Broker builds an architecture for distributed components rather than monolithic systems. It makes the architecture flexible and scalable. Of course, when the Broker pattern is applied, many issues arise, such as component activation, location, security, and so forth. These issues are handled by the services that CORBA provides.

Though the Broker represents a conceptual view of CORBA, you, as a developer, still need a mechanism to access components across the network. Because a remote component can't be directly accessed, CORBA uses the Proxy design pattern for the client/server communication to occur in an easy way, from a developer's point of view.

As noted in the preceding table, the Proxy design pattern provides a placeholder for a component to enable a client to access a component's services. The Proxy design pattern helps the client of a component to access services using a *delegate* rather than using the component directly. The Proxy design pattern is inherent in CORBA itself. A delegate provides many advantages, such as easier access, efficiency, and distribution. Such a delegate is represented by the IDL-generated stubs, which guard a client against an implementation of their servers. They also hide ORB from a developer. Recall that the ORB forwards requests to servers.

The notion of ORB itself is based on the *Forwarder-Receiver* design pattern, which enables it to actually hide the communication protocol from sender and receiver components. In other words, by using this design pattern, a client and server component can communicate with each other transparently. The Forwarder-Receiver design pattern is used to decouple the client and server from the underlying networking mechanism. The client-side ORB and server-side ORB are clearly implementations of this design pattern in CORBA.

Broker, Proxy, Forwarder-Receiver, and Publisher-Subscriber patterns are proposed in the book *Pattern-Oriented Software Architecture: A System of Patterns*, by Frank Buschmann and coauthors (John Wiley and Sons, 1996).

Externalization Service: A Design Pattern

The Externalization Service is a design pattern that OMG has described as a CORBA service. Externalization Service is very much like the *Memento* design pattern proposed in the book *Design Patterns: Elements of Reusable Object-Oriented Software,* by Eric Gamma and his coauthors (Addison-Wesley, 1995).

Externalization Service defines protocols for externalizing and internalizing component data. The service enables a component to externalize its state in a stream of data (in memory, on a disk or file, across the network) and then internalize it into a new instance of the component in the same or a different server process. Thus, externalization/internalization is a two-step process: First, you copy the component to a *stream*. Then, you use the stream to copy the component to a different location. In this way, a stream acts like a transport mechanism for components, enabling you to pass components by using the pass-by-value mechanism. Currently, CORBA implementations support only the pass-by-reference mechanism for components (object references).

The Publisher-Subscriber Design Pattern

The Publisher-Subscriber design pattern is a mechanism to ensure that an interested component (subscriber) has a consistent view of the state of another component (publisher). Publisher-Subscriber enables a publisher to notify any number of subscribers about the changes in the publisher's state. Here is an IDL specification for this pattern:

```
interface CoSubscriber
{
    void notify();
};


exception NotSubscribed{};

interface CoPublisher
{
    void subscribe(in string name,
        in CoSubscriber subscriber);

    void unsubscribe(in string name)
    raises (NotSubscribed);
};
```

A possible implementation of the **CoPublisher** interface would be to keep a registry (such as the Standard Template Library's **map**) of **CoSubscriber**s. Whenever a **CoSubscriber** needs to become a subscriber, the **CoSubscriber** uses the **subscribe()** operation of the **CoPublisher** interface. Similarly, a **CoSubscriber** can call the **unsubscribe()** operation of the **CoPublisher** interface to unsubscribe itself.

NOTE

Decoupled Publishers And Subscribers

In the Publisher-Subscriber pattern, subscribers and publishers are coupled (that is, they know about each other). CORBA also enables you to make a decoupled communication, which is achieved via the Event Services, described later in this chapter's "Event Service" section.

After you understand the preceding description of the Publisher-Subscriber pattern, consider the following advantages of using it:

♦ You can take advantage of interface polymorphism to introduce a hierarchy of subscribers without losing any functionality offered by the design pattern. If you need to make an interface subscriber, derive that interface from the **CoSubscriber** interface.

♦ The publisher has flexibility when it wants to notify its subscribers.

♦ A publisher can have many subscribers. Similarly, a subscriber can subscribe to many publishers.

♦ The pattern can be extended to send some data along, instead of just sending a notification message. If the **notify()** operation can be modified to take **CoMetadata::SeqNVPair** as an **in** parameter, the publisher has flexibility regarding what it wants to notify its subscribers about. (The **CoMetadata::SeqNVPair** type is described later in this chapter's "Name-Value Pairs Using IDL **union**" section.)

The Reference Count Idiom

Idioms are the lowest level of software patterns. They describe how to implement particular components, their functionality or relationships to other components in a given design. An example of a C++ specific idiom is the Reference Counting idiom, which describes how to implement reference counting in C++ to handle deallocation of multiple referenced objects. (Reference counting is implemented in Chapter 5.) The notion of reference counting can be important in distributed computing.

The key concept in *distributed reference counting* is the need for a mechanism that keeps track of the number of connections to a particular distributed component. A *reference count* is an integer value associated with a distributed component. The reference count is incremented when a new reference to the component is created. Similarly, the reference count is decremented when a reference to the component is destroyed. The reference count indicates the number of connections to a component. Thus, reference counting can be used as a way to manage components and proxies. In addition, this mechanism provides the following advantages in distributed computing environments:

♦ *Component usage*—An online service increments a counter every time a client connects to a component. This information is associated with the component, but the information isn't part of the component's interface. You can use a reference count to keep track of the number of clients that are currently using the component.

This helps identify the usage patterns for a particular component. (You can also get the total number of operation invocations performed on the component, but you have to implement that yourself, using an operation count.)

♦ *Load balancing*—In some cases, a client might ask a server to give access to an object reference via an operation call to another component (such as a factory). The factory may have a pool of object references that it can iterate to determine which one has the lowest reference counting, and then return that object reference to the client. Thus, reference counting can be used as a simple mechanism to achieve load balancing.

♦ *Clean-up*—By using a reference count mechanism, your application can determine that a particular component is not currently being accessed by a client. In such a case, you might deallocate the component from the memory, thereby claiming back the resources that the component was utilizing. This is especially important if your application is component-intensive; that is, the application uses many low-granularity components to perform a particular set of computations.

In an ORBacus implementation, the initial reference count of an object (implementation or proxy) reference is one. If the reference count of an object reaches zero, the object is destroyed. A summary of the reference-counting-related operations used by ORBacus is provided in Table 13.2.

CORBA reference-counting mechanisms aren't typically distributed. (Microsoft's *Distributed Component Object Model* or *DCOM* is built around a distributed reference-counting architecture.) In other words, the reference count of a proxy in a client is separate from the reference

Table 13.2 Reference counting semantics.

Operation	Reference count
new interface_impl	Reference count of new implementation is initialized to 1.
ORB::string_to_object()	Reference count of proxy is initialized to 1.
_duplicate(obj)	Reference count of implementation or proxy is incremented by 1.
CORBA_release(obj)	Reference count of implementation or proxy is decremented by 1.
ORB::connect(obj)	Reference count of implementation is incremented by 1.
ORB::disconnect(obj)	Reference count of implementation is decremented by 1.

count of its corresponding implementation instance in a server. This means that if the reference count of a proxy becomes zero, the proxy is destroyed, but the component instance remains unaffected. Analogously, the reference count of any proxy remains unaffected even when its corresponding component instance's reference count becomes zero (and is subsequently destroyed). The CORBA specification doesn't support distributed references for several specific reasons, including:

◆ *Performance problems*—If a client terminates abnormally without properly releasing references, the corresponding server component becomes *stray*, because it has no understanding of the client-crash phenomenon. One way to work around this problem is to have the component sporadically *ping* its clients to determine if they are alive. If the component gets a CORBA-generated system exception, the component may ask the ORB to release itself. As you can see, this ping mechanism results in extra remote calls, thereby causing performance problems.

◆ *Problems with persistent object references*—In CORBA, you can stringify object references to make them persistent. Later, you can destringify the string to get back the object reference (without losing its remote context). Because a stringified object reference can be considered valid even if its connection terminates, supporting both persistent object references and reference counting would be very difficult.

◆ *Error prone*—Distributed reference counting is not automatic and it depends on you to keep the reference count properly updated (by incrementing/decrementing the reference count). If you do not do this correctly, orphaned components (without users) or unwanted deletions of components might occur.

Releasing Proxies And Component Instances

You must remember two rules regarding the release of object references:

◆ Never use **delete** to destroy proxies or component instances. Use only **CORBA_release**.

◆ Never create an automatic instance (nonheap) of a component.

For example, the following code calling **delete** on a proxy obtained with **string_to_object()** is wrong:

```
// Obtain a stringified reference somehow
const char* s = ...;
```

```
//reference count is 1
CORBA_Object_ptr p = orb -> string_to_object(s);

//wrong: reference count is 1
delete p; // Wrong!
```

Instead of **delete**, you must use **CORBA_release()**:

```
// Obtain a stringified reference somehow
const char* s = ...;
CORBA_Object_ptr p = orb -> string_to_object(s);
CORBA_release(p); //okay
```

The following code demonstrates the problem associated with the component instance created on the stack:

```
void foo()
{
    COInterfaceImpl impl; // Wrong!
}
```

The preceding code is wrong because, upon return from **foo()**, the **impl** object is destroyed without calling the **CORBA_release()** function.

You should use the CORBA smart pointers (**_var**) whenever possible:

```
// Obtain a stringified reference somehow
const char* s = ...;
CORBA_Object_var p = orb -> string_to_object(s); //okay
```

In the preceding code segment, no **CORBA_release()** is necessary, because the **_var** will automatically call **CORBA_release()** upon destruction.

The Factory Design Pattern

Sometimes, a client needs to ask for components of types that aren't known at compile time. The Factory design pattern provides an interface for creating components of various types at runtime. It abstracts the creation of components. A factory component provides access to one or more additional components.

In CORBA applications, a client generally uses a factory reference to gain access to the application components. The application publishes the factory in a well-known location (such as the naming server). Then,

Defining Global _var Instances

You must not declare global **_var** type object references. Apart from being a bad programming style, this rule has a technical justification. When you declare a global **_var** type reference, the **_var** reference could be destroyed after the ORB is destroyed. Here's an example.

```
COInterface_var impl; //global instance
int main(int argc, char* argv[], char*[])
{
    CORBA_ORB_var orb = CORBA_ORB_init(argc, argv);
    impl = new COInterfaceImpl;
    return 0;
}
```

After **main()** returns, the **orb** variable is destroyed. However, the component instance isn't destroyed, because the global **impl** variable is still alive, which means that a component instance still exists without ORB being there. This scenario generally results in a crash at the time of program shutdown.

Remember that ORB must be the last object to be destroyed.

---

the client can obtain the published factory object reference from the naming server to gain access to other components on the server. This mechanism is a key element in minimizing the number of object references that need to be published on a naming server. For these reasons, a factory can be an important architectural criterion for the application design as well as for a framework design.

The Factory Interface

Listing 13.2 gives a partial listing of an OMG-specified Lifecycle Services specification. It defines a **GenericFactory** interface from which you can inherit your factory.

Listing 13.2   Specification for GenericFactory.

```
#include <naming/Naming.idl>

module CosLifeCycle
{
    typedef CosNaming::Name Key;
    typedef Object Factory;
    typedef sequence <Factory> Factories;
    typedef struct NVP
    {
        CosNaming::Istring name;
        any value;
    } NameValuePair;
```

```
    typedef sequence <NameValuePair> Criteria;

    exception NoFactory
    {
        Key search_key;
    };

    exception InvalidCriteria
    {
        Criteria invalid_criteria;
    };

    exception CannotMeetCriteria
    {
        Criteria unmet_criteria;
    };

    interface FactoryFinder
    {
        Factories find_factories(in Key factory_key)
        raises(NoFactory);
    };

    interface GenericFactory
    {
        boolean supports(in Key k);

        Object create_object(in Key k,
            in Criteria the_criteria)
        raises( NoFactory, InvalidCriteria,
            CannotMeetCriteria);
    };

    interface SimpleFactory
    {
        Object create_object();
    };
    //...
};
```

Listing 13.2 demonstrates the two types of factories:

◆ *Simple factory*—A COBRA component (factory) that is capable of returning object references for a specific type. You can derive from **SimpleFactory** and implement **create_object()** to return specific types of component references.

NOTE

Naming Service Is A Generic Factory

As Chapter 12 describes, you can register your application component with the Naming Service, which can be used later by a client to obtain the references. In this way, Naming Service behaves like a generic factory, because Naming Service also acts on the key (name) passed to the **resolve()** operation.

♦ *Generic factory*—A CORBA component that is capable of returning object references based on the key and criteria passed to the **create_object()** operation. A generic factory component enables the use of polymorphism by returning object references to different implementations, depending on the input values specified by a client.

As Listing 13.2 shows, the Lifecycle Service also defines a factory for factories, **FactoryFinder**, which is simply a CORBA factory that has a **find_factories()** operation that returns a sequence of object references to other factories, based on the key passed.

Factory Example

The **SimpleFactory** interface in Listing 13.2 is only a suggestive specification; to create a factory, you don't have to derive from the **SimpleFactory** interface. It is generally a good idea to create your own factory specification because it provides you flexibility in creating the components. Here is an example of creating a factory:

```
interface CoAccount
{
    void destroy();
};


interface CoAccountFactory
{
    CoAccount create_account();
};
```

For the **CoAccount** interface, **CoAccountFactory** is defined. The **CoAccount::destroy()** operation allows a client to destroy the **CoAccount** component when the component is no longer needed.

Factory Implementation

The **CoAccount** interface is implemented as follows:

```
class CoAccount_impl : public virtual CoAccount_skel
{
    CORBA_ORB_var orb_;

public:

    void CoAccount_impl(CORBA_ORB_ptr orb)
        : orb_(CORBA_ORB::_duplicate(orb))
    {
```

```
    }

    virtual void destroy()
    {
        orb_ -> disconnect(this);
    }
};
```

The following points are worth noting in the preceding code:

♦ The **CoAccount_impl** class is defined as an implementation of the **CoAccount** interface.

♦ The constructor of the **CoAccount_impl** class takes an ORB parameter and duplicates the parameter.

♦ The **destroy()** operation disconnects the implementation from the object adapter via the **disconnect()** operation call. Consequently, the object adapter no longer holds a reference to the component instance. If no other references to this component instance exist in the server, then the instance is destroyed.

The following is an implementation of the factory:

```
class CoAccountFactory_impl :
    public virtual CoAccountFactory_skel
{
    CORBA_ORB_var orb_;

public:
    void CoAccountFactory_impl(CORBA_ORB_ptr orb)
        : orb_(CORBA_ORB::_duplicate(orb))
    {
    }

    virtual CoAccount_ptr create_account()
    {
        CoAccount_ptr result = new CoAccount_impl(orb_);
        orb_ -> connect(result);
        return result;
    }
};
```

The **CoAccountFactory_impl** class implements the **CoAccountFactory** interface. Every time that the **create_account()** operation is called, it instantiates a new **CoAccount** instance, connects the instance to the object adapter, and returns an object reference to the client.

Memory Leaks In Factories

In the preceding examples, the factory implementation doesn't store any references to the **CoAccount** instances that it creates (because the **create_account()** operation creates the instance and returns it to the client). Therefore, the client is responsible for ensuring that it destroys a **CoAccount** component, by calling **destroy()** when the component is no longer needed. This poses a possibility of memory leaks in the server, because a client might forget to call the **destroy()** operation on the **CoAccount** reference. This can also happen due to a client program crashing before it can invoke the **destroy()** operation. Two possible schemes for handling this issue include:

♦ *Time-out*—Releases an instance when it has not been used for some configurable length of time.

♦ *Expiration*—Invalidates a reference after a certain length of time. After the reference has expired, the client must obtain a new reference.

The implementation of these solutions is beyond the scope of this chapter.

Packaging Components Using Factories

CORBA provides the required infrastructure for component inter-operation; and, as an application designer, you typically focus on component relationships and their collaboration. This is the core of an application design—actually combining components to form a desired application. *Component packaging*, on the other hand, is the process of creating a platform from which components can collaborate with other components, per the application's design. Component packaging is provided by component factories. Because components can exist independently, they provide great flexibility in packaging. However, factory design affects the flexibility and configurability of component packaging.

A few issues and policies about factory design and component packaging are discussed in Chapter 9. For the present discussion, a recap of some of those issues and policies, along with some new issues, is presented here:

♦ *Recycling components*—Factories can either return new instances of components when they are demanded, or recycle those components that no longer are used by the application.

♦ *Load balancing*—The factory component can manage a pool of components and give the client access to them based on some load-balancing logic.

♦ *High availability using factories*—A factory can be implemented in the same process as the component that is created or managed by the factory. This is called an *in-process factory*. A factory can also be implemented in a process that is different from the implementation process of the component that is created or managed by the factory.

This is referred to as an *out-process factory* (the **FactoryFinder** interface can be used to create such factories). If an in-process factory crashes, it causes all the running component instances to crash. If high availability is an application design criterion, you may want to package components in an out-process factory. Factories can support a configurable number of maximum instances of a component in a process.

♦ *Security*—A factory design may require a client to provide security information before the factory component will allow the client to have access to another component.

♦ *Internationalization (I18N)*—Component packaging for different languages affects how a factory can be configured. Generally, you should configure a factory to run in a particular locale, so that all packaged components also share the same locale. Components requiring a different locale must run in a different process; otherwise, this may affect the functionality as well as the performance of the application.

♦ *Performance*—Performance may be a critical parameter when deciding whether to package a particular component in a particular factory. If the application consists of many vertical slices of interacting components, packaging each of these slices in a single factory may be helpful. In other words, the components that interact frequently with each other may be packaged in the same factories. The functionality of a component may generally give a good indication of how it should be packaged. Components that need to check authentication may be packaged in factories that run closer to firewalls and authentication agents. Similarly, components that provide persistence may be packaged in factories running closer to databases.

A factory itself may introduce performance problems by being a bottleneck. If you expect a factory to receive frequent calls to process a component, you need to scale the factory and make it multithreaded.

The preceding list of issues indicates that a good factory design is important for good component packaging. In fact, because a factory addresses a few architectural issues, such as performance, security, and so forth, a factory can be an important architectural element for any generic component framework.

Second Dimension: CORBA Metadata

Metadata is self-describing data. A component's metadata provides for introspection, which includes a description of its interfaces, attributes, and operations. Metadata adds genericity to components. This is why, metadata is considered as the second dimension of the foundation for CORBA frameworks. The following three topics cover metadata:

♦ *IDL* **unions** *and the* **any** *data type*—Useful to create metadata data types in framework development. They can be used as IDL operations' generic parameters to carry application-specific data. Understand that metadata is generic, but at runtime, it is interpreted in an application-specific way.

♦ *Interface repository (IR)*—Discovers existing CORBA interfaces in a system and presents the information to the user. The IR can play a very important role for some tools, such as object browsers and case tools.

♦ *Dynamic invocation interface (DII)*—Allows dynamic creation and invocation of requests to remote components. A client application using the DII mechanism can be compiled with no client stubs at all, thus having no prior knowledge of the target component. Note that the component receiving requests via DII provides the same semantics as the component receiving the operation invocation through the stubs generated from the IDL definition.

Metadata is typically used at runtime (when the components are actually executing in a running system) as generic message data that is exchanged between components in an application-specific manner. This message data can be interpreted by the application that implements the components, thereby enabling the application to treat an otherwise generic interaction as an application-specific dialogue.

Name-Value Pairs Using IDL *union*

An IDL **union** can have a value whose type is not fixed at compile time. By using an IDL **union**, you can create types that can be queried at runtime about their type, or whose type and value can be set at runtime. This is one way of implementing metadata in CORBA. IDL **union**s are convenient for defining interface operations that don't require a fixed set of input values and/or don't provide a fixed set of output values. The actual set of inputs and outputs that is used can be determined at runtime based upon application-processing logic. Listing 13.3 gives an example of implementing metadata by using an IDL **union**.

Listing 13.3   Implementing metadata by using an IDL union.

```
module CoMetadata
{
```

```
enum EBasicType
{
    CO_UNKNOWN, CO_BOOLEAN, CO_CHAR,
    CO_OCTET, CO_SHORT, CO_USHORT,
    CO_LONG, CO_ULONG, CO_FLOAT, CO_DOUBLE,
    CO_STRING, CO_ANY, CO_OBJECT
};


union BasicType switch (EBasicType)
{
    case CO_UNKNOWN: boolean unknown_value;
    case CO_BOOLEAN: boolean boolean_value;
    case CO_CHAR: char char_value;
    case CO_OCTET: octet octet_value;
    case CO_SHORT: short short_value;
    case CO_USHORT: unsigned short ushort_value;
    case CO_LONG: long long_value;
    case CO_ULONG: unsigned long ulong_value;
    case CO_FLOAT: float float_value;
    case CO_DOUBLE: double double_value;
    case CO_STRING: string string_value;
    case CO_ANY: any any_value;
    case CO_OBJECT: Object object_value;
};

struct NVPair
{
    string item_name;
    BasicType value;
};

typedef sequence<NVPair> SeqNVPair;
};
```

The **CoMetadata** module declares a **union** (**BasicType**) that can assume any basic IDL type, including an **any** or an **Object**. This means that the **BasicType** type can represent any value at runtime. Another type, **NVPair**, defines a **struct** that contains an instance **value** of the **BasicType** type and name, **item_name**, of type **string**. At runtime, you can query the **NVPair** to find out its name and type/value by using the **union** instance. As Chapter 9 points out, in the generated C++ code, the **union** has the following characteristics:

♦ It maps to a **class**.

♦ Its members are mapped to accessor and mutator functions (such as **long_value()**).

◆ It has two special overloaded **_d()** member functions that set and return the current value of the discriminator (**EBasicType**).

The **SeqNVPair** type in the **CoMetadata** module can be used to define generic interfaces that don't require a fixed set of input/output values, because the **SeqNVPair** type is capable of representing a variable number of arguments of different types. This is shown later, in this chapter's "From Metaframework To A More Specific Framework" section.

Any And TypeCode

An **any** is a generic data type that can contain any other data type. The type information for the enclosed data type is maintained within the **any** data type; however, to use an **any** as an input or output parameter value, knowledge of the enclosed type isn't required. Knowledge of the enclosed type is only required to obtain the value enclosed in the **any** data type.

You can use type **any** to pass a value of an arbitrary type as a parameter to an operation or to a return value from an operation. Consider the following interface:

```
module CoAnyExample
{
    struct Person
    {
        string name;
        short age;
    };

    interface Test
    {
        void op(in any a);
    };
};
```

The **Test** interface (of the **CoAnyExample** module) has an **op()** operation that accepts a parameter of type **any**. This means that, in a client program, you can construct an **any** containing any type of value that can be specified in IDL, and then pass this **any** in a call to the **op()** operation. The implementation of the **op()** operation must resolve the type of value that the argument **any** contains and then extract the value. (Chapter 10 introduces the various ways of constructing and interpreting an **any**.)

While **any**s are extremely important for specifying interface operations that can accommodate variant data types, the appearance of the type **any** in an interface operation signature conveys no semantic information about the data types that are expected to be enclosed in the **any**. Consequently, you can use a declaration approach to the usage of the **any** data type. This approach declaratively conveys information about the types that are expected to be enclosed in a particular situation in which an **any** is used; for example:

```
struct id
{
    any id_;
};


struct event_data
{
    any event_data_;
};
```

The approach that is shown in the preceding code segment uses **any**, but the approach attaches some semantic meaning with the data by giving meaningful names to the **struct**s.

By using **any**, you can also represent metadata similar to what was shown previously in Listing 13.3:

```
struct NVPair
{
    string name;
    any value;
};


typedef sequence <NameValuePair> SeqNameValuePair;
```

The **SeqNameValuePair** type can denote a variable number of values of varying types.

Recall that the IDL **any** type is represented by the **CORBA_Any** class. This class contains an instance of type **CORBA_TypeCode** that does the job of describing arbitrary, complex IDL types at runtime. Thus, you can use the **CORBA_TypeCode** class while interrogating the type of an instance of **CORBA_Any**. As Chapter 10 describes, the **CORBA_Any** class has a public member function, **type()**, which returns a value of type **CORBA_TypeCode_ptr**.

Interface Repository And Dynamic Invocation Interface

The IR provides distributed access to a collection of objects by using a component's IDL interface. Clients can use the information found in the IR to determine at runtime the component's type and all information about that type. In other words, you can use the IR to determine the runtime type identification (RTTI) of a component. The IR maintains interface definitions as a set of objects that is accessible through a set of IDL-specified interface definitions. The IR stores information by using **TypeCode**s about types that aren't interfaces. Obviously, **TypeCode** is the key to determining the complete structure of a given type.

Essentially, the IR is used to get RTTI information about components so that requests can be issued using the Dynamic Invocation Interface (DII). As discussed earlier, a DII allows dynamic creation and invocation of requests to remote components. A client application using the DII mechanism can be compiled with no client stubs at all, thus having no prior knowledge of the target component. The component receiving requests via DII provides the same semantics as the component receiving the operation invocation through the stubs generated from the IDL definition. In other words, the DII mechanism is used only for clients—a server implementation has no knowledge of whether an operation was invoked as a result of DII calls or stub calls.

Example Scenarios Of Using The DII

The following are two example scenarios in which the DII mechanism can be used:

♦ *Generic object browser using DII*—You can use the DII mechanism to develop an object browsing tool. The tool can discover components that implement specific interfaces, and then give a client access to these components. For example, you can look for all components that implement the **report( )** operation. This scheme is advantageous if a particular design requires certain components to implement certain interfaces.

♦ *Component testing using DII*—Similar to the object browser tool, you can use the DII mechanism to develop an automated test application that discovers components and their interfaces and invokes each operation to the interface by using test data. The test program can store the results, which you can later analyze to determine whether the components' implementation behaved as per the requirements. One advantage of using DII is that the test program doesn't have to be recompiled, because the DII mechanism can discover interfaces dynamically.

Third Dimension: CORBA Service And Facilities

The ORB enables you to write *application interfaces* to represent those components that implement specific tasks for an application. Three points must be noted:

♦ One component may support many interfaces.

♦ One application is typically composed of many components.

♦ New application components can be built by modifying existing components.

Recall that the ORB allows components to communicate with each other. Because everything runs and depends on the ORB, it is key to creating distributed applications. Nevertheless, the ORB alone isn't enough to create distributed applications. To write applications, you typically need services to locate components and manage their lifecycles. You may need system-management services to observe the health of the system and you may need domain-specific interfaces and frameworks to help you do rapid development. Thus, OMA provides additional capabilities in the form of services and facilities that provide both horizontal and vertical capabilities. Generally, the horizontal services are useful to all industries, whereas vertical services are designed to meet the needs of specific industries. (Chapter 12 presents a detailed description of these services.)

You can create component frameworks by combining interfaces for applications, common facilities, and object services. Services can be combined to produce new, powerful services and frameworks. For example, Event Service and Relationship Service can be combined to create workflow frameworks; using CORBA services, such as Transaction Service, you can implement components that act like real-world components.

CORBA Services

CORBA defines 15 different services that augment the basic CORBA architecture. These are horizontal application services, which can be used with different types of applications. Application functionality can be greatly enhanced by leveraging available services. The CORBA services represent a set of preimplemented distributed components that software developers typically need. Chapter 12 provides detailed descriptions of each of the CORBA services. Therefore, this chapter doesn't cover them. However, the following two services are covered

in this chapter because they could be useful in creating the component frameworks:

♦ *Object Property Service (OPS)*—Provides a mechanism to associate
properties (named values) dynamically with components. This service defines operations to create and manipulate sets of name-value
pairs. OPS defines operations to create, delete, and manipulate properties. The names (of named values) are simple IDL strings. The
values are IDL **anys**.

♦ *Event Service*—Supports asynchronous event notifications and event
delivery. Event Service allows components to register dynamically
their interest in an event. The design of this service is scalable and
is suitable for distributed environments.

This chapter also presents a discussion of how to enhance the **Account**
application by using various object services. Refer to the "Adapting
Services For The Banking Application By Using Services And BOM"
section later in the chapter.

Common Facilities

CORBA common facilities cover both horizontal facilities (features
useful to all types of CORBA applications across various industries)
and vertical facilities (functionality that is especially useful to applications within particular vertical markets and industries). *Horizontal
facilities* include user interface and system management facilities, because this functionality is useful to most types of applications, regardless
of the industry in which they are used. *Vertical facilities* might include a
general ledger for use within the accounting industry or automated
shop-floor control facilities for use in the manufacturing industry. Like
CORBA services, OMG specifies only the interfaces for these facilities; the implementations are provided by CORBA vendors, or by the
developers.

The horizontal CORBA facilities are categorized into four types of facilities: user interface, information management, systems management,
and task management. Each facility has a number of basic areas, and
each of these basic areas has a number of subareas that perform specific
services.

The first type of horizontal facility, *user interface*, covers all that relates
to user interfaces, from the tools used to develop them, to the way they
are presented to the user. User interface consists of *user interface styles*,
for the "look and feel" presented to the user by the application, and
user interface enablers, to present the user interface to the user. Enablers
are grouped into five facilities, as shown in Table 13.3.

Table 13.3 User interface enablers.

Enabler	Responsibility
Rendering management	Abstracts user interface components.
Compound presentation	Displays compound documents.
User support	Provides spellchecking, online help, and so on.
Work management system	Maintains a user's work environment and consists of the user's desktop, single logon to the system, and information used by the user.
Task and process automation	Enables users to write scripts to automate their tasks, and use workflows.

The second type of horizontal facility, *information management*, consists of seven concepts, as shown in Table 13.4.

The third type of horizontal facility, *systems management*, provides interfaces for system administration. Systems management consists of ten interfaces, as shown in Table 13.5.

Table 13.4 Concepts of information management.

Concept	Responsibility
Information modeling	Deals essentially with the structure of data.
Information storage retrieval	Includes storage/retrieval for databases, and information retrieval systems, and repositories.
Information interchange	Enables the exchange of data between users and between applications.
Data interchange	Enables the general exchange of data.
Compound interchange	Enables the exchange of data in compound documents.
Data encoding and representation	Enables encodings and translations of data format.
Time operations	Enable manipulations of calendar and time data.

Table 13.5 Interfaces of systems management.

Interface	Responsibility
Instrumentation	Provides the capability to collect data regarding system load, throughput, consumption of resources, and so on.
Data collection	Provides capabilities to log events, and so forth.

(continued)

Table 13.5   Interfaces of systems management *(continued).*

Interface	Responsibility
Security	Provides capabilities for the management of the security system itself (this isn't the same as Security Service).
Quality of service management	Enables you to select the level of service for availability, performance, reliability, and recovery.
Event management	Provides capabilities to register, generate, filter, and forward events in the system (uses Event Service).
Collection management	Enables administrators to deal with collec tions of components to be managed.
Instance management	Provides capabilities to associate components with other components for management purposes.
Scheduling management	Enables you to schedule tasks in a controlled manner (for example, to occur at a certain time or as a response to a particular event).
Policy management	Controls the creation, deletion, and modifica tion of manageable components.
Customization	Enables components to be extended dynamically while retaining type safety.

The fourth type of horizontal facility, *task management*, supports the processing of user tasks. Task management consists of the concepts listed and described in Table 13.6.

Because most applications require facilities such as user interfaces, information storage and retrieval, security, workflow and process management, and so on, the horizontal facilities are generic and thus can be applied in all types of applications, regardless of the industry.

Table 13.6   Concepts of task management.

Concept	Responsibility
Workflow	Enables components to be part of a work process; for example, a purchase process.
Agent	Consists of information objects and associ ated scripts to deal with the information.
Rule Management	Provides capabilities to specify and process rules.
Automation	Enables one component to access key functionality of another component.

Providing details about all of these facilities is beyond the scope of this book (however, you can find more information about these facilities at **www.omg.org/library/cfindx.html**).

In addition to providing horizontal services and facilities, OMG provides specifications for many vertical CORBA facilities. A few vertical-facility examples are listed in Table 13.7.

Object Property Service (OPS)

Recall that a CORBA component supports at least one interface consisting of a fixed set of operations and attributes. However, occasionally, you may need to associate dynamic (runtime) attributes with a component. You can achieve this by using the specifications provided by OPS. OPS provides a mechanism to annotate a component with extra attributes that weren't defined by the component's interface. These attributes are referred to as *properties*. Properties use the **any** data type and can represent any IDL type. In short, OPS does the following:

♦ Provides the ability to dynamically associate named values with components outside the static IDL-type system.

♦ Defines operations to create and manipulate sets of name-value pairs or name-value-mode tuples.

The *CosPropertyService* Module

The **CosPropertyService** module defines an OPS that consists of six interfaces, which are shown in Table 13.8.

Table 13.7   Summary of domain specifications.

Industry	Description
Manufacturing	Represents the integration of manufacturing functions and resources with other aspects of the business enterprise.
Accounting	Provides an interoperable approach to accounting interfaces and seeks to remove the complexity from accounting service providers and end users.
Imagery	Supports the access and interchange of imagery and related data.
Mapping	Provides a cohesive means of manipulating the flow of data from databases through constructed analysis modules into either presentation tools or secondary data applications.
Application Development	Covers the selection, development, building, and evolution of the applications needed to support an enterprise's information systems strategy.

Table 13.8 OPS interfaces.

Interface	Purpose
PropertySet	Provides support for creating, deleting, iterating, and checking for the existence of properties.
PropertySetDef	Provides support for retrieving **PropertySet** constraints and getting and setting property modes.
PropertiesIterator	Provides support for fine-grained enumeration of properties.
PropertyNamesIterator	Provides support for fine-grained enumeration of property names.
PropertySetFactory	Creates **PropertySet**s.
PropertySetDefFactory	Creates **PropertySetDef**s.

A description of all of these interfaces is beyond the scope of this book. However, this chapter looks at two interfaces: **PropertySet** and **PropertySetDef**.

The **CosPropertyService** module also provides a **Property** structure, which consists of two parts—the property's name and its value. The name is simply a CORBA **string**, and the associated value is represented by a CORBA **any**:

```
typedef string PropertyName;

struct Property
{
    PropertyName property_name;
    any property_value;
};


typedef sequence<PropertyName> PropertyNames;
```

As you can see, a **Property** consists of a **property_name** and a **property_value**. The **property_name** attribute is a **string** that names the property. The **property_value** attribute is of type **any** and represents the value assigned to a property. Because the **property_value**'s type is **any**, you can use any value that can be represented in the IDL-type system.

The **CosPropertyService** module also provides a few exceptions that are raised by operations of the **CosPropertyService** interfaces:

```
exception ConstraintNotSupported {};
exception InvalidPropertyName {};
```

```
exception ConflictingProperty {};
exception PropertyNotFound {};
exception UnsupportedTypeCode {};
exception UnsupportedProperty {};
exception UnsupportedMode {};
exception FixedProperty {};
exception ReadOnlyProperty {};
```

The *PropertySet* Interface

As mentioned earlier, the **PropertySet** interface provides support for creating, deleting, iterating, and checking for the existence of properties. The **PropertySet** interface is declared in Listing 13.4.

Listing 13.4   The PropertySet interface.

```
interface PropertySet
{
    void define_property(in PropertyName property_name,
        in any property_value)
    raises(InvalidPropertyName,
        ConflictingProperty,
        UnsupportedTypeCode,
        UnsupportedProperty,
        ReadOnlyProperty);

    any get_property_value(in PropertyName property_name)
    raises(PropertyNotFound, InvalidPropertyName);

    void get_all_properties(in unsigned long how_many,
        out Properties nproperties,
        out PropertiesIterator rest);

    void get_all_property_names(in unsigned long how_many,
        out PropertyNames property_names,
        out PropertyNamesIterator rest);

    unsigned long get_number_of_properties();

    void delete_property(in PropertyName property_name)
    raises(PropertyNotFound, InvalidPropertyName,
        FixedProperty);

    void delete_properties(in PropertyNames property_names)
    raises(MultipleExceptions);

    //...
};
```

The operations of the **PropertySet** interface are described as follows:

♦ **define_property()**—Creates a new property using the name and the value of the property.

♦ **get_property_value()**—Returns the **any** associated with this name or throws an exception if a property with the name doesn't exist.

♦ **get_all_properties()**—Gives a list of all the properties defined within a **PropertySet**. A maximum of **how_many** values is returned in the **nproperties** parameter. Additional values are returned in the **rest** iterator that is of type **PropertiesIterator**:

```
interface PropertiesIterator
{
    void reset();
    boolean next_one(out Property aproperty);
    boolean next_n(in unsigned long how_many,
        out Properties nproperties);
    void destroy();
};
```

♦ **get_all_property_names()**—Gives a list of property names. As with **get_all_properties()**, a maximum of **how_many** names are returned; any additional names are returned by the **rest** iterator. This iterator implements the **PropertyNamesIterator** interface:

```
interface PropertyNamesIterator
{
    void reset();
    boolean next_one(out PropertyName property_name);
    boolean next_n(in unsigned long how_many,
        out PropertyNames property_names);
    void destroy();
};
```

♦ **get_number_of_properties()**—Returns the number of properties in a **PropertySet** instance.

♦ **delete_property()**—Deletes a property from the **PropertySet** instance.

♦ **delete_properties()**—Deletes properties from the **PropertySet** instance.

The *PropertySetDef* Interface

The **PropertySetDef** interface is a derived interface of the **PropertySet** interface that sets and gets the modes (read-only or read/write access) of each property:

```
enum PropertyModeType
{
    normal,
    read_only,
    fixed_normal,
    fixed_readonly,
    undefined
};

interface PropertySetDef : PropertySet
{
    void define_property_with_mode(
        in PropertyName property_name,
        in any property_value,
        in PropertyModeType property_mode)
    raises(InvalidPropertyName,
        ConflictingProperty,
        UnsupportedTypeCode,
        UnsupportedProperty,
        UnsupportedMode,
        ReadOnlyProperty);
    //...
};
```

The **define_property_with_mode()** operation creates a new property by using the name, value, and *property mode* of the property. OPS-defined property modes are described next:

♦ *Normal*—No restrictions to the property.

♦ *Read-only*—Client can read and delete the property, but not update it.

♦ *Fixed-normal*—Property can be modified, but not deleted.

♦ *Fixed-readonly*—Property can only be read.

Example Scenario Of Property Service

You can use OPS to attach user preferences to a component, although user preferences are not defined in the interface. For example, a user can mark a component with language and sorting-order preferences. The user preferences are invented by the user and aren't part of the component's interface.

Event Service

A standard CORBA dialog takes place between two coupled components. In other words, a client's request is directed to a particular component. Therefore, for the request to be delivered, the client must know its component. The client's request generally results in the synchronous execution of an operation on the server. In some scenarios, however, a more decoupled communication model between components is required. For example, a system management tool may need to know whether a disk has run out of space. The application that uses the disk doesn't know about the existence of the system management tool. The application reports that the disk is full, and the system management tool receives that message, which the tool can use to inform the user about the disk running out of space.

This example scenario can be achieved by using *Event Service*, which provides a framework to establish this kind of decoupled interaction between two components. Event Service supports asynchronous event notifications and event delivery between components. The Event Service allows components to register their interest in an event dynamically.

The Event Channel

Event Services use an *event channel* as a mediator component that allows a component to communicate with other components asynchronously. An event channel is a standard CORBA component, and communication with an event channel is accomplished by using standard CORBA requests. Note the following points about event channels and events:

♦ Event Service distributes data in the form of events. The term *event* in this context refers to data that is generated by a source component.

♦ Event Service is anonymous, which means that an application might be notified of an event on a channel, but the application will not know the origin of the event.

♦ The application shows its interest in a particular type of event by registering itself with the event channel.

♦ The Event Service specification defines two distinct kinds of event channels: an *untyped* (generic) event channel, which forwards every event to each of the registered clients by using CORBA **any**s, and a *typed* event channel, which is strongly typed. This book discusses only the untyped event channel.

Event Suppliers And Consumers

An event channel enables decoupled communication between components. An event channel is used by two kinds of components:

- *Supplier*—Produces event data
- *Consumer*—Processes event data

Suppliers and consumers communicate event data by issuing standard CORBA requests. This is done in two ways:

- *Push model*—Allows a supplier of events to initiate the transfer of the event data to consumers. The supplier pushes data to the event channel, which, in turn, pushes data to the interested consumers. In this model, a supplier is referred to as a *push supplier*, and a consumer is referred to as a *push consumer*. The push consumer has a passive role in the event communication, simply waiting for something to happen (the Publisher-Subscriber design pattern, mentioned earlier, is similar to this model). On the other hand, because push suppliers forward data to the event channel, they play an active role in the link to the channel.

- *Pull model*—Allows a consumer of events to request the event data from a supplier. Consumers request the event channel to send data. The event channel, in turn, pulls data from the supplier that supplies an event, if a new event is available. In this model, a supplier is referred to as a *pull supplier*, and a consumer is referred to as a *pull consumer*.

To recap, in the push model, the supplier takes the initiative; in the pull model, the consumer takes the initiative (as shown by Figure 13.1).

The Event Service satisfies the following design principles regarding consumers and suppliers:

- Consumers and suppliers of events support standard IDL interfaces. No need exists to extend CORBA to support the consumer and supplier roles.

- Suppliers can generate events without knowing who is going to receive them. Analogously, consumers can receive events without knowing the identities of the suppliers.

- Multiple consumers of an event and multiple event suppliers can participate in events.

- An event channel is both a consumer and a supplier of events. The channel is a well-known CORBA component. For example, components that use an event channel may locate the channel by looking for it in a naming server.

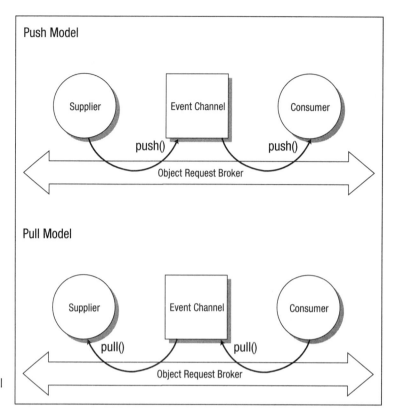

Figure 13.1
Event Service push and pull models.

Event Service Interfaces

The communication models shown in Figure 13.1 are supported by simple interfaces: **PushConsumer**, **PushSupplier**, **PullSupplier**, and **PullConsumer**. These interfaces are defined in an IDL module named **CosEventComm**. The **CosEventComm** module also defines the following exception:

```
exception Disconnected{};
```

Event Channel Policies

A pull consumer has a more active role and periodically polls the event channel to see whether any data exists. Events may occur more frequently than they are polled for by the pull consumer. Consequently, some events might get lost. In such cases, an event channel's buffering policy determines whether events are buffered and what to do with data in case of an event queue overflow. An event channel implementation can feature its own event queue policies. For example, the ORBacus event channel buffers the events in the form of a stack—a certain number of events are stored and, in case of a buffer overflow, the oldest events are discarded.

Push consumers implement the **PushConsumer** interface, which is declared here:

```
interface PushConsumer
{
    void push(in any data) raises(Disconnected);
    void disconnect_push_consumer();
};
```

The following two operations are defined by the **PushConsumer** interface:

♦ **push()**—Used by an event channel to forward events to the consumer.

♦ **disconnect_push_consumer()**—Terminates the event communication. The operation releases resources used at the consumer to support the event communication, and the **PushConsumer** object reference is released.

A pull consumer implements the following (**PullConsumer**) interface:

```
interface PullConsumer
{
    void disconnect_pull_consumer();
};
```

The **disconnect_pull_consumer()** operation terminates the event communication; the operation releases resources used at the consumer to support the event communication, and the **PullConsumer** object reference is disposed.

The following is the **PushSupplier** interface:

```
interface PushSupplier
{
    void disconnect_push_supplier();
};
```

The **disconnect_push_supplier()** operation terminates the event communication; the operation releases resources used at the supplier to support the event communication, and the **PushSupplier** object reference is disposed.

The PullSupplier interface is declared as follows:

```
interface PullSupplier
{
    any pull() raises(Disconnected);

    any try_pull(out boolean has_event)
    raises(Disconnected);

    void disconnect_pull_supplier();
};
```

Here is the description of the preceding operations:

+ **pull()**—Returns the event data to the consumer. The call blocks until the event data is available or an exception is raised. If the event communication has already been disconnected, the **Disconnected** exception is raised.

+ **try_pull()**—Returns the event data and sets the **has_event** parameter to true; if the event isn't available, **try_pull()** sets the **has_event** parameter to false and the event data is returned as **long** with an undefined value. It doesn't block. If the event communication has already been disconnected, the **Disconnected** exception is raised.

+ **disconnect_pull_supplier()**—Terminates the event communication; the operation releases resources used at the supplier to support the event communication, and the **PullSupplier** object reference is disposed.

Example Scenario Of Event Service

One of the applications of Event Service is to implement *change notification*. In this application, an object that can be changed acts as a supplier, parties interested in receiving notifications of changes act as consumers, and an event channel can be used as an intermediary between consumers and the supplier. An event can be generated and propagated to all consumers whenever the object's state is modified. You can implement this by using either the push or the pull model:

+ *Push model*—The object that can be changed supports the **PushSupplier** interface. When a change occurs to the object, it invokes the **push()** operation on the channel. Data is also passed to the **push()** operation. This data characterizes the event. Recall that type of data is **any**, which can be used to carry any data type within the IDL-type system.

+ *Pull model*—All client objects that want to be notified of changes support the **PullConsumer** interface. The consumer may use either the **try_pull()** operation or the **pull()** operation. If **try_pull()** is used, a consumer can periodically poll the channel for events. If **pull()** is used, the consumer's execution thread is blocked until an event is generated by the supplier.

This scenario shows that the generic Event Service forms a basic building block that can be used in providing higher-level services that are specific to an application or a common facilities framework of objects.

Overcoming The Complexity Of Distributed Computing

Experience using CORBA proves that although building small, distributed applications is easy, developing large, distributed applications remains hard. In large application systems, several issues regarding management of interfaces and component lifecycles, component recovery, transactions, consistency, and so forth, become large issues. Obviously, unless building large applications becomes simpler, distributed component systems will not really become popular.

As you know, one of the best ways to reduce the complexity of developing distributed applications is to provide a framework that can take care of the requirements and associated complexity of distributed applications. The framework will simplify the implementation through generalized component interactions and reusable components that are capable of delivering the necessary distributed applications. This framework could be implemented as a BOM, because as you will see later, the BOM can be used to create distributed applications, as well as new frameworks that can be either horizontally or vertically oriented.

The next section defines the architecture that is the base of the BOM example.

Elements Of The BOM Architecture

The BOM architecture consists of two elements, which correspond to the functions needed to implement distributed business applications for diversified requirements:

♦ *Business objects (BOs)*—Implementations of real-world informational business elements, such as Customer, Trader, Employees, Order, and Product.

♦ *Dynamic interfaces*—Representation of a BO's capabilities. A dynamic interface is based on IDL and is bound to a BO by using a C++ member object mechanism. Recall that using member objects is one of the most common C++ techniques of reusing functionality in object-oriented systems. More than one dynamic interface may be bound to a BO.

The notions of BO and dynamic interface are described next.

Business Objects

According to OMG, BOs are representations of the nature and behavior of real world things or concepts in terms that are meaningful to the business. Customers, products, orders, employees, trades, financial instruments, shipping containers, and vehicles are all examples of real-world concepts or things that could be represented by BOs.

A BO represents a significant portion of an overall application system, but nevertheless, is small enough to enable efficient and flexible composition with other BOs to form actual full-fledged applications and application systems.

BOs add value over other representations by providing a way of packaging the essential characteristics of business concepts more completely. It is important to note that BOs can act as participants in business processes, because BOs can perform the required tasks or steps that make up business processes. In this way, BO technology allows the development of objects and processes that mirror their counterparts in the real world. In addition, BOs provide common terms and ideas at a level of detail that can be shared among business and technical people to articulate and understand the business in business terms. In short, a BO:

- Implements a substantial portion of the overall application system's capabilities.

- Represents its capabilities via one or more (IDL-based) dynamic interfaces. Therefore, the BO is capable of efficiently communicating with other BOs over a network.

- Can be developed independently of other BOs.

- Is the fundamental unit of configurability, extensibility, replaceability, and distribution.

Dynamic Interfaces

A BO represents one concept or one business entity. A BO, however, can contain many slices of capabilities; for example, it can participate in Publisher-Subscriber interactions, be a transaction coordinator, and have the capabilities of a bank account. Although you can represent a BO's capabilities by using a single, *big* interface, this can get clumsy, due to the following reasons:

- The definition of the interface can get quite large (it might specify tens of operations), making it difficult for programmers to define new interfaces and comprehend existing interfaces.

- Changing the definition of an interface can be difficult, such as adding new capabilities in a manner that doesn't break existing clients of the BO.

- Informing clients about changes to the definition of the interface can be difficult.

By partitioning a BO's interface into smaller, more modular interfaces, many of these problems can be avoided. Instead of implementing a single, monolithic interface, a BO can implement multiple distinct interfaces that can be bound (explained later) to the BO at runtime. Each of these smaller interfaces, which are easier to define and to comprehend, represents a specific semantic contract that the BO implements.

These smaller interfaces are referred to as *dynamic interfaces of the BO*, although they are no different from the regular IDL-based interface. However, unlike a classical CORBA component, dynamic interfaces aren't part of a BO's IDL declaration.

A client can use a BO object reference to determine which dynamic interfaces the BO currently implements (of course, BO itself is based on an interface). This is accomplished by providing the BO with a common set of basic operations that enables clients to query the BO about which interfaces it implements. If the queried interface is implemented, the client is provided with an interface reference to it. Otherwise, an exception is raised.

BO's Implementation

Based on the concepts previously described, BO's interface can be declared as follows:

```
module CoBOM
{
    typedef string InterfaceName;
    typedef sequence<InterfaceName> SeqInterfaceName;
```

```
    exception NotFound{};

    interface BusinessObject
    {
        Object resolve(in InterfaceName name)
        raises (NotFound);

        SeqInterfaceName list();
    };
};
```

The following is a description of the **CoBOM::BusinessObject** interface:

- **InterfaceName**—The symbolic name of the dynamic interface that is bound to a BO.

- **resolve()**—Enables interrogation of a BO to determine whether the interface specified by **name** is also bound to a BO. The value of **name** must be a fully qualified interface name. If the specified interface is bound, then an interface reference of IDL type **Object** is returned. This reference subsequently can be narrowed so that it can be used to perform operations that are specific to the interface that is the result of the query.

- **NotFound**—An exception that is raised if the interface whose name is specified by **name** in the **resolve()** call isn't bound to the BO.

- **list()**—Lists the names of all the interfaces that are bound to a BO.

CoComponentImpl

The base BO from which a new component's implementation can be derived is shown here (the IDL file of the preceding section is assumed to be compiled using the ORBacus IDL compiler):

```
#include <string>
#include <map>
#include <co_bom_skel.h>

class CoBusinessObjectImpl: public CoBOM_BusinessObject_skel
{
private:

    typedef map<string,CORBA_Object_ptr> INTERFACES;
    typedef INTERFACES::iterator INTERFACE_ITER;
    INTERFACES interfaces_;
```

```
public:

    CoBusinessObjectImpl(){}
    ~CoBusinessObjectImpl();

    //IDL operations
    virtual CORBA_Object_ptr resolve(const char* name);
    virtual CoBOM_SeqInterfaceName* list();

    //local (non-IDL) functions
    void bind(const char* name, CORBA_Object_ptr ref);
    void unbind(const char* name);
};
```

The member functions of the **CoBusinessObjectImpl** class are defined in Listing 13.5.

Listing 13.5   Definitions of the member functions of the CoBusinessObjectImpl class.

```
#include <OB/CORBA.h>
#include <co_bom_impl.h>

CoBusinessObjectImpl::~CoBusinessObjectImpl()
{
    INTERFACE_ITER end=interfaces_.end();

    for (INTERFACE_ITER iter=interfaces_.begin();
        iter!=end; ++iter)
    {
        CORBA_release((*iter).second);
    }
}

CORBA_Object_ptr
CoBusinessObjectImpl::resolve(const char* name)
{
    INTERFACE_ITER iter=interfaces_.find(name);
    if (iter==interfaces_.end())
    {
        throw CoBOM_NotFound();
    }

    return CORBA_Object::_duplicate((*iter).second);
}
```

```
void CoBusinessObjectImpl::bind(const char* name,
    CORBA_Object_ptr ref)
{
    interfaces_[name]=CORBA_Object::_duplicate(ref);
}


CoBOM_SeqInterfaceName* CoBusinessObjectImpl::list()
{
    CoBOM_SeqInterfaceName* names=
        new CoBOM_SeqInterfaceName();

    names->length(interfaces_.size());

    INTERFACE_ITER end=interfaces_.end();

    CORBA_ULong i=0;

    for (INTERFACE_ITER iter=interfaces_.begin();
        iter!=end; ++iter)
    {
        (*names)[i++]=(*iter).first.c_str();
    }

    return names;
}


void CoBusinessObjectImpl::unbind(const char* name)
{
    CORBA_release(interfaces_[name]);
    interfaces_.erase(name);
}
```

Implementation of the **CoBusinessObjectImpl** class is almost self-describing, but the following points are worth noting:

◆ The **CoBusinessObjectImpl** class uses the **map** class to store the pairs of names and the corresponding dynamic interface's object references.

◆ The **resolve()** function is the implementation of the **resolve()** IDL operation, whereas **bind()** is a local member function.

◆ The **bind()** function takes two parameters: the name and object reference of a dynamic interface that you want to bind. The function stores them in the **map** object, which is used later by the **resolve()** call that a client will make.

- Both the **resolve()** and **bind()** functions use **CORBA_ Object::_duplicate()** to increment the reference count of the object reference.

- **unbind()** is a local member function that decrements the reference count of an interface and deletes its entry from the **map** object.

- The destructor of the **CoBusinessObjectImpl** class decrements the reference count of all bound interfaces and deletes their entries from the **map** object.

Using BOM: Developer's Perspective

The **CoComponentImpl::bind()** member function enables BOs to add new interfaces that represent new capabilities, while still supporting older interfaces. Representing a BO's capabilities as a set of bound interfaces enables a client to interrogate a BO to determine which interfaces the BO currently supports, thereby allowing the client to resolve the interfaces it needs to use.

The general model for BO interactions is that every application component is derived from the base **CoComponentImpl** class that supports the **resolve()** member function, which enables a BO's clients to determine whether the BO supports a particular dynamic interface.

As the following example shows, BO extensibility is enabled through the definition of new interfaces. Recall the banking example of Chapter 9—the IDL declaration of the **Account** component is shown here:

```
module CoBank
{
    struct Person
    {
        string name;
        short age;
    };

    interface Account
    {
        readonly attribute float balance;
        readonly attribute Person holder;

        exception NoMoney
        {
            float balance;
        };
```

```
                    void deposit(in float amount);
                    void withdraw(in float amount) raises (NoMoney);
              };
        };
```

The **CoBank::Account** interface is implemented as the **CoBank_AccountImpl** class (see Listing 9.9 in Chapter 9). This interface can be used as a dynamic interface for the following **CoAccount** BO:

```
class CoAccount:public CoBusinessObjectImpl
{
private:

    CoBank_AccountImpl account_;

public:

    CoAccount(CORBA_Float balance,
        const CoBank_Person& name):account_(balance, name)
    {
        bind("CoBank::CoAccount", &account_);
    }
};
```

The preceding code does the following:

♦ The **CoAccount** component is derived from the **CoBusinessObjectImpl** class.

♦ The **resolve()** operation is automatically available to the **CoAccount** component via class derivation. This means that a client can connect to an instance of the **CoBusinessObjectImpl** class via the network.

♦ The **CoBusinessObjectImpl** class contains a member object **account_** of type **CoBank_AccountImpl**.

♦ The constructor of the **CoBusinessObjectImpl** class uses the **CoBusinessObjectImpl::bind()** member function to bind the **account_** instance. Note that the **"CoBank::CoAccount"** name is the fully qualified name of the **Account** interface, of which **CoBank_AccountImpl** is an implementation. As the second argument in the **bind()** call, **&account_** is used to generate an object reference of the **Account** interface.

A server program that uses the preceding **CoAccount** component is shown in Listing 13.6.

Listing 13.6 A server program using the CoAccount BO.

```
int main(int argc, char* argv[], char*[])
{
    try
    {
        // Create ORB and BOA
        CORBA_ORB_var orb = CORBA_ORB_init(argc, argv);
        CORBA_BOA_var boa = orb -> BOA_init(argc, argv);

        CoBank_Person person;
        person.name=(const char*)"vishwa";
        person.age=29;

        CoBOM_BusinessObject_var p =
            new CoAccount(100, person);

        // Save reference
        CORBA_String_var s = orb -> object_to_string(p);

        const char* refFile = "CoAccount.ref";
        ofstream out(refFile);
        if(out.fail())
        {
            cerr << argv[0] << ": can't open `" <<
            refFile << "': "<< strerror(errno) << endl;
            return 1;
        }

        out << s << endl;
        out.close();

        // Run implementation
        boa -> impl_is_ready(
        CORBA_ImplementationDef::_nil());
    }
    catch(CORBA_SystemException& ex)
    {
        OBPrintException(ex);
        return 1;
    }

    return 0;
}
```

The preceding server program is the same as a server program shown in Listing 9.10 in Chapter 9. However, a minor difference appears in the following statement:

```
CoBOM_BusinessObject_var p = new CoAccount(100, person);
```

Because **CoAccount** is derived from the **CoBusinessObjectImpl** class, you can safely assign a pointer to **CoAccount** into a variable of the **CoBOM_BusinessObject_var** type (recall that you should not have automatic or nonheap instances of types that are based on IDL interfaces).

Using BOM: Client's Perspective

The general model for a BO's clients is that the **resolve()** operation is used to determine whether the BO supports a particular dynamic interface. If a BO supports the interface named by the client, then the client is provided with a reference to the specific interface. The client can then use the reference to invoke upon the BO any of the operations defined for the interface. The fact that a BO supports a particular interface implies that the BO implements the semantic contract implied by the interface.

Listing 13.7 gives the client program corresponding to the server program shown in Listing 13.6.

Listing 13.7   Client program to access the CoAccount BO.

```
int main(int argc, char* argv[], char*[])
{
    try
    {
        CORBA_ORB_var orb = CORBA_ORB_init(argc, argv);

        // Get "Account" object
        const char* refFile = "CoAccount.ref";
        ifstream in;
        in.open(refFile);
        if(in.fail())
        {
            cerr << argv[0] << ": can't open `" <<
                refFile << "': "<<
                strerror(errno) << endl;
            return 1;
        }
```

```cpp
        char s[1000];
        in >> s;

        CORBA_Object_var obj = orb -> string_to_object(s);
        assert(!CORBA_is_nil(obj));

        CoBOM_BusinessObject_var bom =
            CoBOM_BusinessObject::_narrow(obj);

        CORBA_Object_var account_obj;

        try
        {
            account_obj =
                bom -> resolve("CoBank::CoAccount");
        }
        catch (const CoBOM_NotFound&)
        {
            cerr << "Interface not bound to the BO"<<endl;
            exit(1);
        }

        CoBank_Account_var account =
            CoBank_Account::_narrow(account_obj);

        assert(!CORBA_is_nil(account));

        cout<<"Initial balance:"<<account->balance()<<endl;
        account->deposit(50);
        cout<<"Balance:"<<account->balance()<<endl;

        account->withdraw(50);
        cout<<"Balance:"<<account->balance()<<endl;

        CoBank_Person_var person=account->holder();
        cout<<"Name:"<<person->name<<endl;
        cout<<"Age:"<<person->age<<endl;

        account->withdraw(1000);
    }
    catch(CORBA_SystemException& ex)
    {
        OBPrintException(ex);
        return 1;
    }
    catch(const CoBank_Account::NoMoney& nm)
```

NOTE

**Dynamic Interfaces
Vs. Naming Service**

Each BO acts like a *mini
naming server*, because a
BO maintains a set of
interfaces. If a client
somehow gets a refer-
ence of a BO, the client
can use that reference to
locate other references
that are contained in the
BO. Obviously, in such a
framework, Naming
Service is used sparingly,
and clients instead rely
on the **resolve()** call.

```
{
    cout<<"No money. Current balance:"<<nm.balance<<endl;
}
catch(...)
{
    cerr << "Unexpected exception " << endl;
    exit(1);
}

return 0;
}
```

In Listing 13.7, the **resolve()** operation is used to query for the
CoBank::CoAccount interface. If the **resolve()** call succeeds, the returned object reference is narrowed into the **CoBank_Account** type
and stored in a variable **account**. Then, the client invokes operations
on **account**.

From Metaframework To A
More Specific Framework

As Listings 13.6 and 13.7 show, BOs are represented by the dynamic
interfaces that they support (though the examples use only one dynamic interface). A BO will support interfaces that enable a high degree
of data and application integration and interoperation. During application development, these interfaces are intended to help developers
to realize the full application features and capabilities that are important to the newer application. In addition, a BO can support interfaces
that are based upon existing standards (such as CORBA services and
common facilities). Such interfaces are referred to as *application interfaces*, because they are specified and implemented to denote particular
application capabilities.

Analogously, the metaframework enables you to define *generic interfaces* that can be specified and implemented independently of any
particular application. The part of an interface that is generic is primarily concerned with representing the patterns of interactions between
BOs. Generic interfaces are demonstrated by the **Request**, **Initializer**
and **Publisher/Subscriber** interfaces, which are shown in Listing 13.8.

Listing 13.8   Generic interfaces for BOM.

```
module CoGenericInterface
{
    interface Initializer
```

NOTE

Interface Is Just A Specification

You must realize that an interface is just a specification that represents an underlying implementation. The implementation of an interface can be different for different BOs. This enables a BO-specific realization of the operations defined for an interface as long as the BO implementation obeys the semantic contract implied by the interface. This is obviously a case of _interface polymorphism._

NOTE

BO Equals Capability Plus Appearance

The generic interfaces of a BO characterize the general capability of the BO. Conversely, the application-specific interfaces of a BO characterize the specific appearance of the BO. The framework (BOM), in general, is intended to provide capability and appearance to BOs, both of which are needed for a complete application.

```
{
    boolean initialize(in CoMetadata::SeqNVPair data);
    boolean deinitialize();
};

interface Subscriber
{
    void notify(in CoMetadata::SeqNVPair data);
};

typedef string SubscriberName;

exception NotSubscribed{};

interface Publisher
{
    void subscribe(in SubscriberName name,
        in Subscriber subscriber);

    void unsubscribe(in SubscriberName name)
    raises (NotSubscribed);
};

typedef string ServiceName;
typedef sequence<ServiceName> SeqServiceName;

exception NoService{};

interface Request
{
    boolean send_and_receive(in ServiceName name,
        in CoMetadata::SeqNVPair indata,
        out CoMetadata::SeqNVPair odata)
    raises (NoService);

    SeqServiceName list();
};
};
```

The following list describes the essential parts of the **CoGeneric-Interface** module:

♦ **CoGenericInterface**—Uses the **CoMetadata** module to make use of the **SeqNVPair** metadata.

NOTE

Adding Business Process Objects To BOM

The *business process object* represents business processes as operations across BOs or related to collections of BOs. Business process objects are generally "stateless" components. A BO can handle short-lived interactions, whereas a business process object can be used to encapsulate long-lived interactions. In fact, the business process object is just a specialization of the BO that is capable of dealing with workflow requirements and some external parameters. It should act like glue between various BOs, and thus support workflow-oriented computing.

♦ **Initializer()**—Represents the initialize code of a BO. The **initialize()** and **deinitialize()** operations can be invoked on a BO at the time of starting and stopping the BO, respectively.

♦ **Subscriber-Publisher**—Same as described earlier in the chapter, except that the **notify()** operation takes one parameter of the **SeqNVPair** type.

♦ **Request**—Represents a specific service that a BO can perform. The **send_and_receive()** operation actually invokes a specific service on BO that is registered with an implementation of the **Request** interface. In addition, the **list()** operation returns the **SeqServiceName** type that represents the services supported by the BO. The **Request** interface is semantically very much similar to the **CoRequest** class that is discussed in Chapter 7, with one distinct difference. Whereas **CoRequest** itself represents input, the **Request** interface's **send_and_receive()** operation carries input as well as output data, using the **CoMetadata::SeqNVPair** metadata.

The preceding declarations of the generic interfaces clearly show that they all use the metadata type. Recall that metadata is typically used at runtime (when the BOs are actually executing in a running system) to exchange data between BOs in an application-specific manner. The metadata is interpreted by the application that implements the BOs, thereby enabling the application to treat otherwise generic interfaces as application-specific interfaces.

After you implement generic interfaces, you can extend BOM by prebinding the generic interfaces to the base BO class. In addition, you can define new derived types of BO; for example, you can create a generic *presentation service component* that provides visual presentation elements. Similarly, you can create a generic *information service component* that is responsible for storing data and maintaining the core "business" rules that ensure the integrity of the data over time.

By adding new capabilities to the metaframework in terms of interfaces and new derived components, you basically move from an abstract world to a less abstract world, which is a *framework*. The newer frameworks will be less abstract and more specific. You can even create vertical frameworks (a banking framework, for example) by using the metaframework. This way, the metaframework provides a perfect platform to accelerate distributed computing. If you use the metaframework to develop applications, your primary task as an application architect is to identify BOs and describe how they fit together to accomplish the desired application and application capabilities. At this level of architecting, you concentrate on interfaces (the surface area) of the BOs rather than on the internal designs and implementation mechanisms. From the application architect's perspective, specifications for a BO consist of four elements, shown in Table 13.9. The component and communication models provide an important basis for specifying BOs.

Adapting Services For The Banking Application By Using Services And BOM

The **Account** component examples shown in Listings 13.6 and 13.7 represent a very lightweight application's BO. The real applications' BOs may use transactions and event mechanisms to provide the required business functionality.

The following is a brief review of how using a few relevant CORBA services can improve the banking example (most of the services aren't readily available; ORBacus provides Naming Service, OPS, and Event Service at no cost):

♦ *Naming Service*—The mechanism to read a stringified object reference from a file shown in the examples is also a very simple mechanism. The applications generally use Naming Service to locate BOs. (The use of Naming Service is demonstrated in Chapter 12.) A highly distributed system must use this service. As mentioned earlier, after you locate a BO, you can locate dynamic interfaces by using the **resolve()** operation.

♦ *Object Trader Service (OTS)*—Banking BOs' factories can be registered with an OTS based on the BOs they support. Therefore, a client can locate factories by using OTS.

♦ *Security Service*—Security Service is essential for the banking application so that many security-related features, such as user identification and authorization, auditing, secure communication, and nonrepudiation, can be applied to make the banking transactions secure and trustworthy.

♦ *Object Transaction Service (OTS)*—OTS is extremely useful to the banking application. You can bind the **Resource** interface of OTS (supports **prepare()**, **commit()**, and **rollback()**) to the **Account** component to make the component a transaction participant.

♦ *Event Service*—Banking BOs quite possibly will receive asynchronous messages from some external data feeds. Thus, Event Service can be used. You can bind an implementation of the **PushConsumer** interface to the **Account** component so that the component can receive the **push()** calls.

♦ *Persistent Object Service (POS)*—Because all banking applications need to store banking data in persistent storage, POS can be used.

♦ *Concurrency Control Service (CCS)*—The **Account** component might be accessed simultaneously. Thus, CCS could prove useful.

♦ *Time Service*—Time Service can be used to ensure that various banking BOs that are located across machines, and even countries, are concurrent with each other with respect to time.

Table 13.9   Constituents of a BO's specification.

Specification element	Description
Component model	Identifies the key BOs and their roles and responsibilities.
Communication model	Identifies interactions between BOs.
Dynamic interfaces	Participate in a particular interaction.
Metadata	Represents BO's application-specific data using generic interfaces.

Chapter Recap

This chapter described the CORBA-based component architecture as a three-dimensional space, summarized as follows:

◆ *First dimension: CORBA design patterns and idioms*—Clear evidence of patterns exists in all levels of CORBA, from high-level CORBA architecture down to detailed design. This chapter presented a few design patterns, such as Factory, Publisher-Subscriber, and so forth. The reference counting mechanism that keeps track of the number of connections to a component was also presented.

◆ *Second dimension: CORBA metadata*—Metadata is typically used at runtime (when the components are actually executing in a running system) as generic message data that is exchanged between components in an application-specific manner. This message data can be interpreted by the application that implements the components, thereby enabling the application to treat an otherwise generic interaction as an application-specific dialogue.

◆ *Third dimension: CORBA services and facilities*—You can create component frameworks by combining interfaces for applications, common facilities, and object services. Services can be combined to produce new, powerful services and frameworks. For example, Event Service and Relationship Service can be combined to create workflow frameworks; by using CORBA services, such as Transaction Service, you can implement components that act like the real-world components.

This three-dimensional space can be referred to as the *foundation for generic BOM*, because it enables you to develop component frameworks by using CORBA. BOM can be used to create distributed applications as well as new frameworks that can be either horizontally or vertically oriented. This chapter presented several BOM concepts, including the following:

♦ A component is a piece of software that can be instantiated as a stateful computational entity that performs certain operations on behalf of its clients.

♦ The interfaces that a component implements can vary during the lifetime of the component.

♦ Interfaces implemented by a component can be distinguished solely by their symbolic names and are referred to as *dynamic interfaces*. A client can use a component's object reference to determine what dynamic interfaces the component currently implements.

♦ Dynamic interfaces also serve as the basis for open application systems.

♦ From the application developer's perspective, a component's capabilities are represented by one or more dynamic interfaces. Each interface represents a semantically related set of operations that the component is capable of performing. Each interface has a distinct name, and a component can bind a set of interfaces to represent its capabilities.

BOM can provide one way to reduce the complexity of developing distributed applications, because it can take care of the requirements and associated complexity of distributed applications. The metaframework provides capability to simplify the implementation, through generalized component interactions and reusable components that are capable of delivering the necessary distributed applications.

Chapter 14

Framework-Centric Application Development

Key Topics:

♦ *Cookbook concepts for frameworks*

♦ *Framework concepts for developing applications*

♦ *Code generation examples*

Object-oriented frameworks bring success to object-oriented programming (OOP). A framework is an abstract design created to solve a set of problems that can be used as a development foundation for newer applications. Recall that object-oriented frameworks enable design-level reuse, because they support reusing the abstract design of an entire application. Thus, framework-centric application development takes advantage of frameworks to magnify the benefits of OOP.

Framework-centric application development provides OOP the following advantages:

♦ Well-defined mechanisms that enable you to reuse frameworks. This is referred to as the *framework usage phase* (also known as the *framework instantiation phase* or *application development phase*), during which you adapt, or reuse, existing frameworks to fulfill a new application's requirements. This phase is the topic of this chapter.

♦ An application construction environment (ACE) that includes a variety of development tools, all of which are designed to accelerate the application development and customization process. For example, a code generator can be provided with a framework to reduce the implementation overhead.

This chapter focuses on framework-centric development from the perspective of a framework developer, rather than a framework user.

Documenting The Framework

One major aspect of reusable software is its documentation. If the framework's documentation doesn't address the requirements of its intended users, those users will not reuse the framework. Because the framework embodies the complexity of the problem that it addresses, a description of the framework is needed. Framework documentation mainly presents descriptions of how to use the framework through recipes and sample programs. Good documentation is the key to maximizing the benefits of writing frameworks, because it encourages as many developers as possible to adapt the frameworks.

The following is a list of reasons why framework documentation is important:

♦ *Learning a framework is difficult*—Framework developers must provide enough information for users to understand how to reuse the framework to develop the applications they want. Framework documentation must clarify users' interactions with the framework.

♦ *Users are looking for problem-solving capabilities*—Framework users are interested in using the framework to solve a particular type of architectural or programming problem. They are not interested in knowing the details of the framework implementation.

The framework documentation must include:

♦ *Purpose of the framework*—Provides information that enables users to determine whether this is the correct framework for their particular situation. It provides information about which problem the framework addresses, and it provides a description of the framework's capabilities.

♦ *Class description document*—Provides a complete and detailed class reference document for all the framework classes that the framework user interacts with. This topic is described in the next section.

♦ *Cookbook*—Describes how the framework is intended to be used (explained further in the "Cookbook" section of this chapter).

♦ *Architecture of the framework*—Provides information that is useful for extending and customizing the framework. Obviously, users need a more detailed and deeper understanding of the framework to extend its functionality and customize it for their particular domain. This document must contain the classes and their relationships, as well as all collaborations between the classes.

Class Description Document

Cookbooks are supported by the *class description document*, which describes the classes and is the key to understanding and using classes in a framework. Table 14.1 presents the structure of a class description document.

An example of a class description document is provided later in the chapter.

Cookbook

Because the built-in prewired flow of control among framework components may be nonintuitive to users, a framework must be supported by the necessary cookbook, enabling users to use the framework easily and successfully. A cookbook consists of *framework adaptation patterns*, also known as *recipes*. If the framework's recipes aren't documented properly for easy (re)use, the framework will not be reused. A recipe consists of five elements, as shown in Table 14.2.

Recipes don't describe the framework architecture or the implementation details. A recipe generally provides information that answers the following two questions:

♦ *What classes must be subclassed for a white-box framework?*—Because a white-box framework is an abstract design and implementation of a family of related applications, you have to derive from the abstract classes of the framework. In addition, the cookbook describes hot hooks to be overridden.

Table 14.1 Structure of the class description document.

Element	Describes
Description	The essence of the class, in plain English
Class declaration	The class's public interface
Member functions	Each member function, including a parameter list and any preconditions

Table 14.2 Recipe elements.

Element	Provides
Purpose	Description of the recipe's capability
Steps	Steps to achieve the purpose of the recipe
Rules of usage	Any rules or constraints that the user should know about
Examples	Examples to back up the steps
Related recipes	References to other, closely related recipes

♦ *What classes should be used from the black-box framework?*—Because black-box frameworks are intended to be used by instantiating the framework classes, the cookbook describes which member functions must be called and in what sequence.

An example of a cookbook recipe is provided later in the chapter.

Rules Of Usage

As a part of the framework documentation, usage rules for a recipe have to be described. A usage rule gives essential information, such as the following, on how to use a particular recipe:

♦ The rules for the creation of objects

♦ The sequence in which a set of member functions must be called

♦ The rules for various constructors and conversion operators

Application Examples

The examples in a framework cookbook are very important. Framework usage examples make the framework more understandable. By reading examples, users can comprehend how the framework can be used. In addition, examples give users an idea of the restrictions and boundaries of the framework.

A framework developer can also include the test programs used while developing the framework as application examples.

CoStruct's Description

Chapters 6 and 7 describe a business component framework (BC framework). The BC framework defines the **CoStruct** and **CoArray** classes to represent the user-defined types (UDTs) in the framework. The classes are described briefly in Chapter 7. The following is a formal description of the (partial) **CoStruct** class in the form of a class description document. A class description of the **CoArray** class is provided in the next section. (Remember that the class description, like the one shown below, must be written for every framework class that the user can access.)

Description

The **CoStruct** class is used to define structures. The **CoStruct** class enables you to assemble simple and composite objects in a tree form and provide a uniform interface to operate on the objects.

Class Declaration

The class declaration is as follows:

```
class CoStruct : public CoType
{
public:

    virtual void registerMembers() = 0;
    //...

protected:

    inline CoStruct();

    inline void registerAttribute(const string& name, CoType*
pt);
    inline void registerAttribute(CoType* pt);
    //...
};
```

Member Functions

Member functions of the **CoStruct** class are described in the next sections.

Class Constructor

The constructor does nothing.

registerMembers( )

This is a pure **virtual** function that is overridden by the user. In the implementation, the function **registerAttribute()** calls are made for all the data members of the derived class.

registerAttribute( )—First Form

Registers data members of the derived class. Parameters are described below:

♦ **name**—The name of the member being registered

♦ **pt**—The pointer to the member being registered

registerAttribute( )—Second Form

Same as the first form, except the **name** parameter is not needed.

CoArray's Description

A (partial) class description of the **CoArray** class may look similar to the example shown here.

Description

The **CoArray** class is used to define a sequence of types. The **CoArray** class is a class template.

Class Declaration

The class declaration is as follows:

```
template <typename T>
class CoArray : public CoType
{
public:

    inline CoArray() throw();
    inline CoArray(const CoArray<T>& va) throw();

    inline T& operator[](size_t n) throw();
    inline const T& operator[](size_t n) const throw();
    inline void add(const T& t) throw();
    //...
};
```

Member Functions

Member functions of the **CoArray** class are described in the next sections.

Class Constructor—First Form

This makes an instance with no element in it.

Class Constructor—Second Form

This is the copy constructor of the **CoArray** class.

operator[]—First Form

This returns an element of the array from the position specified by the parameter, **n**. This function is used to modify an element of the array.

operator[]—Second Form

This returns an element of the array from the position specified by the parameter, **n**. This function can't be used to modify an element of the array.

add( )

This function adds an element to the array at the end.

Cookbook Recipe Examples

Here is a cookbook recipe, "How To Define User-Defined Structures," for the BC framework.

Purpose

This recipe describes how to define user-defined structures.

Steps

Follow these steps to define user-defined structures:

1. Derive from the **CoStruct** class.

2. Declare data member in the derived class.

3. Define the copy constructor.

4. Define the assignment operator.

5. Define the **registerMembers( )** function.

6. In the **registerMembers( )** function, register data members of the derived structure by using the **registerAttribute( )** function.

Rules Of Usage

The following rules are for the usage for the **CoStruct** class:

♦ In all constructors, the **registerMembers( )** function must be called.

♦ The data members of the derived class can be a basic type (**CoLong, CoBoolean**, and so forth) or a user-defined type (**CoString, CoStruct**, or **CoArray**).

Example

The following code is an example of defining user-defined structures:

```
class address : public CoStruct
{
```

```
public:

    CoLong doorNum_;
    CoString street_;
    CoString city_;

    address()
    {
        registerMembers();
    }
    address(const address& other) //required
    {
        doorNum_=other.doorNum_;
        street_=other.street_;
        city_=other.city_;
        registerMembers();
    }
    address& operator=(const address& other) //required
    {
        doorNum_=other.doorNum_;
        street_=other.street_;
        city_=other.city_;
        return *this;
    }

private:

    void registerMembers() throw()
    {
        registerAttribute("doorNum_", &doorNum_);
        registerAttribute("street_", &street_);
        registerAttribute("city_", &city_);
    }
};
```

Related Recipes

"How To Define Arrays" is a related recipe. This cookbook recipe for the BC framework is presented next.

Purpose

This recipe describes how to define an array.

Steps

The steps for defining an array are as follows:

1. Instantiate the **CoArray** class template for the class type for which an array is required.

2. Use the **add()** member function to add data to the instantiated array object.

3. Use the **const operator[]()** function to read data from the array.

4. Use the non-**const operator[]()** function to modify the data in the array.

Rules Of Usage

The rules of usage for the **CoArray** class are as follows:

♦ The **CoArray** class can be instantiated only with the types that are derived from the **CoType** class. For example, you can use **CoArray<CoDouble>**, but not **CoArray<double>** because **double** is not derived from the **CoType** class.

♦ The **add()** function must be called to add data to the array. Don't use the non-**const** version of the **operator[]()** function to add data to an array.

Example

The following code is an example of using the **CoArray** type:

```
CoArray<CoDouble> ad;
ad.add(1.1);
ad.add(1.2);
ad.add(1.3);
ad[2]=1.7; //modifies third element of the array
```

Related Recipes

"How To Define User-Defined Structures" is a related recipe.

Architecture Document For The BC Framework

As mentioned earlier, framework documentation must include a framework architecture, to provide information that is useful for extending and customizing the framework. This architecture document must contain the classes and their relationships, as well as the collaborations between the classes.

Defining the high-level structure of the framework makes describing the behavior of the framework easier. Chapter 6 outlines the foundation components of the BC framework, but it doesn't provide an explicit description of the relationships among the components of the BC framework. The architecture document of the BC framework should include and expand upon the following points:

♦ The internal structure of the BC framework is described by the Broker architectural pattern, because the BC framework enables you to write decoupled components that interact by messages, which is the type of software system that the Broker architectural pattern describes.

♦ A BC is associated with many requests and replies.

♦ A request/reply may be associated with more than one BC.

♦ A BC is always associated with the component manager.

♦ A component manager may be associated with many BCs.

♦ A component manager is a Singleton class.

♦ A BC framework is based on a client/server model, in which the server components (the BCs) register themselves with a component manager and make their services available to clients. Clients access the server components' services by sending requests to the components. However, it is the component manager that locates and instantiates the target BC and forwards the request to that BC, which, in turn, returns a reply to the caller.

Obviously, Unified Modeling Language (UML) notations should be used to depict these relationships, because these relationships mostly involve associations.

Using A Framework

Framework-centric application development differs from application development using class libraries. The primary differences are the following:

♦ *Frameworks provide reusable design*—Frameworks and class libraries are collections of classes. However, frameworks provide rich functionality and strong, prewired connections between classes, which is not the case for class libraries.

♦ *The framework calls you, you don't call the framework*—Because the framework provides strong, prewired connections between classes, the framework controls the runtime behavior for the application. Framework-centric programming requires you to think in a different way because the framework determines when the objects should do their required duties. Conversely, in class-library-based development, you have to provide the entire application structure and make calls to library functions according to the flow of the program.

When you use a framework, you have to adapt the generic functions defined in the framework for a particular application. A particular adaptation of a framework is referred to as a *framework instance*. You can adapt a framework in two ways:

♦ *By class derivation*—You adapt the framework by deriving new classes from the framework and overriding member functions. Frameworks that support this approach are referred to as *white-box frameworks*, because their implementation must be understood before using them.

♦ *By composition*—You adapt the framework to the specific needs of the application by relying on object composition. The framework defines the protocol to enable the object composition. The protocol is defined by the external interface of the classes. Thus, this kind of framework is referred to as a *black-box framework*.

General Steps To Develop An Application Using A Framework

Application development is an important step in realizing the architecture of the framework. Although no specific methodology dictates how to perform framework-centric application development, the development activity necessarily involves implementing hot hooks. To use a framework, you have to use a cookbook that contains *framework adaptation patterns*.

The first step in developing a framework-centric application is to identify the framework to be used. For each application, you need to do the following:

♦ Identify the framework to be used

♦ Identify the primary abstractions

♦ Implement the hot hooks

Hot hooks are the key to reusing a framework and implementing the application. As Chapter 6 describes, a hot hook is just like a C++ pure

virtual function. The framework components are loosely coupled via hot hooks. The behavior of an application's participant is specified by the implementations of hot hooks. Further, hot hooks encourage application developers to think in an object-oriented manner, because they have to think in terms of identifying application-specific classes and implementing hot hooks. This helps the developers understand the design patterns in the framework, thereby improving the understanding of the overall framework.

Example: Using The BC Framework

The primary objective of the BC framework is to describe the partition of applications into a set of interconnectable, collaborative components. Each component implements important aspects of an application. Access to a particular component's application capabilities is mediated by the **CoRequest**s that it supports. **CoRequest**s are what the application developer sees when assembling components to construct fully functional applications. The internal structures of the BC framework classes are described in Chapter 7, which also discusses how the BC framework can be used to develop applications. The following is a recap of the steps required to develop applications using the BC framework:

1. Define requests and replies for BCs. Recall that requests are defined to invoke services of BCs.

2. Define the BCs.

3. Register the BCs with the component manager.

4. Develop a client to invoke the services of the BCs.

Each of these steps must be supported by the framework cookbook. The cookbook must contain four separate recipes to explain how to achieve each of these steps.

Adaptability Of A Framework

A reusable framework isn't used as is, due to its generality property. It has to be adapted to develop new applications. Therefore, ease of use should be an important yardstick when making a framework. A framework without a good degree of adaptability can't be used (nor reused). The following are the ways to increase the adaptability of a framework:

♦ *Documentation*—If a framework isn't supported by proper user documentation, it likely won't be used. If the framework's documentation doesn't meet the requirements of its intended users, the framework won't be reused.

◆ *Application construction environment (ACE)*—Developing an ACE for users enables them to interact with the framework, so that they can easily configure and construct new applications. An ACE (also known as a *toolkit*) is a collection of high-level tools that enables users to interact with a framework. Black-box frameworks can easily be used with an ACE. You can easily build an ACE that lets users choose prebuilt components and connect them, which is a construction method that a black-box framework supports for most applications.

◆ *Code generators*—Because a framework imposes a particular type of coding, code standardization is possible. Coding can be easily derived (and generated) from recipes, to bootstrap the application-implementation process. It is possible (and implemented by many real projects) to develop a code generator for a framework. Code generators are useful to jump-start a new application that is using the framework. The code generator instantiates the framework for you with ready-made code skeletons that you can fill in according to the application's requirements. The concept of code generation is presented next.

Code Generation Example

The section "Example: Using The BC Framework" presented the steps involved in developing an application by using the BC framework. The following sections define each of these steps in the context of code generation, using the example that is presented in Chapter 7.

Step 1: Defining The Request And Reply

Listing 14.1 presents an example that demonstrates how to define the request and reply by using the BC framework.

Listing 14.1   Defining the request and reply.

```
#include <co_component.hpp>
#include <co_factory.hpp>

class openAccount : public CoRequest
{
public:

    CoLong accountNum_;
    CoDouble money_;
    CoString name_;
```

```
        openAccount()
        {
            registerMembers();
            setName("openAccount");
        }
        openAccount(const openAccount& other)
        {
            accountNum_=other.accountNum_;
            money_=other.money_;
            name_=other.name_;
            registerMembers();
        }
        openAccount& operator=(const openAccount& other)
        {
            accountNum_=other.accountNum_;
            money_=other.money_;
            name_=other.name_;
            return *this;
        }

private:

    void registerMembers()
    {
        registerAttribute("accountNum_", &accountNum_);
        registerAttribute("money_", &money_);
        registerAttribute("name_", &name_);
    }
};

class balanceInfo : public CoReply
{
public:

    CoDouble balance_;

    balanceInfo()
    {
        registerMembers();
        setName("balanceInfo");
    }
    balanceInfo(const balanceInfo& other)
    {
        balance_=other.balance_;
        registerMembers();
```

```
    }
    balanceInfo& operator=(const balanceInfo& r)
    {
        balance_=r.balance_;
        return *this;
    }

private:

    void registerMembers()
    {
        registerAttribute("balance_", &balance_);
    }
};
```

Listing 14.1 shows that the complete class declarations of the derived requests and replies can be generated by the code generator if it knows the class member names and their types.

Step 2: Defining A Business Component

Listing 14.2 presents an example that defines an **account** component by using the BC framework.

Listing 14.2   Defining a BC.

```
class account : public CoComponent
{
public:

    account()
    {
    }

private:

    void open()
    {
        cout<<"open():"<<getRequest()->asString()<<endl;

        openAccount* request=
            dynamic_cast<openAccount*>(getRequest());

        balanceInfo* reply=new balanceInfo;
        reply->balance_=50.1234;

        reply->setStatus(12345);
```

```
            setReply(reply);
    }

    void registerServices()
    {
        registerService("openAccount",
            CO_COMPONENT_FUNCTION(&account::open));
    }

    void registerMembers()
    {
    }
};
```

Listing 14.2 shows that most of the parts of the derived component can be generated by the code generator. For example, the **registerServices()** function can be generated if the tool knows the names of the requests and the BC's services. Based on the same input, the skeleton code for the services (such as **open()**) can also be generated.

Step 3: Registering The BC

The following code shows how to register BCs with the component manager:

```
class model
{
public:
    model()
    {
        CoFactory<account>("account");
    }
};
```

The preceding code shows that a **model** class can easily be generated by the code generator if the tool knows the names of the BCs that are to be registered with the component manager.

Step 4: Developing A Client

The following code shows how to develop a client that uses the services of a BC:

```
int main()
{
    model model_;
```

```
    openAccount r;

    r.accountNum_=1234;
    r.money_=13.145;
    r.name_="vishwa";

    CoReply* reply;
    r.sendAndReceive("account", reply);

    balanceInfo* rep=dynamic_cast<balanceInfo*>(reply);

    cout<<reply->asString()<<endl;

    delete reply;
}
```

The preceding code shows that it is not easy to generate the client code. Because the client contains the business logic, generating this code isn't practical.

Chapter Recap

The success of OOP depends on reuse, and the success of reuse depends on an infrastructure, such as that provided by frameworks. A framework enables developers to design applications by using reusable and maintainable building blocks that address application-specific problems. Thus, frameworks enable developers to realize the potential of improved design and code reuse.

The framework usage phase (or framework instantiation phase) results in the development of an application, using the framework as a foundation. In this phase, you adapt the framework to develop an application. To reuse a framework successfully, you must have a set of proper documentation, consisting of these elements:

♦ *Purpose of the framework*—Information about which problem a framework addresses, and a description of the framework's capabilities.

♦ *Class description document*—Class reference document for all the framework's classes. Provides information under the headings "Description," "Class Declaration," and "Member Functions."

♦ *Cookbook*—Describes how the framework is intended to be used. Provides information under the headings "Purpose," "Steps," "Rules of Usage," "Examples," and "Related Recipes."

♦ *Architecture of the framework*—Useful to extend and customize the framework.

This chapter showed an example of developing an application by using the BC framework, which should help you to conceptualize using a framework. This chapter also presented the concept of *code generators*, which are useful for jump-starting new applications that are using frameworks. Because application coding can be easily derived (and generated) from recipes, you can develop a code generator for a framework. The code generator provides ready-made code skeletons that a user can fill in according to the application's requirements.

Chapter 15

Refactoring Framework

An object-oriented framework can be defined as a set of classes that represents an abstract design for solutions to a family of related problems. The presence of a framework influences the development process for the application. Recall that overall framework development has three phases:

♦ *Framework development phase*—Produces a reusable design and related implementation. This phase is described in Chapter 7.

♦ *Framework usage phase*—Application development phase using a framework. You generally adapt the existing framework through inheritance of the abstract classes in the framework. This phase is described in Chapter 14.

♦ *Framework evolution and maintenance phase*—This phase is necessary because the framework is subject to change, due to such things as bugs reported from framework users, identification of new abstractions due to changes in the problem domain, and so forth. Framework evolution and maintenance activities also include *perfective maintenance*, which includes maintainability and adaptability in ways that don't break the requirements of the framework. One aspect of perfective maintenance is *framework restructuring*, which is the behavior-preserving process; this doesn't introduce any bugs into the framework. Framework restructuring is also referred to as *framework refactoring*, which is the topic of this chapter.

A framework sometimes needs to be restructured before it can be reused, to make the framework easier to understand, easier to change, and less vulnerable to errors when future changes are incorporated. An important objective of framework restructuring is to preserve and increase the value of the framework. Restructuring a framework may make possible the addition of more features to an existing framework. In addition, you can make the framework more reusable. Framework restructuring can be applied both in the earlier design and development phases and in the maintenance phase. Framework restructuring may involve splitting complex classes into several simpler classes, and a class may be promoted to a base class for a set of related classes. All of these changes make classes more usable, reusable, adaptable, and maintainable.

Techniques Of Refactoring

Reusable software, such as a framework, is usually the result of many design iterations. Some of these iterations occur after the framework has been reused. The resulting changes affect not only the design of the framework, but also the design of other applications that are built using the framework.

Changing an object-oriented framework involves structural changes, such as moving variables and member functions between classes, and splitting a complex class into several smaller classes. When a structural change is made to a class or set of classes, corresponding changes may also be needed elsewhere in a program, mainly due to type and derivation dependencies. The following are important points about framework refactoring:

♦ Framework refactoring is *not* about adding new features to a framework, *nor* is it about modifying lines of code.

♦ Refactoring doesn't change the behavior of a framework. Refactoring preserves behavior, so that it doesn't break the framework.

♦ Although refactoring doesn't change the behavior of a framework, it can support software design and evolution, by restructuring a framework so that the framework is more changeable.

♦ Refactoring is a maintenance technique that can be used to restructure the framework periodically.

Reuse Elements Can Be Refactored

Languages such as C++ can reduce not only development time, but also the cost of maintenance, thus simplifying the creation of new systems and new versions of old systems. C++ provides a powerful springboard for developing reusable objects. As Chapter 2 points out, the following four features enable reuse in C++:

- *Class*—C++ mechanism to create objects. It is the C++ unit of reusability. Frameworks support design-level reuse by permitting specifications of classes, and by supporting a required degree of abstraction.

- *Class derivation*—C++ mechanism to create object inheritance. It is used to adapt an existing class to a new requirement. Class derivation is also used to implement polymorphism. The combination of class derivation and polymorphism is a major feature supporting the creation of reusable classes in C++. Class derivation can be used in a framework to model various concrete representations of a common abstraction.

- *Class member objects*—C++ mechanism to create object composition. Recall that *composition* is the process of combining many related abstractions into a single abstraction. Whereas inheritance enables you to assemble relevant object abstractions into a hierarchy, composition enables you to fabricate object abstractions to form new abstractions. Composition is a method of reusing an abstraction to create a new abstraction.

- *Templates*—C++ mechanism to construct a family of related classes or functions. Using templates, you can create generic types in C++. Thus, templates facilitate code reuse.

Because an object-oriented framework is both an abstract design of an application and an important object-oriented technique to facilitate design-level reuse, frameworks incorporate the four reuse elements just described. These reuse elements, in fact, are the major refactoring techniques that you can achieve in a framework. The following refactoring techniques can be applied to a framework:

- Abstracting many classes into a base class

- Specializing a base class

- Changing member objects

- Templatizing many classes

These four refactoring techniques are described in the sections to follow.

Many Classes Into A Base Class

The purpose of refactoring techniques is to create an abstract base class for more than one class. One way to do this is to define an abstract base class for a set of concrete classes, and move the common behavior to that base class. The concrete classes inherit their old behavior rather than have that behavior implemented within their member functions. This refactoring guarantees consistency by defining the abstraction in one place. For example, if two classes of a framework are implemented by different project members, these classes may initially appear dissimilar, but you may later find that they share a common abstraction. You can refactor the framework to transfer the commonalties between the two classes into a new base class, which makes the design of the framework easier to understand and reduces future maintenance costs.

Here is an example:

```
class CoWindow
{
private:

    char* title_;
    short color_;

public:

    const char* getTitle() const;
    short getColor() const;
};

class CoButton
{
private:

    char* title_;
    short color_;

public:

    const char* getTitle() const;
    short getColor() const;
};

class CoDialogBox
{
private:

    char* title_;
    short color_;

public:
```

```
    const char* getTitle() const;
    short getColor() const;
};
```

In the preceding code, the **CoWindow**, **CoButton**, and **CoDialogBox** classes share the same behavior. The three classes have **title_** and **color_** data members and corresponding access member functions. You can move these common members to a base class as shown below:

```
class CoGui
{
private:

    char* title_;
    short color_;

public:

    const char* getTitle() const;
    short getColor() const;
};

class CoWindow : public CoGui
{
    //...
};

class CoButton : public CoGui
{
    //...
};

class CoDialogBox : public CoGui
{
    //...
};
```

The preceding code shows a class, **CoGui**, which is made into the **public** base class for the **CoWindow**, **CoButton**, and **CoDialogBox** classes.

Specializing A Base Class

You can break down a large, complex class into several smaller, concrete classes and a base class that represents the general abstraction. An example of a *complex* class is shown in Listing 15.1.

Listing 15.1 An example of a complex class.

```cpp
#include <string>

class CoDataType
{
public:

    enum EType
    {
        CO_NOT_KNOWN, CO_LONG, CO_ULONG, CO_DOUBLE,
        CO_STRING,CO_CHAR, CO_UCHAR
    };

private:

    EType type_;

    long l_;
    unsigned long ul_;

    double d_;
    string s_;

    char c_;
    unsigned char uc_;

public:

    CoDataType(const CoDataType& log) throw();
    CoDataType operator=(const CoDataType& log) throw();

    inline CoDataType(long l) throw();
    inline CoDataType(unsigned long ul) throw();

    inline CoDataType(double d) throw();
    inline CoDataType(const string& s) throw();

    inline CoDataType(char c) throw();
    inline CoDataType(unsigned char uc) throw();

    inline long getLong() const throw();
    inline unsigned long getULong() const throw();

    inline double getDouble() const throw();
```

```
    inline const string& getString() const throw();

    inline char getChar() const throw();
    inline unsigned char getUChar() const throw();

    inline CoDataType::EType d() const throw();

    void print(ostream& os) const throw();
};
```

Listing 15.1 presents a class, **CoDataType**, that attempts to abstract common data types. Instead, this class can better be split as shown in Listing 15.2.

Listing 15.2   Splitting the CoDataType class.

```
class CoDataType
{
public:

    virtual void print(ostream& os) const throw()=0;
};

class CoDouble : public CoDataType
{
private:

    double d_;

public:

    double getValue() const throw();
    void print(ostream& os) const throw();
};

class CoLong : public CoDataType
{
private:

    long d_;

public:

    long getValue() const throw();
    void print(ostream& os) const throw();
};
```

```
//other classes such as CoChar, CoString, and so forth
//...
```

The preceding example splits the big and complex **CoDataType** class into smaller classes, **CoDouble**, **CoLong**, and so forth. Note that the **print( )** member function of the **CoDataType** class has become **virtual** in Listing 15.2 so that the smaller derived classes can override the **print( )** function.

Listing 15.2 shows that the refactoring technique of splitting complex classes into smaller classes supports iterative design of an object-oriented framework. The framework can be extended to handle additional abstractions.

Changing Member Objects

C++'s class member object mechanism enables you to fabricate objects to form new classes. Thus, this mechanism is used as a method of reusing an object. By using this mechanism, you can create complex classes by interconnecting the existing objects with the new class. As Chapter 2 describes, two ways exist to create the new class:

♦ By *delegation mechanism*—A class definition may contain an object of some other class (such an object is referred to as a *class member object*).

♦ By *acquaintance mechanism*—A class definition may contain a pointer or reference to an object of some other class (such an object is referred to as a *member class pointer* or *reference*).

This refactoring mechanism consists of the following three rules, dealing with the restructuring of member object relationships:

♦ Move members from a member object's class to the container classes.

♦ Move members from a container class to the class of one of its member objects.

♦ Convert a derivation relationship into a "containership."

Here is an example:

```
class CoEngine
{
public:

    void accelerate() const throw();
    //...
```

```
};

class CoCar : public CoEngine
{
    //...
};
```

In the preceding example, the **CoCar** class is derived from the **CoEngine** class. The car inherits all the properties of the engine, for example, the **accelerate()** function. However, this relationship can be presented by the containership relationship, because an engine is contained within a car:

```
class CoEngine
{
public:
    void accelerate() const throw();
};

class CoCar
{
private:

    CoEngine engine_;

public:

    void accelerate() const throw()
    {
        engine_.accelerate();
    }
};
```

In the preceding code, the **CoCar** class contains a data member, **engine_**, of the **CoEngine** type, and delegates the **accelerate()** call to the **engine_** data member.

Templatizing Classes

Generic types provide a technique for reusing the functionality of code through parameters. C++ supports generic programming by using templates. Templates are discussed in detail in Chapter 2. Templates (also called *generic* or *parameterized types*) are used to construct a family of related functions or classes. Therefore, in a framework, if you discover a pattern of classes performing similar activities, you may consider

---

Lifecycle Of A Class = Refactoring

Classes are generally domain-dependent or application-dependent. An exercise that is always beneficial is to investigate a project to see whether you can discover new abstract classes that can be reused in later projects or refactored in the current project. Thus, creating abstract classes is both a way of searching for classes for later reuse and a way of cleaning up an existing design.

You can arrange classes in the following way:

♦ Establish a common base class for a set of related classes.

♦ Split big, complex classes into several smaller classes.

♦ Make concrete base classes abstract.

By using these arrangements, you can make classes more reusable and maintainable.

---

creating a class template out of them. You can also use a template-specialization mechanism to provide a different behavior to a particular template instantiation. Listing 15.3 is an example that refactors the classes of Listing 15.2.

Listing 15.3   Refactoring by using templates.

```
class CoDataType
{
public:

    virtual void print(ostream& os) const throw()=0;
};


template <class T>
class CoGenericType : public CoDataType
{
private:

    T d_;

public:

    const T& getValue() const throw();
    void print(ostream& os) const throw();
};


typedef CoGenericType<double> CoDouble;
typedef CoGenericType<long> CoLong;
```

The preceding code creates the **CoGenericType** class template to represent similar types, such as **CoDouble** and **CoLong** (shown in Listing

15.2). The **CoGenericType** class is derived from the nontemplate **CoDataType** class so that the **CoDataType** class still acts as the base class for all the data type classes. You may eliminate the **CoDataType** class if you don't want a hierarchy.

Chapter Recap

Like all software, frameworks evolve. A framework changes primarily to fix bugs, add new features, and refactor. In fact, one of the main characteristics of a framework is that it is easily changeable. Good frameworks are usually the result of many design iterations and structural changes. Implementing these changes is referred to as *refactoring*. This chapter describes four common refactoring techniques:

♦ *Abstract many classes into a base class*—Define an abstract base class for a set of concrete classes and move the common behavior to that base class.

♦ *Specialize a base class*—Break down a large, complex class into several smaller, concrete classes.

♦ *Change member objects*—Convert a derivation relationship into a containership. Also, move members from a member object's class to the container classes, and vice versa.

♦ *Templatize classes*—Make a class template out of similar classes.

Chapter 16

Integrating A Framework With Legacy Components

Key Topics:

- *The concept of legacy integration*

- *Adapting legacy code to CORBA components*

- *Legacy integration in the business object metaframework*

A n object-oriented framework is a development foundation designed for maximum reuse. A framework is an abstract design and implementation structure for an application. The use of a framework accelerates the development process for the application. The following are the three significant phases in framework-centered software development:

- *The framework development phase*—Results in a reusable design and the implementation of a framework. (Framework development is presented in Chapter 7.)

- *The framework usage phase*—Results in the development of an application, using the framework as a foundation. This phase is also referred to as the *framework instantiation phase*. In this phase, you adapt the framework to develop applications. (The framework usage phase is explained in Chapter 14.)

- *The framework evolution and maintenance phase*—Fixes the errors reported from the framework users and adds new abstractions to the framework. (The framework evolution and maintenance phase is discussed in Chapter 15.)

During the framework usage phase, most users (corporations) find that they have a suite of legacy applications that need to cooperate with the new framework-based applications. Replacing all the legacy code simultaneously is impossible, so a mechanism needs to be put in place that enables the legacy and new applications to coexist. The big advantage of the legacy code is that it is robust and tested (and, it works!).

The newly developed code must be capable of working with the existing legacy components. Given a framework's capability to extend, incorporating legacy components is quite possible. The integration between a framework and legacy components may not be an easy task, due not only to the cohesive behavior of the framework that makes replacing a framework class with a legacy class difficult, but also due to potential typing conflicts.

You have a few options available for integrating legacy systems with frameworks, which are briefly discussed in this chapter.

Adapting Legacy Components

A framework presents a design for an application in a particular domain. Based on this design, you develop new applications by generally deriving classes from the framework. However, because a legacy component is not a derived class of the framework class, you can't use it directly with your framework. A *legacy component* is an existing component that does the right thing, but has the wrong interface for your purposes. Because it has the wrong interface, you really can't plug this component into your framework. Therefore, the only way that you can integrate a legacy component with a framework is by adapting the legacy component within the framework's constraints. This is where the Adapter design pattern plays its role. (Chapter 5 presents the Adapter design pattern.)

Recall that the Adapter design pattern provides an existing class with a new interface. It can act as a mediator between the framework and the legacy component—it translates the messages that the framework wants to send into the messages that the legacy component wants to receive. Adapters are implemented by using the underlying operations of the existing legacy implementations.

Chapters 2 and 5 show that Adapters may use either class composition or class derivation to provide new functionality, by adding new member functions. Adapters generally hide the original member functions. An example of the Adapter design pattern is shown in Listing 16.1.

Listing 16.1   An example of the Adapter design pattern.

```
class LAccount
{
public:

    void deposit_money(double money);
    short withdraw_money(double money);
};
```

```
class CoBaseComponent
{
public:

    virtual void deposit(double money)=0;
    virtual void withdraw(double money)=0;
};

class CoAccount : protected LAccount, public CoBaseComponent
{
public:

    class NotEnoughMoney{};
    void deposit(double money);
    void withdraw(double money) throw(NotEnoughMoney);
};

void CoAccount::deposit(double money)
{
    LAccount::deposit_money(money);
}

void CoAccount::withdraw(double money)
throw(CoAccount::NotEnoughMoney)
{
    if (LAccount::withdraw_money(money)==0)
    {
        throw CoAccount::NotEnoughMoney();
    }
}
```

In the preceding code, the **CoAccount** class is the adapter for the legacy **LAccount** class. The **CoAccount** class is derived from the **CoBaseComponent** class as well as from the **LAccount** class, so that it can use the functionality of the **LAccount** class. However, an instance of the **CoAccount** class can't directly invoke the member functions of the **LAccount** class, because the derivation is a **protected** one. The **CoAccount** class provides a different interface to the **LAccount** class by using the member functions of the **LAccount** class. For example, the **deposit()** member function of the **CoAccount** class uses the **deposit_money()** function of the **LAccount** class. Also note that the **CoAccount::withdraw()** function even adapts the error handling of the legacy **LAccount::withdraw_money()** function. You can use the **CoAccount** class wherever the **CoBaseComponent** class is required.

The code in Listing 16.1 shows that although this solution is very suitable, the Adapter design pattern has one disadvantage associated with it. The disadvantage is that, for every member function of the legacy class that needs to be adapted, you have to define a member function that delegates the call to the corresponding member function in the legacy class. This leads to significant implementation overhead for the developer.

Adapting Existing Code For Distributed Components

You can use CORBA as a mechanism to achieve application integration for both new and existing applications. Because the internals of distributed components are hidden from their clients, these components provide a formula for integrating with legacy systems. In the end, these legacy systems can be replaced with newer systems providing the same CORBA interfaces.

The ability to adapt legacy code comes from the fact that CORBA separates the interface from an implementation. Chapter 9 shows the steps of building a CORBA application. Recall that, to write a CORBA application, you must first define the interfaces (which define the capabilities that will be made available by the server and how those capabilities are accessed), implement those interfaces, and compile and run the server.

To implement an interface, a class must be implemented that defines the pure virtual functions listed in the skeleton class generated by the IDL compiler. No restriction applies to how you implement the pure virtual functions, which gives you an opportunity to wrap existing legacy code into the CORBA components. For example, given the following **CoAccount** interface:

```
module CoBank
{
    interface Account
    {
        exception NoMoney
        {
            float balance;
        };

        void deposit(in float amount);
        void withdraw(in float amount) raises (NoMoney);
```

```
    };
};
```

you can define an implementation class **CoBank_AccountImpl** as follows:

```
class CoBank_AccountImpl: public CoBank_Account_skel
{
public:

    virtual void deposit(CORBA_Float amount)
    {
        //your code here
    }
    virtual void withdraw(CORBA_Float amount)
    {
        //your code here
    }
    //...
};
```

This approach is referred to as the *BOAImpl approach,* which gives you a very flexible approach to integrate legacy components within your framework. In particular, in the code of the interface's implementation, you can manipulate any call that it receives, before you pass it on to the legacy code.

CORBA provides another approach, referred to as the *tie approach,* to implement interfaces. The tie approach imposes restrictions regarding when it can be used, and when it can't be used. If an existing legacy component has exactly the correct member functions (each function has exactly the correct name and correct parameter types), the tie approach can be used. In other words, if the existing component does not have exactly the correct member functions, then the tie approach cannot be used. The tie approach uses a delegation mechanism to adapt legacy code to the framework. The tie approach example is presented next.

Tying The Legacy Code

The ORBacus IDL compiler can generate a special class, referred to as a *tie class,* for an interface in the form of a template class (see your ORBacus manual to find out how to do that). For example, for the **CoHello** interface:

```
interface CoHello
{
    void hello();
};
```

a **CoHello_skel_tie** class template is generated as shown in Listing 16.2.

Listing 16.2   The CoHello_skel_tie class template for the CoHello interface.

```
template<class T>
class CoHello_skel_tie : virtual public CoHello_skel
{
    T* ptr_;
    CORBA_Boolean rel_;

    CoHello_skel_tie(const CoHello_skel_tie<T>&) { }
    void operator=(const CoHello_skel_tie<T>&) { }

public:

    CoHello_skel_tie(T* p,
        CORBA_Boolean release = CORBA_TRUE)
        : ptr_(p), rel_(release)
    {
    }

    virtual ~CoHello_skel_tie()
    {
        if(rel_)
        delete ptr_;
    }

    virtual void CoHello()
    {
        ptr_ -> hello();
    }
    //...
};
```

As this partial code listing demonstrates, the **CoHello_skel_tie** class acts like an adapter for the **T** type. Therefore, the **CoHello_skel_tie** class must be instantiated with a class that implements all operations of the **CoHello** interface. The name of this class is generally of the form **<interface-name>_impl_tie**. In contrast to the BOAImpl approach, the class implementing **CoHello**'s (for example,

CoHello_impl_tie) operations doesn't need to be derived from any
skeleton class. Instead, as Listing 16.2 shows, an instance of
CoHello_skel_tie delegates all operation calls to **CoHello_impl_tie**.

Here is the definition of **CoHello_impl_tie**:

```
class CoHello_impl_tie
{
public:
    virtual hello()
    {
        cout<<"hello"<<endl;
    }
};
```

The **CoHello_impl_tie** isn't derived from any other class; it must implement all of **CoHello**'s operations, including its inherited operations.

Creating The CoHello Component

You can represent and create the **CoHello** component as follows:

```
typedef CoHello_skel_tie< CoHello_impl_tie >
    CoHelloComponent;

CoHello_impl_tie* pHelloImpl=new CoHello_impl_tie;

CoHello_var hello =
    new CoHelloComponent(pHelloImpl);
```

A **CoHello_impl_tie** instance **pHelloImpl** is created on the heap and
is passed to the **CoHelloComponent** constructor as an argument. All
operation calls to the exported **hello** object reference are then del-
egated to the **pHelloImpl** instance. Recall that the **pHelloImpl** instance
is of type **CoHello_impl_tie**, and the **CoHello_impl_tie** type is an independent class. This means that if the **CoHello_impl_tie** class is a
legacy component, it can easily be integrated with the new application
or a framework.

Legacy Integration In The Business Object Metaframework (BOM)

Chapter 13 presents the Business Object Metaframework (BOM) that
can serve as the basis for interoperation between contemporary applications and legacy systems. Recall that a BOM-based application system

is represented by a variety of dynamic interfaces rather than by a single, monolithic interface. Such a BOM-based application enables a range of integration and interoperability opportunities between contemporary and legacy systems, because of the following:

♦ Each dynamic interface represents a potential point of integration and interoperation, thus enabling you to control the degree of integration and interoperation.

♦ Each interface "hides" the underlying implementation, enabling you to encapsulate new and legacy systems. Therefore, integration and interoperation can be achieved even if a system was not initially designed for compliance.

Although the effort to encapsulate new and legacy systems might be nontrivial, the use of BOM interfaces enables encapsulation at various degrees of sophistication and completeness. For example, encapsulating only part of a legacy application might be cost-effective, and usually is less costly than developing a new application from scratch.

Chapter Recap

During the framework usage phase, you adapt the framework to develop applications. However, sometimes you need to use the legacy code *as-is* within your framework. Because the legacy components don't follow the framework's rules, they can't be directly incorporated into the framework, which means that you have to adapt the legacy code so that it integrates well with the framework. This chapter focused on the Adapter pattern, and presented the following concepts:

♦ A generic technique for integrating a framework with legacy components is to use the Adapter design pattern and modify the legacy components' interfaces so that they can be plugged into the framework.

♦ Because CORBA provides separation of an implementation from its interface, it provides a perfect mechanism with which to wrap legacy components to make them distributed components. You can use either the BOAImpl approach or the tie approach to achieve this.

♦ BOM provides a good platform to encapsulate legacy applications. The fact that a dynamic interface "hides" the underlying implementation enables contemporary and legacy systems to be encapsulated. Thus, integration and interoperation can be achieved even if a system wasn't originally designed for compliance.

Glossary

This glossary defines frequently used terms related to C++, OOP, CORBA, design patterns, and frameworks. Terms that are used in the book infrequently or in a limited context are not included here.

abstract class—A class with a pure **virtual** function. An abstract class can't be instantiated as a complete object, which makes sense, because an abstract class is just a notion or concept—it has yet to become concrete in the form of a derived class.

abstract data type (ADT)—An object that has the interface only and not the implementation.

abstraction—Characterizes an object and helps distinguish one type of object from other kinds of objects. Abstraction represents the "outside view" of an object.

acquaintance mechanism—A way of reusing a class by containing a pointer or reference to an object of some other class.

activity diagrams—UML diagrams for analyzing use case diagrams, understanding workflow across use cases, and dealing with parallelism.

adaptability—A property of a reusable component. Adaptability means ease of use and clearly is an important yardstick in designing a reusable component.

adaptor—Mechanism to provide an existing component with a different interface (for example, make an STL **stack** out of an STL **list**).

allocator—STL component that encapsulates the information about the memory model for a container.

any—A CORBA generic data type that can contain any other data type. The **any** type is similar to **void*** in C++. It can be used in an operation to pass or return a value of an arbitrary type. The type information for the enclosed data type is maintained within an **any**, but knowledge of the enclosed type isn't required to use an **any** as an input or output parameter value.

architectural pattern—Expresses a fundamental paradigm for structuring software; provides a set of predefined subsystems, as well as rules and guidelines to establish the relationships between these subsystems.

association relationship—Represents a semantic correlation between two classes in a UML diagram. Associations can be bidirectional. They are semantically weak, because they depict general relationships among classes. An association relationship is represented by a line in a UML diagram.

associative containers—STL containers that store elements, based on a key value. They are implemented as class templates and their internal data structures are red-black trees. Associative containers provide an ability for fast retrieval of data based on keys.

bidirectional iterators—STL iterators that can be moved forward or backward and can be used to read or write the elements of the sequence. All STL containers provide at least bidirectional iterators.

black-box framework—Object-composition-based framework.

BOAImpl approach—A way to implement an IDL interface. A class is implemented that defines the pure **virtual** functions listed in the skeleton class generated by the IDL compiler. The BOAImpl approach provides a flexible way to integrate legacy components within a framework.

broker architectural pattern—Describes distributed software systems with decoupled components that interact by remote service invocations. CORBA is based on this pattern.

business objects (BOs)—Implementations of real-world informational business elements, such as Customer, Trader, Employees, Order, and Product.

business process object—Represents the business process as operations across business objects (BOs) or related to collections of BOs. A business process object generally is a "stateless" component. It acts like glue between various BOs, and thus supports workflow-oriented computing.

C-6 classification—A classification scheme for design patterns. This scheme identifies six types of design patterns: Controller, Composer, Connector, Communicator, Converter, and Conductor.

class—A way of defining a new data type, generally known as a user-defined type (UDT). This involves specifying the internal representation of that type, along with the operations that are used to manipulate the type. Classes are C++'s implementation of data abstraction.

class derivation—Involves the creation of a new type from an existing user-defined type in some hierarchical fashion. Class derivation is C++'s implementation of inheritance. Class derivation enables a class to be reusable and extensible.

class diagrams—UML diagrams for modeling the static structure of classes in an object-oriented system; contain classes and their relationships.

class interface—Set of member functions of a class. A class may include zero or more member functions. The caliber of a class depends on how comprehensive and productive this set of member functions is.

class templates—Define a pattern for class definitions. STL container classes are a good example of class templates. Also called a *generic class* or *class generator*.

client—An application that uses the services of a CORBA component; that is, an application that invokes operations on other components by using the component's IOR. Because the client isn't aware of a component's implementation details, the component's implementation changes are transparent to the client.

client stub—An IDL-generated code that allows a client component to access services of a server component (a client stub is also referred to as a *surrogate* or a *proxy*). A stub represents the same set of operations that its IDL contains. A stub is compiled and linked with client code and is used to issue requests.

coding patterns—Programming styles/guidelines that can be applied in any program.

collaboration diagram—UML diagram that shows objects participating in an interaction and depicts the basic relationships among objects.

Collections Service—CORBA service that provides a uniform way to create and manipulate collections of components.

common facility—Defines horizontal and vertical interfaces that are used in most distributed applications. Common facilities are collectively called *CORBAfacilities*.

communicator—Type of design pattern that helps organize communication between components.

component collaboration—Interaction among components.

component diagrams—UML diagrams for modeling components.

component interface—A set of semantically related operations that a component's client can use to access the component's capabilities.

component packaging—Process of creating a platform from which the components can collaborate with other components, as per the application design. Component factories generally provide such platforms. Because components can exist independently, they provide great flexibility in packaging.

componentization—Mapping abstractions and real-world entities into a CORBA component.

composer—Type of design pattern that deals with partitioning an object-oriented system, and decoupling the interface and implementation of classes and objects.

composite—Presents objects in a tree structure. The client can act on the individual objects and the tree uniformly.

composition—A process of combining many related abstractions into a single abstraction. Object composition is one of the most common techniques of reusing functionality in object-oriented systems.

concrete class—A derived class that is not abstract. A concrete class must provide an implementation for its abstract class and is referred to as an *implementation* of an abstract class. A concrete class can be instantiated.

Concurrency Control Service—CORBA service that enables multiple clients to coordinate their access to shared resources.

conductor—Type of design pattern that deals with dynamic interactions among societies of classes and objects.

connector—Type of design pattern that provides control access to services of other components.

consumer—A CORBA component that processes event data.

container—STL object that keeps and manages a set of memory locations of arbitrary types.

container adaptors—Create a new container by mapping the interface of an existing STL container to that of the new container. STL provides three container adaptors: **stack**, **queue**, and **deque**.

controller—Type of design pattern that deals with initializing and configuring classes and objects.

converter—Type of design pattern that converts a class's behavior or interface into another behavior or interface.

CORBA object services—Domain-independent horizontal interfaces that are used in most distributed applications. They are available in the form of CORBA interfaces and come with implementations. Object services are reusable basic building blocks to create distributed object applications. Without object services, writing distributed applications wouldn't be easy. Object services are collectively called *CORBAservices*.

data encapsulation—Refers to combining data and the functions that operate on that data into one composite type. In other words, the data and functions are packaged together in a superior and well-organized bundle (class).

delegation mechanism—A way of reusing a class by containing an object of some other class. Also referred to as *containership*, *has-a relationship*, or *aggregation*.

deployment diagrams—UML diagrams for modeling the productive deployment of a system; present a visual representation of relationships among software and hardware components.

deque—STL class that allows insertion at either end, and provides random access. Abbreviation for *double-ended queue*.

dereferenceable iterator—An iterator **i** for which the expression *i is defined.

design pattern—An abstraction from a general design problem that keeps recurring in specific, nonarbitrary contexts.

distributed component—Encapsulation of data and business logic within objects that can be instantiated and interacted with from anywhere. Access to a particular component's application capabilities is mediated by the object interface that it supports.

distributed reference counting—A mechanism that keeps track of the number of connections to a particular distributed component.

dynamic binding—Provides a common interface for several different classes so that objects of those classes can be manipulated identically by the program. Dynamic binding is C++'s implementation of polymorphism. Also known as *late binding*.

dynamic component model—Adds operations to the interface and describes how a CORBA component interacts with other CORBA components at runtime.

dynamic interfaces—Representation of a BO's capabilities. A dynamic interface is based on IDL and is bound to a BO by using a C++ member object mechanism.

dynamic invocation interface (DII)—Enables requests to be constructed at runtime. Using DII, clients can specify the target IOR, the operation/attribute name, and the parameters to be passed.

dynamic skeleton interface (DSI)—Server-side mechanism to handle dynamic object invocations. DSI does not require the server to be compiled and linked with the skeleton code for an interface to accept client requests.

event—A communication between two components in which one of the components needs to inform the other component about its change of state. This requires that the two components know about each other's interests in events.

event channel—Mediator component that allows a component to communicate with other components asynchronously.

Event Service—CORBA service that supports asynchronous event notifications and event delivery.

Externalization Service—CORBA service that defines protocols for externalizing and internalizing component data.

factory—Provides an interface to create various types of objects at runtime.

forward iterators—STL iterators that can be moved forward and can be used to read or write the elements of the container.

forwarder-receiver—Hides the communication protocol from sender and receiver components. By using this design pattern, client and server components can communicate with each other transparently. The forwarder-receiver design pattern is used to decouple a client and server from the underlying networking mechanism.

framework—A reusable software architecture that comprises both design and code. A framework provides a set of classes that is used as a foundation for solutions to a set of problems.

framework development phase—Results in a reusable design and the implementation of a framework.

framework evolution and maintenance phase—Fixes errors reported by framework users, and adds new features to the framework.

framework usage phase—Results in the development of an application, using the framework as a foundation. Also referred to as the *framework instantiation phase*.

frozen hooks—Functions that consist of a series of hot hooks. Frozen hooks need not be **virtual** functions. They provide a fixed implementation. However, behavior of a frozen hook can vary at runtime, because it depends on hot hooks.

function object—An instance of a class that has the function call operator (()) overloaded. A function object can be used like a function. A template-based function object is referred to as a *generic function object*.

function template—A pattern for function definitions. Provides the capability to write a single function for constructing a family of similar functions.

generality—Property of a reusable component, which must have a broad scope of applicability. If a component can be reused only once, it is not a reusable component.

generalization relationship—A derivation of a class. In UML, a generalization relationship is represented as a solid line with an arrow pointing to the base class.

generic algorithm—STL computational procedure that is able to work on different containers. The generic algorithms include a broad range of fundamental algorithms for the most common kinds of data manipulation, such as searching, sorting, merging, copying, and transforming.

generic factory—A CORBA factory component (supporting the **create_object()** operation) that is capable of returning object references based on a key and some criteria passed to the **create_object()** operation.

generic function object—A template class that overloads the function call operator (**()**). This concept is used in the Standard Template Library (STL).

generic functions—Provide the capability to write a single function that is used to generate similar functions.

genericity—A technique for defining objects that represent structural and behavioral similarity. It is used as a technique for reusing the functionality of code through parameters. It is not the same as abstraction; however, it is key to avoiding the introduction of objects with duplicate behavior. C++ supports generic programming through its template features.

horizontal frameworks—Encapsulate expertise applicable to a variety of applications and domains. These frameworks provide a horizontal slice of functionality that can be applied to different domains.

hot hooks—Just like C++ pure **virtual** functions. Framework components are loosely coupled via hot hooks. Hot hooks provide a connection point at which generic framework objects can communicate with application objects. Hot hooks are a framework's common protocol that enables you to develop the application components.

idioms—Deal with issues related to how a particular design should be implemented. Idioms describe how to implement particular classes and relationships between them within a specific design problem. Idioms are related to a specific programming language, and they comprise aspects of both design and implementation for a particular structure.

implementation repository—Contains information that enables an Object Request Broker (ORB) to locate and launch implementations of components. An implementation repository typically maintains a mapping from a server's name to the executable's name that is used to launch the server.

inheritance—Enables programmers to assemble relevant object abstractions into a hierarchy, to express hierarchical relationships, or commonality, between relevant abstractions.

in-process factory—A factory that is implemented in the same process as the component that is created or managed by the factory.

input iterators—STL iterators that can be moved forward and can be used to read the elements of the container. Moving the iterator from one element of the container to another element takes a length of time proportional to the distance between the two.

interaction diagrams—UML diagrams for modeling interactions within a system.

Interface Definition Language (IDL)—Used to create specifications for a CORBA component. IDL facilitates CORBA's language independence because interfaces described in IDL can be mapped to any supported programming language.

interface polymorphism—Enables a common semantic behavior to be specified across different components using a single interface definition. Although the underlying component implementations may be different, they appear to behave in a manner that is consistent with semantics implied by the interface. Interface polymorphism enables IDL interfaces to serve as conceptual building blocks that can be leveraged throughout a system. Although this leverage doesn't necessarily imply that the underlying component implementations of the interfaces are also leveraged, interface polymorphism does provide a form of reuse, which can be thought of as specification reuse rather than implementation reuse.

interface repository (IR)—A CORBA component that provides persistent storage of module, interface, and type definitions.

Internet Inter-ORB Protocol (IIOP)—Protocol for ORB implementations to communicate with each other. IIOP basically is based on TCP/IP. Using IIOP, a CORBA ORB from one vendor can communicate with an ORB from another vendor. A CORBA-compliant product must implement IIOP. IIOP guarantees interoperability among CORBA products.

interoperable object reference (IOR)—The basis of all communication between components in CORBA. Accessibility of a component is provided through its IOR, which a client must first obtain before it can access a component's services. The client uses the IOR to invoke operations on the component.

inversion of control—Framework calling the functions that a framework user defines. This is also referred to as *flip-flop of control*.

iterator—STL abstraction to provide a mechanism for traversing and examining the elements in a container.

Licensing Service (LS)—CORBA service that enables component vendors to control the use of their intellectual property.

Lifecycle Service—CORBA service that defines operations to create, copy, move, and remove components on ORB.

list—STL container that allows fast insertion anywhere, but provides sequential access only.

map—STL container that supports unique keys and provides fast retrieval of values of another type based on the keys. It provides one-to-one mapping from one type (the key type) to another type (the value type).

marshaling—The process in which the input and output parameters of an operation are mapped into a platform-independent format that can be transmitted over a network.

mediator—Separates the communication between objects.

messages—Operations that act upon objects and that may modify the objects' states.

metadata—Typically used at runtime (when the components are actually executing in a running system) in the form of generic message data that is exchanged between components. This message data can be interpreted by the application that implements the components, thereby enabling the application to treat an otherwise generic interaction as an application-specific dialogue.

metapatterns—C++ reuse concepts that can be applied to most design patterns, to design and implement them. There are two types of metapatterns: hot hooks and frozen hooks.

multimap—STL container that supports multiple copies of keys and provides fast retrieval of values of another type based on the keys.

multiset—STL container that supports multiple copies of keys and provides fast retrieval of the keys.

name binding—Name-to-object association in a Naming Server that is used to attach a name to a component at runtime. The name is used by a CORBA client to locate the component.

naming context—An object that contains a set of name bindings, in which each name is unique. Because a context is an object, it can also be bound to a name in another naming context Binding contexts in other contexts creates a tree that is referred to as a *naming graph*.

Naming Service—CORBA service to provide a client with the capability to locate a component by name rather than using a stringified object reference.

object adapter (OA)—Provides a way to connect component implementations to ORB to receive requests. An OA acts as an intermediary between a component implementation and ORB, providing the mechanism that enables a component implementation to access services provided by ORB.

object dynamics—Interaction among objects. Interactions are mediated by messages that objects exchange with each other. Messages are operations that act upon objects and that may modify the objects' states.

object inheritance—Mechanism to assemble relevant object abstractions into a hierarchy, to express hierarchical relationships between abstractions; that is, to express commonality between relevant abstractions. C++ supports object inheritance through class derivation.

object interaction—Passing of a message from a sender object to a receiver object.

object interface—The specification of an object, conveying its runtime behavior or functionality. An object interface is a set of messages that can be sent to an object to access the object's functionality. C++ provides support for object interfaces through its class mechanism.

Object Management Group (OMG)—The organization that is responsible for defining the Object Management Architecture (OMA), the key to creating distributed components.

Object Property Service (OPS)—CORBA service that provides a mechanism to dynamically associate properties (named values) with components. OPS defines operations to create, delete, and manipulate properties.

Object Query Service (OQS)—CORBA service that enables a component to invoke queries on collections of other components.

Object Request Broker (ORB)—Defines the middleware to carry out component collaboration in a distributed environment. ORB is also referred to as an *object bus*.

object services—Define domain-independent horizontal CORBA interfaces that are used in distributed applications.

Object Transaction Service (OTS)—CORBA service that supports a two-phase commit protocol between components.

OMA object model—Similar to a classical object model, in which a client interacts with a component, and the component provides services. An object model describes a component's behavior and presents the mechanism by which clients are isolated from the component data representations and behavior implementation.

oneway operation—An IDL operation in which the client isn't blocked and continues processing while the target component executes the remote operation.

operation—An identifiable entity that denotes a CORBA component service that can be requested by a client. An operation is just like a C++ member function in a class. Optionally, an operation can specify its exception specification that may be raised by the corresponding implementation in the component.

opportunistic reuse—An act of modifying existing software or a software component to make it fit a current need. Opportunistic reuse has many disadvantages—issues such as testing, configuration management, maintenance, and documentation of the modified components have to be addressed.

out-process factory—A factory that is implemented in a process different from the process in which the component that is created or managed by the factory is implemented.

output iterators—STL iterators that can be moved forward and can be used to write the elements of the container.

past-the-end iterators—Iterators that point past the last element of a range. Past-the-end iterators are never assumed to be dereferenceable.

Persistent Object Service (POS)—CORBA service that provides interfaces for storing and managing the persistent state of components. Although a component defines, manipulates, and manages its state, it can still delegate to POS to perform the actual work related to persistency.

polymorphic classes—Provide an identical interface, but can be implemented to serve different, specific requirements. A polymorphic class declares or inherits at least one **virtual** function.

polymorphism—Ability to send a message to an object without knowing the specific type of the object. C++ implements the concept of polymorphism by using **virtual** functions.

priority_queue—An STL container that can be instantiated with a **vector** or a **deque**. The elements of a **priority_queue** are sorted by using a comparison function object, such as **less**.

programming-by-difference—Process of adapting a base class to work in different situations. The term refers to the fact that the code in the subclass defines the differences between the classes.

property—Extra attribute of a CORBA component that is attached to the component via Property Service. Properties use the **any** data type.

proxy—Design pattern that provides a placeholder for a component to provide access control to the component.

publisher-subscriber—Provides a mechanism to ensure that an interested component (subscriber) has a consistent view of the state of another component (publisher).

pull model—A CORBA event model that allows a consumer of events to request the event data from a supplier. Consumers request the event channel to send data. The event channel, in turn, pulls data from the supplier that supplies an event, if a new event is available.

pure virtual function—Placeholder for the still-unknown derived class function. A **virtual** function can be denoted "pure" by initializing its declaration to zero, possibly followed by the keywords **const** and **throw**.

push model—A CORBA event model that allows a supplier of events to initiate the transfer of the event data to consumers. A supplier pushes data to an event channel that, in turn, pushes data to the interested consumers.

queue—An STL container that can be instantiated with a **list** or a **deque**.

random-access iterators—STL iterators that can be moved from any place to any other place in constant time and can be used to read or write the elements of the supported container. STL containers **vector** and **deque** provide the random access iterators.

refactoring—Act of framework restructuring. Framework refactoring is the behavior-preserving process, which doesn't introduce any defects in the program. The purpose of refactoring is to improve the structure of the framework and make the framework easier to maintain and extend.

reference counting—Keeps track of the number of connections to a particular remote component.

Relationship Service—CORBA service used to allow components to form dynamic relationships (links) between each other. Relationship Service defines two new kinds of objects: *relationships* and *roles*. A role represents a CORBA component in a relationship. A set of related objects forms an *object graph*. The edges of the graph represent relationships.

repository identifiers—Globally identify modules, interfaces, constants, typedefs, exceptions, attributes, and operations.

request—Used by a client to make a request for services on an IOR, resulting in an operation call on the target CORBA component.

resolving a name—The process of determining the object associated with the name in a given context.

reuse—The process of creating software systems from predefined software components. Use is a runtime activity. Reuse is a building-time activity.

Security Service—CORBA service that ensures secure communication between components.

sequence containers—STL classes to store elements in sequential order by grouping a finite set of elements of the same type in a linear arrangement. STL provides three basic kinds of sequence containers: **vector**, **list**, and **deque**.

server—An application that creates CORBA components, publishes the IORs of the components, and provides services to clients. A server has a component implementation that provides the definitions of the data and services.

Server skeleton—An IDL-generated code that allows a component implementation to receive requests from a client. A skeleton represents the same set of operations that its IDL contains.

set—STL container that supports unique keys and provides fast retrieval of the keys.

sidekick function—Serves as a helper for the other class member functions. Generally, sidekick functions are declared as **private**. Preferably, sidekick functions are declared as **const** functions, to guarantee that they don't make any kind of unintentional alterations to the data members.

simple factory—A COBRA component factory that is capable of returning object references of a specific type.

Singleton—An idiom that is applied to a class to ensure that the class can have only one instance at runtime. A Singleton class provides a single point to access its instance.

smart pointers—Objectify the pointers, yet have a pointer-like interface by having overloaded -> and * operators defined. Smart pointers are developed mostly as wrapper classes for pointers.

stack—An STL container that can be instantiated with either a **vector**, **list**, or **deque**.

Standard Template Library (STL)—A C++ library designed for use with a style of programming called generic programming, the essential idea of which is to create reusable components that can be used easily in various combinations, without losing any performance.

state diagrams—UML diagrams for modeling the state space of an object; show the events that cause an object's transition from one state to another.

static binding—Refers to a function call that has all the necessary information at compile time to execute the function. Examples of static binding are normal and C library function calls. Also known as *early binding*.

static component model—Describes the static information of a CORBA component. It is more like an object model, as used in object-oriented analysis and design (OOAD). Its key concepts are interfaces, attributes, hierarchies, and associations between interfaces.

subobject—The embodied base object in a derived object.

supplier—A CORBA component that produces event data.

systematic reuse—Focuses on using frozen assets, or unmodified software components, without altering the source files of the component being reused. Behavior modifications are made through parameter passing, generic instantiations, inheritance, or composition.

systems management—A type of horizontal facilities to provide interfaces for system administration.

template—C++ mechanism to construct a family of related functions or classes. Also called *generic types* or *parameterized types*.

template instantiation—The process in which a class template becomes a real class with real types when its objects are created.

testability of a framework—Describes whether the framework is good at detecting faults at runtime.

tie approach—A way to implement IDL interfaces by C++ delegation mechanism. Using tie approach, the programmer can implement the IDL operations and attributes in a class that does not inherit from the generated skeleton class.

Time Service—CORBA service that enables a user to obtain current time in a distributed environment.

Trader Service—CORBA service that enables a client to locate a component by using some component properties.

Unified Modeling Language (UML)—A language for specifying various attributes of an object-oriented system, such as the static and dynamic characteristics of the system.

unmarshaling—The process in which the marshaled input and output parameters of an IDL operation are converted back to the actual parameters.

usability—Runtime property of a reusable component. Unless a component provides acceptable functionality and efficiency, it cannot be used, and hence cannot be reused.

use case diagrams—UML diagrams for modeling business processes; typically used to characterize the behavior of the complete object-oriented system when interacting with one or more external actors (users).

user interface—A CORBA common facility that covers everything that relates to user interfaces, from the tools used to develop them, to the way they are presented to the user. The user interface consists of user interface styles, for the "look and feel" presented to the user by the application, and the user interface enablers, to present the user interface to the user.

vector—STL class template that allows fast insertion at the end of a sequence and provides random access.

vertical frameworks—Capture knowledge and expertise in a particular application domain. These frameworks encompass a vertical slice of functionality for a particular client domain, such as finance, health care, manufacturing, telecommunications, electronic commerce, or transportation.

virtual functions—C++ technique to delay until runtime the selection of which member function gets called. Such a technique is called late (or dynamic) binding.

warm hooks—A frozen hook of a framework that is also a **virtual** function. It is called a "warm hook" because it can act like either a hot hook or a frozen hook.

white-box framework—Class-derivation-based framework. The programmer can use a white-box framework to develop new applications by deriving new classes from the framework and overriding member functions.

white-box reuse—A way of reusing a base class by adding or overriding member functions to a derived class. Each member function added to a derived class must abide by the internal conventions of its base class.

Recommended Reading

Books On Patterns And Frameworks

Buschmann, F., et al., *Pattern-Oriented Software Architecture: A System of Patterns* (John Wiley and Sons Ltd., U.K., 1996). Describes how patterns occur on three different levels—in software architecture, in design, and in idioms.

Cotter, Sean, et al., *Inside Taligent Technology* (Addison-Wesley, 1995). Provides insights into Taligent's object-oriented programming model and its approach to frameworks, development tools, and so forth.

Gamma, Erich, et al., *Design Patterns: Elements of Reusable Object-Oriented Software* (Addison-Wesley, 1995). Identifies and describes in detail some common object-oriented design problems.

Pree, Wolfgang, *Design Patterns for Object-Oriented Software Development* (Addison-Wesley, 1995). Provides an overview of state-of-the-art approaches in object-oriented technology, as well as practical guidance for their use in software design.

Books On Reuse

Bassett, Paul G., *Framing Software Reuse: Lessons from the Real World* (Yourdon Press Computing Series, September 1996). Presents a discussion of the basic concepts, component properties, technology, methodology, infrastructure, and culture of reuse. Presents the author's successful frame technology that can be used to create language-independent software components that can adapt to each other.

553

Poulin, Jeffrey S., *Measuring Software Reuse: Principles, Practices, and Economic Models* (Addison-Wesley, 1996). Brings together all the latest concepts, tools, and methods for software reuse metrics, presenting concrete, quantitative techniques for accurately measuring the level of reuse in a software project and objectively evaluating its financial benefits.

Books On Objects And UML

Booch, Grady, et al., *The Unified Modeling Language User Guide* (Addison-Wesley, 1998). Provides a guide to all the fundamentals of using UML effectively.

Fowler, Martin, et al., *UML Distilled: Applying the Standard Object Modeling Language* (Addison-Wesley, 1997). Introduces UML, highlighting the key elements of its notation, semantics, and processes.

Graham, Ian, *Object-Oriented Methods* (Addison-Wesley, 1994). An interesting book that provides a comprehensive survey of object technology.

Books On CORBA

Baker, Sean, *CORBA Distributed Objects: Using Orbix* (Addison-Wesley, 1996). Presents various examples of CORBA using C++/Orbix.

Pope, Alan, *The CORBA Reference Guide: Understanding the Common Object Request Broker Architecture* (Addison-Wesley, 1998). Offers an explanation of CORBA and provides a complete reference to the CORBA standard.

Rosenberger, Jeremy L., *Teach Yourself CORBA in 14 Days* (Sams, 1998). Provides the fundamentals of CORBA.

Books On C++ And STL

Liberty, Jesse, et al., *C++ Unleashed: The Comprehensive Solution!* (Sams, 1998). Presents explanations of the core features and complexities of C++.

Lippman, S.B., et al., *C++ Primer* (Addison-Wesley, 1998). Describes the features and programming usage of standard C++.

Meyers, Scott, *Effective C++: 50 Specific Ways to Improve Your Programs and Designs* (Addison-Wesley, 1997). Offers C++ class design and programming tips.

Musser, David R., et al., *STL Tutorial & Reference Guide: C++ Programming With the Standard Template Library* (Addison-Wesley, 1996). Provides a tutorial and reference material on STL.

Stroustrup, B., *The C++ Programming Language* (Addison-Wesley, 1991). A great book by the creator of C++.

Stroustrup, B., *The Design and Evolution of C++* (Addison-Wesley, 1994). Focuses on the principles, processes, and decisions made during the development of the C++ programming language.

Papers

Johnson, R.E., et al., "Designing Reusable Classes." *Journal of Object-Oriented Programming* (June 1988).

Johnson R.E., "Documenting Frameworks Using Patterns." *OOPSLA '92 Proceedings* (1992).

Lajoie R., et al., "Design and Reuse in Object Oriented Frameworks: Patterns, Contracts, and Motifs in Concert." *Proceedings of the 62nd Congress of the Association Canadienne Francaise pour l'Avancement des Sciences* (Montreal, Canada, May 1994).

Vinoski, Steve, "CORBA: Integrating Diverse Applications Within Distributed Heterogeneous Environments." *IEEE Communications Magazine* 35, no. 2 (February 1997).

Online Resources And Information

Appelbaum, Robert, et al., "The CORBA FAQ" at **www.cerfnet.com/~mpcline/corba-faq/**.

Bosch, J., et al., "Object-Oriented Frameworks: Problems and Experiences" at **www.ide.hk-r.se/~michaelm/papers/ex-frame.ps**.

Mattsson, Michael, "Object-Oriented Frameworks—A Survey of Methodological Issues" at **www.ide.hk-r.se/~michaelm/fwpages/files/mattsson-thesis.ps**. Provides a detailed survey about frameworks.

Müller, Peter, "Introduction to OO Programming Using C++" at **www.zib.de/Visual/people/mueller/Course/Tutorial/tutorial.html**.

Opdyke, W.F., "Refactoring Object-Oriented Frameworks" at **ide.hk-r.se/~michaelm/fwpages/files/opdyke-thesis.ps**. Provides a detailed survey of framework refactoring techniques.

Schmidt, Douglas C., "Design Patterns and Pattern Languages" at **www.cs.wustl.edu/~schmidt/patterns.html**.

Schmidt, Douglas C., "Distributed Object Computing with CORBA Middleware" at **www.cs.wustl.edu/~schmidt/corba.html**.

Taligent, Inc., "Building Object-Oriented Frameworks" at **www.ibm.com/java/education/oobuilding/index.html**. A good collection of framework papers.

Weidl, Johannes, "The Standard Template Library Tutorial" at **www.infosys.tuwien.ac.at/Research/Component/tutorial/prwmain.htm**.

Wise, Bowden, "An Overview of the Standard Template Library" (Crossroads, ACM) at **acm.org/crossroads/xrds2-3/ovp.html**.

Informative Web Sites

OMG Home Page at **www.omg.org/**. Makes available a great deal of CORBA-related information and specifications.

ORBacus Home Page at **www.ooc.com/ob/**.

Orbix for Developers at **www.iona.com/products/orbix/manuals/index.html**.

Index